PARTICIPATING ARTISTS

Arahmaiani

Wimo Ambala Bayang

Edwin

F.X Harsono

Budi Kustarto

Jompet Kuswidananto

Rudi Mantofani

I Nyoman Masriadi

Nasirun S.Sn

Garin Nugroho

Eko Nugroho

Erik Pauhrizi

Gotot Prakosa

Angki Purbandono

Mangu Putra

Faozan Rizal

S. Teddy D.

Handiwirman Saputra

Chusin Setiadikara

Pintor Sirait

Putu Sutawijaya

Agus Suwage

Tromarama

Entang Wiharso

Gede Mahendra Yasa

参展艺术家

哈拉海麦尼

维莫·安巴拉·巴扬

艾德文

方济各·沙勿略·哈索诺

布迪·库斯塔图

琼佩特·库斯伟达纳托

鲁迪·曼度凡尼

米斯尼亚迪

那室兰 S.Sn

加林·努格罗

艾柯·努格罗荷

埃里克·穆罕穆德

高托特·普拉考萨

安奇·普班度诺

曼顾·普川

法赞·利泽尔

S. 泰迪·D.

翰迪怀儿曼·萨普川

川森·萨提迪卡亚

平托·西瑞特

普图·苏塔维嘉亚

阿顾思·苏瓦吉

TROMARAMA艺术组合

安塔格·维哈梭

杰德·曼汉德拉·亚萨

INDEX

目录

Foreword | 前言

Indonesia is well known for its thousands of native islands, diverse ethnic groups, religious history, geography, culture, and more. These elements have contributed to a thriving contemporary art landscape in Indonesia, which in the last few years has become very popular in Asia – a trend that cannot be ignored.

The Museum of Contemporary Art, Shanghai is deeply honored to present "Contemporaneity: Contemporary Art of Indonesia" alongside the 2010 World Expo. This is also the first time Indonesian contemporary art has ever been displayed in a Chinese museum, speaking to the prevalence of contemporary Indonesian art. MoCA hopes to seize the opportunity presented by this exhibition to fully introduce the Chinese public to the current art and culture of Indonesia, and to spur on frequent cultural dialogue and cooperation between the two countries.

Ever since the Indonesian new art movement, from 1974 – 1979, contemporary art in Indonesia has been influenced through its more oriented, multi-perspective approach, as its practitioners delve into cultural issues, paying particular attention to social, political, economic, and other issues. These works are richly displayed through multi-media and performance techniques, all of which have caused the art to become extremely diverse. This "Contemporaneity: Contemporary Art of Indonesia" exhibition invites the works of over 20 of Indonesia's most influential contemporary artists in an effort to present the unique style and development process of Indonesian contemporary art.

I wish to extend my greatest thanks to all of the artists, the two curators, Jim Supangkat and Biljana Ciric, AKR Group, the China Gold Charitable Foundation, and the H2 Foundation for Arts and Education for their support of this exhibition, along with Garuda Indonesia, Mandiri Bank, and BMW for actively providing support and assistance. This year marks the 60th anniversary of diplomatic relations between the People's Republic of China and the Republic of Indonesia, and MoCA Shanghai feels deeply honored to be able to bring Indonesian contemporary art to Shanghai during both this special anniversary and the 2010 World Expo, allowing not only the people of Shanghai, but also visitors of the Expo, to enjoy the exhibition.

Thank you to the government of the Republic of Indonesia for their praise and support that has allowed this exhibition to take place during the 2010 World Expo as well as being one of the many art and culture-related events commemorating the 60th anniversary of diplomatic relations between China and Indonesia. We hope that with this exhibition we will provide an opportunity for Chinese artists to engage in close contact with those of Indonesia and their artworks, and hope to contribute to the cultural and artistic exchange between our two countries.

Samuel Kung
Chairman and Director
Museum of Contemporary Art, Shanghai

上海当代艺术馆
MoCA SHANGHAI

有千岛之国美誉的印度尼西亚，其多元的民族、宗教、历史、地理和社会等等因素造就了印尼当代丰富的艺术景观，成为近年来亚洲一股不容忽视的艺术热潮之一。

上海当代艺术馆很荣幸在世博期间为中国观众带来《当代性：印度尼西亚的当代艺术》展览，这也是印尼当代艺术第一次在中国的艺术馆里举办代表当代印尼艺术的大型展览。我们希望借此展览全面地向中国观众介绍当今印尼的艺术与文化，带动两国间更频密的文化对话与合作契机。

1974-1979的印尼新艺术运动，影响着印尼当代艺术以更多面向、多角度的艺术创作方式去探讨文化议题，关注社会、政治和经济等问题，并丰富地展现在媒材和表现技法，使得艺术创作极为多样化。本次《当代性：印度尼西亚的当代艺术》展览邀请了超过20位最具影响力的印尼当代艺术家，着力呈现印尼当代艺术的独特风貌及发展历程。

在此我要感谢参展的艺术家以及Jim Supangkat和Biljana Ciric两位策展人，感谢AKR Group、中国金慈善基金和浩然艺术与教育基金对这次展览的鼎力支持，以及印尼航空公司、曼迪利银行、及BMW积极提供的协助。今年是中华人民共和国与印尼共和国建交60周年。上海当代艺术馆深感荣幸能够在中国与印尼建交60周年及上海世博期间，为上海市民和来自世界各地的民众带来印尼当代艺术展。感谢印尼共和国政府的赞许和支持，让本次展览成为中国上海2010年世博会期间，印尼馆纪念中国与印尼建交60周年的艺术文化活动之一。我们希望藉由本次展览为中国的艺术家提供近距离接触印尼艺术家作品的机会，希望为两国的文化艺术交流做出贡献。

龚明光
上海当代艺术馆主席兼馆长

上海当代艺术馆
MoCA SHANGHAI

Since its founding 50 years ago, AKR Group, based in Indonesia, has grown into a global business with manufacturing facilities, ports and other infrastructure in order to supply the world with quality products and services. AKR Group currently has operations in Indonesia and China, the two fastest growing economies in the region.

The majority shareholder of AKR Group is PT. Arthakencana Rayatama, and he has built up and positioned AKR to become the largest private sector distributor of basic chemicals and petroleum products in Indonesia. AKR is also quickly expanding its reach with investments in 9 major seaports and 6 river ports.

The Group is the second largest producer of Sorbitol in the world with factories in Indonesia and China, exporting to over 80 countries worldwide. It is also a major producer of native starches and their derivatives, which are the main raw materials in FMCG companies with a wide arrangement of uses.

The Group has invested in manufacturing facilities in China and owns 5 river ports in Guangxi (China). AKR Group has also invested in 5 coal concessions of 24,000 Ha in Indonesia. Its property arm owns prime office building in Jakarta, operates 2 world-class hotels in Bali and Manado, and is currently expanding its property business.

PT. Arthakencana Rayatama is the main sponsor of the "Contemporaneity/Contemporary Art in Indonesia" exhibition at the Museum of Contemporary Art, Shanghai. This is one of our corporate, social responsibility initiatives to promote awareness of Indonesian Arts and Culture in China, and beyond. This year marks the 6oth Anniversary of diplomatic relationship between Indonesia and China, even though the cultural and economic contacts between Indonesia and China started almost 600 years ago when Admiral Cheng Ho visited Indonesia on a friendship mission. We hope this exhibition will enhance the 2 countries' understanding of each other, and strengthen our cultural, economic and diplomatic relations to the mutual benefit of the people from both countries.

AKR

AKR Group是一家拥有50年历史的印尼企业，其业务遍布全球，包括制造设备、港口及其他基建项目，为全球客户提供优质的产品和服务。AKR Group目前在发展迅速的印尼和中国均设有运营机构。

AKR Group的大股东为PT Arthakencana Rayatama，该公司将AKR发展为印尼最大的基本化学品和石油产品的私营经销商，并且投资于九个海港和六个河港，积极拓展集团业务。

该集团是全球第二大山梨糖醇生产商，工厂设于印尼和中国，产品出口至全球80多个国家。AKR也是原淀粉及衍生品的主要生产商，该产品用途广泛，而且是快速消费产品公司的重要原材料。

该集团投资于中国的制造厂并拥有广西省的五个河港。AKR Group还投资了印尼五个24,000HA的煤矿开采权。集团的地产部门拥有雅加达黄金地段的写字楼物业，在巴厘岛和美娜多经营两家世界级酒店，目前集团正在积极拓展其房地产业务。

PT. Arthakencana Rayatama是上海当代艺术馆举办的"当代性：印度尼西亚的当代艺术"展览的主要赞助商。这是本公司承担企业社会责任的实际行动之一，目的是在中国和全球推广印尼的艺术和文化。今年是印尼和中国建交60周年，实际上早在600年前郑和将军下西洋时期，印尼和中国已建立了文化和经济交流。我们希望这次展览能加深两国之间的了解，并增强我们的文化、经济和外交往来，让两国人民受惠。

Wait. One must always patiently wait whenever s/he attends the opening ceremony of an art exhibition. Wait for the surprise of viewing the artworks on display; wait for the praise or criticism of the audience; and wait for the phrase: "I wish the Exhibition great success." Because it is only after hearing this phrase that we can then enter the exhibition in order to realize the purpose of our attending the opening ceremony – that is, to see the exhibition. However, because of my impatient character, I usually sneak into the exhibition the night before, or during the hour-long opening speech, to view the exhibition in advance.

October 5, 2009: At a dinner of Indonesian collectors, hosted by Mr. Nick Simunovic, Managing Director and Asia representative of the Gagosian Gallery, I met Mr. Haryanto Adikoesoemo, the Chairman of AKR Group and an art collector. The other sponsor of this exhibition, Chairman of China Gold (Asia) Limited and my good friend, Mr. Honus Tandijono, also attended the dinner. Perhaps under the influence of good wine or our mutual love and fervor for art, we – an entrepreneur, a financier and a lawyer – decided that evening to partner together and work with The Museum of Contemporary Art, Shanghai, to host the first major Indonesian contemporary art exhibition in China to focus on Indonesia's most highly influential contemporary artists in order to exemplify the unique development of contemporary art in Indonesia. I have however entirely forgotten the speech of Mr. Simunovic from that evening.

The value of an exhibition should not, perhaps, be based solely upon its presentation, the academic reputation of the curators, the quality of the artwork, or, least of all, the commercial (or insured) value of such artwork. Instead, I believe that the value of an exhibition is determined by its ultimate impact and influence on its audience, through the promotion of art and cultural exchange. There is a different story and goal for each exhibition. The story of "Contemporaneity / Contemporary Art in Indonesia" is quite simple: it is the result of friendship, the common goal of three friends who hope to promote communication and further understanding between Indonesian and Chinese collectors and artists; to introduce Indonesian contemporary art to friends in the art world; and thereby mark the importance and contemporaneity of Indonesian contemporary art.

The H2 Foundation for Arts and Education supports various charitable projects including the Luo Zhongli Scholarship, the China Academy of Art "Experimental Art" Lecture Series, the China-Taiwan Art Student Exchange Program ("Seed Project"), the Peking University Law School Scholarship and Financial Aid, and other notable charitable projects throughout Asia. "Contemporaneity/Contemporary Art in Indonesia" is an important project sponsored by the Foundation in 2010 to support cultural exchange between China and Indonesia. I would like to thank Haryanto and Honus for their friendship, the support of Samuel Kung, Director of The Museum of Contemporary Art, Shanghai, the dedication of our curators Jim Supangkat and Biljana Ciric, the participation of Indonesian artists and the well wishes from friends.

Now, how to conclude? In an old-fashioned manner: "I wish the Exhibition great success!"

Hallam Chow

罗中立奖学金

H2 FOUNDATION for ARTS and EDUCATION
浩然艺术与教育基金

每次参加展览开幕的时候都需要耐心地等待，等待的是对该展览展示的艺术品的期待，等待的是观众对展览的赞叹或批评，等待的是以上的一句话“祝贺展览完满成功”。因为只能在这句话之后我们才可以进入展场，满足我们到临展览开幕的主要目的——看展览。但不耐烦的我通常会在展览布展时或嘉宾还没完毕他们一小时多的讲词前溜到展览场地先睹为快。

2009年10月5日——在一个由高古轩画廊亚洲代表Nick Simunovic先生安排的印尼收藏家晚宴中，我认识了AKR集团的主席与收藏家Haryanto Adikoesoemo先生。本展览的另一主办方中国金(亚洲)有限公司的主席(及我的好朋友)陈松正先生也在会。一个企业家，一个金融家与一个律师，可能在美酒的影响下，也可能是大家对艺术的真诚热爱下，决定与上海当代艺术馆合作举办在中国第一个大型的印尼当代艺术展，邀请最具影响力的印尼当代艺术家，呈现印尼当代艺术的独特风貌及发展历程。但当天晚上Simunovic先生的发言我却是完全忘掉了。

一个展览的价值不应只是该展览举办的场地，可能也不是策展人的学术地位或艺术品的好与坏，更不应是由艺术品的商业(或保险)价值而定。我相信一个展览的成功在于它最终对观众的影响，对艺术的推广与文化的交流。每个展览的背后都有不同的故事与目的。“当代性：印度尼西亚的当代艺术”的背后故事很纯粹。它是一个友谊的见证——三个朋友对艺术的爱好而定下的一个目标与期待，希望促进中国与印尼两地收藏家与艺术家对双方的认识与理解，在全球关注当代艺术的契机下极力推进印尼当代艺术给各艺术界朋友，从而奠定印尼当代艺术的重要性与当代性。

浩然艺术与教育基金支持的项目包括罗中立奖学金、中国美术学院“实验艺术”讲座系列、中国大陆与台湾艺术学生交流计划(“种子计划”)、北京大学法学院奖学金和助学金，以至亚洲多个地方的其他重要慈善项目。“当代性：印度尼西亚的当代艺术”是浩然艺术与教育基金2010年赞助的主要项目之一。在此我感谢Haryanto与松正的友谊，上海当代艺术馆龚明光馆长对展览的支持，策展人Jim Supangkat与Biljana Ciric的努力，各印尼艺术家的参与及朋友对展览的祝贺。

如何结尾？我只好老土地说一句“祝贺展览完满成功”！

仇浩然

罗中立奖学金

H2 FOUNDATION for ARTS and EDUCATION
浩然艺术与教育基金

China Gold (Asia) Limited is an international financial services company principally engaged in gold trading ("China Gold (Asia)") and is a member of The Chinese Gold & Silver Exchange Society (member no. 140). The management of China Gold (Asia) has worked consistently to build up an investment platform of international standard to provide comprehensive and professional investment and trading services to Greater China and Southeast Asian investors on 99 gold, London gold, London silver and other precious metals.

On numerous occasions China Gold (Asia) has been awarded for its quality professional services, including the Pro Choice Award 2008, the Quality Gold Trading Company Award and the Pro Choice Award 2009. China Gold (Asia) is currently developing securities and other related financial products, and aims to provide its clients with more diversified investment services and a "one-stop shop" financial investment platform, such that our clients may invest in a variety of financial products and thereby achieve substantial investment returns in all respects.

As a global precious metals trading company servicing investors in precious metals, and based on its substantial experience and expertise in precious metals trading as well as a steadfast dedication to quality services and loyalty to servicing our clients, China Gold (Asia) provides professional, timely, honest and unparallel services to investors and assists our clients to benefit from the rapidly changing economic market, and to take advantage of market information and investment opportunity, such that we can maintain long-term strategic partner relationships with our clients.

While developing our business, China Gold (Asia) also remembers our social and corporate responsibilities as an enterprise. The China Gold Charitable Foundation was set up in 2009 to make donations to poverty fighting, youth support, art, education and other charitable causes. "Contemporaneity/Contemporary Art in Indonesia" is an important international exhibition sponsored by China Gold during the Shanghai World Expo 2010. China Gold (Asia) has a close relationship with major financial institutions in Indonesia. As 2010 is also the 60th anniversary of the establishment of diplomatic relations between China and Indonesia, China Gold (Asia) hopes to promote cultural exchange between the two countries by being a principal sponsor of the "Contemporaneity/Contemporary Art in Indonesia" exhibition, and China Gold (Asia) also wishes to further advance the economic cooperation and friendship between the two countries.

China Gold (Asia) Limited
China Gold Charitable Foundation

中国金(亚洲)有限公司是一家以黄金交易为主要业务的国际金融公司(“中国金(亚洲)”)，也是香港金银贸易场140号行员。中国金(亚洲)在各部门努力不懈下，构建出一个具有国际水准认可及肯定的投资平台，为客户提供稳健及全面的贵金属投资服务，竭诚为大中华以及东南亚的投资客户提供专业的香港九九黄金、伦敦金、伦敦银及贵金属的买卖服务。

中国金(亚洲)连续获得【智选品牌大奖2008】，【优质黄金投资公司大奖】及【智选品牌大奖2009】等等殊荣。中国金(亚洲)未来的发展及方向，是为客户提供多元化产品以及一站式的金融平台，现正积极开拓证券及其他相关金融产品的业务，令客户可以更方便地透过中国金(亚洲)的平台进行各种金融产品的投资，协助客户从各方面取得丰厚回报。

作为一家面向全球贵金属投资者的公司，中国金(亚洲)凭借多年经营贵金属业务的经验及专业知识，公平、诚信的专业精神为客户服务，以坚持高标准的道德行为和职业操守，竭力为投资者提供多方位、高水准、诚实、公平、公正的优质服务，帮助投资者在瞬息万变的市场中，都能分秒必争掌握即时市场讯息及投资商机，使公司和投资者之间保持长期的伙伴式关系。

在中国金(亚洲)不断发展的同时，我们也时刻不忘企业的社会责任，并于2009年成立中国金慈善基金为扶贫，扶幼，艺术，教育与文化各方面作捐赠。“当代性：印度尼西亚的当代艺术”是中国金慈善基金2010年在上海世博期间赞助的重要国际文化项目。中国金(亚洲)与印度尼西亚各大金融机构都有良好的合作关系。适逢2010年也是中国与印度尼西亚政府建交60周年，中国金(亚洲)希望就“当代性：印度尼西亚的当代艺术”展览促进中国与印度尼西亚的文化交流，也祝愿两国的经济合作与友谊更进一步。

中国金(亚洲)有限公司
中国金慈善基金

Curatorial Texts | 策展人论述

JIM SUPANGKAT
杰姆·苏潘凯特

Indonesia in Contemporary Art Discourses

当代性话语中的印尼

Contemporary art continues to develop as the discourses around it grow and flourish from the great diversity of thoughts and theories that have been evolving in unison since the 70s that operate collectively against "modernism as institution." [1] This diversity holds true even now. None of these thoughts emerge as paradigms. On the one hand, this allows contemporary art to avoid a singularly dominant position; on the other hand, this makes contemporary art unidentifiable in many ways.

At the beginning of the development of contemporary art, the impact of this diversity went more or less unnoticed, since the idea of an anti-modernism was the foremost signifier of contemporary art. Banal artworks representing this opposition were celebrated. Into the 90s, this celebration was still apparent, allowing for the tradition of international biennials to be seen as important markers of contemporary art development.

However, following four decades of contemporary art development, the ferocity of anti-modernism now seems irrelevant. In this situation, the diversity of contemporary art discourses has lead to a 'problem'. There is a lack of mediation in art criticism, as there are simply too many views and references. Commentating upon this condition, art historian James Elkins puts forward the idea: "Art criticism is massively pro-

自上世纪70年代当代艺术话语进入多元思考和多元理论并行发展的时代以来，当代艺术经历了长足的发展，极大地冲击了“以现代主义为正统”(modernism as institution)的传统。[1]这种多元性保持至今依然未变。没有哪一种思想是以榜样或模板的姿态出现的。一方面，这让当代艺术避免被一种思想所主导；但另一方面，这也让当代艺术变得难以定义。

当代艺术发展伊始，其多元性所产生的影响并未引起广泛的瞩目，因为反现代主义才是当代艺术最显著的标志。只要表现了这种反叛，即使平庸的艺术作品也依然会受到推崇。直到20世纪90年代，人们依然可以感受到这种推崇，也正是这种推崇的力量让国际双年展传统成为当代艺术发展的一个重要标志。

然而，在当代艺术的发展走过了40余年之后，强烈的反现代主义意识如今已显得不那么重要。在这种情况下，当代艺术对话的多元性引出了一个“问题”。

duced, and massively ignored." [2]

Upon entering the early decades of the 21st century, such symptoms seem to be coming to an end. Art fairs have become important milestones in contemporary art developments, highlighting two factors: the development of art markets, and processes of globalization. Previously, art markets have only enjoyed their success in Europe and the United States, especially in the 80s when auction house prices began to grow exponentially. For example, in 1989, Van Gogh's Portrait of Dr Gachet was sold for a price of US$82.5 million, while Renoir's Au Moulin de la Galette fetched US$78.1 million.[3] But after the 90s the growth of the art markets began spreading to all parts of the world, guided by the processes of globalization—following the end of the Cold War, the fall of Berlin Wall, and China's transformation. In 2008, China's art market became the third largest art market in the world. with France being the first, and the USA and the UK as sharing the second position. Since then the main commodity of art markets have been contemporary artworks. Between 2003 and 2007, the augmentation of modern art works stagnated at 5%, while the increase in the number of contemporary art works varied between 10-30%. [4]

By the end of 2008, the Dubai International Financial Center, organizer of the Dubai Art Fair, together with The Financial Times, organized the Global Art Forum, which involved some 80 leading collectors around the world, auction houses, investors and art dealers. The theme of this forum was reminiscent of a manifesto of the present state of contemporary art: "Art is Business."

With regard to this manifesto, global contemporary art seems to have found its foundation: globality. This identification of a global reality particularly emphasizes the reality of the business world that facilitates decentralization and global-local intermingling, all of which gives rise to equality and uniformity. The Boston Consultant Group Inc., in one of its publications, interprets globality thus:

> It's the name for a new and different global reality in which we'll be competing with everyone, from everywhere, for everything. Companies have no centers. The idea of foreignness is foreign. Commerce swirls and market dominance shifts. Western business orthodoxy entwines with eastern business philosophy and creates a whole

太多的观念和视角让艺术批评的斡旋与调和功能丧失殆尽。著名艺术史学家詹姆斯·埃尔金斯(James Elkins)这样评价这一局面："艺术批评大量地被制造出来，也大量地被忽略。" [2]

进入21世纪初叶，这一局面似乎走向终结。艺术博览会成为当代艺术的一个重要里程碑，凸显了两大元素：即艺术市场的发展与全球化。此前，只有欧美地区的艺术市场取得了可观的发展，特别是在80年代，各大拍卖行的价格开始出现巨大的飞跃。1989年，梵高的《加歇医生的肖像》和雷诺阿的《煎饼磨坊的舞会》分别以8250万美元和7810万美元的价格成交。[3]随着全球化的不断推进，进入90年代后，冷战结束、柏林墙倒塌、中国改革开放等一系列重大事件都让世界各地的艺术市场呈现出蓬勃的发展势头。2008年，中国的艺术市场成为全球第三大艺术市场；法国位列第一，美英并列第二。自此，当代艺术作品成为艺术市场当仁不让的主角。2003-2007年间，现代艺术作品的增长率仅为5%，而当代艺术作品的增长率则为10%-30%。[4]

截至2008年底，迪拜艺术节活动的主办方迪拜国际金融中心与《金融时报》共同主办了"全球艺术论坛"，来自全球各地的80余位著名策展人、拍卖行、投资人和艺术商都参加了此次论坛活动。本次论坛的主题体现了当今当代艺术的宣言："艺术是商业"。

根据这一宣言，全球当代艺术似乎找到了自己的根基：全球性(globality)。对于全球现实的这一认知特别强调了商业世界的现实状况，促进地方分权与全球–地方融合，趋向平等与一致。波士顿咨询集团在一份自己的出版物中曾这样对"全球性"做出诠释：

> 这是对全新的、与以往截然不同的全球现实的称呼。在这种新的现实中，我们将与地球每个角落的每个人竞争每件事。公司没有明确的中

new mind-set that embraces profit and competition as well as sustainability and collaboration.[5]

Discussing Contemporaneity

Beyond art markets, there are also other efforts to identify global contemporary art. There are visible differences. This external attempt at identification actually questions the signs of uniformity. Leading art historian Hans Belting commenced such identification by looking at global contemporary art as 'global art', which must be differentiated from 'world art'. For Hans Belting, the idea of 'world art' reflects the hegemonic understanding of modernism.[6]

The nuances of world art stem from modern ideas regarding modernity as of an universal scope. However, world art is really western art, which was claimed to be applicable around the world after it had been confirmed as modern art. This assumption ends as a legitimate claim, as it does not manifest itself in reality. Models and understandings of modern art in Europe and the United States do not exist outside these regions. Although modern art is also known throughout the world, it is impossible to ascertain whether modernism—itself a very complicated discourse—is actually understood and adopted outside Europe and the US. It has never been fully researched whether or not modernism has ever been translated into and/or transformed outside of Europe and the US, thereby becoming a different and disparate form of modernism.

Global art, according to Hans Belting, is not dependent on the sign of the emergence of a reality as predicted by universalism. Global art has emerged as a result of economically-driven reasons. Its development within the realm of the art markets does not concern the concept of uniformity as understood by universalism. Business operations allow global contemporary art to take into consideration the local strengths of art for the very sake of business interests—taking into account public perception, as well as perceptions of the collector and artist—and to then celebrate diversity. Thus, globalism is the anti-thesis to universalism.[7]

Differentiating 'world art' and 'global art' is not accomplished only in order to distinguish modern art from contemporary art. A more significant differentiation in current circles is to differentiate between 'contemporary art' and 'global contemporary art'.

心。“外来”这个概念将不复存在。商业世界将发生巨变，市场的主导力量将发生转变。西方商业正统观念与东方商业哲学相互融合，并将产生一系列关于利润、竞争、可持续性和协作的全新思想。[5]

对话当代性

在艺术市场以外，也有其它试图定义全球当代艺术的努力。其中的区别是明显的。这些来自外部的尝试实际上质疑的是一致性的标志。著名艺术史学家汉斯·贝尔廷(Hans Belting)把全球当代艺术称作“全球艺术”，与“世界艺术”加以严格区别。汉斯·贝尔廷认为“世界艺术”的概念反映了对现代主义的霸权式的理解。[6]

世界艺术的概念源于将现代性放在全球范围内的现代思想。然而，世界艺术实际上是西方艺术，在被确立为现代艺术后宣称自己放之四海皆准。而这一宣言终究只停留在书面，未能在现实世界成立。欧美现代艺术模式和思考脱离了上述两个地区也就不复存在了。虽然全球各地都知道现代艺术的概念，但是我们无法断言现代主义这一极度复杂的对话能够真正在欧美地区以外被理解、被采纳。有一个问题始终没有得到考证，那就是在脱离欧美语境、经过翻译和转型后，“现代主义”是否变成了一种截然不同的概念。

根据汉斯·贝尔廷的说法，全球艺术并非如普遍主义所预测的那样成为现实崛起的标志。全球艺术的崛起主要是受到经济因素的推动。根据普遍主义的说法，它在艺术市场中的发展并不考虑一致性的问题。而商业则让全球当代艺术出于商业利益而将本土优势纳入考虑(将公众观点和收藏家、艺术家的观点都纳入考虑)，并大力颂扬多元性。因此，全球主义与普遍主义是两个相反的概念。[7]

When considered thoroughly, 'contemporary art' is no other than 'world contemporary art'. From this point of view, 'world contemporary art' is the continuity of 'world modern art' even though, in many respects, such a connection is denied, because contemporary art is seen as being an entirely new platform altogether. Such continuity causes 'world contemporary art' to contain a hegemonic understanding as well. Here, world contemporary art again stops at these claims, and it is almost impossible to bequeath such realities outside of Europe and the US. Here, the term 'global contemporary art' becomes very valuable in the search for alternative understandings.

In this search for alternative understandings, the question "what is contemporary art?" must be modified and reformulated as "what is global contemporary art?" The question depends upon the presence of contemporary art around the world as a indisputable fact (which owes to the growth of the art markets). According to Hans Belting, such statements will lead to fundamental points, and arrive at the challenging inquiry: "what is art in a global sense?" [8]

Terry Smith's book, What is Contemporary Art? might be the most comprehensive book describing the signs/indicators of contemporary art development in the 1990s and early 2000s. This book contains a study of the art market within global-local tensions, and discusses the history of art and the growth of museums through the modern-contemporary contention, while also discussing the collision of the North-South flow of growth and development within post-colonial studies.

In my observation, contemporary art as described in this book is discussed both as 'world contemporary art' as well as 'global contemporary art'. Furthermore, I see that there exists a 'space in between', between world contemporary art and global contemporary art. This space in between is reflected in discussions of contemporaneity, which according to Terry Smith is "the most evident attribute of the current world picture." Regarding this matter, he writes:

> Within contemporaneity, it seems to me, at least three sets of forces contend, turning each other incessantly. The first is globalization itself, above all, it thirsts for hegemony in the face of increasing cultural differentiation (the multeity that was released by decolonization), for control of time in the face of the proliferation of asynchronous

对“世界艺术”与“全球艺术”加以区别并不仅仅为了把现代艺术与当代艺术区分开来。更为重要的一个原因是要把“当代艺术”和“全球当代艺术”区分开来。

追根溯源，“当代艺术”与“世界当代艺术”并无区别。从这个意义上讲，“世界当代艺术”是“世界现代艺术”的延续。虽然在很多时候这种延续关系往往由于当代艺术被视为一个全新的平台而被否定，但是这种延续性让“世界当代艺术”保持着一种霸权式的观点。世界当代艺术再次停留在了宣言阶段，无法在欧美地区以外传播开来。而“全球当代艺术”的概念则为寻找另一种表达和视角提供了非常有价值的选择。

在寻找另一种视角的过程中，我们必须对“什么是当代艺术”这个问题作出修正。这里，需要提出的问题变成了“什么是全球当代艺术”。(由于艺术市场的发展，)回答这个问题需要把全球各地的当代艺术发展状况纳入考虑。根据汉斯・贝尔廷的说法，“艺术在全球意义中是什么意思”这个富有挑战性的探究是问题的关键。[8]

特里・史密斯(Terry Smith)的《什么是当代艺术》可能是目前最全面地介绍了上世纪90年代到21世纪初期当代艺术发展的各种标志/指标的书籍了。这本书对处于全球-地方压力下的艺术市场进行了研究，对现当代语境中的艺术史和博物馆发展展开探讨，并讨论了后殖民研究中南北发展的碰撞与冲突。

根据我的理解，当代艺术在本书中包含了“世界当代艺术”和“全球当代艺术”两层含义。此外，我发现在世界当代艺术和全球当代艺术之间有一个“中间地带”。这一中间地带反映在对于当代性的讨论中，特里・史密斯将其称为“……当前世界蓝图中最显著的特征……”。他在书中写道：

> 在我看来，现代性内部至少有三股力量在不断

temporalities, and for continuing exploitation of natural and (to a degree not yet seen) visual resources against the increasing evidence of the inability of those resources to sustain this exploitation. Secondly, the inequity among peoples, classes, and individuals is now so accelerated that it threatens both the desires for dominations entertained by states, ideologies, and religious and the persistent dreams of liberation that continue to inspire individuals and peoples. Thirdly, we are all willynilly immersed in a infoscope—or better, a spectacle, an image economy or a regime of representations—capable of the instant and thoroughly mediated communication of all information and any image anywhere.[9]

As I comprehend it, the tension between globality and multeity as discussed by Terry Smith has now appeared in the form of an image contest regarding global contemporary art. This contest stems from a simple question: Does global contemporary art advocate 'uniformity', or, on the contrary, 'diversity'?

Those who believe in 'uniformity' insist upon 'the present'; they look at it through a spatial lens, causing the understanding of contemporary art to have a fixed and sure meaning. This understanding is not hampered by temporal factors, which will always make any given meaning impermanent and prone to ever-changing conditions.

Emphasizing the spatial factors influences such theories to tend to delimit only 'the present' of contemporary art history (note: other than being influenced by spatial and temporal factors, meanings are also influenced by the history of their understanding). This symptom is reflected in the effort to leave off 'contemporary' as a designation, replacing it with the term 'now'. Thus emerges the term 'art now', which has started to be used widely (especially in art markets). For me, the usage of the term 'art now' is almost like returning to the identification of 'the cutting edge' of modernist avant-gardism.

In this way, the understanding of contemporaneity, which is "the quality of belonging in the same period of time" and "the quality of being current or of the present," has no problem at all[10]. As such, all the artists in the world (and especially the current generation) are contemporaries as a result of existing together in the present moment. Together, they practice "the" contemporary art that represents the signifiers of glo-

地进行角逐。首先是全球化——面对日益显著的文化差异(殖民统治的瓦解所带来的多元性)时对于主导权的追求；面对异步时间性扩张时对于时间控制权的追求；以及面对越来越多的证据显示自然和视觉资源无以为继时，对于继续开发自然资源并(以前所未见的程度)探索视觉资源的追求。第二，民族、阶级和个体之间的不平等性日益加剧，对政府、意识形态和宗教的统治地位以及赋予个体和民族以灵感的自由理想造成威胁。第三，我们心甘情愿地沉浸在一种镜像中——或者说，一种景观、一种形象经济、一种表现政体——有能力对任何地方的任何信息和图像进行即时彻底传达沟通。[9]

在我的理解中，特里・史密斯所谈到的全球性与多元性之间竞争关系现在开始以全球当代艺术竞争这种直观的形式出现。这一竞争源于一个简单的问题：全球当代艺术究竟提倡“一致性”还是“多元性”呢?

主张“一致性”的人坚持“当前”，关注空间因素，对于当代艺术的意义有固定而明确的理解与定义。这种理解不会受到时间因素的制约，因此能够保持恒定而不易发生变化。

对于空间因素的重视也让这种主张容易决定当代艺术史的“今天”(注：除了受到空间、时间因素的影响，意义也受到历史认知的影响)。这也反映在用“当代”取代“现在”作为时间节点的举动中。由此也产生了一个新的词汇“art now”(当代艺术)，并已广泛地被接受和运用(特别是在艺术市场中)。在我看来，“art now”的出现就好像又重新回到了现代前卫主义时期的“the cutting edge”(最前沿)。

根据这种主张，对现代性的理解——即“属于同一时代”且“属于当前”——就不会有任何问题了[10]。因此，全球所有艺术家(特别是当代艺术家)都是同时代

bality.

Contrary to this, I believe that global contemporary art actually reiterates/affirms diversity, as its scope in reality has undergone great expansion. This diversity is what has distinguished global contemporary art from world contemporary art. I am able to see the importance of temporal factors in the understanding of contemporary art following its 40 years' development. Thus, it is important to find the alterations in the meaning of contemporary art that are usually to be found in the shifting of language and signs. The search for alterations of meaning must not dismiss the historical exploration of contemporary art as well.

Contemporaneity is a term in which shifts/changes in language and signs can be found. The premise of this investigation is the realization that contemporaneity is not a 'safe' term, as understood in terms of art now. Contemporaneity is a 'problematic term'. Upon this conviction, I tend to open discussions of contemporaneity by positioning it on a level of mediation. This is the position of the discourse around contemporaneity.

My proposal for the aforementioned investigation is to delve into what I call 'art sensibility', or the notion of art at large through a pluralist perspective. The idea is to reactivate the awareness that is now beginning to fade, to acknowledge artistic sensibility as a universal indication, but to refute the art phenomenon as a single-substantive reality that has an essence that involves an absolute and universal truth.

In the development of contemporary art, an attempt to broach the problematic subject of contemporaneity was embarked upon by Jean-Hubert Martin through an outrageous exhibition: Les Magiciens de la Terre at Centre Georges Pompidou, Paris, in 1989. In this exhibition, Jean-Hubert Martin located contemporary artworks next to traditional works of art, amongst them being such things as: earthen installations by Tibetan priests, and the paintings of the women of Uttar Pradesh, India, using a canvas-like painting medium.

That exhibition led to a long-standing controversy, one that has been much discussed for many years now in the realm of contemporary art. Jean-Hubert Martin has received continuous attacks from all corners. Following this exhibition, experiments like the one he had done became absent from the development of contemporary art. This indicates one of the

人，身处同一个时间段。他们共同实践这种具有全球性特征的当代艺术。

与此相反，我相信随着全球当代艺术的范围在现实中的一不断的扩充，它实际上重申/证实了多元性。多元性是将全球当代艺术与世界当代艺术区分开来的关键点。在当代艺术40余年的发展历程中，我们看到了时间因素的重要性。要定义全球当代艺术，就要擅于在语言符号的转变中发现当代艺术含义的变化。对于变化的探寻不能抹煞对于当代艺术的历史探索。

“现代性”这个词里包含了语言符号的更替/变化。而开展这一研究的一大前提便是认识到现代性并不是一个“安全”的字眼。跟“art now”一样，“现代性”是一个“有问题的词语”。基于这一论断，我希望开放关于现代性的讨论，把它放到一个可以探讨并调整的水平上。以下便是针对现代性展开的一些讨论。

针对上述研究，我的建议是深入探究“艺术情感”，即多元视角下的艺术概念。再次唤起已经开始消退的意识，将艺术情感看作一种普遍现象，但是要驳斥把艺术现象视作一种包含绝对的、普遍的真理的单物质现实。

在当代艺术的发展过程中，让-休伯特·马丁(Jean-Hubert Martin)以1989年在法国蓬皮杜艺术中心举办的一场名为“大地魔术师”(Les Magiciens de la Terre)的另类展览为契机，进行了探讨现代性这一争议主题的尝试。在这次展览中，让-休伯特·马丁将当代艺术作品与传统艺术作品并置展示，其中包括西藏大地艺术和印尼北方邦女性以类似帆布的材质作为媒介创作的绘画等。

展览引起了巨大的争议，其激发的讨论在当代艺术界持续多年。让-休伯特·马丁不断受到来自世界各地的攻击。在这次展览后，他所开展的各种艺术实验开

most common tendencies in understanding multeity, leading to questions and shedding the inquiries that Jean-Hubert Martin was unable to answer: like, "Can contemporary art be the equivalent of the 'presentation of ethnic arts'?" This question can never be discussed fully; at all times it leads to a deadlock.

In the development of modern art, this question can be answered immediately and firmly: "No", because in modernism, modernity is understood to be the contradiction of traditionalism. Within the development of contemporary art (which has defied modernism), this question should really offer a different answer. However, in reality, this question is unanswerable as well. This shows how modernism—and even colonial visions—continue to wield influence over the development of contemporary art.

The problem of this inquiry is upon the word 'quality', as it pertains to the context of contemporaneity. Within contemporary art discourses, 'quality' relies upon art in a Western sense, believed to be different from 'quality' as reliant upon ethnic art sensibilities. There exists no platform to simultaneously discuss art in a Western sense and ethnic art sensibilities, because ethnic art studies are fenced inside the sphere of ethnology and anthropology from the colonial era and into our current period. This dilemma demonstrates modern thinking sensibility, where the commensurability underlying all modern thought in its search for truth clashes with the incommensurability thesis held by ethnologists and anthropologists. [11]

Even though I am not abandoning the problem of ethnic art sensibilities, I tend not to search for an answer to such an inquiry. I tend to look for a way to circumnavigate this problem by comparing the development of contemporary art inside and outside Europe and the United States in order to search for differences and similarities as well. Contemporary art is an area in which this search can be implemented. Within modern art there is no space to make such differentiations. [12]

As it does not take only spatial factors into account, the differentiation does not stop at the present. This type of differentiation searches for language signs that reveal the alterations of meaning in the context of contemporary art. This type of differentiation, which takes into account temporal factors, involves studies that take into account the history of contemporary art, again, inside and outside Europe and the United

始从当代艺术发展史中缺席。这显示出对于多元性的一种普遍的理解趋势，引出了让-休伯特·马丁无法回答的质疑与询问：当代艺术能够与“当前的民族艺术”相提并论吗？人们从未就这一问题展开过全面而深入的讨论，各种探索与努力都陷入僵局。

在现代艺术的发展过程中，这一问题可以迅速得到明确的回答：“不能”，因为在现代主义中，现代性与传统性是两个相反的概念。而在当代艺术的发展中(对现代主义进行了反抗)，这一问题本应该拥有截然不同的答案。但是，事实上这个问题还是无解。这显示出现代主义、甚至殖民主义观念对当代艺术的发展有持续性的影响。

这个问题的核心在于当代性语境中的“品质”(quality)。在当代艺术对话中，西方意义上的“品质”与民族艺术的“品质”不同。没有哪一个平台能够同时探讨西方意义上的艺术和民族艺术，因为自殖民时代至今，民族艺术便一直被限制在民族学和人类学的研究框架内。这一进退维谷的窘境显示出现代艺术思想——即作为所有探求真理的现代思想之基础的可比性——与民族学家和人类学家所持有的不可比性论点之间有着显著的冲突。[11]

虽然我并未放弃民族艺术这一问题，但是我却并不打算探寻问题的答案。我更倾向于找到一个纵览全球的方法，把欧美内外的当代艺术发展进行比较，找出不同点和共同点。当代艺术正是可以完成这种探求的领域。而现代艺术领域中则根本不存在形成差异的空间。[12]

差异化把空间因素纳入考虑，因此它并不会只停留在当前。寻求语言符号类的差异化显示出在当代艺术语境中意义的变化。此类差异化也将时间因素纳入考量，包括了欧美内外当代艺术史研究。这一差异化甚至对当代艺术崛起前的艺术发展进行反思，其中包括

States. This differentiation can even re-consider the developments of art before the emergence of contemporary art, including developments in the 19th century, from which modern thinking sensibilities and colonial visions stem.

From this differentiation, one may observe differences and similarities within artistic developments inside and outside of Europe and the United States since the 19th century. One may observe that this development hinges upon the translation of art in a Western sense. Regarding such developments happening outside of Europe and the United States, observers may discover that there are no distinct boundaries between modern art sensibilities and ethnic art sensibilities. It is also observable that the difference between modern art and contemporary art is also less distinct. Thus, the occurrence of ethnic art sensibilities in contemporary art is a natural evolution of previous developments, not a contention between modernism-pluralism.

In the end, it will become evident that the question of whether contemporary art is similar or dissimilar to present ethnic arts will not be a dilemma. The answer to this can demonstrate multeity in global contemporary art.

The Emergence of Contemporary Art

The first symptoms of contemporary art in the United States emerged in the 60s; this was marked by such works as 200 Campbell's Soup Cans (1962) by Andy Warhol, Jasper John's Numbers (1962), and Ed Ruscha's Noise (1963). [13] These creations gave rise to controversy as they highlighted popular culture. In the future, this genre would come to be identified as Pop Art, and this genre stirred quite a bit of controversy because the prevailing modernist sensibilities of that time believed that culture must remain outside the context of art. Against this, Pop Art works highlighted culture. Even more so, Pop Art highlighted popular culture, which modernists thought to reflect low-brow tastes—from which comes the term kitsch.

In Germany, some early symptoms of contemporary art emerged in the form of Joseph Beuys' banal works of art, towards the end of the 60s. His works were protests and reactions towards the condition of German's art world, shadowed by guilt after Nazism's dark, historical legacy since the end of World War II. This guilt caused the depolitization of art, which is reflected in German's post-WW II modern art works.

现代思想和殖民主义观点萌芽的19世纪艺术的发展。

从这种差异化中，我们或许可以看到19世纪以来欧美内外艺术发展的共同点和不同点。我们也可以发现这种发展依赖于西方意义上的艺术翻译与诠释。至于欧洲和美国以外的艺术发展，观察人士会发现在现代艺术思考与民族艺术思想之间并没有鲜明的界限。此外，我们还会发现现代艺术与当代艺术之间的差异并不那么显著。因此，我们可以说当代艺术中民族艺术的出现是先前发展过程的自然演变结果，而非现代主义–多元主义之间竞争的产物。

最后，我们可以清楚地看到“当代艺术能够与‘当前的民族艺术’相提并论吗”这个问题并不难回答。问题的答案就在全球当代艺术的多元性中。

当代艺术的兴起

上世纪60年代，以安迪·沃霍尔的“两百个汤厨浓汤罐头”(200 Campbell's Soup Cans, 1962)、贾斯珀·约翰的“数字”(Numbers, 1962)和埃德·拉斯德的“噪音”(Noise, 1963)为代表的一批作家与作品的出现标志着当代艺术在美国萌芽[13]。这些作品强调的是大众文化，在当时引起了巨大的争议与关注。之后这一类型的作为被统称为“波普艺术”，其引起争议的原因在于当时处于主导地位的现代主义相信文化(必须)保持在艺术的语境之外。波普艺术作品则着重凸显了被认为应该在艺术范畴以外的文化。此外，由于波普艺术凸显的是流行文化、大众文化，现代主义者因此认为波普的低级趣味——是低俗的艺术(kitsch)。

在德国，20世纪60年代末期约瑟夫·博伊斯的世俗作品标志着当代艺术的崛起。他的作品是对德国艺术界的回应与抗议。自二战结束以来，德国艺术界一直处于纳粹黑暗历史阴霾的笼罩之下。这种负疚感

Artists took great care when portraying/addressing socio-political problems. This was the reason why German's modern art works were controlled by modernism-fueled abstractism/abstraction. Beuys stated that his protests were of a moral position, not a political one. Parallel to Beuys' stance, there emerged the Neo-Expressionism movement in Germany, introducing such names as Georg Baselitz and Anselm Kiefer.[14]

At the beginning of the 1970s as well, a number of Italian artists followed Beuys' footsteps by creating banal and 'dirty' artworks. Italian critic Germano Celant named this new 'trend' in Italian art as Arte Provera, which involved the tendency to delve into material mutability, and aiming to discover new media and forms of expressions in order to display an overlooked reality.[15]

When contemporary art began spreading to many parts of the world the signs found within these art practices were amongst those that were actively assimilated, as they were visual symbols easily understandable as a new, collective mode of expression—something that was alluring for many artists, especially when these languages became a 'trend'.

Such is the pattern of world contemporary art, which is still currently applicable. At the beginning of its inception, Warhol and Beuys' 'discoveries' were used to identify contemporary art works around the world. Nowadays, trends in global contemporary art are replete with 'discoveries' by Damien Hirst, Ashley Bickerton, Jeff Koons, Matthew Barney, Ron Mueck, and many others like them.

The emergence of contemporary art is not merely the emergence of new ways of expression. The emergence of contemporary art has a complex cognitive background, the understanding of which requires actuality, not just learning through theoretical suggestions. One of these backgrounds that I think will be difficult to understand outside of Europe and the United States is the perception of art history and the museum.

In contemporary art discourses, this problem is almost always overlooked. It is overshadowed by the contention between modernism and post-modernism. This occurs despite the fact that the problem regarding art history and the museum is a fundamental problem in the emergence of contemporary art in

让艺术产生了“去政治化”倾向，并在德国后二战时期现代艺术作品中有所体现。艺术家在表现/解决社会政治问题时显得格外小心谨慎。这也就是为什么充满现代主义特征的抽象主义在德国现代艺术作品中占主导地位。博伊斯声称他的抗议是一种道德立场而不是政治立场。“新表现主义运动”在德国的崛起涌现出了乔治・巴塞利兹(Georg Baselitz)和安森・基弗(Anselm Kiefer)等艺术家，他们所持的艺术见解与立场与博伊斯有共通之处。[14]

1970年代初，一批意大利艺术家追随博伊斯的脚步，开始创作世俗而“肮脏”的艺术作品。意大利评论家杰马诺・切兰特(Germano Celant)将这股意大利艺术发展新动向称之为“贫穷艺术”(Arte Provera)——探求材料的可变性以挖掘新的媒介和艺术语言表达，从而来展现被忽视的现实。[15]

当当代艺术开始在全球兴起，这些艺术实践中的符号更趋同化，这些视觉符号成为一种容易理解的全新的集体表达方式——对艺术家们有着巨大的吸引力。这一情况在这些视觉语言成为一种“趋势”的大背景后显得尤其突出。

这一世界当代艺术模式至今依然适用。在崛起之初，沃霍尔和博伊斯等人的“发现”被用来鉴别和定义全球各地的当代艺术作品。而如今的达明恩・赫斯特、阿什利・比克顿、杰夫・昆斯、马修・巴尼、让・穆克等人的“发现”则又为全球当代艺术提供了更多新鲜的血液。

当代艺术的崛起并不仅仅是新的表达方式的崛起。当代艺术的崛起有一个复杂的认知背景，要理解这一背景则需要现实的支持，而不能仅仅是通过理论来进行学习。在这些背景中，其中有一项我觉得欧美以外地区的人难以理解，那就是对于艺术史和美术馆的认识。

Europe and the United States.

It is common knowledge that the practice of art history as it emerged at the end of the 19th century was one of many attempts to understand the meaning of art in life. The basis of this thought was that great works produced by great artists throughout the course of history may reveal the meaning of art. Unlike the Aesthetics and those belonging to the realm of philosophy, art history was an empirical study stemming from linear historicism, itself a modern principle.

In his text Re:Post, Hal Foster presents the idea that art history originates from research into the collections belonging to Europe's largest museums, themselves built by Europe's royal and noble families, which retain European artworks that hail from the 16th century and beyond. All of such collections are comprised of paintings and sculptures. Thus, art history up until the development of late modern art only inquired after art that was made according to these two mediums, which causes Hal Foster to posit that the context of art history is the museum, and entirely not about culture or art in society.[16]

Modernism is a concept based upon this history of art. Modernism affirms art history and the museum as modern art institutions. Through such an institution, modernism does not only study art history in search of the meaning of art, but—and involving art historians, curators, and critics—it attempts to control the development of modern art. This is what is then known as "modernism as institution," which has been subsequently criticized as an act of 'domination'. And so, through this critique, contemporary art emerges.

Conflicts that gave rise to contemporary art are difficult to understand outside of Europe and the United States because the tradition that one must believe in the supremacy of art history and the museum does not exist. This is reflected also in the lack of museums outside Europe and the United States, as well as the lack of intensity in the study of art history.

James Elkins points out this reality in his introduction to the book he edited, Is Art History Global?. Looking at the statistics provided, it can be understood that outside of Europe and the United States the presence of an art historical institution is arguably next to none.[17]

Outside of Europe and the United States, the muse-

在当代艺术对话中，这个问题几乎完全被忽略，完全被遮掩在现代主义和后现代主义争论的阴影之中。而当代艺术在欧美崛起时，艺术史和美术馆是一个根本性的问题。

人们普遍把19世纪末的艺术史视作理解生活艺术含义的一种尝试。这一思想的根本理念是：伟大的艺术家在历史进程中创作的伟大的作品能够体现艺术的意义。不同于美学或哲学，艺术史是基于线性历史主义这一现代原则发展起来的实证研究。

哈尔·福斯特(Hal Foster)在《再次：后》(Re: Post)一文中对起源于由欧洲皇室建立、从16世纪以来便从事欧洲艺术品保存的大型欧洲博物馆的馆藏研究的艺术史进行了详细阐述。这些馆藏只有两大种类：绘画与雕塑。因此，直到现代艺术发展到后期，艺术史所关注的艺术也都是围绕着绘画和雕塑。哈尔·福斯特指出，艺术史的语境是博物馆，而完全无关乎社会文化或艺术。[16]

现代主义是一个以艺术史为基础的概念。现代主义进一步肯定了艺术史与博物馆是现代艺术正统机制。通过这样一种机制，现代主义不仅仅通过研究艺术史来探索艺术的意义。通过这样的机制——加上艺术史学家、策展人和评论家的共同参与——其目的在于控制现代艺术的发展。这便是所谓的“以现代主义为正统”。之后“以现代主义为正统”被批判为“霸权”。正是在这种批评下产生了当代艺术。

欧美以外的地区很难理解这些导致当代艺术产生的冲突与争辩，因为这些地区原本就不存在把艺术史和博物馆放在至高无上地位的传统。这一点从欧美以外地区博物馆数量匮乏且对艺术史的研究也毫不热衷便可窥知一二。

詹姆斯·埃尔金斯在其主编的《艺术史是全球性的

um tradition causes yet another problem: that is, the presence of ethnological museums that are separate from art museums. These two types of museums are separate because ethnology and art history are two different fields of study. Although artifacts and ethnic objects usually found in ethnological museums do display/demonstrate artistic sensibilities, these objects are never thought to be works of art in their own right. There are currently no studies on how artists outside of Europe and the United States perceive this duality. They cannot possibly deny that the artifacts and ethnic objects inside the ethnological museums are part of their history, but they are equally unable to view them as works of art.

In the midst of such circumstances, how can the contention between art history and the art museum as its context (as it occurs in Europe and the United States) really be understood?

The Emergence of Contemporary Art in Indonesia

To demonstrate the development of contemporary art outside of Europe and the United States, I will highlight the case of Indonesia, the indicators of which I know in detail. In this situation, we can clearly perceive the similarities and differences of the development of contemporary art inside and outside of Europe and the United States.

The first signs of contemporary art in Indonesia emerged in 1975, through the Indonesian New Art Movement (Gerakan Seni Rupa Baru Indonesia), initiated by artists from what were, at that time, Indonesia's two largest art academies. This movement then organized a number of exhibitions in several cities in Indonesia between 1970-1979.

In their 1979 exhibition at the Jakarta Art Center, Taman Ismail Marzuki, the movement launched their book, Gerakan Seni Rupa Baru Indonesia, containing texts from members of the movement and the polemics caused by their exhibitions between 1975-1979. This book also contains the movement's manifesto.

Through this manifesto, the Indonesian New Art Movement can be seen as marking the emergence of contemporary art in this particular location. This movement rejected the concept of fine art, replacing it with new art, reflecting media exploration. The move-

吗？》(Is Art History Global?)一书导言中指出了这一现象。从书中列举的数据我们可以看到，在欧美以外的地区艺术史机构的数量几乎接近于零。[17]

在欧美以外地区，博物馆传统还引发了另外一个问题：民族学博物馆与美术馆完全是两个分离的体系。两类博物馆之所以分离是因为民族学和艺术史隶属于两个截然不同的研究领域。虽然民族博物馆里展示的古器物和民俗物件也具有艺术性，但是这些物件并没有被当成艺术品看待。没有人就欧美以外的艺术家如何看待这种二元性展开过研究。他们无法否认民族博物馆内展出的古器物和民俗物件是历史的一部分，但是他们也同样无法把这些看作是艺术品。

面对这样的情况，以艺术史与美术馆为语境的论辩(发生在欧美)如何能够被真正地理解呢?

当代艺术在印尼兴起

我将以自己最为熟悉的印尼艺术发展为例来详尽说明欧美以外的当代艺术发展进程，从中我们能清楚地看到欧美地区和欧美以外地区当代艺术发展的相同和不同点。

印尼的当代艺术兴起于1975年，以“印尼新艺术运动”(Indonesian New Art Movement)为标志，由本土两大艺术学府的艺术家们发起的，并在1970年至1979年间在各大城市举办了多场作品展。

1979年在T.I.M雅加达艺术中心举办展览期间，新艺术运动的艺术家们出版了《印尼新艺术运动》一书，收录了1975年至1979年间艺术家们的创作文本以及由各类艺术展引发的思考辩论。另外，新艺术运动宣言也包含其中。

宣言指出，“印尼新艺术运动”标志着当代艺术在印尼的崛起。该运动摈弃传统意义上的美术，代之以的

ment also criticized formalism, as well as abstractism/abstraction, declaring the importance of the idea and social issues (or context). In the movement's manifesto, it reads:

> In creating, to throw away as far as possible art forms that have existed until now (the movement recognized it as 'old art'), that is, art limited around: painting, sculpture, and graphics. In the Indonesian New Art Movement, penetration between these forms of art, bringing forth art works that cannot be categorized into these established art forms, is seen as legitimate (new art). [.....] To believe in actual social issues as the more important issues to be discussed, rather than personal sentiments. In as much that the wealth of idea is more significant than a master's skill in cultivating elements of form. [19]

The Indonesian New Art Movement reflects the academic rebellion that was not understood by the Indonesian art world at that time. Thus, the banal works that were created, reflecting this rebellion, were condemned by almost everyone in the Indonesian art world, because they could not understand the thought process that went into such works. This symptom revealed how modernism's influence and the universalistic ideology were only to be found within a small circle of art academies.

In his book Modern Asian Art, John Clark placed the Indonesian New Art Movement within the ranks of Asian-based rebellions, reflecting the adaptation of the avant-garde spirit. Throughout Asia, adaptations such as these could be found only within small groups of artists. However, in his studies, John Clark concluded that these small groups have always played a role in affecting development and change within modern Asian art since the 20th century. [20]

In addition to revealing many of the similarities and differences within the emergence of contemporary art in Europe and the United States, the emergence of the Indonesian New Art Movement also demonstrated a different set of cognitive underpinnings. In rejecting universalism, this movement had their own reasons that could not be fully and equally compared to the rejection of universalism in the emergence of contemporary art in Europe and the United States. This rejection of universalism reflected identity politics. In the movement's manifesto, this rejection is reflected in one of the passages:

新艺术形式，其具体表现为对媒介的进一步探索。另外，形式主义、抽象主义等艺术手法受到批判；理念和对社会民生的关注的重要性日益凸显。宣言的原文写到：

> 在创作过程中，尽可能地要摒弃前人的艺术创作形式(即新艺术运动中所说的“旧艺术”)，即不能仅局限于绘画、雕塑和手绘等艺术创作。“印尼新艺术运动”主张对传统艺术形式的借鉴融合，但又不隶属于其中任何一个流派——这理所当然就是“新艺术”……它主张放眼社会万象，而非局限于个人情愫，丰富的理念比娴熟的技艺重要得多。[19]

印尼新艺术运动所体现的学术叛逆在当时并不为印尼艺术界理解。因此，带有反叛情结的作品几乎被批得体无完肤。因为人们无从得知作品背后的故事，也不能理解作者的构思。这种状况表明，现代化的影响力和普遍主义在艺术圈里接受程度相当有限。

约翰·克拉克(John Clark)在他的《现代亚洲艺术》(Modern Asian Art)一书把“印尼新艺术运动”归类为以亚洲为策源地的艺术反叛，体现了一种经过改良的前卫精神。在整个亚洲，这种改良也只在一小部分艺术家身上体现。然而他的研究表明，正是这少数人影响并改变了20世纪亚洲现代艺术的进程。[20]

除了展现与欧美当代艺术的异同点外，“印尼新艺术运动”的兴起开辟了一个新的认知高度——它不主张艺术的普遍性，但又与反对欧美当代艺术的普遍主义不尽相同，反映出一种身份政治。宣言如是说：

> 为发展名副其实的“印尼”艺术，我们应把新艺术发展史列为优先考虑，从拉登·萨勒(Raden Saleh)开始着手……为进一步发展以印尼本土批评家、史学家、思想家提出的文本和理论为基础

> To aspire the development of art that is "Indonesian", by prioritizing knowledge on the history of new art, beginning with Raden Saleh. [....]. To aspire the development of art based upon texts and theories by Indonesian persons, be they critics, historians, or thinkers. To intensely reject opinions stating: that development in Indonesian art is part of world art history, opinions stating that art is universal [....][21]

This declaration showed that by rejecting universalism, the Indonesian New Art Movement was more interested in puzzling over hegemony rather than the debate between the universalist and pluralist. Furthermore, the rejection of the history of art within the abovementioned declaration is far different from the rejection of art history found in Hal Foster's study. The rejection of art history in/by the Indonesian New Art Movement demonstrated rejection over the domination of (world) art history. This movement even began questioning the local art history.

In the 1970s, knowledge about contemporary art was not widespread in Indonesia, especially with regard to questions/issues involving marginalization, notions of 'the other', problems concerning the difference between the developments inside and outside of Europe and the United States, as well as post-colonial issues. Only during the 1990s did these thoughts begin to surface as issues and references in texts on contemporary art in Indonesia.

There are similarities that at first seem coincidental, such as the critical stance taken upon the de-politicization of art that also served as the background to Joseph Beuys' rebellious work. In the Indonesian New Art Movement's manifesto, it is noted as: "To believe in actual social issues as the more important issues to be discussed."

However, the critical stances toward depoliticization themselves had different backgrounds. The Indonesian New Art Movement's critical stance stemmed from the political problems in Indonesia, specifically. This movement emerged after ten years of following political changes in Indonesia from 1965 onward, shifting from a political system that was dominated by socialism to one of liberal politics. This change had involved a bloody revolution between military power and many left-wing movements. It had led to a military government, one that was keen to perform large-scale detentions of members of the Indonesian

> 的印尼艺术创作；坚决反对任何有关“印尼艺术是世界艺术史的一部分”、“艺术具有普遍性”等论调……[21]

此声明体现了“印尼新艺术运动”一贯反对艺术普遍性的主张，它更像是个对艺术霸权踌躇满志的人，而非游走在普遍主义和多元主义论辩的边缘。另外，上述宣言中对艺术史的否定也绝不等同于哈尔·福斯特的理论。“印尼新艺术运动”旨在反对(世界)艺术史的主导地位，并开始对本土艺术发展史提出质疑。

早在20世纪70年代，当代艺术理念在印尼尚不为人所知，尤其是关于“边缘化”(marginalization)、“他者”(the other)、欧美各国和其他国家艺术发展的异同以及后殖民研究等问题。直到90年代，这些理念才以文本话题和指代的形式涌入印尼当代艺术作品中。

乍一看在某些方面二者不谋而合，比如“去政治化”的政治立场似乎与约瑟夫·博伊斯作品的反叛互为呼应。在上述宣言中也明确提倡，“真实世界的社会万象更为重要……”

然而，印尼新艺术运动“去政治化”的批评立场有着截然不同的出发点。它根植于印尼本国的政治问题。1965年，印尼国内政局巨变，自由政治取代社会主义，其间历经血雨腥风的军事革命以及左翼运动。“印尼新艺术运动”于10年后诞生。革命后建立的军政府，对印尼共产党和相关组织成员实行大面积拘捕迫害，并对任何同情共产党、社会主义和左派路线的人实行“白色恐怖”统治。军政府正式在法律上明文禁止任何形式的共产主义运动，并辅以高压手段残忍迫害。

这种“白色恐怖”影响深远——人们对政治议事恐惧万分，艺术家们也难以幸免。由此引发了在艺术领域内“去政治化”的思考。自此以后政治和社会议题成

Communist Party (Partai Komunis Indonesia) as well as its affiliated organizations. This new government had operated upon the basis of a politics of intimidation directed towards anyone showing sympathy for communism, socialism, and other left-wing ideologies. The government had by then formally—that is, legally—banned communism in any form, exercising a repressive form of politics in order to ensure the application of this ban.

This intimidation had widespread effects. Fear existed in the minds of the people who were afraid to question topical political issues; and the artists were not immune to this either. This condition led to a de-politicization of art. Political and social issues disappeared from the art lexicon.

In the midst of this situation, a number of artists embarked upon the search for an Indonesian identity by adapting many aspects of Indonesian traditional art forms, or by drawing attention to symbols of ancient history showing/representing Indonesia's supremacy. This nationalistic, heroic tendency received commendation from the ultra-nationalist military government.

The Indonesian New Art Movement criticized the depoliticization of art and suggested that the artists have left all social responsibility behind by doing so (which was also considered an immoral attitude). This reaction fermented a dislike to dishonest/untruthful forms of expression.

The background to this critical stance is reflected in a text by Hardi, a member of the movement, writing in the book Gerakan Seni Rupa Baru Indonesia. He wrote down his experience traveling around Europe between 1977-1978, where he witnessed Joseph Beuys' work in Documenta VI, and expressed his amazement. However, he did not view it as an early sign of contemporary art. He correlates Joseph Beuys' thoughts with those of Soedjojono, a pioneer of Indonesian modern art at the beginning of 20th century, known to be a nationalist artist who also advocated universal humanism.

To legitimize his viewpoint, Hardi focuses on traditional theater performances in East Javanese society, the format of which is aimed at criticizing authority and siding with the people. He notes the many risks faced by members of this traditional theater troupe during the colonial years up until the time of Indonesian independence. At that point then, the artists had fiercely

为艺术创作的禁区。

在这种情况下，一批艺术家开始了对印尼民族身份性的探索。他们应用多种印尼传统艺术形式，在展现民族优越性的远古历史作品中寻找灵感。这种积极主张民族自豪感、描绘民族英武形象的艺术受到极端民族主义的军政府当局的褒奖。

印尼新艺术运动批判所谓的“去政治化”艺术，认为那些艺术家没有履行自己的社会责任(并斥其为不道德的态度)。这表明了他们对虚伪艺术形式的唾弃。

新艺术运动艺术家哈迪(Hardi)在《印尼新艺术运动》一书中谈到这一批判性观点产生的背景时表示，1977年至1978年间，他游历欧洲各国，期间还参观第六届文献展(Documenta VI)，其中约瑟夫・博伊斯的作品令他惊叹不已。然而，哈迪并不认为这是当代艺术萌芽的标志。接着，他把20世纪初印尼现代艺术先驱苏若约诺(Soedjojono)和民族主义艺术家约瑟夫・博伊斯的普世人文主义思想进行了比较。

为了使自己的主张合法化，哈迪把目光投向了东爪哇群岛上的传统戏剧表演，这是种旨在批判当局反映社会民生的艺术形式。他提出，传统戏剧社所面临的挑战自殖民时期到印尼民族独立后一直存在。即使是不断被压迫甚至迫害，戏剧表演者们坚定地艺术立场从未动摇。[22]

哈迪的视角表明，在艺术学界之外滋生出了一种现代艺术，而这种艺术对现代化是持批判性的态度。除了民族性的一面，它也展现出同情弱势群体、维护被压迫者利益的一面。这种艺术表现形式是基于通过民族主义精神展现普世价值观的新的尝试。[23]

哈迪的观点表明现代艺术发展和印尼当代艺术并没有严格的分界线。由此看来，印尼新艺术运动——当代

defended their stance even when they had been repeatedly punished/penalized and persecuted. [22]

Hardi's angle is an indicator that outside of the art academies there grew a type of modern art that was actually critical of modernism. Not only nationalistic, this form of modern art also demonstrated a very strong tendency to side/defend with the oppressed. This expression of modern art was built upon the foundation of a certain morality that attempted to understand universal humanism through nationalism. [23]

Hardi's text shows that there really is no strict division between the development of modern art in relation to contemporary art in Indonesia. From this point of view, the Indonesian New Art Movement—signaling the emergence of contemporary art—has returned to the basis of Indonesian modern art which was lost in the 70s due to the intimidation tactics practiced by the dictatorial military government, using nationalism as a tool of power.

Another similarity that is seemingly quite coincidental can be found in the emergence of a type of Pop Art in works by the artists of the Indonesian New Art Movement. This symptom was not rooted in the desire to put forward popular culture. This symptom emerged as a result of Indonesia's exposure to the world, following two decades of being utterly locked in. This openness/exposure then led to culture shock. [24]

Up until 1965, the socialist government under President Soekarno had cut off Indonesia's ties with the international world. In this situation, Indonesia's visual world underwent a certain diminishment. There were no Western movies, no billboards and neon-signs, no magazines, books and printed materials showing the advancements in the world of design. All products containing signs of a 'Western aesthetic' were denied circulation, and were believed to spread liberal-capitalist ideals.

This situation ended in 1965. The liberal-militaristic government under President Suharto opened up Indonesia. Thus emerged a new wave of activity aimed at building the country's failing economy. In the hunt for a 7.5% economic growth rate, Indonesia opened its doors as wide as possible to multinational investment firms, which began to flow in almost immediately at the beginning of the 1970s.

艺术萌芽的标志——实质是返璞归真、追本溯源，回到了20世纪70年代前没有军政府独裁统治、以民族主义作为宣传利器的时代。

另一个不谋而合的相似点体现在印尼新艺术运动作品中波普艺术元素的出现。这种流行艺术并没有推广流行文化的原始冲动，而是基于印尼闭关锁国二十年后重新拥抱世界的现实。这次开放带来了重大的文化冲击。[24]

从苏加诺上台一直到1965年，他领导的社会主义政权切断了印尼与国际社会的一切联系。在这种情况下，印尼的视觉艺术领域受到诸多限制：在国内，禁止放映西方电影，没有广告牌，没有霓虹灯，杂志、书刊等一切体现现代设计理念的印刷品都难觅踪影。所有打上“西方美学”烙印的产品都因体现自由资本主义的价值观被禁止发售流通。

直到1965年苏哈托总统建立起自由军事政府，上述情况才成为历史。此时重振经济雄风乃当务之急；为完成当局制定的7.5%的经济增长目标，印尼重新开放国门，尽最大努力引入外资。70年代初跨国投资公司迅速进入印尼市场。

急速的转变让印尼重新认识了世界。各类五花八门的杂志、印刷品、摄影作品、广告牌、宣传品如雨后春笋般涌出，极大地丰富和取悦了人们的感官，甚至出现了购买外国杂志的浪潮和青少年沉溺国际流行文化的现象——孩子们珍藏海报，对名牌、流行元素和广告形象如数家珍。

面对如此大的视觉冲击和变幻，一些日惹的年轻画家感到震撼——之前苍白的画面变得如此多娇，并在不断更新丰富中。和其他年少年一样，这些年轻的艺术家们开始收集剪切杂志封面、广告图片、T恤、照片和海报。渐渐地，他们觉得用手头的收藏品也能用来

This abrupt change altered the visual world that was previously impoverished. Magazines, printed materials, photographs, billboards, and advertisements appeared almost out of nowhere, stimulating visual sensation, and affecting people's sensorial faculties. A certain foreign-magazine buying fever gripped the society at that time, and thus emerged a measure of greed in the teenage audience for the world of pop. They hoarded posters, logos of famous products, popular symbols and advertising images.

In the midst of this condition, a few young painters in Yogyakarta underwent some shock, facing a changing visual reality. The visual world around them suddenly became very colorful. Their experience became extremely enriched. Like the teenagers, these young artists collected cuttings of magazine covers, advertising pictures, t-shirts, photographs, and posters. And in this situation emerged the idea to use this collection to create new things.

Suatmaji was the first painter to explore this condition. In the 1970s, he began to create collages out of photographs, advertising images, logos of well-known products, as well as popular symbols, haphazardly placed on his canvases. He felt that the pictures, photos, and magazine covers around him were good enough as they were and that he did not need to look for other ideas.

With his ability to paint realistically, Suatmadji was compelled to create a realistic painting copying those advertising images and the torn out magazine pages. Upon canvas, he connected these paintings, attaching the real photographs and torn magazine pages. In this way, he represented an illusion of adhesion, by blurring the boundaries marking the difference between what was actually pasted on and what was painted.

Dede Eri Supria brought realistic art to the Indonesian New Art Movement when he joined in 1977. In his paintings, Dede Eri Supria not only blurred the difference between painting and torn out magazines. His ability to paint realistically made it possible for him to blur the boundaries between realistic paintings and three-dimensional objects as well.

This activity jump-started a large wave of work, especially in the city of Yogyakarta. It owed itself to the ability to paint realistically, due to the education system in this city's higher education academy for art (now

创作一些东西。

苏阿特玛吉(Suatmaji)是其中的先行者。早在20世纪70年代，他就开始用照片、广告图像、名牌商标，流行标识随意地制作成拼贴画。在他看来，这些图像、照片和杂志封面本身就是极好的创作素材，都不必另觅他山之石。

苏阿特玛吉凭借扎实的功底，创造出一幅幅现实主义的作品，有的是模仿了广告图像，有的灵感则来自旧杂志。在画布上，他尽情挥洒，将这些画和真实的影像、旧杂志联系起来。由此创造出虚幻的衔接，拼贴画和手绘画的界限也变得模糊起来。

1977年，迪德・埃里・苏普里尔(Dede Eri Supria)将现实主义艺术形式引入到印尼新艺术运动中来。在迪德・埃里・苏普里尔的作品里，他凭借高超的技艺，不仅把绘画作品和旧杂志有机地结合起来，甚至还使得现实派绘画和三维实体变得界限模糊。

这种趋势随之发展壮大并形成社会浪潮，尤其在日惹——印尼最高艺术殿堂(现称为印尼艺术学院艺术和设计系)所在地。印尼艺术学院的教育模式和对现实派绘画教学的精益求精是此浪潮发展壮大的重要原因。其实早在1950年学院成立之初，这种方法已经得到应用。到了60年代，社会现实主义得到了当局社会主义政府的肯定。

因此，日惹的艺术院校毕业生精通现实主义绘画。当他们对广告图像有着浓厚兴趣并产生强烈的模仿欲望时，在此基础上应用现实主义的绘画技艺也并不是什么难事。

以现实主义绘画技巧为表达语言直到今天都是长盛不衰的经典手法。除了展示各类流行文化偶像，这种手法也常用于超现实主义表达阴郁消极的主题。

the Faculty of Art and Design at the Indonesian Art Institute). They have always been known to be very meticulous in the instruction of realistic painting. This method began its implementation in 1950, the year of the Institute's inception. This instruction received affirmation in the 1960s when social realism received its commendation from the ruling socialist government at that time.

Thus, most of Yogyakarta's higher education alumni were very adept in realistic painting. When they became interested in advertisements and felt compelled to copy them, these artists did not meet any obstacles in putting them into application, particularly because they had mastered realistic painting techniques.

The tendency to use realistic painting techniques as a language of expression holds firm even through till today. In addition to displaying the various icons of popular culture, this language of expression is also used to display surrealistic spaces in otherwise bleak expressions.

Studies of the emergence of contemporary art in Indonesia demonstrate clearly the similarities and differences compared to the emergence of contemporary art in Europe and the United States. From this 'window' we may see the development of art at large in Indonesia showing, again, both similarities and differences.

Art in an Indonesian Sense

The Indonesian New Art Movement's manifesto, which can be used as source material to question the current contemporaneity, is a declaration that demonstrates a consciousness of local art history. In the movement's manifesto it is noted: "To aspire the development of an art that is 'Indonesian', by prioritizing knowledge on the history of new art, beginning with Raden Saleh."

Raden Saleh was an Indonesian painter who lived in the 19th century (1807-1880). At that time, Indonesia was still a colony of the Dutch empire. Raden Saleh was known as the only native/indigenous painter appointed as painter to the Dutch empire.

Raden Saleh was a romanticist, who had traveled to various European countries, living in the Netherlands (1829-1839), Germany (1839-1844), and Paris,

对印尼当代艺术崛起与发展的研究清晰地展现出其与欧美当代艺术历史进程的异同。通过这样一扇“窗户”，我们也能再现印尼整体艺术的发展及其异同点。

印尼语境中的艺术

“印尼新艺术运动”的宣言对时下艺术领域的当代性提出了质疑，同时也是具本土艺术史上的一次觉醒。宣言强调：“应从萨勒开始，梳理新兴艺术的发展历史，以此弘扬‘印尼’本土艺术。”

萨勒(Raden Saleh, 1807-1880)是19世纪的印尼画家。当时印尼仍是荷兰帝国的殖民地，而萨勒也是当时获得荷兰帝国任命的唯一印尼本土画家。

萨勒是浪漫派画家，曾周游欧洲列国，先后在荷兰(1929-1939)、德国(1939-1844)和法国巴黎(1844-1851)居住。他的绘画作品《蒂博尼哥罗王子被俘》(1857)描绘了反抗残暴殖民统治斗争中的关键之役。这幅作品的风格与弗朗西斯科・戈雅的《1808年5月3日》(1815)相似，而后者再现了一个反抗西班牙统治的农民在生命最后时刻面对行刑队伍的场面。

在约翰・克拉克的研究中，萨勒的《蒂博尼哥罗王子被俘》显示出19世纪亚洲各国现代思潮、爱国主义和艺术觉醒的萌芽迹象。约翰・克拉克写道：

> 当代艺术话语中相对化的产生条件，直接由一个国家的自治程度建构产生。国民性话语建立在殖民地的本土话语之上，而民主主义话语则使自己区别于殖民统治，以形成国民性话语。其最初的表现方式可见萨勒于1850年创作的《1825-1830爪哇战争后蒂博尼哥罗王子为德・科克将军将军所俘》……。[26]

1990年至今，我在若干文章中都提出过与约翰・克拉克类似的观点，即萨勒的集体绘画代表了19世纪印

France (1844-1851). His painting, The Capture of Prince Diponegoro (1857), depicts the critical point of the fight against colonial tyrannical politics. This painting can be seen in similar light to Francisco Goya's The Third of May (1815), which shows the final moments of a peasant facing a firing squad for defying the power of the Spanish monarchy.

In John Clark's study, Raden Saleh's The Capture of Prince Diponegoro represents the emergent signs of modern thought, the embryo of nationalism and artistic consciousness in Asia in the 19th century. John Clark writes:

> The condition under which the relativisation of existing art discourses took place are directly structured by the degree of type of state autonomy. The discourse of the national is founded on the local context of the colonial. Nationalist discourse distinguishes itself from the colonial order to found the national. Among the earliest expressions of this is Raden Saleh 1850's dipiction of The Capture of Prince Diponegoro by General De Kock after the Java War of 1825-1830 [...] [26]

Parallel to John Clark's exposition, I have put forward, in a number of publications since the 1990s, that Raden Saleh's collective paintings signal the presence of art in a Western sense in Indonesia in the 19th century.

Raden Saleh was a nobleman from the Javanese Classical Tradition, which was emergent in the 19th century (note: Javanese Tradition is one of Indonesia's ethnic traditions). The Javanese Classical Tradition in the 19th century was a mestizo tradition, created by the Dutch colonial government together with Javanese noblemen. In this tradition, one will be able to find many signs of cultural translation—the adaptation of certain lifestyles, ways of thinking, and systems of government. One of them being the translation of art in a Western sense.

This translation is reflected by the introduction of the term "kagunan" into the Javanese language, which can be found in the High Javanese Language Dictionary Baoesastra Jawa. [27] We do not know when this term was conceived, but this term can be found in old scripts written by the royal scribe, Ronggowarsito (1802-1873).

尼本土艺术(此处对艺术的定义是按照西方观念的)的萌芽。

萨勒是一名贵族，他的创作风格源于19世纪的爪哇古典传统(爪哇传统风格是印尼的民族传统风格之一)。19世纪的爪哇古典传统风格是一种兼容并蓄的多元风格，受荷兰殖民政府和爪哇贵族两方影响。在这种风格中，人们可以发现诸多文化移植的特征——如移风易俗的生活方式、思维方法、行政体系，其中之一就是对西方观念中的艺术的翻译与引进。

为了如实反映这种多元观念的交融，我们不妨借助一个爪哇语名词“kagunan”。这个词可在高级爪哇语词典《鲍氏爪哇》(Baoesastra Jawa)[27]中查得，词源不得而知，但可在爪哇宫廷作家朗哥瓦西多(1802-1873)的手稿中找到。

其他若干历史记录中，我们亦可觅得该词的踪迹，这进一步印证了它是在19世纪中期出现的。例如：荷兰皇家艺术与科学院的塔克·罗尔达(Taco Roorda)教授、德尔福特(Delft，爪哇学先驱)和萨斯特拉-塔玛(Sastra-Tama，精通爪哇语写作的平民)的共同合作项目，该项目于1848年进行，旨在拓展爪哇语的语言结构。项目的实施方案于1833年起草，由位于爪哇岛(时为荷兰殖民政府行政中心)的爪哇语学院负责规划设计。[28]

“Kagunan”一词显示出爪哇人试图定义“艺术现象”的尝试。而这一尝试在印尼其他民族的文化传统中绝无仅有。同世界各民族的文化一样，印尼民族文化传统并不认同这种对艺术的定义。因此，从“kagunan”这个词的构词法明显带有西方思潮的印记。

从语言学的角度分析，“kagunan”的词源要追溯到公元前500年古希腊语中的单词“mousikě technĕ”(缪

There are several historical notes that can strengthen the signs of this term's appearance in the middle of the 19th century. Among others are the collaborative works of Professor Taco Roorda from the Royal Academie, and Delft (a pioneer in Javanology) with Sastra-Tama (a nobleman who mastered the written Javanese language) in developing the structure of Javanese language. This happened in 1848. This developmental project was started in 1833 by the inception of the Instituut voor het Javaansche Taal (Institute for Javanese Language) in Java, the administrative center of the Dutch colonial government.[28]

The term kagunan in Javanese language reflects the attempts to define the art phenomenon. The attempt to define the art phenomenon cannot be found in other ethnic traditions in Indonesia. Like all other ethnic cultures in the world, Indonesian ethnic traditions do not recognize the definition of art. Thus, as seen from the method of its inception, kagunan has been influenced by Western thought traditions.

Through a linguistic inquiry we can observe that the term kagunan utilizes the term mousikě technĕ of the Ancient Greek language (500 BC) as its source. The term mousikě technĕ is in many ways the basis for thinking about art in Western culture. It is first translated into the term 'artes liberals,' or 'liberal arts' in Latin, which was then reformulated as the term 'art' in English, which has now become the ideological foundation of art in a Western sense.[29]

The creation and the meaning of kagunan are close to the creation and meaning of mousikě technĕ. The base word of this term is 'technĕ', which means "a work that has use and benefit." The root word of kagunan is guna, which has the same meaning with the base word of mousikě technĕ. In Baoesastra Jawa, the word 'guna' is also noted to mean: character, skill, having distinction, a beneficial product or useful product. Meanwhile, the literal meaning of kagunan is also close to the understanding of mousikě, that is: inspiration, or a poetic urge.

Though coming from the same source, the artistic sensibility behind the term kagunan is not the same as the art sensibilities behind the word art in English. The understanding of mousikě technĕ is that of a mental activity, distinguished from an activity of physical toil. In kagunan, these two activities cannot be separated. The artistic sensibilities behind the English word art emphasizes this aspect of mental activity

斯的艺术)。该词可谓西方文化中文艺思想的基石，它最早在拉丁语中译作“文艺”(artes liberales或liberal arts)，随后在英语中译作“艺术”，并成为了西方观念中艺术思想体系的基础。[29]

“Kagunan”的形成和词义同“mousikĕ technĕ”非常接近。后者的主体部分为“technĕ”，意为“有用或有益的作品”。“kagunan”的词根是“guna”，意义与“technĕ”相同。在《鲍氏爪哇》词典中，“guna”还表示“性格”、“技巧”、“有鲜明特征”、“有益的产品”、“有用的产品”。此外，“kagunan”的字面意思还与“mousikĕ”相似，即“灵感”或“创作欲”。

虽然系出同源，但“kagunan”语义中包含的艺术感知力与英语单词“art”中的艺术感知力却不尽相同。“Mousikĕ technĕ”代表了思维活动，与体力活动不同，而“kagunan”则包含了思维和体力两层意思。正如18世纪时期黑格尔、康德、舍勒和叔本华作品中所提到的“mousikĕ technĕ”，英语“art”中包含的艺术感知力更侧重于思维活动(思想、脑力劳动)。

受印尼民族艺术感知力的影响，“kagunan”词义中兼有脑力活动和体力劳动的双重涵义。现已证明，该词提升了“手工艺”的地位。在《鲍氏爪哇》词典中，“kagunan”的释义为：“绘画、雕刻、创造音乐的技艺，是一种有用的能力。”[30]

这也反映出“kagunan”词义所包含的艺术感知力与18世纪美学理论(在德国广为接受)有相似之处，而这理论又最终被黑格尔、康德、舍勒和叔本华等人抛弃。对于美学思想中的艺术感知力，维基百科有如下阐释：

艺术是为了唤起某种感觉或情感而有目的地组织

(thought, mind-work) of mousikě techně as reflected in the works of Hegel, Kant, Scheler, and Schopenhauer in the 18th century.

The tendency to not distinguish between mental activity and physical toil in the term kagunan reveals the influence of ethnic art sensibilities. Here, it is demonstrated that kagunan elevates craftsmanship. In Baoesastra Jawa the definition of kagunan is thus: "the skill to create pictures, carving, and music composition and a useful capacity."[30]

This symptom reveals how the artistic sensibilities behind kagunan are close to the artistic sensibilities of the Aesthetics in the 18th century (especially in its expansion in Germany), which was actually abandoned by Hegel, Kant, Scheler, and Schopenhauer. Regarding the artistic sensibilities of aesthetic thought, Wikipedia records:

> Art is the process or product of deliberately arranging elements in a way that appeals to the senses or emotions. It encompasses a diverse range of human activities, creations and modes of expression, including music and literature.
>
> [...] Traditionally, the term art was used to refer to any skill or mastery.

Craftsmanship, in the definition of kagunan, cannot be seen as based upon the current understanding of art, which tends to see it as the skills of handiwork, which are separate from mind-work. I view craftsmanship as centered upon the thoughts of Richard Sennett, who provocatively states that "making is thinking."

Richard Sennett is a second-wave Pragmatist—which is currently still progressing, especially in Europe—which continues the agenda of pragmatic cognition regarding homo faber (man as maker). [31] In his book, The Craftsman, published in 2008, Richard Sennett posits:

> "Craftsmanship" may sugggest a way of life that waned with the advent of industrial Society—but this is misleading. Craftsmanship names an eduring, basic human impulse, the desire to do a job well for its own sake. Craftsmanship cuts a far wider swath than skilled manual labor [.....]. The Craftsman explores dimensions of skill, commitment, and judgement in a particular way.

> 素材的过程或产物。其范畴极为广泛，涉及人类活动、创造发明和表现手法(包括音乐和文学)。
>
> ……传统观念中，艺术这个词是用来指代技巧或精通程度的。

按“kagunan”的定义，我们不能将“手工艺”的意义等同于当今人们对“艺术”的理解。这种理解割裂了脑力劳动而更侧重于手工技巧。而我对“手工艺”的理解则基于理查德·桑内特(Richard Sennett)的理论，他曾提出颇有争议的观点：“创作即思考”。

理查德·桑内特是第二次实用主义浪潮的参与者——该运动延续至今，尤以欧洲为甚，他始终不移地坚持“人即制造者”[31]的实用主义认知纲要，在2008年出版的著作《巧匠》(The Craftsman)中，他提出了这一设想：

> “手工艺”也许代表一种随着工业社会发展而逐渐没落的生活——但这会让人产生误解。手工艺包含的是一种持久而基本的人类冲动，一种出于对工作热爱而把工作干好的意愿。它的含义远比“熟练的手工劳动”广泛……《巧匠》以独特方式探究技巧、义务和判断力方面的问题。这些问题主要集中在双手与大脑的紧密联系中。每一名优秀的匠人都能在实际操作和思考之间建立起联系。这种联系会演化成持久的习惯，随后这些习惯会在寻找问题和解决问题之间建立起规律。[32]

“Kagunan”含义中的“手工艺”即包含上述认知理解过程。就定义而言，“kagunan”表示“用来表达美的思想与知觉的共生”，其本土内涵再次得到证明。在爪哇哲学中，更确切地说，几乎在所有印尼民族思想传统中，这种思想和知觉的共生与道德伦理有关，反映了对善良的和积极的思考的认同尝试。

It focuses on intimate connection between hand and head. Every good craftsman conducts a dialogue between concrete practices and thinking; this dialogue evolves into sustaining habits, and these habits establish a rythm between problem solving and problem finding.[32]

Craftsmanship in kagunan carries such a cognitive understanding. Definition-wise, kagunan is noted as "the simultaneous development of thought and feeling based on the expression of beauty." This again demonstrates the locality of content. In Javanese philosophy—and almost all thoughts of ethnic traditions in Indonesia—this simultaneous development of thought and feeling reflects the attempt to recognize goodness and positive thinking, as related to moral ethics.

The artistic sensibilities behind kagunan endure even until now in Indonesia because its very underlying logic forms the foundation for the understanding of the terms 'art' in the Indonesian lanaguage. Bahasa Indonesia is a modern language conceived together with Indonesia as a nation and country in the beginning of the 20th century, as a development of the Malay language system, the lingua franca in the Far East prior to the colonial period. [33]

In 2008, the Indonesian National Gallery in Jakarta organized a grand exhibition of Indonesian art to celebrate 100 years of national awakening (which 'occurred' in 1908). In this exhibition, the artistic sensibility behind 'Seni' (art)—with kagunan as its basis, which emerged in the 19th century—was distributed to all Indonesian artists that have received acknowledgement. The aim was to seek a certain accord. This exhibition presented 354 artists from four generations (the majority of whom were all well-known Indonesian artists). The exhibition title, Manifesto, is also the declaration of Indonesian artists with regard to art in an Indonesian sense. [34]

The basis of this manifesto results from the confusion in the usage of the word seni as the Indonesian translation to the term "art," as used in the world of global art. The confusion results from the fact that the term "art" has two translations in the Indonesian language: (1) "seni" (art); and (2) "seni rupa" (visual art). In the English language, both are alike, whereas in the Indonesian language they are differentiated. In the exhibition, Manifesto, this confusion was explored through a linguistic inquiry, demonstrating the distinction be-

时至今日，“kagunan”包含的艺术感知力仍存在于印尼社会，因为对这个词的理解奠定了印尼语言中对“艺术”这一概念的认知基础。印尼语属于现代语言，它由马来语(在殖民时期前远东的通用语)发展而来，并在20世纪初期与印尼的国家和民族共同成型。[33]

2008年，为庆祝民族觉醒100周年(“开始”于1908年)，位于雅加达的印尼国家画廊举办了一场大型印尼艺术展。展览期间，“艺术”背后艺术感知力的思想——以“kagunan”为基础，起源于19世纪——被传递给所有获得认可的印尼艺术家。这样做旨在寻求共识。这场展览展出了四代共计354名艺术家的作品(大部分是著名印尼艺术家)。展览名称“宣言”代表了印尼艺术家以印尼认知观念审视艺术的宣言。[34]

在全球艺术语境中，“art”一词的印尼译文“seni”所引起的意义上的混淆成为本次宣言展的一大主线。“art”在印尼语中有两种翻译：(1)“seni”(艺术)；(2)“seni rupa”(视觉艺术)。在英语中，两者意义相近；在印尼语中则不同。在取名为“宣言”的展览中，主办方通过语言学的角度分析辨明了两者区别，使这种混淆得以解决。

英语中，艺术与视觉艺术的相似度由英文“艺术”的物体属性所决定。这样的艺术感知力使视觉艺术(拥有实体形态的艺术表达)成为识别艺术现象的主要方式。[35]

印尼语中，“seni rupa”(视觉艺术)由“艺术”(seni)和“视觉的”(rupa)两个词构成，其中“seni”为名词，位于“首位/前位”，而“rupa”则用来形容“seni”，为修饰语。作修饰语的“rupa”可视作形容词(修饰名词“seni”的形容词)。如此，“seni rupa”便与英语中的“visual art”等同起来。

tween the two terms.

In the English language, the analogousness of art and visual art is hinged upon its very thing-ness that is present in the English notion of "art." This artistic sensibility makes visual art (an artistic expression that retains a concrete form) into a primary way to identify artistic phenomena. [35]

In the Indonesian language, the term "seni rupa" (visual art) is made up of two words: "seni" (art), and "rupa" (visual). The word "seni" is a noun, in the 'head'/'leading' position. The word "rupa" describes the word "seni," as a modifier. The word "rupa" as a modifier can be viewed as an adjective, the adjective that modifies the noun 'seni'. Here, the word "seni rupa" becomes equal to the understanding of "visual art" in the English language.

However, the word "rupa" in the term "seni rupa" can also be seen as an adverb (a verb, an adjective, or a noun that explains the noun "seni"). Here the adverb "rupa" (an adjective) has the same status with the other noun-adverbs like dance, theater, and music, and the adjective-adverbs like painting, sculpting, drawing. These analogous, adverbial forms show the perception that views "seni rupa" (visual art) as having an equal position to other artistic expressions (dance, music, and literature). Art, in this case 'visual art', is not the primary way of viewing artistic phenomena.

The important part in this linguistic inquiry is that the primacy of all art expressions is placed upon the word "seni" and not upon its adverbial forms. "Seni" or "art" is an abstract noun that demonstrates a person's mental quality. Upon weighing this definition, such mental quality is located between sensibility and sensitivity, reflecting spiritual knowledge, which Wikipedia notes as having three levels: imagination, inspiration, and intuition. When examining its level of thought, this mental quality is close to pragmatism and far from logocentric philosophy that is concerned with the search for universal truth.[36]

This art, in an Indonesian sense, forms the basis of artistic development since the early 20th century until now, as the cause of its entire line of development—within both eras, the modern and contemporary—as differentiated from the developments in Europe and the United States.

然而，"seni rupa"中的"rupa"也可视作一个副词(一个动词或副词，或者一个用来解释名词"seni"的名词)。在此副词"rupa"(一个形容词)与其他名-副词如舞蹈、剧场和音乐，或者与其他形容-副词如油画、雕刻和绘画等同。这些功能类似的副词形式显示出将"seni rupa"与其他艺术表现形式(舞蹈、音乐和文学)等同的观念。艺术，或者这里所说的"视觉艺术"，便不是考量艺术现象的主要方式。

语言分析的重要性在于所有艺术表现手法的重心都集中在"seni"的名词形式上，而非它的副词形式。无论英语"art"还是印尼语的"seni"都是彰显个人思维状态的抽象名词。细想这个定义，思维状态其实介于感知能力和敏感程度之间，它反映了一个人的心智程度。维基百科将其分为三个维度：想象力、灵感和直觉。当我们开始检验其程度时，这种思维状态就更接近于实用主义的本质，而背离了以追求普遍真理为目标的理性中心论。[36]

印尼语中对艺术的理解，为20世纪初叶至今的艺术发展打下了基础，促进了现代和当代两大领域艺术的勃发，这与欧美的艺术发展又是大相径庭的。

印尼观念中的艺术范畴介于西方观念和印尼民族艺术感知力之间。因此，"印尼观念中的艺术范畴能否与民族艺术感知力等而言之"并非是无法解答的难题。我们可以像理解印尼和西方观念中的艺术差异那样，轻而易举地区分其中的异同。这一现象体现了全球当代艺术的多元性，因此对于当代性理解的争议——正如"大地魔术师"展后引起的关注——永远不会有答案。

结语

综上所述，特里·史密斯的专著进行了一次有益的尝试。他几乎对当代艺术的每一个方面都进行了探索，但是却从未就何谓当代艺术提出过真正明确的结论。

Art in an Indonesian sense is located between art in a Western sense and ethnic art sensibilities. Thus the question: "Can art in the Indoensian sense be equated to ethnic art sensibilities?" is not a problematic question that cannot be answered. The similarities and differences can easily be identified, and it is as easy as it is to understand the differences and similarities of art in an Indonesian sense and art in a Western sense. This is a sign of multeity in global contemporary art. Here, the controversy behind the understanding of contemporaneity—like what was evidenced during and after the exhibition of Les Magiciens de la Terre—will never surface.

In Closing

For me, Terry Smith's book is a welcome exposition. Terry Smith explores almost all corners of contemporary art, but never offers any clear conclusion as to what contemporary art really is. This book inspires me to liken the emergence of contemporary art with the 'Big Bang' theory within cosmology. After 40 years of growth, fragments of contemporary art that have escaped from the 'big bang of modernism' are beginning to undergo a process of stabilization, and are beginning to become comprehensible.

Understanding the development of art outside Europe and the United States is like finding the dark side of a moon that has heretofore remained hidden from sight, but it is nevertheless important to the understanding of said moon. However, like the celestial objects—galaxies, constellations, and the solar system with its attendant planets—the particles within contemporary art are understood without there being any structural understanding of art. Art is a universal symptom that resides within human life, throughout all ages and all cultures. It can be experienced through diverse ways of expression, reflecting one's consciousness of diverse art forms. However, art can never be fully identified. Like the way that the universe reflects God's omnipotence, likewise it can never be fully understood, but can definitely be experienced.

他的专著启发了我把当代艺术的崛起比作“宇宙大爆炸”理论。在经历了40余年的发展后，脱胎于“现代主义大爆炸”的当代艺术的碎片开始进入一个稳定化的过程，逐渐变得更可以为大家所理解。

要去了解欧美以外地区艺术发展情况就好比发现月亮背着光的阴影面，虽然困难，但是对于了解整个月球却具有非常重要的意义。然而，跟银河、星座、太阳系和行星共同组成的天体星系一样，对于当代艺术粒子的理解不可以脱离对艺术的结构性理解。不论身处哪个时代、哪种文化环境，艺术都是人类生活中一个普遍的常驻元素。我们可以通过多元的表达方式来体验艺术，通过各种艺术形式来呈现我们的思考与想法。然而，艺术却从未被完整地定义过。就如宇宙展现了上帝的全能，虽然不可能完全被理解，但是绝对能够被感知。

1 Regarding "modernism as institution", see: Brian Wallis, "What's Wrong with this Picture, An Introduction" in Art After Modernism, Rethinking Representation. Brian Wallis (ed.). The New Museum of Contemporary Art NY. 1992. p.xii.

2 Quoted by Micahel Schreyach in his text, "The Recovery of Criticism" in The State of Art Criticism. James Elkin, Micahael Newman (ed.). Routledge. NY. 2008.

3 "Art is Money". The World and I. October 1990.

4 Special Report. The Economist. Nov-Dec. 2009.

5 Globality – Competing with Everyone from Everywhere for Everything. Jointly written by Harold L. Sirkin, James W. Hemerling, and Arindam K. Bhattacharya. Business Plus. NY. 2008. pp 1-2.

6 "Contemporary Art as Global Art, A Critical Estimate," Hans Belting. in The Global Art World. Audiences, Markets and Museums. Hans Belting, Andrea Buddensieg (ed.). Hatje Cantz. Ostfinden. 2009. pp. 38-73.

7 Ibid.

8 Keynote speech in "A New Geography of Art in the Making" Seminar, held in Center for Art and Media, Karlsruhe; with Göethe Institute. Hongkong 21- 22 Mei, 2009.

9 What is Contemporary Art? Terry Smith. University of Chicago. Chicago-London.2009. pp. 5-6

10 Wikipedia.

11 This symptom can be seen in text by Dennis Dutton, "But They Don't Have Our Concept of Art" in Teories of Art Today. Noël Caroll. (ed). The University of Wisconsin Press. London. 2000. pp.217-238

12 In 1990, the exhibition "Modern Indonesian Art, Three Generation of Tradition and Change" curated by Joseph Fisher, Astri Wright (USA), and Helena Spanjard (the Netherlands), part of the Festival of Indonesia in United States, was turned down by art museums in the United States. The curators were advised to submit their exhibition proposal to anthropological museums, since most of the pieces on show demonstrated ethnic markings/signs.

13 Art Today. Edward Lucie-Smith. Phaidon, London. 1999. p. 10.

14 Contemporary Art. Klaus Honeff. Taschen. Koln. 1992. p 41.

15 Opcit. P 47.

16 In Art after Modernism. Opcit. pp. 189-201.

17 Is Art History Global ? James Elkins (ed.) Routledge. NY. 2007. pp.v – viii.

18 They, Jim Supangkat, Hardi, B. Munni Ardhi, Harsono, Siti Adyati, Nanik Mirna, Pandu Sudewo, Ris Purwana, Anyool

1 关于"以现代主义为正统"，参见：《哪里错了？——导论》，布莱恩・瓦里斯著，收录于《现代主义之后的艺术：反思与重现》(布莱恩・瓦里斯主编)，新当代艺术博物馆，纽约，1992，p.xii

2 引自《批评的复苏》，迈克尔・斯克雷亚克著，收录于《艺术批评现状》(詹姆斯・埃尔金斯、迈克尔・纽曼主编)，Routledge出版社，纽约，2008

3 《艺术就是金钱》，《世界与我》杂志，1990年10月

4 2009.特别报道，《经济学人》，2009年11-12月

5 《全球性——与地球每个角落的每个人竞争每件事》，哈罗德・L・塞金、詹姆斯・W・何莫林、奥林丹・K・巴塔查亚合著，Business Plus出版社，纽约，2008，pp 1-2

6 《当代艺术・全球艺术：一份批判性评估》，汉斯・贝尔廷著，收录于《全球艺术世界：观众、市场与博物馆》(汉斯・贝尔廷、安吉拉・白蒂斯格主编)，Hatje Cantz出版社，Ostfinden，2009，pp. 38-73

7 同上

8 汉斯・贝尔廷在"艺术新版图"研讨会上的发言，卡尔斯鲁厄市艺术媒体中心/香港歌德学院联合主办，2009年5月21-22日

9 《什么是当代艺术》，泰瑞・史密斯著，芝加哥大学出版社，芝加哥–伦敦，2009，pp. 5-6

10 维基百科

11 参见丹尼斯・杜顿(Dennis Dutton)著《但是他们没有我们的艺术观念》，收录于《当代艺术理论》(诺埃尔・卡罗尔主编)，威斯康辛大学出版社，伦敦，2000，pp.217-238

12 1990年，作为美国印尼艺术节的相关活动，由约瑟夫・费雪、阿斯特里・怀特(美国)和海伦娜・斯潘贾德(荷兰)所共同策划的"现代印尼艺术，三代的传统和变革"被美国各大艺术馆拒之门外。由于大部分展出作品具有鲜明的民族特征/记号，三位策展人被建议向人类博物馆提交展览方案。

13 《艺术・当代》，爱德华・路西–史密斯著，Phaidon出版社，伦敦，1999，p. 10

14 《当代艺术》，克劳斯・霍内夫著，Taschen出版社，科隆，1992，p 41

15 前引书，P 47

16 《现代主义后的艺术》，前引书，pp. 189-201

17 《艺术史是全球性的吗？》，詹姆斯・埃尔金斯主编，Routledge出版社，纽约，2007，pp.v-viii

18 "他们"包括：Jim Supangkat, Hardi, B. Munni Ardhi, Harsono, Siti Adyati, Nanik Mirna, Pandu Sudewo, Ris Purwana, Anyool Subroto, Bachtiar Zainul等。

19 《印尼新艺术运动》。杰姆・苏潘凯特主编，Gramedia出版社，雅加达，1979年，p.xix

20 《现代亚洲艺术》，约翰・克拉克著，Craftsman House出版社，悉尼，1998年，p. 226.

Subroto, and Bachtiar Zainul.

19 Gerakan Seni Rupa Baru Indonesia. Jim Supangkat (ed.). Gramedia, Jakarta.1979. p.xix

20 Modern Asian Art. John Clark. Craftsman House, Sydney. 1998.p. 226.

21 Gerakan Seni Rupa Baru. Ibid

22 Opcit.pp. 4-17.

23 It can be seen as the paradigm of modern Indonesian art stemming from Sodjojono's thoughts. In 1946, Soedjojono wrote "[…] We can tell ourselves that we are internationalists, after we are able to become nationalists. How can an artist […] want to show his love to the international world, when he is unable to love his brethren and country? […]" Written in text titled, "Seorang Seniman Dengan Sendirinya Harus Seorang Nasionalis" ("An artist must, by default, be a nationalist"). In his anthology, Seni Lukis, Kesenian dan Seniman. Indonesia Sekarang, Yogyakarta. 1946. pp 22-27.

24 "Painstaking Realism in Indonesian Contemporary Painting". Curatorial Introduction. Jim Supangkat. Katalog Pameran The Mutation. The Japan Foundation Forum, Tokyo. August 1997. pp.33-41

25 Indonesian Modern Art and Beyond. Jim Supangkat. Indonesia Fine Art Foundation,Jakarta. 1997. p 22.

26 Modern Asian Art. Opcit. p.241.

27 Baoesastra Jawa. Pigeaud.Th. (et.al). JB Wolters. Groningen –Batavia, 1939.

28 Di Negeri Penjajah – Orang Indonesia di Negeri Balenda 1600-1950. Harry A.Poeze. KITLV-Jakarta.2008.p.16

29 Keywords. A Vocabulary of Culture and Society. Raymond Williams Fontana Press. London.1988. pp.32-33, pp.40-43.

30 See Sanento Yuliman's text in this catalog.

31 The first wave of Pragmatism emerged in the US at the end of the 18th century, in reaction to European idealistic thoughts which tend to break down abstract questions, searching for universally-applicable truths. Pragmatism has a tendency to want to solve life's (day-to-day) problems and challenges. Some of Pragmatism's first exponents are: C.S. Peirce, William James, and John Dewey. Pragmatism's second wave emerged following the end of World War II, evolving, until now, through several generations of Pragmatists. Current Pragmatists, other than Richard Sennett, include names such as Hans Joas, Richard Rorty, and Richard Bernstein. Both the first- and the second-wave of Pragmatism continuously question homo faber (man as maker) within the context of work and production systems/regimes.

21 《印尼新艺术运动》，同上

22 前引书，pp. 4-17

23 这可以看成是从苏若约诺开始的印尼现代艺术的模式。1946年，苏若约诺写到“【……】我们只有先成为民族主义者后才有可能成为国际主义者。如果一个艺术家都无法爱自己的同胞，自己的祖国，他又怎么可能爱这个世界呢？”(引子《一个艺术家必须先是个民族主义者》，选自苏若约诺文集《绘画艺术、艺术与艺术家》，印尼Sekarang出版社，日惹，1946，pp 22-27)

24 《印尼当代绘画中历经苦难的现实主义》(“突变”展览画册策展前言)，杰姆・苏潘凯特著，日本基金会论坛，东京，1997年8月，pp.33-41

25 《印尼现代艺术及其他》，杰姆・苏潘凯特著，印尼美术基金会，雅加达，1997年，p 22

26 《现代亚洲艺术》，约翰・克拉克著，Craftsman House出版社，悉尼，1998年，p.241。

27 《鲍氏爪哇》，Pigeaud.Th等编，Groningen: J.B. Wolters出版社，雅加达，1939年

28 《荷属东印度1600-1950》，Harry A. Poeze著，KITLV出版社，雅加达，2008，p.16

29 《关键词：文化与社会词汇》，Raymond Williams著，Fontana出版社，伦敦，1988年，pp.32-33，pp.40-43

30 参见画册中收录的萨能托・于利曼的文章。

31 实用主义第一次浪潮在18世纪末期兴起于美国，其目的为对抗可能无法面对抽象问题的欧洲理想主义思潮，并寻求普适真理。实用主义是试图解决(每日)生活实际问题和挑战的思潮，初期拥护者有：C.S. 皮尔斯，威廉・詹姆斯，和约翰・杜威。第二次实用主义浪潮自二战结束后开始，迄今已发展多代实用主义者。时下成员除理查德・桑内特外，还包括汉斯・约阿斯，理查德・罗缇，以及理查德・伯恩斯坦。两代实用主义者均质疑工作和生产体系中“人即制造者”之语。第一次浪潮试图用19世纪萌芽的社会主义分析此问题。第二次浪潮则摒弃此法，更倾向于用探究工作和生产体系中不同人每日生活的各个方面。

32 《巧匠》，理查德・桑内特著，Allen Lane出版社，伦敦，2008，p.9

33 印尼是一个后殖民国家，其疆域曾被荷兰帝国占领长达300年之久。在二战中，自1942至1945年间，印尼被日本入侵者所统治。1945年二战结束后，不久领土被宣布成为“印度尼西亚”。将殖民地当地居民视为一个国家民族的概念最早起源于20世纪初。由此，“印尼”并非指一个单独的民族或种族团体。今天在印尼，有约350个种族团体使用约500种语言，他们之间并无清晰可辨的区别。

34 《艺术宣言》(策展前言)，J杰姆・苏潘凯特著，《宣言——印尼视觉艺术大展》画册，印尼国家画廊，2008年5-6

The first wave tends to view it through socialism which was growing in the 19th century. Pragmatism's second wave departed from this paradigm, more inclined to explore the various personal dan daily aspects of work and production systems.

32 The Craftsman. Richard Sennett. Allen Lane. London.2008. p.9

33 Indonesia is a post-colonial country. It's territory is comprised of what was the colonial territory of the Dutch Empire for 300 years. During World War II, between 1942-1945, this territory fell under the control of the Japanese Empire. Soon after the end of World War II in 1945, this territory is declared to be the territory of "Indonesia". The concept of viewing the residents within this colonial territory as a nation emerged in the beginning of the 20th century. Thus "Indonesia" do not point to a certain race or ethnic group. Currently, in Indonesia, there are around 350 ethnic groups with relationships that cannot be clearly drawn out between one and the other. This 350 ethnic groups utilize around 500 languages.

34 "Manifesto Seni". Curatorial Introduction. Jim Supangkat. Katalog Manifesto - Pameran Besar Seni Rupa Indonesia. Indonesia National Gallery. Mei-June 2008. pp.27-28.

35 "But They Don't Have Our Concept of Art". Theoreis of Art Today. Ibid.p.225

36 In my assessment, there are differences between thoughts behind the expression of modern art and the thoughts behind the expression of contemporary art. Modern art, ending with Abstractism/Abstract Art reflects a logocentric thinking that is epistemologic. Contemporary art which is increasingly inquiring about the day-to-day (through craftsmanship), reflects pragmatism.

月，pp.27-28

35 《但是他们没有我们的艺术观念》，收录于《当代艺术理论》，同注[11]，p225。

36 我认为，对于现代艺术表达和当代艺术表达背后的思想是有区别的。现代艺术最终走向抽象艺术，反映了认识论的理性中心主义。当代艺术则不断关注每日生活(通过手工技艺)，反映了实用主义趋向。

BILJANA CIRIC
比利安娜・思瑞克

Individuals as Medium - New Models of Mondialite

个体媒介——世界性的新模式

It is very difficult from a curatorial perspective to produce a sense of reality through an exhibition that represents a single country and it's current emissions of thought and visual culture, which will be presented in another country that doesn't really understand the current state of Indonesian social and cultural development. Contemporaneity - Contemporary art in Indonesia intends to work the structure of the exhibition around individual artists and their artistic oeuvre, providing insight into some of the most important individuals in contemporary culture, with particular emphasis on film and visual arts.

In this exhibition the curator's role is to act as the medium through which we all try to provide a platform that could be the starting point for a future, more in depth understanding of cultural practitioners in Indonesia.

This exhibition does not attempt to evaluate what is Indonesian, but to look at the contemporary art practice in Indonesia as a possible model of reference for many cultures that are not considered as central powers with respect to contemporary visual art, but who perhaps in last few decades have developed their own models that are very unique to their particular locality and existence, and who could serve as

从策展的角度讲，倘若要在一个不了解印尼社会和文化现状的国度举办一场展览，试图真实重现印尼风土人情及其思想和艺术的发展，这样的尝试将会举步维艰。而《当代性——印度尼西亚当代艺术展》则将通过展出印尼个体艺术家及其作品的方式，以电影和视觉艺术为重点，介绍当代文化中最具影响力的个人感悟。

此次展览中，策展人扮演中间人的角色。凭借此中间人，人们得以着手搭建一个深入了解印尼文艺创作者的平台。

该展览并非以评价印尼特色艺术为目的，而着眼于印尼当代艺术创作，并将其视为多元文化的衡量模式，这些文化在当代视觉艺术中并非中坚，但却在近几十年内自立门户，所创风格因其风土人情别具特色，并为世界艺坛注入一股新鲜活力。

我们可从爱多尔德・格列森特(Edouard Glissant)对“世界性”(mondialité)问题的思考来审视此风格。“世界性”是“全球性”的形式之一，其意义与

activators for the establishment of a more vibrant dialogue on the global level through such models.

This model could be seen from perspective of Eduard Glissant's musings on mondiality, or mondialite, a form of globality which is very different from the term globalization that we all experience today in many aspects as a condition that we all have contributed to and achieved. But globality can be understood as a resistance to globalization through a global dialogue that produces difference. These differences are our valuable contributions to the world that brings the possibilities of creating new models and formats.

As Glissant stated in one of his interviews: "I can change by changing with the other, without losing myself and without compromising myself. It's hard to imagine and it's hard to accept, and I think this is the role of art, literature and thought to provoke this change, which is fundamental and without which no other change would be possible. I don't believe any political, military, economic or cultural solution is possible in this world without this change to the imaginary.

The change to the imaginary starts with the individual and his/her effort to produce new, effective models of institutions, production, and the development of new relationships, and re-connecting with tradition as a strategy for the future.

The Indonesian cultural milieu went through drastic changes after 1998, with the change of a political regime that actually requested cultural practitioners to look at the arts and visual culture and it's contribution from different lines of perspective, unlike during Suharto regime.

As art shed its more or less underground nature after the fall of the Suharto régime, it's main enemy, artists were left in a void, tryng to find their own position in a new social system. In a certain way, the practices that began in the mid-90's were of a collective strength, and in terms of the artist community after 2000, set the stage for more concrete dimensions as to the development of artists' organizations that had clear missions and goals.

Individual artistic practices changed in many respects, looking into the inner-relations within sociaty. At the

时下流行的“全球化”迥异，后者是一种人们不断施加影响和受到影响的状态。“全球性”则通过全球范围内的对话，凸显地域差异，并对“全球化”产生抑制作用。这类差异可谓人类对世界文化的珍贵贡献，因为其促成了新型模式和新兴格局的产生。

格列森特曾在接受采访时表示：“我能通过改变他人来改变自己，但我不会在这种改变中迷失，亦不会妥协。”此话颇让人费解也让人无法接受，不过，我认为是艺术、文学和思想催生了上述变革，这三者至关重要，其存在保证了变革的可能。假使没有这种思想层次的变革，世间的政治、军事、经济或文化等领域就不存在任何变革的可能性。

思想层次的变革始于个人，包括其创造的新型有效的组织、产品形式，新型关系的发展，以及对传统的重新融合，并以此作为应对未来的新策略。

1998年以来，印尼文化环境历经剧变，新政权希望文艺工作者从不同视角审视艺术、视觉文化及其影响，这与苏哈托时代的状况迥异。

印尼艺术自其大敌——苏哈托政权垮台后，神秘而不为人知的本质渐渐褪去，艺术家们感到空虚失落，并努力寻找他们在新社会体制中的位置。从某种意义上说，二十世纪九十年代中叶开始的一系列创作代表了这种共同努力。而2000年后建立的艺术家社团，则为各类肩负明确使命和目标的艺人团体，提供了更为坚实广阔的舞台。

个人艺术创作曾经历多方改变，这种改变直指社会内部深层关系。与此同时，印尼社会环境也从军事政权转化为一个受市场力量驱动的体系，迫使艺术家想方设法适应艺术市场，满足产品需求，这与其他形式话语的发展无明显关联。

有学者认为，对一些国家及其当代艺术创作的发展，

same time, the social envirnoment also changed from a miltary system to one shaped by market forces, which also forced artists to invent new strategies for dealing with the art market and production demands that were not neccesarily connected to the development of any discourse.

Some researchers point out how the world is actually less interconnected today than during the 19th century, especially when discussing the Asian region, although there are many parallels and comparative studies that could be drawn between many countries and their development of contemporary art practices. For example, Chinese contemporary art lost it's underground position in 2000 with the acceptance of contemporary works of art to be éligible to participate in the Shanghai Biennial. This meant that contemporary art in China lost it's undergound status, but was also not completely accepted into the offical institutional system, leaving artists in a position of being in between, which could be taken as a main point of departure for how artists began to change their perspectives about themselves, their own existence, and art. These kinds of parralels in the region could also serve as a point of departure for a discussions that could be important to the construction and identification of its own critical contexts. Many of the countries in the region share similar issues that can be viewed at the larger regional level, and it would be fruitful to consider how each country is positioned within the region and also the larger global context.

On the other hand, new media has introduce many new aspects and issues that the generation before didn't face or have to navigate. The interference caused by mass media culture that is then channeled through artworks, or artists using mass media tools, can be identified in recent genereations of artists like the collective Tromarama, where members of the group worked with musical bands in order to produce videos that overlap popular culture production and the desire to find new ways of collaboration between and within different fields. This example is an interesting of an artistic startegy implemented not only in the visual art field, but by searching for the thin line between the visual arts and pop culture, a line that is a very important mirror today for reflecting contemporary reality.

尽管人们可以找到许多相似或可以比较的案例，但是当今世界，尤其是亚洲地区各国的联动反而少于19世纪。例如，在2000年“上海双年展”正式接纳并展出当代艺术创作后，中国的当代艺术便告别了原先不为人知的地下境地。虽然这些艺术不再神秘，但是他们并未被正统学院体系全盘接受，当代艺术家也因此夹在中间带。这是他们开始审视自我、自身存在感和艺术的一大主要出发点。同一地区不同国度之间的相似点，或许能引发探讨，这对各国自身文化环境的建构和认同也是至关重要的。我们可以用更广义的区域概念来看待同一地区内不同国家的相似案例，这样一来，考量每个国家在该区域、甚至更大的国际背景中所扮演的角色，或许能让我们获益匪浅。

此外，新媒体也带来了诸多史无前例的方式或需要应对的问题。大众传媒文化带来的影响已经深入艺术作品，而利用大众传媒工具进行的创作，在近几代艺术家——如印尼艺术家组合“特罗玛拉马”(Tromarama)的作品中也屡见不鲜。该组合成员与乐队合作，并拍摄视频，这既是大众文化的产物，也是寻求不同艺术领域合作的探索。这是个生动的例子，他们的艺术手法不但属于视觉艺术领域，还对视觉艺术和大众文化之间狭窄的边界进行了探索，而这条边界恰恰是一面反映当代现实的重要镜鉴。

在对印尼艺术场景进行研究时，我很惊讶地发现存在这样一类自发组织，通过各种存在和发展模式，它们力求成为当代艺术领域的主流，同时也想深入其他研究、展览等人们关注的共同区域。这种艺术机构模式由一小部分个人制作，其中许多为艺术家，他们对打造独立于政府援助之外的创作空间饶有兴趣。

此次展览的联合策展人杰姆·苏潘凯特(Jim Supankat)谈到，约翰·克拉克(John Clark)曾在其文章《现代亚洲艺术》中讨论过亚洲各国的新文艺运动、以及运动的反叛本质和前卫精神对于现代性发展的影响。20世纪的印尼，自发组织如“Ruang

While conducting my research into the Indonesian art scene I was suprised to find the existance of such self-organization that, through a congloméràtion of alternative models of existing and surviving, is striving to become a main force in the field of contemporary art, and includes some of the most interesting gathering spaces for research and exhibiting. These models are run by a small number of individuals, many of whom are artists that are interested to create a scene that is a possible space for development beyond or outside of any governemental support.

As co-curator, Jim Supankat mentioned how John Clark, in his text Modern Asian Art, discussess the New Art Movement in Asia and their rebellious nature with an avant-garde spirit affecting the development of modernity. In the 20th century, these self-organized entities like Ruang Rupa, Kunzi, Mes 56, and the Cemeti Art House were actually providing the new models that in a way were resistant to globalization, but at the same maintained a very active dialogue with it. These new models provided new modes of exchange for different channels of thoughts and ideas that has come to set the discussion in a very different situation. On the other hand, it's surounding envirnoment, as it is without the support of the local gouvernment, brings forth a parallell to the Chinese art scene that moves the artist into a more complex role, one that is not only of an artist, but also researcher, activist, entrepreneur, exhibition organizer, collector, cultural worker, and so on. This multiplicity of roles in the very specific environment of Asian countries allowed the artists to have a very important role as the main activators of the art scene. These actions usually require some form of collective dimension, but to a certain extent also represent individual voices that very well may be shared. And so it makes it difficult to make a clear desctinction between the private and collective. This issue was brought up in many of the discussions that I had with artists about the existence of a third sphere that is very important in their life, the sphere between the public and the private, which actually belongs to the community. That third sphere makes the practitioners active in the very understanding of the needs and possibilties for action. The sense of community, not only of an art community, but one of very different groups, are that in which these practitioners are active and this develops an art that is more concerned with the unstable medium of interaction.

Rupa”、“Kunci”、“Mes 56”、“Cemeti艺术之家”(Cemeti Art House)等纷纷为对抗“全球化”提供了新的模式与平台，但同时也在同“全球化”开展积极的对话。这些新模式为不同渠道的思想和创意提供了全新的交流方式，创造了完全不同的对话场所。此外，它不受当地政府资助的情况，这一点也与中国艺术环境颇为相似：中国的艺术家身兼多职，他们往往还是研究人员、活动家、企业家、展览组织者、收藏家、文化从业者等等。亚洲各国独特环境所赋予角色以多样性，使得艺术家肩负了艺术界重要催化剂与推动者的重要角色。这既要求集体合作，但在某种程度上也反映了共同的个人主张，因此很难明确区分个人和集体的概念。在同许多艺术家谈到第三领域在生活中存在的重要性时，我都提及了这个话题，这个领域介于公共和私人区域之间，属团体性质。第三领域让创作者在对行动需要和可能性的理解中积极主动。团体不仅指艺术团体，而且包括完全不同的组织，创作者在此可以主动发挥想象进行创作，由此催生了一种更为关注不稳定的介入媒介的艺术。

这类团体对艺术界及其多样性的发展影响甚大，尤其自1998年苏哈托政权垮台以来。他们采用的手法最早见于Cemeti艺术之家和他们的各类活动中。

本次展览将通过展出艺术家近期作品，集中反映其个人世界，并通过分组展览的形式，详尽呈现其创作理念。展览展示当今印尼文化环境，呈现在更为广义的文化环境里，个人对艺术家地位的理解，并揭示作品主题，从而将主题扩展至印尼之外更广的区域。

为了进一步探讨艺术家的工作环境和创作策略中使用的文化和社会元素，本次展览特邀一批艺术家展示其个人档案，并将此展示命名为《再活一千年》。每名受邀的艺术家须负责各自的展示，档案资料包括相关的个人历史，凡是对艺术家本人的整体艺术观、人生观有影响的材料都将纳入展示，形式包括杂志、电影、书籍、藏品、照片、工艺品，以及其他任何与艺

These communities actually made a very strong impact on the development of the art scene and it's diversity, especially after 1998 and the fall of the Suharto regime. One of the earliest models for these kinds of approaches could be seen in the organization of the Cemeti Art House and their various activities.

This exhibition will focus on presenting an artist's individual universe through one or a series of his/her recent works and to present his/her ideas in the most complete way within a group exhibition structure. The exhibition not only shows the current Indonesian cultural milieu, but also portrays the individual standpoints in a wider cultural conception of an artist's position in society, and the issues concerned or raised through his/her works, surpassing the limitation of issues pertinent only to Indonesia.

In order to provide a deeper insight into the cultural and social elements of the working environment and strategies of artists, the exhibition will also include a presentation of personal archives from certain artists, the presentation of which is titled "Live Another Thousand Years." Each artist will be invited to curate his/her own presentation of archival materials related to his/her personal history, which might include any material that the artist finds to be influential in the shaping of his/her viewpoints and his/her understanding of art and life in general, including such things as magazines, films, books, memorabilia, photographs, artifacts or anything else that might establish a possible link with his/her artistic approach.

Through these personal perspectives, we the curators hope to avoid a traditional, retrospective presentation only through the works of art. Rather we hope to emphasize life and a sense of its everydayness that will allow the audience to gain a better insight into the different approaches to art-making today, and to shed light on the broader spectrum of social transformation in recent years.

The title, "Live Another Thousand Years," is inspired by the poem "Aku" of Chairil Anwar, one of the most famous and influential Indonesian poets, who died in 1949 when he was just 27 years old. Anwar's poem reminds us of the importance of belief in what we are doing and the urgency to not only express ourselves, but to act. Many of the represented artists are not

术家表现手法的形成过程有关的物品。

作为策展人，我们期望通过上述方法避免把这种梳理做成以作品为单一渠道的传统回顾展。我们希望强调生活及其每天的内容，让观众更好地理解当今艺术创作的不同手法，从更广阔的视角反映当今社会变迁。

标题《再活一千年》的灵感源于诗歌《我》(Aku)的启发，这首诗由印尼最具影响的诗人凯里尔・安哇尔(Chairil Anwar)所作。安哇尔卒于1949年，时年仅27岁。《我》提醒世人信仰自己的事业，在表达自我的同时，更要行动起来。受邀的艺术家不仅是艺术家，他们的工作远不止艺术创作，他们还是活动家、历史编撰者、医者、企业家等等。就这一点来说，本次展览及其展品尤为重要，它也呼应了安哇尔的诗句："我想再活一千年。"

以艺术家的作品或提供的其他形式物品为例，我们将简要介绍一下上文中提及的创作模式。

安奇・普班度诺(Angki Purbandono)是"MES 56"(专业摄影艺术空间)的核心成员之一，他以创作扫描成像的照片著称。这次他将展示过去五年中在印尼各地拍摄的"疯狂"系列照片，这套摄影作品记录的对象是发了疯的人，以及他们每天的生活。同时，我们还将展示其《超越范思哲》项目书，该系列涵盖上百张相片，由安奇每日拍摄积累而成，耗时若干年。作品在反映露宿街头人群的生活状况的同时，对他们坦诚的生活和创造力致以了敬意。安奇正在进行的另一创作是收集跳蚤市场和反映印尼历史电影的照片。作为此次个人档案的一部分，他将展示一部分收藏的电影照片。这项收集老照片的工作将会逐渐形成一个相片博物馆，印尼的影像历史将在此得以保存。

哈拉海麦尼(Arahmaiani)的作品以反映政治社会面貌著称，目前她正在与玉树(中国青海省地震灾区)当地的团体合作完成"旗帜"项目。她将选择那些需要倾

only artists, and their works go far beyond mere artistic practice—they are activists, history re-rewriters, healers, entrepreneurs, and many other roles. This is what makes the artists in this Exhibition and their work important, and echoing the words of Chairil Anwar: "I want to live another thousand years."

Through individual examples of the artists' work and other forms of contribution, we will outline some of the working models that were mentioned in this text previously.

Angki Purbandono, one of the core members of MES 56 (an art space devoted specifically to photography), although known for his scanned photographic images, will show part of his Madness series that he has been shooting over the last five years around Indonesia, capturing people who have gone mad, and their daily existence. Containing the hudreds of phototographs that the artist took over the years on a daily basis, we will also show the Beyond Versace Project Book that displays the outfits of people living on the streets, making a kind of homage to their creativity and the bareness of their human existence. One of Angki's ongoing projects is to collect old photographs from flea markets and films that capture and reflect the history of the image in Indonesia. As part of the archive he will show a small portion of his collection of films. His ongoing collection of old photographs is building of a muséum of images that will preserve the visual history of Indonesia.

Arahmaiani, known for her political and social involvement in the arts and beyond, will continue her ongoing Flag project, working with a community in Yu Shu, the earthquake devastated area in Qing Hai in the northwest of China. The artist will select communities that are in need to have their voices heard, and through their work together they will attempt to define a community of key words that are connected to their current status. The artist uses herself as a medium between the weak and the powerful, by trying to channel the message of the weak and overcome the barriers of stereotypes. She is both attached to the community, but also maintains a distance that she needs to preserve, making the artist the sole action-maker who is able to question everything. For the archive portion, Arahmaiani, with her unique way of life, will present her suitcase and various performance

诉和被倾听的团体，通过合作并联系自身状况，寻找关键字来定义这个团体。她视自己为弱势群体和强势群体之间的桥梁，努力传达弱势群体的心声，并尽力革除思维定势的阻挠。她虽然隶属该团体，但却保持应有距离，让自己成为质疑一切的行动者。在哈拉海麦尼将展示的档案资料中，受其独特生活方式影响，我们将会看到她的手提箱和几件演出服装，这些都是她随身携带的物品。作为第一批参与国际展览的艺术家，哈拉海麦尼至今对西方和印尼文化持批判态度，因为这些文化中至今存在诸多成见，尤其对穆斯林文化存在偏见。哈拉海麦尼的文化活动丰富，作品涉及写作、视觉艺术，并参与活动组织工作。

日惹艺术家艾柯・努格罗荷(Eko Nugroho)同样将团体合作的概念视作其创作灵感的重要来源和重要组成部分。十几年前，在创作生涯早期，他创办了《长肉》(Daging Tumbuh)漫画杂志，该杂志用复印机印制，半年一期，手工发行，共印150份。刊物制作过程中，艾柯会随机邀请一些人表达他们的看法，这些人或来自他的村子，或是打扫清真寺的。他在日惹经营的店铺是一个临街的店面，名叫“为大米而战”(Fight for Rice)。这家店也成为他结交年轻艺术家、设计师和音乐家的场所，他们在此合作或买卖小玩意、T恤或者音乐等私人物品。所售之物旨在增强个人创作能力。我们可以从他的展品中察觉到一种较为玩世不恭的角色设定，这角色的外形通常混合了人形、机器人和怪物，但抹除了各自原有的特征，增添了看似寻常的外观。这样一来，这个角色便可代表你我，甚至任何人。

方济各・沙勿略・哈索诺(FX Harsono)是20世纪七十年代“新艺术运动”的成员，过去十年中，他不断创作涉及其印籍华裔身份的作品，力图唤起人们对那一段从未提及、但却存在过的、对印尼影响深远的历史的意识。他的创作始于1948年其父在勿里达(Blitar)制作的一本家庭相册。这本相册为当地发生的屠杀华

costumes, which are things that she carries around with herself. Although one of the first artists to start taking part in international exhibitions, Arahmaiani is still critical of the West and of her own culture, because of the existing stereotypes, especially with regard to muslim culture. Arahmaini has developed a very rich cultural practice through her writings, visual artworks, and her work as an activist.

Eko Nugroho is based in Jogya and also takes the concept of community as a very important source and intégral aspect of his work. Since early on in his career, some ten years ago, he created Daging Tumbuh, a magazine made from photocopies that he still runs, publishing it every half a year, and which he distributes by hand, all 150 copies. For this, Eko invites random people to contribute and express themselves, random people from his village, or even the person cleaning the mosque. His store that he runs in Jogja is called Fight for Rice and is a small storefront that is also one of his attempts at involving young artists, designers, and musicians to collaborate and sell their own personal merchandise, from objects and t-shirts, to music. All of which is on sale as an attempt to strengthen independent creativity. For his his work in the exhibition he produces a very cynical setting with characters that are usually a combination of human form, robot, and monster, yet stripping away their actual identity, and creating a setting that appears normal. In this way his characters could be you or me, or anyone at all.

FX Harsono was a member of the New Art Movement back in the 70's who, in the last ten years, has been creating bodies of work that are related to his identity as an Indonesian Chinese person, thereby trying to bring awareness to a part of history that is never mentioned, but exists and has left significant traces in Indonesia. The artist started the work around his own family photo album that his father put together in Blitar around 1948. This is importnat as evidence of the massacre of many Chinese in that area. Most of the works that the artist has produced require the establishment of a relationship with the subject, or of rediscovering their expérience, which then becomes source material and a point of departure. His collection for the archive is a personal collection of archival material related to himself and people that he has interviewed for his project. In a way, it is a museum

人惨案提供了重要依据。哈索诺的大量作品都以这个主题或这段历史的场面再现为基础，这也是他创作的源头和起点。在展示部分，我们将看到关于他个人，以及他为这个项目所采访的对象的档案。总之，这部分展览将是一段涵盖几代印籍华人的另类史。他的作品通过其保留的目击者口供和记录文献组成，力图为这段失落的历史提供铁证。

阿顾思・苏瓦吉(Agus Suwage)在其作品中反映了我们对他人爱憎情感间的内在联系。他的玩世不恭表现在他让自己化作一面镜子映照你我。他对音乐痴迷，每日沉浸其中，而这个专业爱好也为其大多数作品标题提供了灵感。他的作品反映了生活的荒诞和快乐。

要谈论S・泰迪(S. Teddy)的作品则有些困难，甚至连他本人都会觉得困难，因此让我用文字来写，难度自不待言。我们能在其所属乐队的活动中了解到他的作品，他有时是个活跃的表演者，有时又摇身一变，成为一个坐在一边抽烟的普通人，毫不起眼。最可贵的是他对艺术和美好的生活怀有强烈信念。

琼佩特(Jompet)在戏剧、声音和音乐方面的经验，使他能在创作中融入含有戏剧特征的舞台装置艺术。他的力作之一是《爪哇之战》，作品取材自加拉西(Garasi)剧场版演出，参与其中的艺术家们在剧中从多个角度审视了爪哇的历史。琼佩特以爪哇皇家士兵的制服为例，证明爪哇文化作为一种模式，可通过自身方式对不同文化的影响进行取舍。这是艺术家文化研究的出发点，他们通过考察当地舞蹈、口述历史等方面，研究文化的发源及其表现形式探讨他所说的第三种现实。第三种现实是在转型中的文化状态和它制造新的现实的可能行。新的现实是艺术家关注的第三种现实通过他们一系列的新的作品探讨。

加林・努格罗(Garin Nugroho)、艾德文(Edwin)、法赞・利泽尔(Faozan Rizal)和高托特・普拉考萨(Gotot Prakosa)是本次展览特邀的四位电影导演，分别代表

of an alternative history that covers a few different genereations of Indonesian Chinese living in Indonesia. His work attempts to be the voice of testemony of this unwitten part of history that he preserves through oral records from the witnesses, and even more so through his documentary work.

Through his work, Agus Suwage has maintained a certain internal relationship of a guy you love to hate. His sense of cynicism comes out in the way that he uses himeself as a mirror to each and every one of us. His obsession with music is a source from which he gets most of the titles for his work and which takes up most of his day, as it is his professional hobby. His work is largely devoted to life, it's absurdity as well as it 's pleasures.

S. Teddy's work is actually a bit difficult to talk about, even for himself, and especially for myself as I try to write about it. A description of his work can be glimpsed in his activities with his band at large, where at times he will be on stage as an active performer, or at other times just a guy sitting and smoking a cigarrette. What is important is that he has a strong belief in art and providing a better more fulfilling life.

Jompet's involevement in the theater, and in sound and music, has led him to produce his own staged installations that contain theatrical textures. One of his most important projects is War of Java, which comes from a Garasi Theater production in which the artists were involved, which looks at the history of Java in its many different aspects. The artist takes Javanese culture as a model that through it's own strategy, can negotiate the influences of different cultures and uses the example of Java's royal soldier uniform. This was a point of departure for the artists in order to keep investigating culture: its traditional roots, and manifestation today, by exploring the areas of dance, oral history, and many other aspects. His project for the archive looks at the gray areas, as the artists referred to them, the areas in which we work as cultural practitioners, as a special project in this publication.

Garin Nugroho, Edwin, Faozan Rizal and Gotot Prakosa are four filmmakers that were invited to present their films as part of the exhibition, providing insight into a few different generations of film directors. Gotot Prakosa started making his films in the 70s, and the

不同时期电影导演的见解。其中包括自20世纪七十年代开始拍摄电影的高托特・普拉考萨，也包括如艾德文一般年轻的导演。四位导演都是印尼地区独立电影界的重量级人物。

对于“窗”(Jendela)艺术团体成员的作品，本次展览将展出鲁迪・曼托法尼(Rudi Mantofani)、米斯尼亚迪(Masradi)和翰迪怀儿曼・萨普川(Handiwirman Saputra)的创作。翰迪怀儿曼收藏人们弃之不用的废弃物，如破损的橡胶、一块海绵等，这些都成为他创作迷你雕塑的材料，也是他绘画和其他创作的基础。他在作品中融入了一种独特的视觉语言，这增加了观众从最佳观测点进行分析的不确定性——虽然面前的图像烂熟于心，但却无法琢磨。

上述作品及其他诸多创作皆起到了连接个人艺术活动和集体合作观念的桥梁作用，当然这只是此次展览的一部分。

与中国十年前的情形类似，印尼艺术家们已在市场上引起瞩目，近年来拍卖行竞标他们作品的买家也屡见不鲜。然而，本土团体、个人、组织和集体创作到底对这一现状有多大贡献，答案仍不得而知。此次展览亦期望通过讨论差异的对话，在亚洲和更为广阔的全球环境之间搭建起当代艺术创作探讨的桥梁。

show also introduces younger filmmakers and their work, like that of Edwin. These four filmmakers are very important individuals in the création of an independant film field in Indoensia and the region

Among the members of the Jendela Group, the exhibition presents Rudi Mantofani, Masradi, and Handiwirman Saputra. Handiwirman's collection of useless objects that would be considered waste to most people, things like a broken rubber gym, or a piece of thread from a sponge, become materials that he to create miniature sculptures. These then become points of departure for his paintings and other objects. The artist creates a unique visual language through his body of work that introduces a certain uncertainty as to the procès of codifying that takes place from the viewer's vantage point, since the imagery seems familiar but is difficult to define.

These and many other practices are the very work that connects individual action and the over-arching collective notion that is but only part of this exhibition.

Similar to what happened with Chinese art ten yaers ago, Indonesian artists have attracted much attention from the market, and there is much press about their numbers at the auction houses in recent years. Yet, the work of the many local communities, the individuals, organizarions and collectives that all contributed to the development of this scene is still rather unknown. This exhibition hopes to bridge a discussion of contemporary art practice within Asia and in the larger global context by producing a dialogue around difference.

Essays | 文章

ANTARIKSA
安塔瑞克沙

Between Revolutionary Stronghold and Laboratory of the West: Political Positions in Indonesian Fine Arts in the 50's

在革命要塞与西方实验室之间：20世纪50年代印尼艺术的政治地位

Yogyakarta was the principal art center in Java during the 1950s. In Claire Holt's report, Art in Indonesia (1968), she states that there were a total of seventy-four registered art-related organizations in Yogyakarta in 1955. Of that number, fourteen were general groups – and this included student-initiated organizations with common ethnic backgrounds, seventeen dancing clubs, sixteen music clubs, twelve drama clubs, and seven fine art clubs. These organizations dealt with traditional or modern art forms. In addition to these organizations, campus-based student bodies had not been idle in their respective colleges. Overall, it is estimated that two-thirds to three-quarters of Java's painters lived in Yogyakarta.

Hersri Setiawan, former Secretary General of LEKRA (Lembaga Kebudayaan Rakyat, People's Culture Organization) Central Java, vividly captured the artist's world of that time in his unpublished writings Tembang Turba. "In the early 50's, numerous budding 'artists' and 'men of letters' would declare themselves 'artists' after trying their hand at sketching self-portraits or composing verses about moonlight or love. The attributes of a typical liberal artist's look included

日惹在20世纪50年代是爪哇省的艺术重镇。根据克莱尔·霍尔特(Claire Holt)的专题报告《印尼艺术》(1968)的统计，1955年日惹有正式记录的艺术组织共有74个，其中14个为普通团体(包括由相同种族背景学生组成的团体)、17个舞蹈社团、16个音乐社团、12个戏剧社团和7个美术社团。这些艺术组织围绕着传统或现代艺术形式开展活动。此外，以校园为基础的学生社团也不甘示弱、纷纷活跃于各大院校。估计当时居住在日惹的艺术家人数占爪哇艺术家总数的2/3至3/4。

中爪哇省"印尼人民文化协会"(LEKRA)前秘书长赫斯黎·史迪亚万(Hersri Setiawan)曾在自己的一篇未公开发表的文章中对当时的艺术界做了生动的描写："50年代早期，许多刚刚展露头角的'画家'和'文人'在画了几幅自画像或创作了几句花好月圆、浓情蜜意的诗文之后就纷纷开始以'艺术家'自居了。桀骜不羁艺术家的典型打扮必须具备以下几个特征：一头乱蓬蓬的长发、衣衫褴褛、不修边

shaggy, unwashed, long hair, dressing in nothing but rags, patched here and there. The artists were not too fond of taking a shower either, because water and soap, so they say, killed inspiration. They would trawl through the city in search of glimmering inspirations amidst the debauched darkness of the city square. Deceive and steal, they would say, like Chairil." [1]

Hersri spoke about Yogyakarta's transformation from a political center to a cultural center along with its genuine as well as fake extremists. "I don't know about other cities, but that was what became of Yogyakarta then. This is due to the influence of the artist's bohemian wave in '45 as well as Yogya's history as the Revolution Capital. Ever since the central government office moved back to Jakarta, Yogya had lost its status as 'political center' but gained its title as the 'campus town' and 'the center of national culture', inheriting with it the good and bad remnants from the extremities of the war for independence." During the later half of 1940s, Yogya, as the Revolution Capital, was swarmed with refugees from all across the nation who felt the threat of a common enemy. Day and night, the 'extremists' – NICA's term for youth guerillas, the supporters of the new republic – were seen in every corner of the city. NICA's definition of 'extremists' pointed at those who violated the rust en orde (security and order) they had imposed on the people, while the laymen's definition of the same word merely described their physical attribute: unshaven, long haired, mustached men, carrying cartridge rounds and hand grenades wherever they went. Of course, there were the fakes among the true extremists who struggled for the nation's cause.

The two most important artists' organizations of the time, SIM and Pelukis Rakyat, operated from their headquarters in Yogyakarta. According to Claire Holt there were "no fitting '-isms' available at that time to describe the variety of their artistic style, not least 'Indonesianism'." Works from this period were marked by the relationship between Society and Nature; one can easily distinguish an artist from the other through their respective working methods and ideological orientation.

幅。这些艺术家通常都不喜欢洗澡，因为根据他们的说法，水和肥皂会扼杀灵感。他们会在城市的堕落与黑暗中开展撒网式的搜索，只为找寻那星星点点的灵感曙光。欺骗、偷窃，他们会说，这就像凯里尔一样。”[1]

赫斯黎也提到了日惹从政治中心向文化中心的转型过程，并对其中涌现的真正的和假冒的极端分子进行了描述。“我不知道别的城市情况如何，但是当时的日惹是这样的。这既是受到了1945年波希米亚艺术浪潮的影响，也因为日惹在历史上一直是一座革命之都。自从中央政府迁回雅加达后，日惹便失去了其作为‘政治中心’的地位，逐渐发展成为‘大学城’和‘全国文化中心’，但是，日惹还是继承了独立战争时期极端分子遗留下来的各种好的与不好的习气。20世纪40年代后期，作为革命之都，全国各地受到共同敌人的威胁的难民大量涌入日惹。荷兰兵将年轻的游击队员和新共和国的支持者们统称为‘极端分子’。日以继夜地，这些极端分子神出鬼没却又无所不在，城市的每一个角落都有他们的身影。荷兰兵定义中的‘极端分子’指的是那些破坏他们在殖民地的安全与秩序的人；而一般意义上对于‘极端分子’的定义往往只对他们的外在特征进行了描述：胡子拉碴、一头长发、身材魁梧，无论走到哪里都带着子弹和手榴弹。当然，也有一些冒牌货混入了为民族解放事业奋斗的极端分子的队伍。

当时两大最重要的艺术家组织分别是SIM和Pelukis Rakyat，它们的总部都设在日惹。克莱尔・霍尔特称那一时期没有任何‘现成的主义’可以来描述它们多元的艺术风格。‘印尼主义’或许是最接近确切的一个表述。”这一时期的论著多围绕着社会与自然之间的关系。人们可以轻松地根据艺术家不同的工作方法和意识导向对他们进行区分。

苏加诺和PKI(印尼共产党)赞同LEKRA所倡导的意识形态，是50年代最重要的两股艺术赞助力量。苏加

Two of the biggest art patrons in the 1950's were Soekarno and PKI (Partai Komunis Indonesia or Indonesian Communist Party), who share LEKRA's ideologies. Soekarno's definition on nationalism is Marhaenist Nationalism, while PKI's nationalism is Communist nationalism, commonly referred to as "People's Marxism" by many observers.

A Dutch scholar, Saskia Eleonora Wieringa in Penghancuran Gerakan Perampuan di Indonesia (1999) believed that the populist ideology of Soekarno's Marhaenism emphasized homogeneity and mutual cooperation. Revolution is the dream of an everlasting struggle. The sentiment of nationality is shaped by this condition, to face the common enemy, the colonial Dutch, overlooking the difference between the co-operating factions. Soekarno's populism is based on his charismatic leadership, aimed at creating mythical unity to defend against external threats. In the mean time, PKI focused on class struggle (even though its ideology was not as steadfast Marxism as expected, considering its Communist roots). The PKI leaders focused mainly on building a tremendous base of mass supporters from all over the country, instead of building a party whose cadres were educated, eloquent, dedicated and consistent in working on class struggle. By creating this huge "communist family," PKI extracted certain elements of Javanese values, such as harmony, which was also a foundation of Soekarno's Marhaenism.

President Soekarno, in his enthusiasm in collecting diverse works of art since the 40's, also played a role as one of the biggest patron of artists. Pierre Labrousse, in "The Second Life of Bung Karno: Analysis of the Myth, 1979-1981" (1994), writes that Soekarno once said: "Buying and collecting paintings and works of arts are not comparable with collecting jewelry or accumulating gold… collecting works of art means preserving authentic national legacy." Though Soekarno's taste may not always be as consistent as they may seem, it was nonetheless respected and often became the "benchmark" for what artists understood as the "Indonesian emotion" and "authentic national legacy."

诺对于民族主义的定义属于平民民族主义，而PKI对于民族主义的定义则属于共产民族主义，也常被称作“人民马克思主义”。

荷兰学者Saskia Eleonora Wieringa在《印尼妇女运动消亡史》(Penghancuran Gerakan Perampuan di Indonesia, 1999)一书中提出：苏加诺的平民主义(Marhaenism)强调同质性和相互合作。革命是一个永恒的奋斗梦想。民族情感正是在这种情况下培养起来的：面对共同的敌人——荷兰殖民者——各个合作派系之间的分歧与区别显得无足轻重。苏加诺的“平民主义”建立在自己独特的具有强大感染力的领导风范基础之上，旨在打造一个抵御外辱的神话般团结的整体。与此同时，PKI更多地关注阶级斗争(虽然考虑到PKI的共产主义本质，它的意识主张其实并没有达到马克思主义所要求的坚定不移的高度)。PKI领导人更多地关注于从社会各界吸收支持者，从而奠定PKI广泛的社会基础；而在政党建设方面投入的精力则相对较少，也忽略了对干部修养、口才、奉献精神和对于阶级斗争的连贯性的培养。在建立这样一个“共产主义大家族”的过程中，PKI也吸收了爪哇人民的一部分价值理念，例如和谐融洽。而这也正是苏加诺提出的“平民主义”的一个基础理论。

1940年以来，由于对艺术品收藏的热情，苏加诺总统一直是最为重要的艺术赞助人之一。皮埃尔·拉布鲁斯(Pierre Labrousse)在《苏加诺的第二次生命：迷思分析(1979-1981)》(1994)一书中写道：苏加诺曾说过“购买、收藏画作和其他艺术品与收集珠宝或黄金是不一样的，收藏艺术品也是在保护纯正的民族遗产。”虽然苏加诺的艺术品味时有变化，前后并一致，但是他的选择常常被艺术家视作“印尼情感”与“纯正民族遗产”的风向标。

雕塑家艾德希·苏纳索(Edhi Sunarso)是Pelukis Rakyat的成员。回忆当年的情景，艾德希讲述了苏加诺如何运用自己对艺术的影响力来对他担任设计的纪念碑

Edhi Sunarso, a sculptor and member of Pelukis Rakyat, relates how Soekarno played his role as the inspiration for his monumental projects. Edhi says: "Back then, I was working on the Monumen Dirgantara project. I had various designs to show, but none satisfied Bung Karno. Then he said to me, 'we haven't the means to manufactures any planes, least of all the fighting kind, but during revolution, we have all the courage to fly them. So make a statue that evokes this spirit of courage. That's all we've got. Once again, what have we got? We have spirit. We have Gatutkaca!' Then he posed like Gatutkaca right in front of me, 'Hurry! Make the sketch. Here, like this!' he said. Then there it was, I made the statue."

The most influential sanggar (or art sanggar-cum-commune) such as SIM and Pelukis Rakyat, depended partly on Soekarno's version of nationalism, and partly on PKI's version. Due to their members' involvement in PKI's activities, these sanggar were often called "left-wing sanggar." The truth is, the political attitudes among their members remained diverse because they had never imposed any particular political attitude towards them. This is not the case with the later sanggar like Bumi Tarung, for example, which forced its members to take up LEKRA membership as well.

Compared to the-association-of-professionals-looking Persagi, other associations had a more traditional bind – such as sanggar and etc – towards their members. These sanggar resembled the kind of education developed in Taman Siswa, except that it was run with a looser control system. The leaders and the young, unmarried painters normally lived in these sanggar. The learning process at the sanggar was based on the principle of togetherness, and so the leaders and senior painters would mentor the juniors.

A sanggar would receive their income from their sales at art fairs and other instances, as well as donations from the government. These were spent on basic materials required to run such initiatives. A SIM member, Hendra Gunawan, left the sanggar because he disagreed with the organization's subsidy distribution

项目进行指导。艾德希表示："当时我正为Dirgantara纪念碑项目担任设计。我给苏加诺看了很多设计稿，但是没有一个能让他满意的。后来他跟我说'我们没有能力造飞机，特别是战斗机。但是在大革命期间，我们却满怀着驾驶飞机的勇气。我们要创造一件能够激发这种勇气与精神的雕塑。这是我们的全部。我们拥有些什么？我们有的就是一股精神。我们有爪哇神(Gatutkaca)！'然后他就在我面前摆了一个爪哇神的姿势。'快！赶紧画下来。就像这样！'他说道。于是我就按照这个姿势创作了纪念碑。"

SIM、Pelukis Rakyat等最具影响力的艺术学会(sanggar)、或曰艺术公社(art sanggar-cum-commune)既采纳苏加诺对于民族主义的定义，也采纳PKI对于民族主义的定义。由于成员们投身PKI的各种活动，这些艺术学会也被冠以"左翼艺术学会"之名。而事实上，成员之间的政治态度和见解并不统一，他们从不将任何一种政治态度强加于别人。而到了后期出现的如Bumi Tarung等艺术学会，情况就发生了转变。后期的艺术团体强行要求成员必须接受并遵循LEKRA的思想。

相比专业协会性质的Persagi(印尼画家协会)，艺术学会等其他协会与成员之间的关系更为传统。这些艺术学会与塔曼·西斯哇(Taman Siswa，意为"学生的花园")校园团体的教育模式相似，而其内部的管理原则则更为自由。学会领导人和年轻的未婚画家往往住在艺术学会内。艺术学会的学习基于团结互助的原则，因此领导人和年长的画家会担任年轻画家的导师，为他们提供指导。

艺术学会的收入来源主要来自于各种艺术博览会上的作品交易和政府的捐助。收入用于为开展各种活动所需的基本材料与设备提供支持。亨德拉·古那旺(Hendra Gunawan)曾是SIM的成员，后来由于不赞同学会的政府津贴分配政策而选择离开了学会。苏若约诺(Sudjojono)强调根据成员的特点进行分

policy that they received from the government. Sudjojono emphasized categorization according to members' merits, classifying them into four classes: A, B, C and D, based on their achievements and position as an artist. Hendra strongly opposed this model and demanded a classification scheme based on the status, either familial or marital, of all members. In his demand, he stated that married members should receive 200 rupiahs per month, while the unmarried ones, 100 rupiahs; their merit as artists shouldn't count. This disagreement was recorded by Claire Holt.

Hendra Gunawan left and founded Pelukis Rakyat and applied his system there. On the rare occasion when it did not make enough money, Hendra or Affandi would dip into their private funds to keep their sanggar running. In fact, according to Edhi Sunarso, Hendra's wife would sometimes sell her batik clothes to help with funding.

With the good reputation he had enjoyed during his time as leader of Persagi, Sudjojono held a high, steady position in the history of modern fine arts of Indonesia. Agus Darmawan T reports that Hendra Gunawan once acknowledged Sudjojono as the artist "who brought Indonesian fine art to new heights, and, to where it rightfully should be," ("Hendra Gunawan dan Pikiran-pikiran yang Terempas", Kompas, Oct 5, 2001). Claire Holt describes Sudjojono as "a versatile, determined and eloquent man, whom, at the same time, is torn between art and politic." Holt believes Sudjojono had acquired a good education under the Dutch regime and had read European philosophy and literature. Is it no wonder then that Sudjojono, with such a background, would urge artists to be politically conscious and praised Picasso and Diego Rivera as role models. He firmly believed that arts must be devoted to the cause of social and political struggle.

However, Holt might be wrong in saying that Sudjojono began to support communism after the War for Independence, or during the 50's, at least if that conclusion is to be deducted from testimonials by

类——根据他们作为艺术家的成就和地位依次分为A、B、C、D四类。亨德拉强烈反对这一模式，并提出建立一个以成员家庭或婚姻状态为基础的分类标准。他提出，已婚成员应每月获得200卢比，而未婚成员获100卢比。而他们作为艺术家所取得的成就不应该纳入考量。克莱尔·霍尔特在报告中也记录了这一分歧。

亨德拉·古那旺离开SIM后成立了Pelukis Rakyat，在这里实践了他的理想。Pelukis Rakyat成立之后几乎没有遭遇过资金短缺，而一旦偶尔出现此类问题，亨德拉和阿梵迪会动用自己的个人资金来维持学会的运作。事实上，根据艾德希·苏纳索的说法，亨德拉的妻子有时会典当自己的蜡染衣服(batik clothes)来帮助学会筹款。

在领导Persagi时期获得的巨大威望与荣誉为苏若约诺在印尼现代艺术史上赢得了崇高的地位。阿顾思·达玛旺·T(Agus Darmawan T)写道：亨德拉·古那旺称苏若约诺是一名“将印尼艺术带上全新的高度并走上正确的发展道路”的艺术家(载于《亨德拉·古那旺与批判思考》，《罗盘报》2001年10月5日)。克莱尔·霍尔特(Claire Holt)将苏若约诺描述为“多才多艺、意志坚定、口才出众，而同时他又在艺术与政治之间左右为难”。根据霍尔特的研究，苏若约诺在荷兰统治时期接受过良好的教育，通晓欧洲哲学与文学。拥有这样的背景，苏若约诺鼓励艺术家培养政治意识、并将毕加索和迭戈·里维拉推崇为楷模也就不足为奇了。他坚信艺术家应投身于社会与政治斗争的宏大事业中。

然而，霍尔特称苏若约诺在印尼独立战争后或50年代开始支持共产主义，这一点值得商榷，至少与欧·海·德扬(Oey Hay Djoen)、约瑟夫·伊萨克(Joesoef Isak)、索布隆·艾迪特(Sobron Aidit)、巴苏基·雷索波沃(Basuki Resobowo)等人的说辞不符。在一次雅加达“文化网络”(Jaringan Kerja Budaya)组织

Oey Hay Djoen, Joesoef Isak, Sobron Aidit and Basuki Resobowo. In a discussion just outside the Jaringan Kerja Budaya headquarters in Jakarta, Oey Hay Djoen, once a member of Central Secretary of LEKRA, said that Sudjojono had been a communist since 1945. Joesoef Isak, a leading journalist, gave another hint that by the end of the 40's Sudjojono had aligned his sympathy with the communists. Joesoef said, as reported by Hafis Azhari in Biografi Joesoef Isak (draft of the book, unpublished), that after the Madiun Incident in 1948, which ended with the execution of Musso and the arrest of Amir Sjarifudin, Sudjojono met with Soekarno in Yogyakarta. At that time, the Dutch had just released Soekarno from exile on Bangka Island. Even during those dire times, Soekarno could not resist the temptation of owning a painting by Sudjojono. Both men agreed to exchange a painting for clothes. Sudjojono then looked Soekarno in the eye and asked in Dutch:

"Mas Karno, ben jij nog steeds een Marxist?"

Soekarno seemed a little offended by that and retorted: "Naturlijk Jon Ik ben nog steeds een Marxist!"

Sudjojono then asked, "En waarom blijtbt je maar stil, terwijl jouw vrienden die Marxisten waren doodgeschoten werdwn?"

Meaning: "Mas Karno, are you still a Marxist?"

"Naturally, I am still a Marxist!"

"Then, why did you let your comrades get shot dead?"

This last question struck Soekarno deeply. He remained stunned for some time and finally broke into tears.

Sudjojono's sympathy towards communism might have been sparked ever since the 30's, or possibly before. Sobron Aidit records in "Taman Siswa" (unpublished) that Taman Siswa back then was like a lair for PKI members; Sudjojono was educated there and

的讨论中，LEKRA前中央秘书处成员欧·海·德扬(Oey Hay Djoen)说道苏若约诺1945年加入共产党。知名记者约瑟夫·伊萨克(Joesoef Isak)则曾经暗示过苏若约诺在40年代后期就表现出对于共产党的同情与支持。哈菲斯·阿兹哈里(Hafis Azhari)在《Joesoef Isak传》(手稿，未出版)中提到Joesoef曾说过在1948年发生"茉莉芬(Madiun)事件"并导致穆索(Musso)被枪决、埃米尔·斯亚里服丁(Amir Sjarifudin)被捕后，苏若约诺与苏加诺在日惹会面。当时，荷兰刚刚赦免了流放邦加岛的苏加诺。即使在如此崎岖多舛的年代，苏加诺依然无法抗拒拥有一副苏若约诺画作的诱惑。两人约定用衣服来交换画作。接着，苏若约诺直视着苏加诺的眼睛用荷兰语问道：

"Mas Karno, ben jij nog steeds een Marxist?"

这句提问显然冒犯了苏加诺，他随即反驳道："Naturlijk Jon Ik ben nog steeds een Marxist!"

苏若约诺接着问："En waarom blijtbt je maar stil, terwijl jouw vrienden die Marxisten waren doodgeschoten werdwn?"

这段对话可以翻译为：

"苏加诺先生，你还是一名马克思主义者吗？"

"当然，我仍然还是一名马克思主义者！"

"那么，你为什么眼睁睁看着自己的同志中弹牺牲？"

最后一个问题深深地刺痛了苏加诺。好一会儿他都无法从震惊中缓过来，泪水滑过他的脸颊。

苏若约诺对于共产主义的同情或许可以追溯到20世纪30年代甚至更早一些的时候。索布隆·艾迪特在《塔曼·西斯哇》(未出版)一文中曾提到塔曼·西斯哇在当时可以说是PKI成员的一个秘密据点。苏若约诺曾在那里接受教育并最终回到那里教学。

eventually returned to lecture there.

Basuki Resobowo's testimonial "Bercermin Dimuka Kaca: Seniman, Seni dan Masyarakat" (2005) about his meeting with Sudjojono in 1936, also gives a similar picture of Sudjojono's intimate relationship with the ideology. Basuki relates: "I knew he'd come back from his journeys overseas. I came to him and asked, 'Why you had come back so soon! How far did you go?'" In typical Sudjojono habit, upon seeing his good friend, he happily dragged his sleeves to a nearby inn to drink coffee and have a long, nice talk. He told him: "I only went as far as Singapore. I cancelled the plan to go to Europe. In Singapore I met some Indonesian expatriates who advised me to go back to the country instead of wasting my time there. Youths are needed during times like these, when war is imminent in Indonesia." With the belief of an artist, he went on: "They've got a point there. Artists must not be apathetic, we must take part in the crucial political developments in the history of the Indonesian people." Sudjojono believed that time and place played a part in the process of creation of a work of art, though not a determining component.

If this talk between Basuki and Sudjojono had taken place in 1936, then chances are this meeting in Singapore with the "Indonesian expatriates" had influenced Sudjojono's ideology during the Persagi era. The identity of these "Indonesian Expatriates" remains a mystery, but it must be noted that Singapore, during those times, was an escape for activists, especially the communist activists who sought refugee after failed communist coups from 1926 to 1927, when PKI became a forbidden party.

Hendra Gunawan, on the other hand, was different from Sudjojono. Holt described Hendra Gunawan as "more open-minded and not as dogmatic as Sudjojono." Hendra Gunawan had been interested in the integration of arts and politics before the 50's. In Agus Hermawan T's records, he paid his respects to Sudjojono and admits: "If I were to tell the truth about the person who brought Indonesian fine arts to new heights, then, that man is Sudjojono. Thanks to this

巴苏基・雷索波沃在《前车之鉴：艺术家、艺术与社会》(Bercermin Dimuka Kaca: Seniman, Seni dan Masyarakat，2005)提到了他与苏若约诺1936年的一次会面，也让大家再次看到了苏若约诺与共产主义思想之间的密切关系。巴苏基写道：“我知道他结束了自己的海外游历回到印尼。我问他‘你为什么那么快就回来了！你到底走了多远？’”跟往常一样，遇见好友苏若约诺总是很高兴地把袖管捋起，然后一起到附近的小酒馆边喝着咖啡边进行一番长谈。他告诉巴苏基“我最远只到了新加坡。我取消了前往欧洲的计划。在新加坡我与几个印尼侨民见面，他们建议我回国而不要在那里浪费时间。国内战争一触即发，此时尤其需要年轻人回来报效祖国。”出于艺术家的信仰，他继续道“他们提到了一个重点。艺术家决不能漠不关心。在印尼政治发展的关键时刻，我们应该积极投入到这段人民历史中去。”苏若约诺相信时间与地点在艺术创作的过程中虽然不是决定性的元素，但是都扮演着重要的角色。

如果巴苏基和苏若约诺的这段对话发生在1936年，那么很有可能在新加坡与“印尼侨民”的那次会面对Persagi时期苏若约诺的思想认识产生了影响。这些“印尼侨民”的真实身份至今依然成谜，但是会面地点在新加坡这一点值得注意。新加坡在那一时期是很多政治活动家的庇护所，特别是在1926-1927年PKI被禁、共产主义政变失败后，许多共产主义活动家都选择前往新加坡避难。

亨德拉・古那旺(Hendra Gunawan)则与苏若约诺不同。霍尔特将亨德拉・古那旺描述为“思想更开放，不像苏若约诺那么教条主义”。亨德拉・古那旺在50年代前便已经表现出对艺术与政治融合的兴趣。阿顾思・达玛旺・T在自己的文章中表达对于苏若约诺的敬意，并承认“如果要说谁把印尼艺术带上了一个全新的高度，那个人一定是苏若约诺。他为画家们开启了一片新的创作天地。很多画家都或直接或间接地接受过他的教导。他

fellow many painters learnt the lesson, in person or by other people. He believed that an artist must not just stand there; he must not be passive. An artist must organize himself as not to turn all his attention to simply creating while ignoring other movements, as these movements are essential in generating a revolution. That's the least of it."

Hendra explored further on the existence of an artist in the middle of a revolution and his position in politics. He said that SIM, Penulis Rakyat, and the individuals like Soerono, made passionate posters to advance the revolution. This made Dutch artists question the local community in a hardened tone: "Must you get involved with politics?"

Hendra Gunawan answered, "That's right. We must…. Politics that is wrong will bend arts. And the right politics will nurture the arts."

The important position that sanggars like SIM and Pelukis Rakyat occupied in the development of art was then brought to the recently founded art schools in Yogyakarta. The sanggar painters played a significant role in the art schools for a time. The most important art schools in Indonesia in the 50's were the Academy of Fine Arts of Indonesia (ASRI, Akademi Seni Rupa Indonesia) in Yogyakarta, founded in January 1950, and the Department of Architecture and Fine Arts of Bandung Institute of Technology (ITB, Institut Teknologi Bandung).

Most lecturers were sanggar painters who had no academic background in ASRI and was said to have fashioned their teaching methods after the sanggar model. The school lacked studio spaces so painting sessions had to be conducted outside. The academy also saw to it that its teachers not only taught artistic skills but also imparted their political understanding and attitudes to their students. Some influential teachers, like Sudjojono, Affandi, Hendra Gunawan, Abdulsalam, Harijadi, Suromo, Trubus and Ng. Sembiring, succeeded in persuading their students to join SIM, Pelukis Rakyat, or LEKRA, and even PKI. As "Western" art and techniques only made their way into the

认为艺术家绝不能袖手旁观地站在一边；艺术家决不能消极被动、漠不关心。艺术家在创作的过程中决不能忽略其他各种社会政治运动的进展，因为这些运动往往是推动革命的关键因素。这样的自我要求是最起码的。”

亨德拉则进一步探讨了革命中艺术家的意义以及他们在政治中的地位。他表示，SIM、Penulis Rakyat这样的艺术学会以及苏若约诺等艺术家纷纷创作各种饱含热情的海报作品宣传革命。这让荷兰艺术家用强硬的口气向本土艺术社团提出了这样一个问题：

“我们必须参与到政治中去吗？”

亨德拉·古那旺的回答是：“没错。我们必须……错误的政治会压制并扭曲艺术。而正确的政治则能够滋养艺术。”

SIM和Pelukis Rakyat等艺术学会在印尼艺术发展史上的重要地位也促使各种艺术院校在日惹兴起。学会画家长期以来在艺术院校中扮演着重要的角色。20世纪50年代，印尼最权威的两所艺术院校分别是1950年创立于日惹的印尼艺术学院(ASRI)和万隆技术学院(ITB)的建筑与艺术系。

这些院校的讲师多为学会画家，他们本身没有ASRI的学院背景，其讲授方法也多借鉴艺术学会的模式。由于学校没有工作室空间，绘画课程必须在户外进行。学院也认为教师不应只是传授技艺，而且也应该向学生传播他们自己对于政治的理解与态度。苏若约诺、阿梵迪、亨德拉·古那旺、阿布杜萨拉姆(Abdulsalam)、哈里亚蒂(Harijadi)、苏若莫(Suromo)、特鲁布斯(Trubus)以及Ng·塞姆毕林恩(Ng. Sembiring)等一批具有影响力的教师成功地引导学生们加入了SIM、Pelukis Rakyat、LEKRA甚至PKI。由于“西方”艺术与技巧在50年代中期才出现在印尼艺术院校的课堂中，其对于战时艺术所产生的影响力无法与艺术学会教师的影响力相提并论。

classrooms in the mid 50's, it did not hold the same influence to war-time art as compared to the sanggar teachers.

In Bandung, according to Holt, "the artists were conquered by art itself." Art schools in Bandung already had excellent studios and classrooms. Art education was taught according to the Western model. Compared to the more politically inclined Yogyakarta, Bandung was more interested in methods and theories of aesthetics. The most influential teacher in Bandung was a Dutch painter, Ries Mulder. In Holt's reports, Mulder described his teaching method as providing an introduction to the formal visual language in its widest possible sense, the possibility of line, tone, color, shape and space, and their function in artistic expression as applied during the different periods in different parts of the world.

Mulder admitted: "in criticizing my students' work, apart from formal and technical advice, I limit myself from the development of their personal efforts in developing their work. It's a fact I fully realize that the element of personal influence is inevitable, but nobody with profound knowledge of the situation developing here, will deny that I had managed to control these influence to the extent that it can work indirectly. My students influence one another on a stronger level compared to my influence on them."

Mulder further told his students: "You are free to find yourselves without obstacles, or prejudice, or sentiments without daily pressures that you are 'Indonesian'. Why would you hide this independence from other people?"

Helena Spanjaard, in her "Bandung, the Laboratory of the West?" (1990) called the works of Ries' students – Ahmad Sadali, But Mochtar, Popo Iskandar and Mochtar Apin, among others – as "Ries Mulder's cubism." After the mid-50's, the works of these Bandung painters were becoming more diverse in terms of their form and content, but they generally painted in an abstract style.

根据霍尔特的记载，在万隆“艺术家被艺术本身所征服”。万隆的艺术院校拥有一流的工作室和教室，遵循西方模式开展艺术教育。比起政治气氛浓郁的日惹，万隆对于美学方法和理论更感兴趣。荷兰画家瑞斯·穆尔德(Ries Mulder)是万隆最具影响力的导师。在霍尔特的报告中，穆尔德将自己的教学方法描述为“在可能的最广泛的意义上对正规视觉语言进行引导式的介绍，让学生了解线条、色调、色彩、形状与空间的各种可能性，以及不同时期、不同地点它们在艺术表达中的不同作用”。

穆尔德表示“在点评学生作品的时候，除了给出技术性的指导建议，我不会影响他们对作品的个性化理解与诠释。我很清楚个人的影响力的因素是不可避免的。但是所有了解印尼局势的人都不会否认我努力把这些影响力控制在不会对作品产生直接作用的范围内。换言之，个人影响力只是间接地发挥作用。学生们对彼此的影响远比我对他们的影响深刻的多。”

穆尔德还告诉学生：“你们完全可以在没有阻碍、没有偏见、没有压力的情况下自由地表达你们是‘印尼人’。你们为什么要对别人隐藏这样的独立性呢？”

海伦娜·斯帕嘉德 (Helena Spanjaard) 在她的著作《万隆，西方实验室？》(1990)中将瑞斯学生艾哈迈德·萨塔利(Ahmad Sadali)、布特·莫什塔(But Mochtar)、帕波·伊斯坎达尔(Popo Iskandar)、莫什塔·阿皮尼(Mochtar Apin)等人的作品称之为“瑞斯立体派”。50年代后，这些万隆画家在创作形式和内容上更趋多元，不过一个普遍的倾向是他们的风格逐渐走向抽象。

日惹艺术家常说万隆画家的作品——也就是瑞斯学生的作品——缺乏思想性。他们把万隆艺术家的作品称之为“西方艺术”——是个人主义的，在表达上亦更为抽象。而日惹的艺术则是“印尼艺术”——是社会主义的，在表达上属于现实主义。基于这些特点，亨

Artists from Yogyakarta would often say that the work of Bandung painters – Ries' students – lacked ideological content. They called the works by Bandung artists "Western art" that was individualistic and tended to be akin to the abstract expressionists, whereas Yogyakarta's art is "Indonesian art," socialist and realist in their expressions. Based on these characteristics, Hendra Gunawan would always claim Yogyakarta as the "center of nationalist art, the stronghold of revolution."

Observers would generally say that the works of Yogyakartan painters – for example, the works of Hendra Gunawan, Affandi, or Sudjojono – are indeed extraordinary realist and expressionist works. These works are mostly social documentations of the war years against the Dutch, portraying troops, refugees, senior citizens, children, and profound self portraits. Such works were exhibited in the open several times as an acknowledgement of the struggle for independence.

Trisno Sumarjo, an art critic, in his "Bandung Mengabdi Laboratorium Barat," classifies two kinds of modern Indonesian art: first, spontaneous art, native of the country, born by the spirit and the experience of Indonesia; the other, imitation or artificial arts in the classrooms of Western "laboratories." Trisno condemns the fine arts in Bandung that are, in his point of view, "shallow," "bloodless," and smell like "the air of European laboratories," as the victims of foreign teachers who support modernism. In the mean time, an LKN (Lembaga Kebudayaan Nasional, National's Culture Organization) officer, Sitor Situmorang, believes that Bandung artists have developed a shallow modernism, directly taken from the taste of Western bourgeoisie. Western painting, he proceeds, is in crisis and is no more than a trick, a game of perspective, composition and color contrast. Modern art has no meaning, delivers no message and doesn't have a point of view that relates to the world, unlike Yogyakartan paintings. This modern art, he says, is only a visual expression of the private life of the painter and will never fulfill its cultural function in Indonesia.

德拉·古那旺始终把日惹称为"民族主义艺术中心，革命的要塞据点"。

人们一般认为亨德拉·古那旺、阿梵迪、苏若约诺等日惹艺术家的作品属于现实主义和表现主义范畴。他们的作品多是对印尼独立战争的社会纪实，往往以部队、难民、老年人、孩童为主题，有时也进行自画像创作。这些作品多次在公开场合进行露天展示，作为对独立战争的纪念。

艺术评论家特里斯诺·苏玛迦(Trisno Sumarjo)在《万隆，西方实验室的奴仆》(Bandung Mengabdi Laboratorium Barat)一文中将印尼现代艺术分为两类：第一类是自发型的艺术，土生土长，凸显印尼精神与体现；第二类是从西方"实验室"的课堂中发展出来的模仿艺术、或曰人造艺术。特里斯诺批判万隆艺术"肤浅"、"冷漠"、带着"欧洲实验室的气息"，受到支持现代主义的外国教师的荼毒。与此同时，印尼国家文化协会LKN负责人西托尔·西杜莫朗(Sitor Situmorang)也表示，万隆艺术家所打造的是一种肤浅的现代主义，直接脱胎于西方资产阶级的品味。他接着说道，"西方绘画处于危机之中。那不过是一个戏法，是一场透视、构图和色彩反差的游戏。现代艺术没有内涵，不传递任何讯息，也没有自己的世界观，与日惹的绘画作品完全不一样。这种现代艺术只是一种画家个人生活的视觉表达，不能满足印尼的文化发展与表达的需要。"

其他研究人员则喜欢把50年代的印尼艺术界视作为一场"为人民而艺术"与"为艺术而艺术"两种概念之间的较量。万隆的艺术西方化倾向可以看作是"为艺术而艺术"的代表，而日惹艺术中浓郁的民族主义色彩则是"为人民而艺术"的代表。这也是为何日惹成为LEKRA理念发展的最佳地点。

1 凯里尔·安哇尔(Chairil Anwar)，上世纪40年代杰出的印尼诗人。

Other observers are keener to call the arena of Indonesian fine arts during the 50's as a contest between the concept of "art for the people's sake" and "art for art's sake." The tendency towards Western art, as was happening in Bandung, is a representation of this art for art's sake; on the contrary, the high sentiment of citizenship and nationalism in Yogyakarta represented the view of art for the people's sake. This is one reason why Yogyakarta became a perfect place for the growth of LEKRA's notions.

1 Chairil Anwar is the prominent Indonesian poet during the 40's.

TONY GODFREY
托尼·高夫雷

Indonesian Art Understood As Global Art – Or Not

Indonesia is the world's fourth largest country, it has an extensive and buoyant art scene, yet its art is rarely seen beyond its own boundaries. Before I moved to Asia, during twenty-five years of being a London-based art critic, but one with strong global interests, I had only heard of two Indonesian artists – Heri Dono and Jim Supangkat. Why should this be? Why is Indonesian art so invisible? And a second question that inevitably follows from that is: "Why should the rest of the world get to know what is happening in Indonesia?"

Economically, the market for Indonesian art is dynamic, but hermetic – it is totally enclosed. This is not unique: in Europe for example Italian art is sent from Italy to Sotheby's and Christie's in London to be sold; Italian collectors fly to London, buy it, and take it back to Italy. So likewise Indonesian art is sent to Hong Kong to be sold, and then once sold, almost invariably returned to Indonesia. Indonesian artists can survive without collectors from overseas: many seem to not expect an international reputation, and indeed seem to not be bothered by being

印尼艺术，全球艺术——是，抑或不是？

作为全球第四人口大国，印尼艺术的发展可谓朝气蓬勃、百花齐放。然而，印尼艺术却鲜少走出国门到更广泛的国际舞台上展示。在迁居亚洲之前，虽然我在伦敦担任艺术评论家已经长达25年之久。虽然我也保持着对全球艺术发展的敏锐触角，但是我却只听说过两位印尼艺术家的名字——他们是赫利·多诺(Heri Dono)和杰姆·苏潘凯特(Jim Supangkat)。为什么会出现这样的局面呢？为什么人们没有途径去看、去了解印尼艺术呢？而紧随其后的一个不可避免的问题就是"世界为什么应该去了解印尼呢？"

从经济的角度来说，印尼艺术市场既充满活力又极具神秘色彩——这个市场几乎完全对外封闭。这样的情况倒也并非孤例，无独有偶：以欧洲为例，意大利的艺术品就是先从意大利运往伦敦的苏富比和佳士得拍卖行进行拍卖；接着，意大利收藏家们飞往伦敦、买下作品，然后再将其运回意大利。印尼艺术品的买卖情况与此十分类似。首先，作品被运往香港进行出售，而一旦交易完成，几乎无一例外会被运回印尼。

"local."

Indonesia, or more specifically, the two culture towns of Jogja and Bandung, are comfort zones – in both a positive and a negative sense. There are friendships, enough discussions for many participants, and sufficient cliques to create an internal tension. I, like those few others from other countries who have discovered the dynamism and good will of Indonesian artists, relish my visits. But very little art from other countries gets transmitted to Bandung or Jogjakarta, and the artists themselves do not often get outside: in an age of global travel Indonesian artists are among the least well travelled. Relatively few artists speak English – the language in which most art discourse appears. And, of course, the dismal exchange rate (currently over 1300 rupiah to the yuan, and over 9000 to the US dollar) is not an incentive to travel abroad.

Being linked historically to a minor European power (Holland) has also added a degree of marginalisation; I'm sorry but I am not going to learn Dutch to learn about early modern Indonesian art. Since 1700 Holland has been a historical backwater and as a result her colonies (or ex colonies) have been regarded with much less interest than those of the dominant colonial powers France and England.

History matters. The turbulent history of Indonesia since 1942, when the Japanese arrived and overturned the colonial government, has been inspirational to artists but has also in some respects trapped them. The prestige that accompanied early modernists like Hendra, Sudjojono and Affandi as freedom fighters was crucial in giving art in Indonesia a role in "nation-building," and the prestige of those artists still reflects, however weakly, on contemporary artists. At times Indonesian art has, understandably, been obsessed with its own history, but for everyone in the West who knows of the Sukarno Indonesian struggle for independence

即使没有海外收藏家的介入，印尼艺术家依然有足够的生存空间：他们之中相当一部分人似乎并不期待在国际舞台上声名鹊起，而怡然自得于做好“本土”艺术家。

印尼、或者更明确一点地说——印尼的两大文化重镇日惹和万隆——可以被称之为舒适区。这可谓有利有弊。这里有友谊、有探讨，也有各种不同的派系和圈子，都使得其内部充满张力与活力。跟少数几个发现印尼艺术家的创作活力与美好意愿的外国人一样，我十分珍惜也很享受自己的印尼之行。但是，别国艺术几乎无法进入万隆或日惹，而印尼艺术家们又很少走出国门：在旅行和游历日益变得全球化的时代，印尼艺术家可算得上是大门不出、二门不迈的典型了。会说英语的艺术家人数也相对较少——而英语可以说是当前艺术对话的垄断性语言。当然，悬殊的汇率(印尼卢比对人民币和美元分别约为1300:1和9000:1)也是抑制印尼艺术家国外看看走走的一大原因。

印尼与荷兰有着密切的历史渊源。而荷兰在欧洲列强中相对弱势的地位也在一定程度上加剧了印尼的被边缘化：很抱歉，我不会为了去更多地了解早期的印尼现代艺术而学习荷兰语。自1700年以来，历史上的荷兰便一直处于相对闭塞的状态。而作为荷兰的殖民地(或者说前殖民地)，印尼所获得的关注与兴趣程度远不如英法列强的殖民地。

历史的影响力举足轻重。1942年日本出兵入侵印尼，在推翻了当时的荷兰殖民政府后开始对印尼实行殖民统治。这段动荡而血腥的历史为很多艺术家提供了创作灵感，但在某种程度上，这也限制了他们的创作。亨德拉(Hendra)、苏若约诺(Sudjojono)、阿梵迪(Affandi)等现代主义先驱作为自由斗士的名望一举奠定了艺术在印尼“国家建设”中的关键地位——前辈艺术大师的声望在当今虽已式微，但是依然在当代艺术家身上有所体现。印尼艺术在很长一段时间内都以本国的历史为关注焦点，这一点其实无可厚非、也

and good government, a thousand know of Mao Tse Tung and the birth of the People's Republic of China. Indonesia's history is little known and this can be (unnecessarily) a barrier to understanding the art produced there.

Dominated by collectors rather than museums, Indonesian art has tended to be personality focused, expressionist and instinctual rather than conceptually driven. This has perhaps made theory-led curators from the West to assume (incorrectly) that it is old fashioned.

Perhaps the biggest barrier to Indonesian art, now becoming better known on the international circuit, is that it is insufficiently exotic. There is of course a good market for paintings of Balinese women with no tops on, but we shouldn't take that seriously. Heri Dono and others may reference wayang kulit – often in the case of younger artists this is merged with the more "up-to-date" Manga – but there is never any reference to tribal art still produced in Sumatra, Borneo (Kalimintan) and Irian. That may still intrigue many artists in the West but Indonesian artists are oblivious to it. Nor could any serious artist paint a beautiful landscape with rice fields with happy peasants and mountains behind. Such mooie Indies art was the soft pornography of Dutch colonialism and to be avoided now.

But it is above all this lack of exoticism that makes Indonesian art so interesting: art from Indonesia is about the same issues, forces and problems that face the rest of the world, but seen from a different perspective. For example, that perennial subject, the condition of the artist. Here as elsewhere he or she is someone normally displaced from his or her home context, someone who must work alone in a highly social setting, someone from what can be a profoundly religious society (Islam, Christian, animist) encountering a flagrantly secular capitalist society. Many of these artists have moved from Su-

并不难理解。但是对于西方受众来说，知道苏加诺(Sukarno)总统带领印尼追求独立解放并最终建立自治政府的人数不及知道毛泽东带领中国人民建立中华人民共和国人数的千分之一。大家对于印尼历史普遍感到陌生，而这是妨碍大家了解印尼艺术的(不必要的)障碍。

由于是收藏家而非博物馆占据着主导的地位，印尼艺术更倾向于关注个性，它往往是表现主义的、直观的，而不是以理论来带动发展。这或许也让偏重理论的西方策展人产生了这样一个(不正确的)想法：即印尼艺术是传统而老派的。

此外，阻碍印尼艺术在国际舞台上获得更多关注和知名度的另一大原因在于其缺乏“异国情调”。当然，半裸的巴厘女子画像拥有不错的市场——但是我们不应该把这当作一个严肃的题材来对待。赫利·多诺等艺术家会借鉴印尼传统皮影戏(wayang kulit)——年轻一代艺术家则常常会采用更具“现代性”的漫画的形式。但是，苏门答腊、婆罗洲(加里曼丹岛)和伊里安岛上现在依然流传着的部落艺术却从来不曾出现在当代艺术家的创作中。这些艺术对于很多西方艺术家来说具有相当大的吸引力，但是印尼艺术家却似乎对此视而不见。也没有任何一位严肃的艺术家会创作一幅以稻田、欢乐的农夫和起伏的山峦为主题的绘画作品。此类“美丽印度”(mooie Indies)流派的艺术风格被认为是对荷兰殖民主义的软性讴歌，如今俨然成为艺术创作需要规避的禁区。

但是，也正是“异国情调”的缺位让印尼艺术显得如此有趣：印尼艺术所探讨的问题和话题在全球范围内具有普遍意义，但有意思的是，印尼艺术家则从一个不同的视角来看待这些问题和话题。举例来说，一个经常出现的主题便是关于艺术家处境的探讨。与别处一样，在这里他/她往往也是一个从家乡语境中抽离、流离失所的人；必须在一个大社会环境中独自一人埋头工作；拥有深刻的宗教社会背景(伊斯兰教

matra or Bali to Java, or from small towns to larger metropolitan centres. This has been, of course, a dominant condition for many artists – the English landscape tradition was made by people who had moved to London. As for loneliness, one artist speaks for many of them when he talks about the difficulty of making art, normally a lonely, self-centred activity, in the context of what is a still a very communal society, and in many respects a gentle society. There is a precarious balance between the loneliness of art making and the communal nature of many studios where other artists wander in and chat or flick through the pictures of magazines, and where the artist's children will play or dump their toys. Many artists work outside or, if they work indoors, leave their door open.

It is significant how many of the artists in Jogja live on the Southern edges of the town where padi fields predominate still and the housing is low level and clustered tightly together. Here a kampong life still exists where life flows unbroken between the open rooms and the pathways between houses. It is a potent symbol for a communal life that is being eroded by modern life: as Eko Nugroho points out, increasingly in the kampongs people sit behind closed doors watching TV – being internally colonised by a distant and effectively virtual culture. His work, perhaps above all others, stands against this passivity, involving his whole community as makers and participants in his productions.

Spirituality and a sense of the magic of things are less easy to identify but equally important. (The Italian word Maggia would be a better word than the English "Magic" here because it suggests something everyday rather than perverse and deliberately conjured.) Very few of these artists can be described as devout Muslims and the most that Islam can be said to give them is a general sense of harmony, aspiration and good will. The artists focus on the material world without being materialists. In

徒、基督教教徒、万物有灵论者)，与万恶的世俗资本主义社会相遭遇。很多艺术家从苏门答腊岛、巴厘岛移居爪哇，或者从小城镇移居大都市。当然，这是许多艺术家都面临的一个共同处境——英国风景画的传统也是由那些移居伦敦的人所建立的。至于孤独，当一位艺术家谈起艺术创作的艰辛，他往往说出了很多艺术家的心声。艺术创作是一项孤独的、以自我为中心的活动，它在一个高度共享而平和的社会语境中发生。在艺术创作的孤独感与许多工作室的共享本质之间存在着一种不稳定的平衡关系。在这些工作室中，其他艺术家会走进来进行交谈或浏览一下杂志上的图片；艺术家的孩子们会在这里玩耍或者把玩具丢得满地都是。很多艺术家都选择在室外开展工作，而如果他们选择在室内进行创作，他们也会把门开着。

日惹南部地貌仍以稻田(padi)为主，楼房低矮而密集。究竟有多少艺术家居住在日惹南部城镇，这个问题具有重要的意义。在这里，一种田野乡间(kampong)的生活方式依然存在，生活如同流水一般在房屋与房屋之间开放的房间和走道之中不间断地徜徉。这可以说是共享生活的有力证明，而这种生活正日益遭受现代生活的侵蚀：正如艾柯・努格罗荷(Eko Nugroho)所指出的，田野乡间的居民越来越多地选择关起门来看电视——被一种遥远而虚幻的文化进行着内部殖民。与其他艺术家相比，努格罗荷的作品更鲜明地与这种被动性进行较量和抵制，让他所在的整个社区都作为创作者参与到他的作品中来。

要明确地指出精神性和对于事物魅力(magic)的感知比较困难，但是这两点却同样重要。(在这里，使用意大利语"Maggia"或许比英语"Magic"更贴切，因为"Maggia"意指日常的、非反常或特意制造出来的。)这批艺术家中几乎没有人可以被称为虔诚的穆斯林，伊斯兰教义对于他们最大的影响或许还是在宏观意义上培养了他们的和睦、善良与抱负。这些艺术家将关注的焦点放在物质世界上，但是自己本身却

short, spiritual belief is manifested in an attitude towards things of this world. It would be very easy to describe many art objects, such as those of Handiwirman, for example, as surreal, but that would be inadequate. Certainly surrealism has been an influence, but "magic realism" may be a more appropriate term for this attitude to the object, which is often connected to narrativity. This is accentuated in Handirwirman's case by the way he takes images of his objects and uses them as actors in his paintings. Objects matter.

And the art market – Indonesian as elsewhere – always wants objects, especially paintings. Many of Masriadi's paintings joke with his mordant humour on the zeal of collectors, their competitive desire to obtain his works. Because the auctions are one of the major sites to see Indonesian art – unlike in the West, it is where much Indonesian art is first exhibited – and because Indonesian art magazines are unusually fascinated by prices it is no surprise that the artists are unusually aware of the status of the artworks as consumables and emblems of value.

All the issues that dominate art elsewhere appear here too: Budi Kustarto and Puto Sutawijaya, with a fascination in the human body; humour in Angki Purbandono's super noodle theory photographs. His work is an indicator too of a curiosity in photography in Southeast Asia: that it is becoming an art form in the age of digitalisation, not before it. As a result, the play that scanning, digitally dislocating or enhancing allows seems central. Photography here is about acting rather than representing.

Memory and the act of mourning is one of the key themes of this exhibition, but it is of course a theme of much good art today – from Anselm Kiefer to Zhang Xiaogang, from Christian Boltanski to Huang Yong Ping. F.X. Harsono, like other artists, returns frequently to the 1998 attacks on ethnic Chinese in Jakarta as a problem area, a point when something

并不是唯物主义者。简言之，精神信仰体现在对于世界万物的态度之中。我们很容易把艺术品形容为“超现实”。萨普川・翰迪怀儿曼(Saputra Handiwirman)的作品就是一例。但是，仅仅用“超现实”来描述是不够的。当然，超现实主义的确产生了深远的影响，但是用“魔幻现实主义”(magic realism)来形容这种对于叙事对象的态度或许更为贴切。这一点在翰迪怀儿曼的作品中展露无遗。通过对物体的图像化记录并将其应用于自己的绘画作品中，翰迪怀儿曼向我们显示了对象的重要性。

印尼的艺术市场与其他地方一样，总是想要作品，特别是绘画作品。收藏家的热忱以及他们对获得作品所展开的激烈的竞争中蕴含着一种犀利的幽默感，米斯尼亚迪(Masriadi)的许多画作正是都拿这种幽默来开玩笑。一方面，拍卖行变成了观摩印尼艺术的一个重要场合——与西方艺术不同，拍卖行是很多印尼艺术作品首次展示的舞台，另一方面，印尼的各种艺术杂志又往往唯作品成交价格马首是瞻，在两个因素的综合作用下，艺术家往往把艺术品视作消费品和价值的象征也就不足为奇了。

所有在世界其他地方占据主导地位的艺术议题也都在这里出现：布迪・库斯塔图(Budi Kustarto)和普图・苏塔维嘉亚(Puto Sutawi jaya)对于人体的迷恋；安奇・普班度诺(Angki Purbandono)超级面条理论摄影的幽默感。普班度诺的作品同时也是东南亚摄影艺术的一个指标：成为数字化时代中的一种艺术形式。此时的摄影更多的是关乎表演而非真实再现。

回忆与悼念是本次展览的一个重要主题，当然这也是当今艺术的一个常见的主题——从安森・基弗(Anselm Kiefer)到张晓刚、从克里斯蒂安・波尔坦斯基(Christian Boltanski)到黄永砯。与其他艺术家一样，当印尼历史上发生了有必要反复审视并彻底杜绝的恶性事件时，方济各・沙勿略・哈索诺(F.X.Harsono)经常会以作品的形式重回1998年

bad emerged in Indonesian history that needs to be examined again and again, and eventually exorcised.

But, of course – and this must be emphasised – a lot of this art has no overt relationship to 'subjects' or issues. It is about, or rather we should say "infused" with, wit, vitality, beauty, elegance and poetry. Although there is much that we will better appreciate in this art by knowing the historical and social context in which it was made, this is on the whole a sociable art that is complex but reasonably easy to understand and enjoy.

雅加达发生针对华人的暴乱的现场。

不过，有一点必须强调的是，很多时候这些艺术与"主题"或事件之间并没有任何明显的联系。作品所表现的是——或者说作品的表达中"充满了"——睿智、活力、魅力、优雅与诗意。虽然对于作品的历史和社会语境有所了解将有助于我们更好地欣赏并理解印尼艺术，但是总的来说，这是一种随和的、容易沟通的艺术——虽然有其复杂性，但却不难理解，可以让人很轻松地便沉浸到作品之中。

SIMON GUAN
肖蒙

Contemporaneity: An Interpretation of an Experience

当代性：一种经历的诠释

To interpret the term "contemporaneity" is rather intriguing. Perhaps an easier way is to try to understand it in the context of its Chinese version, although there seems to be no exact translation.

The New Oxford English-Chinese Dictionary defines "contemporaneity" as: the quality or state of existing or occurring in the same period of time. Wordnet states it as "the quality of belonging to the same period of time," or "the quality of being current or of the present." For the Chinese version, Google translates the term as "时代性" (shi dai xing). ICIBA(爱词霸), a popular web translation tool, puts it as "同时代" (tong shi dai). The English-Chinese Dictionary, the most authoritative one in China, edited by Professor Lu Gu-shun, defines it as: 同时期(性), 同时代(性), 同时发生(性). In a playful way, translated back into English, they mean "being in the same period of time or era" or "occurring at the same time."

To put those definitions in the context of the development of contemporary art in the world, the

要翻译"contemporaneity"这一词的确有些难度。词典里没有与之直接对应的译文，却更像是对该词的解释。如果把这词放在中文语境中也许更容易理解。

新牛津英汉词典定义"contemporaneity"为"同时存在或发生的性质或状态"。网上词典Wordnet定义为"当前性或现在性"。Google将该词译成"时代性"。"爱词霸"(ICIBA)则译成"同时代"。由陆谷孙教授主编的中国最权威的《英汉大词典》将其释义为"同时期(性)、同时代(性)、同时发生(性)"。

如将这些解释放在当代艺术的背景中，释义该词似乎不再是个问题。看似更像是某种宣言。艺术评论家对当代艺术的观点通常是直白的：单一化的、由男性白人主导的现代主义艺术已寿终正寝，取而代之的是由背景大不相同的一群艺术家所带来的多样性的混合艺术形式。

当我们将眼光投向欧美以外的当代艺术较活跃的国家，我们不难发现那些国家正在发生的变化：新的

term seems less of a defining problem but rather a manifesto. The general art critic's view of contemporary art is candid: the linear, singular, white and male-dominant practices of modernism have finally declined, replaced by this multi-faceted and diversified development with a hybrid complexity of art forms produced by people of widely differing backgrounds and attachments.

Take a quick look at the contemporary art development in a number of active nations outside of Europe and the US, where some new form of democracy is being shaped and fast growth of economy is observed. Artists from China, Cuba, Russia, and even South Africa, for example, have been bringing new voices, perspectives, ideas and styles onto the global art stage. The extraordinary proliferation of the art phenomena generated by such artists is increasingly widespread: biennials being one official expression for the general public. The same forces also catalyzed the springing up of new museums like mushrooms as part of the new ferment of globalized art production and consumption.

China, Russia, and Cuba, all developing away from their identities as Communist nations in the era of a new world order, differ from one another as Russia being the most post-Communist state. China, following the end of the Cultural Revolution, developed first on multiple paths from socialist realism, religious themes, or even Marxist humanism, and then engaged rapidly with the new and fast-growing consumer culture that soon resulted in the rapid emergence of great wealth and inequality. In both China and Cuba, capitalist-communist propaganda art has been produced, if you want to compare the work of Wang Guangyi and Jose Angel Toirac. Such coincidence is not surprising, for both the governments have loosened their grip on their planning economies, allowing private enterprises to flourish.

Gao Minglu noted that, as the capitalist devel-

民主形式在成形，经济正高速发展。例如：中国、古巴、俄罗斯甚至南非。这些国家的艺术家正将新的观点、期望、理念以及风格带上全球艺术舞台。由这些艺术家们产生的丰富多彩的艺术现象正迅速蔓延扩展：双年展就是面向大众的官方表述。这些艺术家也促就了一大批新型美术馆的诞生，如雨后春笋般，成为全球化的艺术生产及消费的催化剂。

中国、俄罗斯和古巴都源自于世界新秩序时代的共产主义国家，但又各不相同：俄罗斯属于后共产主义国家。中国自文革结束后率先走上社会现实主义，宗教派别，甚至马克思人文主义的多元化发展道路；加上快速发展的消费文化，乃至贫富悬殊扩大。就中国和古巴而论，王广义和何塞・安吉尔・托拉克(Jose Angel Toirac)的作品各自呈现出资本主义－社会主义的宣传式艺术。此类巧合不足为奇，因为两国政府放开了原有的计划经济，使得私营经济体得以蓬勃发展。

高名潞指出，随着资本主义在中国的发展，像王广义那样的艺术家开始脱离曾经是那么宏伟的精神主题和人文主题，转而取悦于媒体以及致力于商业化的成功。或者更确切地说，是迎合西方口味。不难发现，像谷文达、蔡国强、徐冰等一些功成名就的中国当代艺术家大多居住或活跃于纽约、巴黎、伦敦和柏林，因为那里不仅是世界文化中心而且是艺术市场及藏家的活跃之地。

他们是中国迄今为止最成功的艺术出口。蔡国强和徐冰用中国的古代发明火药和印刷术作为他们主要的表现介质。从西方的观点看，这些形式映射了中国的元素：表现传统？的确！突显民族性？或许。蔡国强、徐冰、谷文达和王广义都先成名于欧美。他们是否可以被归类为中国当代艺术发展的领军人物还是属于西方观念中的世界当代艺术家，值得商榷。相反，栗宪庭描述的“泼皮式”先锋派(如方力均和岳敏君)的作品却可以不折不扣地冠以与世界各地同一时期出现的地道的中国当代艺术。

opment in China accelerated, artists like Wang Guangyi began to move away from the once grand spiritual and humanistic themes and toward pleasing the media saturated world and achieving success in the art market; or, to be more specific, appealing to the Western eye. Bear in mind, the most successful Chinese contemporary artists today, such as Gu Wenda, Cai Guoqiang, Xu Bing, and many others, are either living or practicing in the main cultural centers of the globe, like New York, Paris, London and Berlin, where the supportive art markets and collectors are.

They are China's most successful exports in art. Cai Guoqiang and Xu Bing adopt Chinese ancient inventions as their main medium of expression: gunpowder and print, which in the Western sense are reflections of Chinese phenomena: Traditional? Yes; Ethnical? Probably! Both Cai and Xu, together with Gu and Wang gained their fame in Europe and the US. Whether they can be grouped together as representatives of Chinese contemporary art development or world contemporary art in the Western sense remains a question. Whereas other manifestos, as Li Xianting described, such as the "anti-heroist" avant-garde (Fang Lijun and Yue Minjun), can be safely labeled as the new Chinese contemporary art that emerged at about the same period of time as elsewhere.

In a broader view, the evolution of contemporary art in Asian countries is seen progressing at different paces. While the unprecedented changes in China's economic, social and cultural life over the past decades have evoked highly ambitious and experimental responses from Chinese artists, Indonesian contemporary art that emerged in the late 70s seems to have developed at a relatively steadier speed. Different from those Chinese contemporary artists, Indonesian contemporary art has much deeper roots in its own soil, whether due to the political changes under the different regimes or

在一些亚洲国家里，当代艺术的沿革各不相同。中国在过去的几十年中经历了前所未有的经济、社会和文化的演变，催生了一大批心气颇高、勇于尝试的艺术家。而起始于七十年代后期的印尼当代艺术相对发展得更稳健些。不同于那些中国当代艺术家，印尼的当代艺术更深地植根于本土，这或许起因于各时期的政治变化，又或许源自于印尼丰厚的文化遗产。此外，有本国的艺术评论家们和藏家们的大力支持，印尼本土的艺术市场十分活跃。从这一方面来说，印尼的当代艺术家们并不太积极寻求赢得本土之外的认可。

在欧美之外的当代艺术似乎同时间在全球范围内如蓝筹股般遍地开花。欧美和欧美以外的当代艺术分界不再像现代艺术那样的边际分明。从西方眼光看，来自印尼的当代艺术或许具有本土意识。然而，这次展览所带来的不完全如此。当我十年前开始接触印尼当代艺术时，我被其多元化和全球性所震撼。人们通常以为来自如印尼、中国这些国家的当代艺术会有明显的本土烙印，事实并非如此。然而，这也不能就此断言它没有本土味道，而应该说“伪装”得更巧妙。

中国当代艺术的出现或许要晚于自七十年代兴起的西方当代艺术十多年。如前所述，那些领军人物多数成名于国外，所以中国的当代艺术是更具本土性还是全球性，已无需多议。但要确切地证实何时出现、如何出现，却有些难度。高名潞曾经说过，要写一部中国当代艺术史甚为困难。无论高名潞等人在《中国当代艺术史1985-1986》中如何编织各路流派，将其置于全球当代艺术的背景中来审视，他们显然缺乏地标式的作品或成就。当时所谓的“85新潮”无非是一群在读或刚从国内各艺术院校毕业的年轻人，在“资本主义式”经济发展初期对西方后现代主义艺术的不成熟的诠释。他们或许带些“当代特质”，但在西方的当代艺术语境里仍值得探讨。

就艺术词汇学论，或更确切地说，就当代艺术语意而论，“contemporaneity” (当代性)不是一种风格，

its cultural heritage rich with Indonesian identities, and it also has a strong art market within the country, which is both celebrated by the art critics and supported by the collectors, which, in a way, might prevent those artists from seeking so vigorously recognition outside of Indonesia.

Global contemporary art that has emerged outside of the US and Europe is multiplying with blue-chip standard contemporaneously. The space in the contemporary art world between inside and outside of the US and Europe is no longer so distinctive as in the Modern Art period. Contemporary art from Indonesia may, in Western senses, bear their ethnic sensibilities and yet in reality as clearly reflected in this exhibition the answer is not entirely clear. In my initial encounters with Indonesian contemporary art, about ten years ago, I was amazed at its pluralism and globalism, but with much less exposition of ethnicity, which one might expect from a nation like Indonesia or China. However, it does not mean that ethnicity is not obviously seen, but rather cleverly "disguised" in the spaces in between.

The Chinese contemporary art that may have occurred more than a decade later than that which emerged in Europe and the US beginning in the 70s, seems less of an issue in this discussion as to whether or not they are more ethnic or more global, given the fact as aforementioned that those pioneers are mostly active outside China. It is still hard to determine when and how it came into being. Gao Minglu once said that it was very difficult to write a book about the history of Chinese contemporary art. No matter how Gao and others were trying to plot those trends in their book History of Chinese Contemporary Art 1985-1986, it is simply impossible to identify the landmarks if they are to be viewed in the global scene of contemporary art. The new art wave of the so-called "'85 Movement," is generally comprehended as the beginning of Chinese contemporary art, and it is in fact an imma-

或流派，更不是一种审美价值观。在本人看来，它不应属于一种“性质”，而是一种“状态”：一种同时间在发生的进行中的状态。它揭示了一个事实：一种当代的经历，即我们当下的生活、工作和体验。无论你是艺术家、评论家或观众，不管你愿不愿意，你已经是当下经历的一分子。

最近一次去纽约出差，我在闲暇时有意不去MET或MoMA，而是去了Chelsea和Soho逛画廊。那里成百家画廊突显出全球性艺术正在攻入世界当代艺术的中心地带。来自美国以外的艺术家带着某种本土文化特征的作品成了画廊的主导。有意思的是，曾经是区别明显的“世界当代艺术”和“全球当代艺术”似乎更具多重性了。

我们可以乐此不疲地继续讨论当代艺术到底是什么，何时以及如何在世界上出现。然而要取得一种共识似乎不难：当代的艺术家无论在何地、以何种方式，只要他们在同一时期进行艺术创作，他们便是在经历一种状态：即当代性。这就是本次艺术展览所要带给大家的。

ture interpretation of Western post-modernism with certain "contemporary characters" by a group of students or fresh graduates from art academies in China in the dawn of "capitalist" economic boom. It indeed remains a question in the Western discourse of contemporary art.

In artistic terms, or, to be more specific, in the context of contemporary art, "contemporaniety" is not a style, nor a school, nor an aesthetic value. In my understanding, it is not a "quality" (性质) but rather a "state" (状态): a state of occurring or happening at the same period of time, which undoubtedly reveals a fact: an experience of being contemporary. It is in this very moment that we are living, practicing and experiencing. Like it or not, you (whether an artist, an art critic, or an audience) are already a part of it as being contemporaneous.

During a recent business trip to New York, I purposely avoided spending my leisure time in the Met or at MOMA, but took a very exhaustive excursion of gallery hopping in Chelsea and Soho. Amongst the hundreds of the galleries, there's an obvious sign of emerging global art invading the center of the contemporary art world: artists from the outside of the US are a dominant phenomenon with their works of certain ethnic and cultural sensibilities. Ironically, the once quite distinctive in-between space of "world contemporary art" and "global contemporary art" is probably becoming more pluralized.

We can continue to discuss those phenomena to understand what exactly contemporary art is, and to comprehend when and how it actually started around the world. One conclusion that can be easily drawn is that if a contemporary artist is performing in the same period of time as others no matter where and how, all of them are experiencing the state of being contemporaneous. And this is exactly what this exhibition wants to bring to you.

SUSAN INGHAM
苏珊·英格汉姆

Indonesian Art, Entering The Global

In the aftermath of modernity, art has indeed only one option: to be contemporary. But "being contemporary" these days means much more than a mindless embrace of the present.[1]

In his book, What is Contemporary Art? Professor Terry Smith describes contemporary art as "an intense, expansionist, proliferating global subculture, with its own values and discourse." [2] Contending forces compete within contemporaneity, one of which, as Smith recognized, has had particular relevance for non-European, post-colonial and Asian cultures; as he put it, the pressure to enter the globalized dialogue was tempered by a post-colonial necessity for cultural differentiation. He stated that the "globalizing character is essential to it (Contemporary Art), but it also mobilizes nationalities, and even localisms." [3] It is as if the very forces that provide an outlet for the expression of local issues and interests are the same forces that attempt to make these issues conform to a global standard. These are, therefore, potentially contending forces within Contemporary Art.

By the 1990s it became clear that international communications and cultural traffic was changing radically. The term 'globalization' was used to describe this transformation and in the fine arts it was marked by the exchange of information and imagery through ever expanding technologies, fuelled by

印尼艺术，走向全球

在经历了现代性的洗礼后，艺术只有一个选择：走向"当代"。但是，走向"当代"绝不仅仅意味着不假思索又盲目地投身现代性的怀抱。[1]

在《什么是当代艺术》一书中，特里·史密斯(Terry Smith)教授将当代艺术描述为"……一种强烈、极富扩张性、迅速蔓延的全球性亚文化，拥有自己的价值理念和语汇……"[2]。在当代性的各种角逐力量中，史密斯指出其中一股与非欧洲、后殖民和亚洲文化关系尤其密切，用他的话来说，后殖民时代文化差异的必要性缓解了融入全球化对话的压力。史密斯表示"全球化对于它(当代艺术)是一个必要的特征，但是也带动了民族性和地方性的传播……"[3]看起来，推动本土化问题表达的力量也正是推动这些问题向全球统一标准靠拢的力量，因此，也是当代艺术内部潜在的竞争力量。

进入20世纪90年代后，我们很清楚地看到国际交流与文化沟通正发生巨变。人们将这一转型称为"全球化"。而在艺术领域，全球化则表现为信息与影像通过不断进步的技术进行交流；现当代艺术公共组织与机构数量锐增；以及集合了全球艺术家的各种大型综合展览的大量涌现。昆士兰美术馆亚太三年展

an increasing number of public institutions geared towards modern and contemporary art, and an extraordinary number of large-scale survey exhibitions providing opportunities for artists to travel the globe in order to attend them. Christine Clark, the project manager for the Asia-Pacific Triennial, held by the Queensland Art Gallery, and selector of Indonesian artists in the 90s, wrote: "international exhibitions during the 1990s are part of a larger process of globalization and can be seen as a response to the stimulation and pressure of global culture." [4] Late 20th century Contemporary Art provided an opportunity for a small group of Indonesian artists to find an outlet on the global stage for local and national issues that were suppressed at home; and yet to enter this dialogue, the artists and their artworks had to conform to the requirements of those international exhibitions.

The defining moment in Indonesian history, which marks an impact on Indonesian modern and contemporary art, was the establishment of the Orde Baru, or the New Order regime, installed by President Suharto after the overthrow of Sukarno in 1965. The regime dominated modern Indonesian culture for three decades, influencing attitudes that persist into the present. The traditional, particularly Javanese, arts and crafts, the wayang, gamelan, batik materials and historic architecture and sculpture, were favoured as they were considered to represent Indonesian identity and assist the government in welding a national and cultural unity in an archipelago of diverse ethnic groups. These arts also projected a benign and uncontentious image of the regime for tourism and economic purposes. So, existing art institutions, such as the Museum Nasional that was originally founded by the Dutch, continue to preserve these arts, while attempts to found a similar institution to promote Indonesian modern and contemporary art has been met with limited results.

Modern art arrived relatively later in Indonesian cultural circles and was strongly identified with merdeka, or freedom and independence from colonial

项目负责人克里斯汀・克拉克(Christine Clark)在90年代负责挑选参展的印尼参展艺术家和作品，他曾写道："……20世纪90年代的国际展览是全球化大进程的一个组成部分，可以看作是对全球化文化所带来的刺激与压力做出的回应。"[4]一方面，20世纪后期，当代艺术为一小部分印尼艺术家提供了在全球舞台上呈现在国内受到镇压的各种本国事件和本土化问题的途径；另一方面，要加入这一对话，艺术家和他们的艺术又必须符合国际展览的要求。

印尼历史上对印尼现当代艺术产生重大影响的决定性时刻是1965年苏哈托推翻苏加诺政府并建立"新秩序"(Orde Baru)政权。"新秩序"政权对现代印尼文化的主导与统治长达30年之久，影响力至今犹在。传统皮影戏(wayang)、甘美兰音乐(gamelan)、印尼蜡染(batik)等传统爪哇民间工艺以及印尼历史建筑和雕塑在这一时期备受推崇，因为这些被认为体现了印尼的身份性，有助于政府在这个拥有多元民族的群岛上打造文化整体性。此外，这样的艺术形式也打造了一幅恬美怡人的印尼风情名片，推动了旅游和经济的发展。因此，诸如原先由荷兰人创立的国家博物馆等艺术机构还是继续保留了这些艺术形式，而希望建立类似机构以推动印尼现当代艺术的尝试则未获成功。

在印尼文化圈，现代艺术可谓姗姗来迟。而且，不同于亚洲很多国家以前卫美学实验作为对现代艺术的响应，在印尼现代艺术中，推翻殖民统治后的自由与独立性(merdeka)表现得尤其突出。与西方不同，印尼现代主义并未排斥过去的艺术传统。正如昆士兰艺术馆现代艺术策展人朱莉・艾文顿(Julie Ewington)所言，前现代、现代和后现代等各种时代在印尼的日常经验和艺术中共存。[5]

1965年苏哈托通过政变上台后，国家一度处于暴力与政治迫害阴影笼罩之下，反映在艺术人文领域上就是印尼现代主义分化为两股势力。社会/政治艺术支持者转向地下，而关注形式和装饰性元素的艺术则成

control, rather than some avant-garde aesthetic of experimentation—a response to modern art that occurred in many Asian countries. Indonesian Modernism did not reject the artistic traditions of the past as in the West, for, as Julie Ewington, curator of Modern art at the Queensland Art Gallery, wrote: the pre-modern, modern and postmodern eras co-exist in everyday Indonesian experience as well as in the arts. [5]

The political coup of 1965, when Suharto was installed, was followed by terrible violence and persecution, which in the arts, effectively split Indonesian Modernism into two streams. Supporters of sociopolitical art were driven underground, while art with a focus on formal and decorative elements became the mainstream modern art in Indonesia. Modern, decorative and abstract art was supported by a voraciously expanding art market; it was the predominant style taught in art schools, and, when permission was sought to exhibit, politically neutral art was favoured by those with the power of authorization. Politically sensitive art or art which implied a criticism of the regime became potentially dangerous to exhibit and did not find an adequate outlet in Indonesia until after the fall of Suharto in 1998. The New Order regime continued to suppress dissent, more vigorously in literature than the visual arts, as the brutal detention of Indonesia's most prominent modern writer Pramoedya Ananta Toer, on the island of Buru, testifies. Nevertheless, Indonesian artists, such as the major modern painter Hendra Gunawan, were imprisoned, and in Hendra's case from 1965 until 1978. [6] The artist Hardi wrote: "there was still fear of recriminations if artists expressed their attitudes to social problems through their work," [7] and Semsar Siahaan, perhaps one of the most controversial activist-artists in the 1980s, had his exhibition in Yogyakarta in 1988 closed by the police on the grounds that he was "staging the exhibition to humiliate the authorities." [8]

Yet by the 1980s the media revolution was beyond the control of censorship in Indonesia and information was flooding in through film, television and print.

为印尼现代艺术的主流。现代、装饰性和抽象艺术受到急速扩张的艺术市场的热切支持与追捧，成为艺术院校的主导风格；而在申请展览许可时，不涉及政治意味的艺术最易受到当局的青睐与喜爱。展示蕴含敏感政治题材或对当局有批评意味的艺术作品具有潜在的危险性。这些艺术作品直到1998年苏哈托下台后才得以在印尼获得展示的舞台。“新秩序”政权不断镇压持不同政见者，文学领域遭到的镇压更甚于视觉艺术领域，印尼著名现代作家普拉姆迪亚·阿南达·杜尔(Pramoedya Ananta Toer)被关押在布鲁岛便是一例；但是，印尼艺术家也遭到迫害，著名现代画家亨德拉·古那旺(Hendra Gunawan)于1965年至1978年被囚禁长达13年之久。[6]艺术家哈地(Hardi)写道：“……艺术家如果在作品中表达了他们对于社会问题的态度就有遭到谴责甚至提告的危险……”[7]。赛门萨·希亚哈恩(Semsar Siahaan)可以说是80年代最具争议性的激进艺术家之一。1988年他在日惹举办的展览被警方以“展览令当局蒙羞”为由强行关闭。[8]

而80年代的媒体革命有效地抵制了印尼审查制度的管制，信息通过电影、电视、印刷品等渠道如洪水一般涌入印尼。一小部分艺术家开始致力于探索各种富有当代性的议题。1975年，“新艺术运动”(Gerakan Seni Rupa Baru)的成员宣称席卷印尼城市的现代化浪潮是真正的印尼文化。杰姆·苏潘凯特(Jim Supangkat)也是“新艺术运动”的成员，他称这个团体标志着印尼艺术的转折点，特别是他们对于装置艺术的运用标志着与现代艺术及其充满争议的以绘画和雕塑为先的等级排序的区别。苏潘凯特在1993年发表在澳大利亚期刊《艺术与亚太》(创刊号)的专文中提到“当代艺术”时称：

> 当代艺术于1975年在印尼萌芽，当时，一个年轻艺术家团体发起了一场“印尼新艺术运动”。这次运动可以视作介绍并引进各种当代原则的

Small groups of artists became interested in exploring contemporary issues, beginning in 1975 with the members of Gerakan Seni Rupa Baru, the New Art Movement, who claimed that true Indonesian culture was in the modernization that was engulfing urban Indonesians. Jim Supangkat argued that this group, of which he was a member, marked a turning point in Indonesian art, and their art, particularly with its use of installations, signified a break with modern art and its conventional hierarchy prioritizing painting and sculpture. In his article in the first edition of the Australian journal, Art and Asia Pacific in 1993, he called this art 'contemporary art', saying:

> Contemporary art emerged in Indonesia in 1975 when a group of young artists organized a movement known as the Indonesian New Art Movement. This movement can be regarded as the pioneer in introducing contemporary principles…Even so, it took nearly ten years for contemporary art to flower in Indonesia. And it will be another ten years before installation art is regularly exhibited and discussed. [9]

Terry Smith describes how "in the years around 1989, shifts from modern to contemporary art occurred in every cultural milieu throughout the world, and did so distinctively in each." [10] If the term Postmodernism is used at all, Smith considers the term to be a marker of the transition between the two. The debate over Postmodernism developed in Indonsia in the early 1990s and exploded around the 9th Jakarta Art Biennale in 1993, curated by Supangkat, who held that the predominance of installation art was a feature of Postmodernism; but since then few have revisited these arguments and many contend that the debate remains unresolved.

The public response to contemporary and experimental art in Indonesia was illustrated by Astri Wright's description of Heri Dono's solo exhibition in Jakarta in June 1988. Wright reported that no Indonesian critic reviewed the exhibition and no works sold until her review was published in the

> 先锋创举……但即使如此，当代艺术在印尼从萌芽到成熟花了将近10年的时间。而装置艺术成为常态性展出和讨论的艺术形式则还需要另一个10年。[9]

特里・史密斯写道："……在1989年前后，全球各地的文化大环境都经历着从现代向当代的过渡，而其具体过程却是千差万别。"[10]如果"后现代主义"一词确实用得上，史密斯认为这个词标志着两者之间的过渡。关于"后现代主义"的争论最早于90年代早期在印尼出现，并于1993年第9届雅加达艺术双年展时达到顶点。作为策展人，苏潘凯特认为装置艺术的主导地位是后现代主义的一大特征。但是此后这一话题鲜少被重提，论辩也一直处于悬而未决的状态。

通过阿斯特里・莱特(Astri Wright)对1988年6月在雅加达举行的赫利・多诺(Heri Dono)个展的描述，我们可以了解公众对当代艺术和实验艺术的反应。莱特记录道，在她的评论文章发表在英语报刊《雅加达邮报》之前，没有任何印尼评论家评论这次展览，也没有一件作品成交。而她的文章发表后，10个小型作品中有9件成交，都由外国人和印尼侨民购买。[11]不论是绘画、装置还是行为，甚至包括他的传统皮影戏作品，赫利・多诺都将自己对苏哈托政权暴力镇压的探究与呈现隐藏在幽默的外衣下。虽然在国内被禁，但是带有实验媒体性质作品内涵获得了国际展览策划人的青睐。昆士兰美术馆副馆长卡罗琳・特纳(Caroline Turner)是亚太三年展项目的联合发起人，同时也是亚太三年展印尼参展艺术挑选人。她曾说过："很多例子都说明海外曝光(对印尼艺术家来说)具有非常重要的意义，有助于他们奠定自己在印尼国内的合法地位，同时又帮助他们有更多机会与全球各地的艺术家和知识分子见面，并让他们的作品为更广泛的观众群所认识……"[12]

参加了1993年在昆士兰美术馆举行的第1届亚太三年展的印尼艺术家们向大家展现了印尼艺术正在经历的

English language Jakarta Post, and then nine of the ten small works that sold were bought by foreigners and expats. [11] Heri Dono's work, whether painting, installation, or performance, including his wayang shadow puppet plays, used humour to disguise his exploration of the repressive aspects of the Suharto regime; and while effectively silenced at home, this content executed in experimental media found favour with the taste-makers for international exhibitions. Caroline Turner, then Deputy Director of the Queensland Art Gallery, co-founder of the Asia-Pacific Triennial Project and a selector of Indonesian art for the Asia-Pacific Triennial said: "In many cases, exposure overseas was of great significance for (Indonesian artists) in legitimizing their role within Indonesia, in enabling them to meet with like-minded artists and intellectuals internationally, and allowing their work to reach a wider audience." [12]

The Indonesian artists selected for the first Asia-Pacific Triennial at the Queensland Art Gallery in 1993 illustrate the transition from the modern to the contemporary that was occurring in Indonesian art. Of the nine Indonesian artists invited to exhibit, five artists submitted paintings that were in the tradition of modern art while three artists focused on installation work. A.D. Pirous and Srihardi Soedarsono, artists who had been extraordinarily successful in the Indonesian art market, presented abstract paintings of rich colours and surface textures. Three other painters referred indirectly to conditions in Indonesia: Dede Eri Supria, for example, depicted 'the concrete jungle' springing up in Indonsian cities, and Ivan Sagito explored the pspychological dimensions within the repressed Indonesian society. But it was the artists, Heri Dono, Dadang Christanto and FX Harsono who specifically used their art to explore cultural issues and voice criticism of the social and political regime through installations and performance.

Heri Dono's work, Gamelan of Rumour, was an installation of mechanically-operated hammers striking a gong – like pieces laid out on the floor in a way similar to a traditional gamelan orchestra, yet there

从现代向当代的过渡。在9位获邀参展的印尼艺术家中，5位带来了传统的现代绘画作品，3位则将关注的焦点放在装置作品上。阿都・雅里・比劳斯(A.D. Pirous)、斯里哈迪・苏达索诺(Srihadi Soedarsono)等在印尼艺术市场取得巨大成功的艺术家带来了色彩丰富、表面纹理细腻的抽象绘画作品。其他三位画家则以隐喻的笔触表现了印尼的大环境，例如，苏芮亚(Dede Eri Supria)描绘了正在印尼各个城市萌芽崛起的“混凝土丛林”；而艾温・萨吉特(Ivan Sagito)则对压抑的印尼社会所面临的心理困境进行了一番探究。但是，是赫利・多诺、达旦・克里斯坦托(Dadang Christanto)、方济各・沙勿略・哈索诺(FX Harsono)这些艺术家用他们的艺术来探索了各种文化议题，并通过装置和行为来表达对社会政治制度的批判之声。

赫利・多诺的装置作品《甘美兰的谣言》用机械控制的锤击打锣——模仿传统甘美兰乐团的表演形式，但是现场没有任何音乐家而且装置传出的声音也不是音乐。这个作品涉及赫利经常探讨的两大主题：其一是那些必须机械地遵守指示的人所感到的无力感；其二则正如作品标题所指出的——真相与谣言之间的困惑以及政府公告与公众认知之间的差异。方济各・沙勿略・哈索诺的作品则延续了他对于环境开发和农村社会被破坏的关切。以《只是权利》为名，作品呈现了绑在斜靠在香蕉叶的一扇门上的布偶。达旦・克里斯坦托的装置把用竹子、棕榈叶等天然材料做成的挂钩穿过的一系列悬空柱子，让人联想到原住民纪念柱。达旦是印尼华裔，这个作品与他的其他作品一样，是为1965年大屠杀中遇难的同胞们的公开请愿。不过他的作品超越了个人经验，表现出对所有苏哈托政权下的受害人、甚至全球各地的受害人的关切。长长的作品标题以“献给那些被杀害的人”，并继续道：

> 献给那些：
> 贫穷的人

were no musicians and the sound emitting from the work was not musical. Two themes surfaced in this work, which Heri often explored: the first being the powerlessness of the people who must function automatically when instructed, and the second, signalled by the title, the confusion between truth and rumour, the gap between government announcements and public understanding. FX Harsono's work was a continuation of his concern about the exploitation of the environment and the damage done to rural communities. Titled Just the Rights, his work depicted rag figures bound to sections of a door, which was leaning against banana fronds. Dadang Christanto's installation was a series of suspended posts pierced by pegs also made from natural materials such as bamboo and palm leaf, and which were reminiscent of indigenous memorial poles. This work, as is of all Dadang's work, was an explicit plea for the victims of the bloodbath in 1965 of which his ethnic Chinese family was one of many; his work extends from the personal to all the victims of Suharto's regime, and victims everywhere. The long title began with: For those who have been killed, and continued,

For those:
Who are poor
Who are suffer(ing)
Who are oppressed
Who are voiceless
Who are powerless
Who are burdened
Who are victims of violence
Who are victims of a dupe
Who are victims of injustice.

It was a powerful piece and Dadang continued to be selected for later Triennials in Queensland, eventually making his home there. Dadang and Heri became part of a small band of Indonesian artists who entered the discourse of international contemporary art, globe-trotting between biennials, while Indonesian Modernist painters ceased to be selected.

Biennials, the generic term for regular survey exhibi-

受难的人
遭受压迫的人
沉默的人
无力的人
承受重担的人
暴力的受害人
谎言的受害人
不公的受害人

作品非常有张力，也让达旦随后再次入选昆士兰举办的亚太三年展，并最终选择在那里定居。达旦和赫利成为全球各种双年展活动的常客，而此时印尼现代主义画家的作品则没有再入选国际展览。

作为大型国际综合展最常见的模式之一，双年展提出了自己的标准与要求。双年展需要将国家、政治、经济等方面纳入通盘考虑，因此会青睐令人印象深刻、能够为观众带来视觉惊艳的实验媒体艺术作品。纽约亚洲艺术博物馆馆长兼全球艺术项目副主席招颖思写道："……国际策展人对于专注于实验媒体的艺术家比较感兴趣，因为这符合他们进步的当代艺术的愿景。"[13]大型综合展览的理念起源于西方，第一次视觉艺术双年展活动于19世纪后期在威尼斯举行。西方艺术机构的认可与他们提供的可观资金和人脉支持让展览一路走来畅通无阻。而当双年展在欧美中心地区以外发展时，其模式依然保持不变，仍然由同一批联络人和策展人在这个国际网络系统中活动。观察人士开始提出美学实践的"跨国标准"。他们的语气有时是批判性质的，例如，英国保守派艺术评论家彼得·福勒(Peter Fuller)创造了"BICCA"(Biennale International Club Class Art，双年展国际俱乐部级艺术)一词，暗喻同一批策展人在全球各地飞来飞去，所有艺术都开始出现同质化的倾向。

国际双年展的邀约让艺术家有机会融入国际辩论中去，而与其他艺术家的联络又推动了理念的交流与相互的交叉影响。英语将发挥重要的作用。印尼艺术家

tions of international art, imposed their own requirements on artists. They had national, political and economic interests to serve so tended to favour a certain type of impressive art in experimental media that provided a spectacle for the audience. Melissa Chiu, Museum Director for the Asia Society, New York, and Vice President of their Global Art Programs, wrote that "international curators (were) interested almost exclusively in artists working in experimental media, which matched their own ideas of more progressive contemporary art." [13] The concept of large-scale survey exhibitions was established in the West with the first biennial of visual art in Venice in the late 19th century, and recognition from Western institutions with their considerable financial backing and powerful connections have continued to provide the imprimatur. When biennials developed outside the Euro-American centers, the model remained the same and international networking systems developed between them using the same contacts and curators. Observers began to speak of a 'transnational standard' of aesthetic practices, sometimes critically, as in the well-known phrase, 'BICCA', or 'Biennial International Club Class Art', coined by the conservative British art critic, Peter Fuller, which implied that the same curators flew around the world and all art was beginning to look the same.

Invitations to international biennials exposed artists to international debates, and contact with other artists resulted in the exchange of ideas and cross influences. It helped to speak English and Indonesian artists and curators found they needed English to participate in international forums, and to obtain residencies and scholarships, even those offered by the Netherlands, their own ex-colonial power. [14] There was a pressure on artists to conform to the requirements of international exhibitions and develop the skills necessary for making submissions or explaining their work. In the case of Nindityo Adipurnomo, he was the only Indonesian artist selected for the Fukuoka Triennial in 2002, because his submission addressed the curatorial brief of 'collaboration', his work having involved the participation of local Indo-

和策展人发现如果自己要参与国际论坛、要获得驻地项目或奖学金，哪怕这些项目和奖金是由前殖民帝国荷兰提供的，他们仍然需要掌握英语。[14]艺术家面临着满足国际展览要求的压力，为提交作品方案或解释作品耗费了大量精力。以宁帝久・阿蒂朴诺莫(Nindityo Adipurnomo)为例，他是唯一入选2002年福冈三年展的印尼艺术家，因为他的方案符合“协作”的策展理念，在作品中融合了印尼本土手工艺者的参与。双年展似乎更倾向于带有民族气息的艺术作品，印尼艺术家纷纷意识到海外策展人对“民族身份性”和“本土色彩”情有独钟。宁帝久・阿蒂朴诺莫曾说：“他们试图评判什么是‘印尼’，因此他们在找寻一些富有异国情调的东西。”在一张拍摄于福冈三年展的照片中，他的图片旁边是一张传统印尼皮影戏人偶的图像，虽然他的作品与皮影戏毫无关系。

本土问题和历史需要解释，而这样的解释很可能“遗失在翻译中”。阿斯穆酋・伊利安托(Asmudjo Irianto)在一篇关于1999年在加利福尼亚举行的“过渡印尼”展专题论文中提到，如果美国观众觉得作品的主题难以理解丝毫不令人意外。他写道：

> 大部分作品是对社会悲剧的叙事，有好几层隐含的意味；它们所表现的各种具体问题和景象让美国观众感到非常陌生。只有对印尼国内的环境有所了解的人才能够理解——而且，他不仅需要了解印尼的社会、文化和政治环境，还需要对印尼的艺术界有所了解。[15]

面对各式各样的展览要求与规模，国际策展人和展品挑选人所追求的本土身份性正面临着消失殆尽的危险。有些艺术品不适合在美术馆环境中进行展示：或许是因为易碎易损，或者因为体积过大——虽然美术馆的再现能力令人啧啧称奇。它们或许是针对某一艺术事件的无政府主义作品，亦或者其内涵表达取决于特定的地点和时代，而一旦经过再现，作品本来的原始能量就被消解了。在1996年的亚太三年展上，迪

nesian craftsmen. Biennials seemed to favour art that imparted an aura of its source and Indonesian artists became aware that overseas curators had a predilection for 'national identity' and art with 'local color'. Nindityo Adipurnomo said: "They try to evaluate what is 'Indonesian', so they're looking for something exotic". In an image taken for the Fukuoka Triennial, his profile is equated with the Wayang figure protruding from his back pack, although his work did not relate to the Wayang.

Local issues and histories needed explanation and references can be 'lost in translation'. Asmudjo Irianto, in an article about the Pancaroba Indonesia exhibition held in California in 1999, said that it would not be surprising if American audiences found the subject matter difficult. He wrote:

> Most works represent a narrative of social tragedy and have many layers of other hidden meanings; they represent specific problems and particular iconographies that are unfamiliar to American audiences, and which can only be understood through a knowledge of local conditions in Indonesia - and not only of Indonesia's social, cultural and political milieu, but also its art world. [15]

The very quality of local identity that global art selectors sought was in danger of being lost in the requirements and scale of the exhibitions. Certain artworks are not conducive to museum display: they may be too fragile or architectural in scale, although it has been remarkable what museums have been able to recreate. They may be the anarchic product of an art happening or they may be dependent on their original site or time when they are recreated; in short, their raw energy is diffused. Tisna Sanjaya's installation, The Monument of thirty-three years of Thinking with the Knee, in the Asia-Pacific Triennial in 1996, was constructed from remnants of a community action where large up-side-down bamboo figures had been marched around Bandung and then placed in significant public spaces. A bamboo screen in the center of the work shows Habibie,

斯纳・森加亚(Tisna Sanjaya)的参展作品是装置《用膝盖思考三十三年纪念碑》。这个作品是利用社团行动的遗物来构建完成的，一根根大型倒立竹像排列在万隆街头，接着又在各个重要公共空间进行展示。作品中间的一个竹子屏风上是苏哈托的继任者哈比比亲吻苏哈托手背的画面。"用膝盖思考"是一句印尼谚语，意为向强权屈服而不用脑思考，自甘愚蠢。而"三十三年"则直指苏哈托执政的年数。屏风被安放在迪斯纳家的前院里，作为对目前政治腐败的批判。但是警方和当地穆斯林原教主义者都提出了反对意见。画面上人物佩戴的黑色穆斯林毛毡帽(Peci)让人联想到穆斯林男性的服装，从而将其视为对伊斯兰教的一种批判。[16]与作品相关的历史背景在当时具有重要的意义，但是，一旦将作品转移到海外艺术机构展示，观众就必须借助解释来理解作品，而作品所蕴含的能量与传达出来的迫切性也就被极大地削弱了。国际论坛与展览的本质在于将众多作品并排呈现以获得最大的关注，这一点恰恰会扼杀个性化的信息传达。

全球当代艺术对不同社区间的对话做出了重要贡献；也推动了艺术品跨越语言与经验的隔阂在更广的范围内产生情感影响力。国际展览为各国国内的社会政治问题提供了一个展示与讨论的平台，但是特里・史密斯提出的全球化倾向与具体的本土历史与思考的表达之间存在着矛盾。虽然两方面的诉求都很重要，但是在本土表达和全球认知之间还是可能出现分歧；在忧国忧民与娱乐大众、真实传达与吸引眼球之间会发生讯息的遗失。

Suharto's nominated successor, kissing Suharto's hand. 'Thinking with the knee' is an Indonesian proverb that meant bending to another's authority and not using your brain, that is, to be stupid, and the 'thirty-three years' directly referred to Suharto's years in power. The screen had been installed in the front garden of Tisna's house as a criticism of current political corruption, but the police and local Muslim fundamentalists objected, seeing it more as a criticism of Islam because the figures were wearing the Peci, or the black Javanese cap that has become associated with male Muslim dress. [16] The histories associated with the work had considerable meaning at that time and in that place but, removed to an overseas institution, interpretation was needed for the audience and the urgency and energy of the piece were diminished. The very nature of international forums with so many pieces side by side, clamouring for attention, can mute the individual messages.

Global Contemporary Art has contributed to important dialogues between communities, and major works of art have had emotional impact across borders of language and experience. While international exhibitions provide a platform for the social and political issues of home, there is a tension between the globalizing tendencies identified by Terry Smith and the expression of particular local preoccupations and histories. Although both aspects are significant, there can be a disparity between an image with local meaning and an image, which is universally understood, and loss can occur between angst and entertainment and between message and spectacle.

1 Terry Smith, What is Contemporary Art? University of Chicago Press, 2009, p.1.

2 Ibid, pp 241.

3 Ibid, pp242.

4 Christine Clark, "When the alternative becomes the mainstream: operating globally without national infrastructure", in Cemeti Art House, 15 years Cemeti Art House: exploring vacuum, 1988-2003, Yogyakarta, Cemeti Art House, 2003, p. 122.

5 Julie Ewington, 1995, "Five Elements - An abbreviated account of installation art in South-East Asia", Art and Asia Pacific, Vol. 2, No. 1, p.114.

6 Astri Wright, Soul, spirit, and mountain preoccupations of contemporary Indonesian painters, Kuala Lumpur, Oxford University Press, 1994, note in particular Chapter 8 concerning the life and experience of Gunawan.

7 Brita Lee Miklouho - Maklai lists a number of cases of repression in the arts in the 1970s in her work, 1991, Exposing Society's Wounds: Some Aspects of Contemporary Indonesian Art since 1966, Discipline of Asian Studies, The Flinders University of South Australia, Adelaide, pp.69 – 77.

8 Purnomo, Setianingsih,1995, The Voice of the Muted People in Modern Indonesian Art, Masters (Honours) thesis, The University of Western Sydney, Nepean, Faculty of Visual and Performing Arts, Art History Department, p. 88, footnote.

9 Jim Supangkat, 1993, "Indonesia Report, A different Modern Art", Art and AsiaPacific, (Issue September 1993, inaugural edition), pp. 20 - 24. The journal, originally published by Fine Arts Press, Sydney, Australia in 1993, later became Art AsiaPacific and in 2003 was purchased and relaunched from New York.

10 Terry Smith, op. cit. pp.6 – 7.

11 Wright, A. 1994, Soul, spirit, and mountain preoccupations of contemporary Indonesian painters, Kuala Lumpur, Oxford University Press, footnote, p. 238.

12 Turner, C., ed., 2005, Art and Social Change: Contemporary Art in Asia and the Pacific, Pandanus Books, Research School of Pacific and Asian Studies, The Australian National University, p.211.

13 Melissa Chiu, "Asian Contemporary Art: An Introduction", c Oxford University Press, 2005, Grove Art Online.

14 General scholarships in the Netherlands require a high level of English language, note the Netherlands Education Centre website. The Rijksakademie, which has provided residencies for Indonesian artists including Nindityo Adipurnomo, also stated that their language requirement was English. Email, receptie@rijksakademie.nl 06/02/2006.

15 Asmudjo Jono Irianto, "An Unsettled Season, political art of Indonesia", Art AsiaPacific, no. 28, 2000, p.83. The Pancaroba Indonesia exhibition was held in 1999 at the Pacific Bridge Contemporary Southeast Asian Art gallery in Oakland, California.

16 Interview, Tisna Sanjaya in his home in Bandung, 04/07/2001. See also Asmudjo Irianto, "Tisna Sanjaya: The monument of thirty-three years of thinking with the knee", in Queensland Art Gallery 1996, The second Asia-Pacific Triennial of Contemporary Art, Queensland Art Gallery, p.66.

1 《什么是当代艺术？》，特里・史密斯著，芝加哥大学出版社，2009，p.1

2 同上，p.241

3 同上，p.242

4 《当替代变成主流：无关国家基础设施的全球化运作》，克里斯汀・克拉克著，《Cemeti艺术之家15年：探索真空，1988-2003》，Cemeti艺术之家，日惹，2003，p.122

5 《五大元素——东南亚装置艺术简谈》，朱莉・艾文顿，《艺术与亚太》，1995，第2卷第1号，p.114

6 《灵魂、精神与山峦：印尼现代画家的关注焦点》，阿斯特里・莱特著，吉隆坡，牛津大学出版社，1994，书中第八章介绍了古那旺的生平与经历。

7 Brita Lee Miklouho-Maklai在自己的作品中列举了一些20世纪70年代发生在艺术界的镇压案例。《揭示社会创伤：1966年以来印尼当代艺术的一些方面》，1999，弗林德斯大学亚洲研究系，阿德雷德，澳大利亚，pp.69-77

8 《来自印尼现代艺术的无声的声音》(硕士论文)，p.88脚注，Purnomo，Setianingsih著，西悉尼大学内匹安学院艺术史系视觉艺术与表演艺术专业，1995

9 《印尼报告：一种不同的现代艺术》，杰姆・苏潘凯特著，刊载于《艺术与亚太》(1993年9月创刊号)，pp.20-24。《艺术与亚太》原先由悉尼艺术出版社于1993年创办，后改名为《艺术・亚太》并于2003年被收购并由纽约发行。

10 特里・史密斯，同注1，pp.6-7

11 《灵魂、精神与山峦：印尼现代画家的关注焦点》，阿斯特里・莱特著，吉隆坡，牛津大学出版社，1994，p.238脚注

12 《艺术与社会变迁：当代艺术在亚太》，卡罗琳・特纳主编，Pandanus出版社，澳大利亚国立大学亚太研究院，2005，p.211

13 《亚洲当代艺术：导论》，招颖思著，牛津大学出版社，2005(Grove Art Online)

14 荷兰教育中心网站上特别指出奖学金项目要求申请者有良好的英语技能。曾经为宁帝久・阿蒂朴诺莫等印尼艺术家提供过驻地项目的荷兰皇家美术学院也声明要求的语言为英语。Email: receptie@rijksakademie.nl 06/02/2006

15 《动荡的季节：印尼政治艺术》，阿斯穆酋・伊利安托，刊载于《艺术・亚太》，2000年第28期，p.83。"过渡印尼"展1999年在加州奥克兰的太平洋之桥东南亚当代艺术画廊举行。

16 选自迪斯纳・森加亚访谈(04/07/2001，万隆家中)。也可参见阿斯穆酋・伊利安托著《迪斯纳・森加亚：用膝盖思考三十三年纪念碑》，昆士兰美术馆，1996，第二届亚太当代艺术三年展，昆士兰美术馆，p.66

NURAINI JULIASTUTI
努拉伊妮·朱丽阿斯图缇

Alternative Space as the New Cultural Movement: The Landscape of Creativity

The word "alternative" in Indonesia was previously known in the phrase "alternative media" ("media alternatif") as a term that used to describe the media that showed some opposition to the New Order regime. The use of the word has expanded over the past ten years. It has become part of the vocabulary of culture, and is now used to refer to spaces for new voices in literature, film, and visual arts in three Indonesian cities—Jakarta, Bandung, and Yogyakarta—in particular.

During the New Order era, the field of art and culture was controlled by formal institutions. Under the dominance of formal cultural authorities, local people were forced into two positions. First, as consumers of cultural products offered by formal spaces. By consumers I mean, for example, an audience of people visiting visual art exhibitions and enjoying theater in Taman Budaya (Cultural Center), which are available in all Indonesian provinces. Second, as cultural producers and active users required by authorities holding power of those spaces to adjust their cultural expressions accordingly.

The dominating role of formal spaces started to

新文化运动的替代空间：创意景观

“替代”(alternative)一词最早是通过“替代性媒体”(media alternatif)这个短语出现在印尼的。所谓“替代性媒体”指的是在当时发出反对“新秩序政权”声音的媒体。过去十年来，“替代”一词出现的频率越来越高，使用的范围也越来越广，已经发展成为文化语汇的一部分，并特别被用来指代印尼三大城市——雅加达、万隆、日惹——新兴的文学、电影和视觉艺术空间。

在“新秩序”政权统治期间，政府对艺术和文化领域实行管制。在正统文化权威的统治下，印尼人民只能扮演两种角色。其一是作为官方艺术空间所提供之文化产品的消费者。所谓“消费者”指的是参观展览的观众或在印尼各省的文化中心(Taman Budaya)充当戏剧演出的观众等。其二则是作为文化的生产者和积极的使用者，并根据对这些空间拥有控制权的当局的要求对自己的文化表达进行相应的调整。

20世纪90年代，官方艺术空间的统治地位开始削弱。以日惹的视觉艺术领域为例，1988年Cemeti艺

weaken in the 1990s. In the visual art scene in Yogyakarta for example, the foundation of Cemeti Art House in 1988 served as a challenge to powerful spaces. It was born as a response to the absence of space for contemporary visual art production, and provided a space for contemporary visual art voices, which did not fit into existing art spaces, such as Taman Budaya and the National Museum.

New rooms for artistic and cultural products slowly formed. Posters containing information about exhibitions that were not in galleries, but rather in small flats or cafes, were distributed. Some of these new spaces have been developing and establishing their roles as alternative spaces ever since, such as Kedai Kebun Forum and Via-Via. Both are restaurant-gallery spaces. Even now, the number of multi-functional spaces, like restaurant-galleries, cafe-library-discussion space-galleries, and distro-galleries is increasing.

The demise of the New Order government has not only been followed by the increase of alternative spaces, but also by the more active role of local people at the level of cultural production.

Of the new spaces in the visual arts and film, some notable examples in Yogyakarta are Ruang Mes 56: a space for art photography, and Kinoki: a space for film. There are also spaces built for art-related and cultural discourses. Cemeti Art Foundation—now known as Indonesian Visual Arts Archive (IVAA)—is a space focusing on the documentation and research of visual art. Kunci is a space that produces newsletters and a website to discuss Indonesian contemporary social and cultural issues. Rumah Sinema is a space focusing on film studies.

Central to the existence of alternative spaces are the youth as the initiators of the spaces. Not only have these alternative spaces demonstrated new ways of discussing/experiencing art and culture, they also create a landscape of creativity.

The Inner-workings of Alternative Spaces

术之家(Cemeti Art House)的创立对强势的传统空间提出了挑战。Cemeti艺术之家的出现弥补了现代视觉艺术空间的空白，为与文化中心和国家博物馆等现有艺术空间格格不入的现代视觉艺术提供了展示、发声的平台。

艺术文化产品的新空间慢慢形成。展览逐渐走出传统的美术馆空间，开始在一些小型公寓或咖啡馆举办，而印有相关展览宣传信息的海报也得以在四处发放张贴。诸如Kedai Kebun Forum和Via-Via等新空间经过不断的发展，逐步奠定了自己替代空间(alternative space)的地位。Kedai Kebun Forum和Via-Via都是餐馆兼画廊型的艺术空间。时至今日，餐馆兼画廊、咖啡馆/图书馆/讨论空间兼画廊和精品店兼画廊等多功能空间的数量依然呈上升态势。

“新秩序”政权垮台后不仅替代空间的数量进一步增加，而且印尼人民在文化生产方面开始扮演起更为积极的角色。

在日惹诸多视觉艺术与电影的新空间中，最具影响力和知名度的两个分别是艺术摄影空间Ruang Mes 56和电影空间Kinoki。此外，还有一些专供进行艺术文化对话的空间。“印尼视觉艺术档案”(IVAA，原Cemeti艺术基金会)是一个专注于视觉艺术记录与研究的空间。Kunci空间则通过简报和网站等渠道对当代各种社会文化事项展开讨论。Rumah Sinema则是专门的电影研究空间。

以年轻人为空间的创始人是替代空间的一个重要特点。这些新的替代空间不仅展示了探讨艺术与文化的新途径，而且打造了一幅全新的创意景观。

替代空间所开展的工作

在空间创始人眼中，“替代”是一个非常灵活的词。经营一个替代空间意味着自由地运用这一语汇，根据

In the hands of its founders, "alternative" becomes an elastic term. Organizing an alternative space means the freedom to employ the term, to stretch and to flex it according to the situation that one is facing.

Founded in 2005, Kinoki began its activity by providing space for alternative film screenings. It then developed activities created to nurture fresh ideas of young filmmakers, and to form reading communities on film and video production, such as holding filmmaking and film criticism workshops, and publishing a periodical newsletter on film called Ikonik. If a space is considered a physical room for an activity, looking at Kinoki's scope of activities, it is a space that is moving freely from physical to non-physical space.

Conversely, there are spaces that are moving from non-physical to physical space. Formerly known as a newsletter, Kunci develops activities that require real spaces such as book discussions, organizing community history workshops, and making exhibitions. Like Kunci, IVAA not only performs as a visual arts documentation centre, it organizes activities such as inviting artists to discuss their visual concepts, organizes exhibitions in its office, and publishes a periodical newsletter on visual arts.

Alternative spaces must be flexible in creating activities that can be adjusted to ever-changing foci and contexts. This includes flexibility in finding funding to support the running of the space and the capability of its members to perform various activities.

This brings me to a discussion of the other character of an alternative space, that is, its openness and willingness to build a network with other alternative spaces. Mostly initiated as personal and group initiatives, the seeds of alternative spaces find their best places to grow outside state art institutions and universities. With their inherent non-formal character, a particular activity of an alternative space is developing collaboration with another space not necessarily working in the same field. For example, Kinoki col-

具体情况不断对空间进行挑战或调整。

Kinoki电影空间成立于1995年，为小众电影提供了一个展示的平台。随后，Kinoki也参与组织了各种旨在培养年轻电影人更多新鲜理念的活动，并创立了电影与视频作品阅读社团。此外，Kinoki不仅组织电影制作与电影评鉴工作坊，还出版了一份名为《Ikonik》的电影期刊。如果艺术空间被视作活动的实体空间，那么反观Kinoki所组织的各种活动，我们会发现Kinoki已经从实体空间向概念空间转变。

不过也有相反的情况，有些艺术空间则是从概念空间转变为实体空间。Kunci便是一例。Kunci最初只以简报的形式出现，后来逐渐开始组织读书会、社团历史工作坊和展览等需要实体空间的活动。无独有偶，IVAA也不仅只扮演着视觉艺术文献中心的角色，同时也邀请艺术家就视觉概念开展座谈、在自己的空间内举办各种展览、并出版了一份视觉艺术刊物。

替代空间在组织活动方面必须具有高度的灵活性，以便根据关注的焦点与内容的变化而进行调整。这里所谓的灵活性也包括在寻找资金方面具有灵活性，为空间的经营以及提高组织活动的能力提供支持。

这就引出了替代空间的另一大特点：与其它替代空间建立合作网络的开放性。大多数替代空间成立之初都是个人或团队性质的，官方艺术机构与大学院校之外才是替代空间萌芽与发展的最佳地点。与生俱来的民间性质让替代空间能够开展一些特别的活动，其中之一便是可以与分属不同领域的其他空间建立合作。例如，Kinoki与Kunci曾合作举办东南亚电影展映与座谈系列活动。此外，Kunci还与IVAA合作举办了以“1990年代的印尼年轻媒体”为主题的系列展览和座谈活动。

替代空间之间密切的关系也折射出它们非商业性的性质，组织的活动往往遵循低成本战略。它们所实践的

laborates with Kunci to create film screenings and a discussion series on Southeast Asian film. Kunci collaborates with IVAA to create discussions and an exhibition on "Indonesian youth media in the 1990s."

The close relationship between alternative spaces reflects their non-commercial character, and a low cost strategy for running their activities. They practice a form of networking economy.

Alternative spaces show the desire to appropriate modern cultural and lifestyle expressions as part of their new work mediums. The popularity of cafe-culture in Indonesia has inspired alternative spaces to build cafes to cover some of their operational costs. Kinoki and IVAA, for example, are spaces with cafes adjacent to their offices.

Kinoki owns a small shop selling VCDs and DVDs of films produced by young filmmakers, uniquely designed t-shirts made by local designers, and various newsletters published by alternative spaces and youth groups based in Yogyakarta and other cities. IVAA developed a similar shop selling various alternative magazines, comic books, video art DVDs and other things made by local visual artists. These "distro-like" shops show the confluence of an alternative space and creative industry. An alternative space has expanded its reach to accommodate and to distribute creative products.

These spaces choose new media to support their activities, such as Mailing list, Blogspot and Facebook. For Kinoki and IVAA, the profit obtained from their cafes is not big. For an alternative space funded by international funding agencies like IVAA, perhaps building a cafe is not really a necessary step to take. The real benefit they have gained by having cafes is through their provision of spaces for discussions and meeting-centers for the organization's communities. Likewise, a mailing list owned by Kunci, a blogspot of Kinoki, and a Facebook of IVAA are used not only as mediums to inform their communities about their activities, but also as ways of knowledge-sharing among their community members.

是一种网络经济模式。

替代空间展示了以表达现代文化与生活方式作为新的艺术媒体的愿景。咖啡文化在印尼的兴起赋予替代空间发展以新的启发，很多空间纷纷开设咖啡馆以补贴部分运营成本。例如，Kinoki和IVAA的空间内都设有咖啡馆。

Kinoki拥有一家小型商店，出售年轻电影人制作的VCD和DVD、本土设计师特别设计的各款潮T以及日惹和其它城市替代空间和年轻艺术团体出版的各种期刊杂志。IVAA也开设了一家类似的商店，出售艺术类期刊、漫画书、视频艺术DVD以及其他本土视觉艺术家的作品。这种“精品店”模式的商店显示了替代空间与创意产业的新的结合点。替代空间将触角伸向了推广并销售创意产品。

这些空间纷纷选择新的媒介渠道来为自己的活动提供支持，邮件列表、博客和Facebook等新兴媒介都成为它们的宣传推广渠道。Kinoki和IVAA咖啡馆的收入在其总收入中所占的比重不大。从经济效益的角度上讲，对于IVAA这样由国际资金出资扶持的替代空间，开设咖啡馆或许并没有十分的必要。但是咖啡馆最大的好处是为IVAA组织的各种社团座谈和讨论活动提供了空间。同样的，Kunci的邮件列表和博客、IVAA的Facebook帐号都不仅成为发布社团活动信息的渠道，也是成员之间分享信息、抒发感想的园地。

替代空间承认印尼的年轻一代是艺术大社区中的一员。当前，替代空间的发展融合了几代艺术家的共同努力。一方面是经历过“新秩序”时代、迫切希望看到文化运动转型的一代；另一方面是出生于80年代的年轻一代，他们大多在千禧年之后进入大学学习。印尼的80后出生之时正值“新秩序”政权最辉煌的年代，而他们进入大学之际又适逢印尼改革运动(Reformasi)的尾声——这场发生在20世纪最后几年的政治运动见证了“新秩序”军事政权的垮台。年轻一代对

An alternative space acknowledges the new generation of Indonesian youth as part of its community. In the latest development of alternative spaces, there has been a mixture of generations. On the one hand, the generation that experienced the New Order, who urgently needed a cultural movement transformation, and on the other hand, Indonesian youth born in the 1980s, who started their college in or after the year 2000. The latter is the generation that was born in the heyday of the New Order era and who started their university life when Reformasi—the last few years of the 20th century, which saw the destruction of the military-backed New Oder—had already passed. They experience it only by reading the stories and documentation in the mass media. The mixing of generations opens up a possibility for the new youthful generation to create new alternative spaces. In short, the two generations need each other.

The strength of alternative spaces to develop a new cultural movement lies in the combination of the capability to build a network with other creative spaces, and their potential to form cultural communities.

Old Enemy: The Dilemma of Being "Alternative"

The existence of new spaces in Jakarta, Bandung, and Yogyakarta has interested the youth in other cities. They started to form networks and copy the types of spaces. However, despite the proliferation of alternative spaces, is this just a small-scale cultural movement performed by educated middle class youth living in Indonesian urban areas? Is being "alternative" only a new middle-class phenomenon? Does the existence of alternative spaces actually make any difference to freedom in the art scene? Are the alternative communities using their networks for constructive change? I want to briefly refer to a recent case in the Indonesian film scene as a pointer here to my concerns.

Recently, the Masyarakat Film Indonesia (Indonesian Film Society)—a Jakarta-based working group that consists of film workers and cultural activists that

于这些历史事件的认识与体验多依赖书本和大众媒体。几代艺术家的融合为年轻一代创立新的替代空间提供了更多可能性。新老两代艺术家互相需要。

替代空间推动新的文化运动的能量主要来自于两个方面，一是与其他创意空间构建网络的能力，二是组建各种文化社团的潜力。

宿敌："替代"的困境

雅加达、万隆和日惹的新兴空间也引起了其他城市年轻人的浓烈兴趣。他们纷纷仿效这样的空间形式并开始构建网络。虽然替代空间蓬勃发展，但是那会不会只是生活在印尼大都市、接受过高等教育的中产阶级年轻人搞出来的小规模文化运动呢？所谓"替代"是否只是一种新的中产阶级现象？替代空间的存在是否真的让艺术自由呈现出新的面貌？替代社区是否运用它们的网络来推动建设性的变化的发生？说到这里，我想用最近发生在印尼电影界的一个事例来说明我的担忧。

雅加达"印尼电影协会"(Masyarakat Film Indonesia)是由电影工作者和文化界人士共同组成的专业电影协会，旨在全面改善印尼电影大环境。该协会最近提出对1992年颁布的电影法案进行修订。他们提出的修改意见包括取消电影审查委员会(Lembaga Sensor Film)。作为电影人，他们认为审查委员会的存在抑制了文化产品的发展。然而，印尼电影协会的提议既没有获得电影界也没有获得替代空间运动中成立起来的新兴文化社团的普遍响应与支持。从中我们看到了一个令人遗憾的事实：即使在电影社区内部也没有形成对于文化产品(此例中为电影)的统一意见，也没有就它们与政府之间(密切)的关系和与社会其他方面的关系达成共识。

这显示出替代空间和社团的影响力还是非常有限的。举例来说，越来越多的年轻机构与组织将电影作为一种启

works for the betterment of the condition of Indonesian film—requested a review of the Film Acts of 1992. One of their recommendations was the closure of the Lembaga Sensor Film (Film Censorship Board). As filmmakers, they considered the Censor Board to be repressive of the flow of their cultural product. However, their courageous effort to review the Film Act lacked strong support from both film communities and new cultural communities formed by the alternative spaces movement. This reflects the sad truth that, even among the film communities themselves, there is no solid view regarding the life of cultural products—in this case, a film—and their relationship with the state, which remains strong, and with other aspects of society.

This suggests that the impact of alternative spaces and communities is limited. For example, the movement to look at the audio-visual medium in new ways—the use of a film as a medium to open new awareness as shown by youth organizations, the popularity of "low-budget and strong message film" among youth film-makers, and the new spaces for new discourses on film as shown by new film spaces and publications—has failed to bring its existence to a broader scale, and to transform its spirit into new critical voices. The alternative spaces and communities are not united, or are not powerful enough. As a united body, they have failed to recognize a creeping back of "New Order style" cultural repression to mute the voice of cultural products considered dangerous. Perhaps this is the dilemma of being "alternative." Alternative spaces gain greater freedom, and can express it, but cannot collectively see the threats to that freedom.

Despite the fact that I acknowledge the great potential of alternative spaces, I will end this essay with a pessimistic note: that the alternative space movement is still at the level of exploration of new arts and cultural discourses, and the freedom of consumption. However, in the flow of freedom, these new spaces are floating towards destinations that they have not yet clearly formulated.

发新的思想意识的媒介、带有强烈意识色彩的低成本电影在年轻电影人中日益流行、同时，新的电影空间和出版物也为开展电影对话提供了更多新的场合。然而，这场新的视听媒介运动并未在更广泛的范围内产生影响，也未能将运动的精神转化为新的批判之声。替代空间和社团还不够团结。作为一个整体，他们未能察觉到一股旨在封杀“危险”文化产品的“新秩序时代式”文化镇压暗流正在涌动。这或许也正是“替代”所面临的困境。一方面，替代空间获得了自由、也能够表达自由之声；但另一方面，作为一个整体，它们无法看到对于这种自由的威胁。

虽然我也相信替代空间蕴藏着巨大的潜力，但是我却仍然要以略显悲观的论调为本文作结：替代空间依然处在一个对新的艺术形式、文化对话以及消费自由的探索阶段。然而，在这股自由的潮流中，新兴空间的未来将走向何方依然不明朗。

SANENTO YULIMAN
萨能托·于利曼

The Waving Hands on the Rock

岩石上的巧手

"Lukis" in Its Original Sense

The word 'lukis' is found in a number of languages of the Indonesian archipelago. The word exists, for example, in the Malay language of Minangkabau (lukih). It is also found in Javanese. Along the way, the meanings of words might change. We should therefore ask: What did the Javanese word of "lukis" originally mean?

The question can be answered by turning to, for example, the written language of Kawi or ancient Javanese. Here, apart from meaning "to paint", the word anglukis also meant "to carve" (L. Mardiwarsito, Kamus Jawa Kuna Indonesia, Nusa Indah: Ende, 1981). The word anglukis in the New Javanese language still contained this meaning (see W.J.S. Poerwadaminta, Baosastra Djawa, Pakempalan Triwikrama: Yogyakarta, 1930). Back then, "to paint" did not only mean making visual creations by drawing lines and applying colors, but also carving.

To gain better insight about how our ancestors viewed the task of "painting" (melukis), we could turn to the ancient book of Tantu Panggelaran (The Site of Exposure), written in the sixteenth century. One

"Lukis" 之追根溯源

印尼群岛很多语言中都有"lukis"一词。例如，在米南加保族的马来语和爪哇语中都有这个词。在不同的语言中，这个词的意义会发生一些变化。因此，我们必须要问：爪哇语"lukis"最初是什么意思?

要回答这个问题，我们可以参阅一些古爪哇语(Kawi)文献。除了表示"绘画"，"anglukis"还有"雕刻"的意思(L. Mardiwarsito，《印尼古爪哇语词典》，Nusa Indah: Ende, 1981)。在现代爪哇语中，"anglukis"依然有这层意思(参见W.J.S. Poerwadaminta, Baosastra Djawa, Pakempalan Triwikrama: 日惹, 1930)。在当时，"绘画"并不仅仅表示通过线条和色彩来进行视觉艺术创作，也包括通过雕刻来创作。

要更好地了解我们的祖先是如何看待"绘画"(melukis)这一行为的，我们可以参阅16世纪的古籍《众神》(Tantu Panggelaran)。其中有一项记载特别有意思，它提到万神之神巴塔拉古鲁(Batara particularly interesting part is the one that tells of Batara Guru ordering the gods to come down to the Island of Java to teach the Javanese a number of skills. It informs us that the ancient Javanese viewed various skills as originating from the gods. The blacksmithing skill originated from the god Brahma; goldsmithing, god Mahadewa; homebuilding, god Wismakarma; and the skills of thread spinning, weaving, and dressing up, from goddess Sri. One could imagine how people valued such skills highly as they believed it was the gods themselves who first taught them these skills, by becoming the first artisans.

Among the gods, one was sent to Java to become painter. He was Bagawan Ciptagupta (or Guru Ciptagupta), who as a painter was called empu Ciptangkara (or "master" Ciptangkara). Batara Guru ordered him thus:

> "Bagawan Ciptagupta manglukisa, hamarnah-marnah halengkara sakarupaka ri cipta, masarana mpune tanganta; matangnya mpu Ciptangkara ngarananta nglukis."
> (Paint, Bagawan Ciptagupta; create beautiful image, in harmony with the shapes in your mind, by using your empu, your thumb, the axis of your hand; and thus as a painter you shall be called empu Ciptangkara)

Painting was thus seen as the work of arranging (hamarnah-marnah) beautiful images (lengkara or adornment), in line with the shapes that originated in thoughts.

One should also note the name of the painter-god. In the heavens (i.e. in the realm of the spirits), he was called Ciptagupta or "Hidden Image". In the real world (the physical world), he was called Ciptangkara, or the Maker of Images, or One who Gives Shapes to Images. "Cipta", in its archaic sense, meant thoughts, ideas, or dreams. (Take note of the Indonesian phrase of "mengheningkan cipta" or "silencing the thoughts", as well as the word of "cipta" in Sundanese or Javanese.)

Why does Batara Guru say "by using your empu, your thumb"? Apparently, the author of Tantu Panggelaran wished to explain the origin of the word "empu" used to address painters. The title of "empu"

Guru)命令诸神下凡教授爪哇岛人民各种技能。从中我们可以看到，古代爪哇人认为人类的各种技能和本领都来自于天神：Brahma神把锻铁技术传授给人类、Mahadewa神、Wismakarma神和Sri女神则分别掌管着炼金、建筑和纺纱、编织、剪裁等技术。由于大家都信奉众天神是第一批能工巧匠，而且是他们把各种技艺传授给人类，我们可以想象当时的人们是多么崇敬这些技艺。

在诸神当中，有一个被派往爪哇并成为一名画家。他就是Ciptagupta古鲁(Bagawan Ciptagupta)。作为画家，他又被称为"empu Ciptangkara"(Ciptangkara大师)。巴塔拉古鲁命令他：

> "Bagawan Ciptagupta manglukisa, hamarnah-marnah halengkara sakarupaka ri cipta, masarana mpune tanganta; matangnya mpu Ciptangkara ngarananta nglukis."
> (绘画，Ciptagupta古鲁；创造美丽的图像，将心中美好和谐的画面尽情展现，通过你的empu、你的巧手；作为画家，你应该被尊称为"empu Ciptangkara"。)

绘画在当时被视为根据心中的想法与愿景对美丽的图像进行排列组合。

画神的名字也值得注意。在天国(神灵的疆域)，他被称为"Ciptagupta"，即"隐藏的图像"。而在现实的世界(俗世)，他被则称为"Ciptangkara"，即"图像缔造者"或"赋予朦胧以形像的人"。在古语中，"cipta"是思想、想法或梦想的意思。(印尼短语"mengheningkan cipta"(沉默的思考)和巽他语、爪哇语中"cipta"一词都表此意。)

巴塔拉古鲁为什么要说"通过你的empu、你的巧手"？显然，《众神》的作者希望解释用来指涉画家的"empu"一词的本源。铁匠这一称谓中也有"empu"一词，这可以被解释为：因为铁匠用自

for blacksmiths was also explained that way: because the blacksmiths used their big toes to hold one of their tools. We could also apply this train of thoughts to explain the title of empu given to literary masters: their thumbs were used to hold their writing instruments.

It is not important whether or not such etymology is correct. What is interesting for our study here is the fact that, first, the painter was given the title of "empu" or "master", and, second, the title was linked with manual dexterity or manual work.

By combining the information from the dictionary and from Tantu Panggelaran, we gain a better picture about our ancestors' view on painting, which we could define into two classes:

a) To paint is to turn thoughts, ideas, or dreams into visual arrangements or creations, which are beautiful or able to please our sense of sights;

b) The creation is made by drawing lines and applying colors, or by carving, using tools that are held by the hand or clasped by the fingers.

Today, we have firmly differentiated between the definitions of "to paint" and "to carve", and between painting and carving. There is a strong belief about the equivalence between the Indonesian word of "melukis" and "to paint", and between "lukisan" and "painting". In truth, the Anglo-Saxon terms (to paint, painting) contain the understanding of paints, or the tool itself, while the Indonesian terms (melukis, lukisan) did not originally have that meaning.

As we revisit the painting tradition in Indonesia, we do not intend to use the word "painting" like it was used in the sixteenth century. We are not going to talk about carvings, even the colored ones. Many people are aware about the carving traditions that exist almost all over Indonesia. On the contrary, in general people do not know about the painting tradition (in its contemporary sense) in the Indonesian regions—and this includes our art experts. Usually, these experts know more about the painting tradition in Europe.

Among the traditions that we are going to consider

己的大拇指来拿工具。我们可以用同样的逻辑来解释为何文学大师也被冠以“empu”的称号：他们用拇指来握笔。

词源考证正确与否并不重要。我们的研究中一个有意思的事实是，其一，画家被授予“empu”或者说“大师”的头衔；其二，这个头衔又与精巧手工艺和手工艺产品息息相关。

把词典定义和《众神》的记载相结合，我们能够更全面地了解祖先对于绘画的理解，其中包含两层意思：

a) 绘画就是将思想、理念和梦想转化为视觉化的排列组合和创造，能够带来美好和愉悦的视觉体验；

b) 绘画作品既是线条和色彩的融合；也可以借助双手和工具雕刻而成。

如今，无论是创作过程还是最终呈现的作品，我们都对“绘画”和“雕刻”进行了严格的区别。但是，我们相信在印尼语中，“melukis”(上漆)和“lukisan”(绘画)是同义的。事实上，在盎格鲁撒克逊语中，(上漆、绘画)这些短语包含画和绘画工具的意思，而印尼语中(melukis、lukisan)最初并没有这层含义。

在我们对印尼绘画传统进行回顾的时候，我们并无意采用绘画一词在16世纪时的意义。我们并不打算谈论雕刻作品，哪怕是彩绘雕刻作品。很多人都对印尼的雕刻传统十分了解。而大部分人并不了解印尼的绘画传统(现代词义上的绘画)——甚至包括我们的艺术专家。通常，这些专家反而对欧洲的绘画传统了解更多。

在我们要讨论的各种传统中，有一些早已在印尼群岛出现。因此我们会提到岩石和洞穴中的绘画作品。好几个岛屿都发现了这样的艺术作品。我们还会提到满者伯夷王朝(Majapahit)时期的绘画作品，虽然关于这

are the traditions that had existed here in the Indonesian archipelago, as far as we can know about them. That is why we are going to talk about paintings on rocks and in caves, which have been discovered on several islands. We are also going to talk about paintings in Majapahit, although we can only rely on scarce written sources. We will then move from one Indonesian island to the next, seeking and recording the traditions.

The Waving Hands on the Rock

History tells us how the urge to paint had been fulfilled before the discovery of cloth and paper, the materials that are today seen as the most fitting and "appropriate" painting holders. The oldest paintings we know of were made on rocks and cave walls. The most famous of the prehistoric paintings are the Lascaux cave paintings in France, from 15,000 years ago, and the Altamira cave painting in Spain, which is about 13,000 years ago. Such "cave paintings" are also found in many eastern regions of the Indonesian archipelago. To the west, so far they are only found in South Sumatra.

In Irian Jaya, the cave and rock paintings have been found in several places. The easternmost sites where the cave paintings can still be found are the Gumaimit and Penfelu caves around Lake Sentanl, in the northern coast of Irian. Rather to the west, but still in the northern part, they are found in the caves on Muamuran and Roon islands in Saireri Bay. To the west of this large island, one must mention the Bay of Berau, which forms the "mouth" of the head of the island, which is shaped like a bizzare animal. To the south of the bay, on the coast, at the Abba promontory near Darembang, another set of rock paintings has also been found.

Such paintings have also been discovered on the cave walls in Sorrora and on Wamerei Island. On the south coast of Irian, one can encounter such rock paintings in Dudumunir cave on Arguni Island, as well as on Namatote Island and around the bays of Triton and Bitsyari. On one of the small islands in the Islands of Kei, another wall of rock with paintings has also been found. If we sail across the Banda Sea to the south, after we pass the islands of Tanimbar, Babar, and Leti, we will reach the island of Timor.

些作品的书面记载非常有限。我们将对印尼群岛逐一进行观察分析，探寻并记录这些传统。

岩石上的巧手

历史向我们展示了早在画布与纸张这两种被视为最“适合”承载绘画的材料发明之前我们的祖先是如何实现自己绘画的愿望的。已知的最古老的绘画作品出现在岩石和洞穴里。法国的拉斯科(Lascaux)洞穴壁画和西班牙的阿尔塔米拉(Altamira)洞穴壁画是最著名的两处史前绘画，距今分别已有15,000年和13,000年。印尼群岛东部地区也发现了好几处这样的洞穴壁画。而在西部地区，目前只在南苏门答腊地区发现过此类绘画。

在伊里安查亚地区，多处都发现了洞穴和岩石绘画。伊里安北部海岸圣塔尼湖附近的Gumaimit和Penfelu等处的洞穴绘画是目前最东部的发现地点。在北部地区，Saireri海湾Muamuran和Roon岛的洞穴中也发现了此类绘画。而说到西部地区就不得不提Berau海湾，这个海湾好似岛屿的“嘴巴”，让整个岛屿看起来就好像一个诡异的动物。而在海湾南部，Darembang附近的Abba海岬也发现了一组岩石绘画。

在Sorrora岛和Wamerei岛也发现了此类洞穴壁画。在伊里安岛到南部海岸，人们在Arguni岛的Dudumunir洞穴内、Namatote岛上以及Triton和Bitsyari海湾地区都发现了岩石画。在Kei群岛上也发现了一处岩石壁画。如果我们从Banda海向南航行，在越过Tanimbar、Babar和Leti三岛后，我们到达了帝汶岛。而在帝汶岛东部Tutuala区北海岸，岩石和洞穴岩壁也有绘画。Banda海北部的Seram岛和Nusa Ina岛也有几处岩石绘画。在北部海岸，Sulaeman湾五处峭壁都有岩石壁画。与此同时，南部海岸Tala河沿岸至Elpaputih湾也发现了好几处此类绘画。而在西北地区，也发现了此类古代绘画——最后，我们来到了

To the east of the island, in Tutuala on the northern coast, there are rocks and cave walls embellished with paintings. The Seram Island or Nusa Ina in the northern part of Banda Sea is also home to several rock paintings. On the northern coast, the paintings can be found on five different cliffs in Sulaeman Bay. Meanwhile, the southern coast hosts such paintings along the river of Tala, which goes toward the Elpaputih Bay. To the north-west of the island, there are also such ancient paintings—and we finally arrive at South Sulawesi, home to cave paintings in the caves of Patogere, Lambattorang, Burung, and Pattae near Maros, as well as in Jarie cave near Saripa.

Not all the paintings are accessible to visitors. Some of the paintings in Burung cave, for example, are located eight meters above the ground. In the islands of Kei and in Irian, there are paintings on the rock at the height of four meters above the sea level. Some of the paintings in Irian were even made on the cliff, ten to fifteen meters above the sea level. One can thus deduce that the ancient painters reached such sites through water in the era prior to the raising of the land. H.R. van Heekeren estimated that the paintings found in the Indonesian archipelago are around 4,000 years old.

The one feature of the paintings that would immediately capture our attention is the abundant presence of hand silhouettes. The silhouettes were made by placing the hand on the rock surface and applying ocher on the area around it. Such hand silhouettes are found among the cave paintings in South Sulawesi, on the cliffs at the Sulaeman Bay in Seram, in the Bay of Berau in Irian, on Arguni Island, the Islands of Kei, and in East Timor.

The Lambattorang cave in South Sulawesi is home to at least forty hand silhouettes. Apart from these silhouettes, the motifs that have been found in abundance in many places are those of the human figures, boats, the sun or the moon, and birds (in Irian, Kei, and Seram). On the cliff of the Abba promontory in the bay of Berau, there are also the motifs of fish, turtles, man-lizard (the combination of the shape of a lizard and that of a man) and foot stamps. In south Sulawesi, apart from the motifs of hand silhouettes, there are also the shapes of babirusa (Babyrousa babirusa) found in the caves of

南苏拉威西岛，这里拥有Patogere、Lambattorang、Burung、Pattae和Jarie等多处著名洞穴壁画。

并不是所有岩石和洞穴壁画可以向参观者开放。例如，Burung洞穴中的部分壁画位于高于地面8米的地方。而在Kei和伊里安岛上也有好几处岩石绘画位于海平面以上4米的位置。伊里安岛上甚至发现了一些悬崖峭壁上的绘画，比海平面高出10-15米。从中我们可以得出这样的结论，古代画家是在海岛升高之前从水路到达这些地点完成创作的。根据荷兰考古学家H.R. van Heekeren博士的判断，印尼群岛发现的绘画作品距今大约有4000年的历史。

这些绘画作品最引人注目的一大特点是大量的手印剪影。把手放在岩石表面然后在周围涂上赭土，于是在岩石上留下了这些手印。南苏拉威西岛的各处洞穴壁画中都可以发现这类手印剪影，包括Seram岛的Sulaeman海湾、伊里安岛的Berau海湾、Arguni岛、Kei岛和东帝汶岛的悬崖峭壁上。

位于南苏拉威西岛的Lambattorang洞穴中至少发现了40个手印剪影。除了手印，常见的图案还包括人形、船、太阳、月亮和鸟(伊里安岛、Kei岛、Seram岛)。在Berau海湾的Abba海岬峭壁上，还发现了鱼类、海龟、人形蜥蜴(人与蜥蜴结合的形象)、脚印等图案。在南苏拉威西，除了手印剪影，在Pattae、Lambattorang和Patogere等洞穴中还发现了鹿豚的图案。除了容易辨识的物体和生物形象，这些绘画中还有一些非具象的图案，或一些杂乱的图形、以及优美却模糊的线条(曾在伊里安岛Abba海岬地区出现)。

此外，画面上还出现了几何图形(Kei岛)。在伊里安北部地区发现的绘画则是非具象的(它们未表现任何具体的物体或生物图形)，主要由曲线、圆圈和螺旋线构成。蜥蜴图案也是常见的图案之一。人、动物和各种物体的图像通常是通过线条构成简单的示意图来

Pattae, Lambattorang, and Patogere. Besides the motifs that we can recognize as images of objects or creatures, there are also non-representative motifs, or ones that do not depict anything and consist of mere doodles or, in contrast to the doodling lines, of firm and graceful lines (as found in the area of the Abba promontory in Irian).

Then there are also geometric shapes (in the islands of Kei). The paintings in the northern region of Irian are non-representational (i.e. they do not represent shapes of objects or creatures) and consist mainly of curves, circles, and spirals. The motifs of lizard are found here and there. The shapes of humans and animals, as well as of objects, are generally depicted using lines, forming simple diagrams. At the bay of Abba, however, we can see pictures of fishes with impressions of movements, which are further strengthened by the curves and convexities of the rock.

On the ceiling of Pattae cave, one can see a 50-cm-long painting of a jumping babirusa, with an arrow pierced into its heart. The depictions of the fish and babirusa diverge from the diagram-like pattern: the two animals seem alive. This shows that the painter had a shrewd perception regarding the reality around him and could capture the essence (the characteristic shapes) of the animals that he or she was painting. The painter(s) used three kinds of colors: red, black, and white. In general, the colors were used to make outlines, but sometimes they are also used to fill planes, for example the areas around the hand outlines (red, ocher), or the faces of human figures found on the islands of Kei (red, ocher).

Rock paintings can be very impressive. At the bay of Abba, Irian, for example, we have found a rock surface full of a variety of motifs, but with the dominating presence of hand outlines with outstretched fingers, seemingly waving in the dark. We cannot, however, say that the wall or cliff surface constitutes one complete painting. The motifs found there do not seem interconnected, and neither do they seem to have been arranged in a certain composition, much less reveal a clear order. Each motif seems to appear as a self-standing expression instead of forming one whole idea alongside the other shapes. Here and there newer pictures were painted over the older

表示。而在Abba海湾，我们还发现了动态的鱼群图案，而岩石的弧度和凹凸感更加强了这种动感。

在Pattae洞穴的顶部，我们可以看到一幅50厘米长的绘画，上面画着一只跳跃的鹿豚，一个箭头穿过了它的心脏。对于鱼和鹿豚的描绘与其他示意图类的图案不同：这两个动物看起来栩栩如生。这显示出画家对于周遭的现实世界敏锐的观察，而且有能力捕捉他/她所描绘的动物的精髓(典型的形象)。画家主要运用了三种色彩：红、黑、白。一般来说，色彩被用来勾勒线条，但是有时也用颜色才填充平面，例如手印周围的区域(红色、赭土)或Kei岛上发现的人形图案的脸部(红色、赭土)。

岩石绘画可以让人留下深刻的印象。以伊里安岛Abba海湾为例，我们发现了一块表面充满各种图案的岩石，但是手印轮廓和伸出的五指剪影主导了整个画面，看起来好似在黑暗中挥手致意。然而，我们不能说岩壁和悬崖表面构成了一幅完整的绘画。各种图案看起来并没有任何内部联系，也找不到特别的构图原则，更不用说清晰的条理了。每个图案看起来都是独立的表达，而非与其他图案共同构成一个宏观的理念。旧的图案还常常被新的图案所覆盖。有时也会出现一些表现整体理念的图案，例如在一幅几个人泛舟而行的画面下面是鱼群的图案，而上面则是一个圆圈，很可能是太阳的象征(Arguni岛绘画)。

有些图案常常成对出现，如蜥蜴或人形蜥蜴与象征太阳的圆圈(Berau海湾)。这些图案的成对出现透露出两种图案之间观念上的关联。关于岩石绘画的意义和功能依然没有定论，这也是由于如今居住在这里的人并不是当初开创这一绘画传统的居民的后代。

从这些古代遗迹中，我们可以整理出这样的故事线索：这些绘画作品是由外国人或一组盲人旅行者在他们攀岩的途中用双手留下的痕迹。因为有些手印并没有完整的手指形象，就如Jarie洞穴壁画上所显示的；

ones. Sometimes there are also motifs revealing a unity of ideas, for example the depiction of several persons on a boat, below them are pictures of fish, and above them is a circle, which perhaps refers to the sun (the painting on the island of Arguni).

There are also two motifs that often appear side by side, for example the motif of lizard, or the man-lizard, and the circle that perhaps symbolizes the sun (the bay of Berau). Their presence together betrays a conceptual link between the two motifs. The meaning and function of the rock paintings are a matter of conjecture, especially because the people living in the region today are not the descendants of the people who owned this ancient painting tradition.

The stories that we can now gather about these ancient remains say that the paintings were made by foreigners, or a group of blind travelers, who in their journey groped the rock and cliffs and left traces of their hands. Because some of the outlined hands do not have complete fingers, as seen in the pictures in Jarie cave, and because there are societies with the tradition of cutting fingers as a sign of grief, or as the mark of a widow, can we then conclude that the hand outlines found in the rock paintings in the Indonesian archipelago are signs of grief, eternal proofs of the loyalty of wives whose husbands had died? We cannot be certain about that, especially because many of the hand outlines show complete fingers.

The motifs of lizards and man-lizard are certainly fascinating. The shamans who dance using masks and clothes that resemble certain animals are common in the rituals of simple societies. Do the motifs of man-lizard represent the shamans in such rituals?

Josef Roder, who in 1938 analyzed the prehistoric paintings in the western regions of Irian, wrote an interesting report. In the surrounding areas he found woodcarvings representing lizards. The locals made offerings before the woodcarvings, and included in the offerings were fish bones. It had been said that the rituals were done "so that the number of the fish would not decline". The locals called the lizards "matutua" or "elders", whom the local mythology views as having an origin that is related to the sun. Matutua was the ruler of all fish.

而有些社团有以切断手指以示悲痛或作为寡妇身份象征的传统。那么我们是否可以得出这样的结论：印尼群岛上发现的岩石壁画上的手印是悲痛的标志、是妻子对亡夫保持忠诚的永恒象征吗？我们无法确定，因为还有很多手印显示出完整的十指。

蜥蜴和人形蜥蜴的图案尤其迷人。带着面具、穿着动物式样外衣起舞的僧人模仿着各种动物，这是很多社团中常见的仪式。人形蜥蜴图案是否象征着某种特殊的仪式呢？

1938年，德国考古学家约瑟夫・罗德尔(Josef Roder)对在伊里安西部地区发现的史前绘画进行了分析，并撰写了一份有趣的专题报告。在绘画的周边区域他发现了象征蜥蜴的木刻。当地居民把贡品放在这些木刻前面，贡品的内容包括鱼骨。据传仪式是为了"鱼类的数量不会减少"。当地居民把蜥蜴称之为"长者"(matutua)，根据当地神话，蜥蜴的起源与太阳有千丝万缕的联系。"Matutua"还统治着所有的鱼类。

对于蜥蜴的信仰在群岛古代文化中非常普遍，甚至远至波利尼西亚群岛都可以找到这样的痕迹。举例来说，根据传统的信仰，汤加(Tonga)岛(波利尼西亚)的居民有一种叫做"atua"的天神(注意这个名字)，他住在蜥蜴和鱼群里面。我们也知道巴塔克(Batak)族人对于蜥蜴神(Boraspati ni Tano)的信仰，他们相信蜥蜴神住在土地中并掌管着土地肥沃程度，并会以蜥蜴的形象出现。

通过比较研究，我们逐渐掌握了蜥蜴图案和人形蜥蜴神灵以及其他与捕鱼、狩猎(鹿豚)等古代贸易相关图案的意义。或许这些图画是仪式的一部分，祈愿捕鱼和狩猎行动会取得成功，也祈愿族人获得充足的食物资源。

正如我在本文开头所说，在印尼群岛的西部地区只

Beliefs related with lizard manifestations were common in the ancient cultures of the archipelago, and spread as far as the Polynesia. In the old belief of the residents of Tonga islands (in Polynesia), for example, there was a kind of god called "atua" (note the name) who could live inside certain lizards and fish. We also know of the old beliefs of the Batak people about Boraspati ni Tano, who lived in the earth and ruled the soil and its fertility, and was able to make an appearance in the form of a lizard.

With such a comparative study, we gradually capture the meaning of the lizard motif and that of the supernatural being—the man-lizard—as well as the other motifs that were linked with the ancient trades of fishing and hunting (the babirusa). Perhaps the paintings with such motifs were complementary to the rituals related to the hope that the fishing and hunting expeditions would be a success, and the hope about the sustainability of the food sources.

As I have mentioned in the beginning of this essay, in the western region of the Indonesian archipelago, the prehistoric paintings have been found only in South Sumatra. On the walls of two ancient tombs in the village of Tanjung Ara, Pasemah, there are damaged paintings in black, white, red, and yellow. Two of the paintings can still be recognized as depicting a man with a buffalo, while another painting seemingly depicts a man with an elephant. The figures of man and the buffalo were depicted in thick and curving outlines, with strong geometric patterns, and in dynamic and forceful arrangement. Such sturdiness is in harmony with the rough and fierce face of the man and the burly appearance of the buffalo. The one who lay buried in the tomb must have been an important leader who was seen by the community as a strong and brave hero. The depicted subjects (the men and the animals) as well as the dynamic and forceful styles are in line with the styles of the stone sculptures often found in the area of Pasemah, and enable us to estimate that the paintings were from the bronze period, around 300 BCE.

Painting Technology in the Era of the Temples

The Hindu-Indonesian culture left behind numerous buildings and carvings, and many of them became a source of wonderment to the world. With regards

有南苏门答腊省发现了史前绘画。在帕塞马坦君亚拉(Tanjung Ara)村庄里的两处古代墓穴壁上，有一些破损的黑、白、红、黄四色绘画。其中有两幅依然可以辨认，一幅画着一个男人和一头水牛，而另一幅则画着一个男人和一头大象。男人与水牛都用厚重的曲线线条描绘，具有强烈的几何感，充满活力与动感。粗旷坚毅的线条与男人严峻的脸庞和水牛魁梧的身躯相得益彰。墓葬的主人一定是一位显赫的首长，被族人公认为顽强勇敢的英雄。画面的主体(男人与动物)以及动感而奔放的风格与帕塞马地区发现的石雕艺术风格非常吻合，由此我们做出判断，这些绘画创作于公元前300年的青铜时期。

庙宇时代的绘画技术

印度-印尼文化为我们留下了大量建筑和雕刻作品，其中很多都让世界惊叹不已。然而，在研究其中的绘画作品时，我们必须接受这样一个现实：对于过往我们知之甚少，而且掌握的也多是二手信息。金属板上的雕刻画——以公元8、9世纪的中爪哇作品和13世纪的巴厘岛作品为例——所体现出的绘画传统比雕刻手法本身更丰富、更耐人寻味。在金属板上雕刻图案并非易事，而且金属板雕刻画的需求量也不大。创作这样的绘画不仅需要柔韧而常见的材料，还需要更多元的绘画需求的支持。

在16世纪中期首次出版的(Coimbra，1552)卡斯塔尼达(Castaneda)葡语作品第三卷，有一段标记为1511年的记录非常有意思。其中提到爪哇国王(满者伯夷国王)将一副画作和其他珍品一起献给了当时刚刚接管马六甲海峡的葡军船长阿方索·德·阿布奎(Alfonzo D'albuquerque)和葡国民众。

书中记载道："在一匹如beirami长纱一般长的织布上，画家描绘了国王出行的盛况，四轮马车和四轮象车浩浩荡荡，国王端坐车内，四周环绕着四面旗帜，随从左右相侍。每一个细节都如此清晰、自然，堪称

to painting, however, we must be satisfied with only a limited knowledge of the past, and one that we receive from second-hand sources at that. The scratched images on metal plates—one from Central Java, from the eighth or ninth century, and another from Bali from the thirteenth century—indicate a more extensive drawing tradition that was richer than the metal scratchings themselves. To engrave images on metal plates is not an easy task, and there were not many demands for it. The drawing skills necessary to do that must be supported by a drawing tradition using more accessible and pliable materials, and used for a variety of needs.

In the third volume of the Portuguese book of Castaneda, which was first published in the mid-16th century (Coimbra, 1552), there is an interesting record with the year mark of 1511, which says of a painting that along with other objects were sent from "the great king of Java", i.e. the king of Majapahit, in honor of Alfonzo D'albuquerque, the captain and Portuguese general who just took over Malacca at the time.

It was thus reported that there was: "a piece of fabric as long as a beirami, on it was depicted all the King's splendor, with wooden carriages drawn by horses, and elephants carrying similar carriages, and the king sits in carriages with four flags, accompanied by his entourage. Everything looks so clear and natural that it is impossible to improve."

There are several things that we can learn from this brief report.

First, the inclusion of a painting among the gifts of honor by a king to a foreign envoy shows that among the Majapahit nobility, painting was seen as a valuable object.

Second, it was reported that the painting "depicted all the King's splendor" and that "the king sits in carriages". The reporter was certainly talking about a narrative painting that told of an event (or perhaps a fragment of a scene?) by depicting a series of scenes. It is thus understandable that the painting is stretched out, as long as a beirami cloth, or a long cloth that in the past was seen as highly valuable in the area of Kambai and surroundings.

完美。"

从这段简短的描述中，我们可以得出以下几个结论。

首先，这幅画被作为珍品被国王献给外国使节，这说明在满者伯夷王朝时期，绘画的地位是非常崇高的。

第二，根据记载，这幅画"描绘了国王出行的盛况"并显示"国王端坐车内"。记录者所描述的显然是一副叙事性的绘画，通过一系列场景的描绘来表现一个事件(或一个片段)。从中我们也了解到画卷的长度如贝拉米(beirami)长纱一般，而在古时候的贡拜地区贝拉米长纱是尊贵的象征。

第三，记录者特别写道"每一个细节都如此清晰"。这一点显然与来自欧洲的记录者平时之所见有很大的区别，不然这样的描述就显得多余了。换言之，记录者对满者伯夷绘画的精细留下了深刻的印象。

欧洲绘画中某些流传了一两百年的传统元素，也就是造成"缺乏清晰细节"的原因，在满者伯夷时期的绘画作品中并没有出现。例如从明到暗的渐变，这会让物体的全部或部分隐藏在阴影和暗处。而"大气透视"(atmospheric perspective)原理则会让观众产生站得越远画面越模糊的视觉体验。

同样，距离透视会让远方的物体显得更小、不完整、而且缺少细节。在满者伯夷时期的绘画作品中，为了更好地突出细节的清晰，线条扮演了重要的角色：每一个图形都是通过茁实平整的线条来勾勒的。线与线之间的区域均匀地涂上颜色，没有明暗之别，而物体的形状也不会过度渲染。画面上没有延展空间。因此，画面中的一切看起来都非常清晰、仿佛就在眼前。

第四，葡萄牙记录者的观点显然受到当时西方绘画风格的影响，如果他当时看到的是如今在巴芝丹、东爪哇、古弄辛度的瓦那萨利和中爪哇地区依然保存着的

Third, the report tells us of a painting in which "everything looks clear", and this would certainly be superfluous unless the clarity was so special that it was starkingly different from what the reporter—who was a European—usually saw. In other words, the reporter was impressed by the clear depictions of the Majapahit painting.

Some of the elements that had been common in European paintings for a century or two, which would give rise to a "lack of clarity", were thus absent in the Majapahit painting. For example the gradual transition from brightness to darkness, which would hide the objects, or parts of them, in the shadows or darkness. Then there is the element of the atmospheric perspective, which would make an object look vague the farther away it is from the viewer.

Similarly, the distance perspective will make far-flung objects appear small, incomplete, and lacking details. In the Majapahit painting, in order to achieve the impression of clarity, lines played a significant role: every single shape was depicted in firm and tidy lines. The colors filled the areas within the boundaries of these lines, in equal strength, with neither light nor shadow, and the volumes of the objects were not strongly depicted. There was no space that seemed to be extended far beyond. Therefore, everything looked clear and close-by.

Fourth, there was scant possibility for the Portuguese reporter, whose perceptions and observations had certainly been accustomed to the European paintings of the era, to express his fascination with the words "everything looks so clear and natural that it is impossible to improve" had what he was seeing been a painting in the style of the wayang beber, which we still have in Pacitan, East Java, and Wanasari Gunungkidul, Central Java.

The painting gift for D'Albuquerque seemed to have the style that was distinct from that of the wayang. The Portuguese report does not record the materials used to make the colors, certainly because the information had been unavailable to them. Today, among the Javanese and Balinese traditional painters, there are people who are still aware of the ancient recipe of making color pigments. White is achieved from ground burnt bones. The yellow pigment is from atal

贝柏戏(wayang bebe)风格的绘画作品，那么他不太可能会发出“每一个细节都如此清晰、自然，堪称完美”的赞叹。

献给阿方索・德・阿布奎的画作在风格上与印尼传统皮影戏哇扬戏(wayang)有显著的区别。葡语文献中没有记载制作颜料的原料，显然这是因为他们并不知道颜料的配方。直到今日，爪哇和巴厘的民间画家依然遵循古法制作颜料。白色通过焚烧骨头获得；黄色、亮红、深红、蓝色、黑色则分别从赭石、黏土、红铅、绿叶、烟灰等原料中提取。溶剂和定色剂则取材自天然果实。

根据艺术史学家Brandes的考证，古代爪哇人用虫漆来制作黑色颜料。通过这些颜料的综合调配，我们可以进一步获得绿、紫、棕、灰等色调。当然，织布也并非古代唯一的作画工具。在木板上绘画也很常见。除了板材和布料，还有一种树皮做成的类纸材料(daluwang)也经常被用来作画。

我们知道，巴芝丹地区至今依然保存着贝柏戏风格的绘画，这些画距今至少已有一百年的历史(根据继承者的说法，这些画已经传承了12个世代)。而这些画正是在树皮纸上创作的。古代巴厘绘画也是如此。19世纪时，爪哇人、特别是东爪哇波诺罗戈县地区的居民仍然使用树皮纸来绘画。

树皮纸由一种名叫“古鲁甘”(gluga)的树皮制成。在古爪哇语中，我们可以找到许多与绘画技术相关的词汇：daluwang、dalancang、mangsi、hatal、laka、kepuh、galuga、gumaluga等。

采用天然原料(石头、泥土、植物、烟灰等)制作颜料的方法以及用树皮制作纸张的方法依然在印尼群岛某些偏远而古老的印度文化族群中得以保存。这显示出这些技术历史之悠久甚至可以追溯到印度文化产生影响力之前。15世纪伊始，一个名叫马欢的中国人来

batu; light red from napal (a kind of clay); red dye from gelinggam or gluga plant (Broussonetia papyfera); blue from the tarum or nila leaves; and black pigment, or mangsi, from oil lamp soot. For the solvent and fixer, the water from abu jangkang or the burnt fruit of the kepuh tree (Sterculia foetida) is used alongside ancur.

According to Brandes, the ancient Javanese recipe used laka or lak (instead of ancur) for the black pigment. From these pigments, one can get other hues such as green, violet, brown, and grey. Certainly, fabric was not the only material used to hold the paintings in the past. Wooden boards were always easy to get. Apart from boards and fabric, there was also a kind of paper-like material, known as daluwang or dalancang (or jeluang in Indonesian), or what people in Java knew in the past as "kertas gendong" (or, literally, "carrying paper").

We know that the wayang beber painting that today is still stored in Pacitan, and is at least a hundred years old (or according to the beneficiary: twelve generations old), was made using this kertas gendong material. The same is true for several old Balinese paintings. In Java in the nineteenth century, people still made daluwang paper in several places, the best known of these was Ponorogo, East Java.

Daluwang was made of the bark of gluga (or gelinggam) tree. In the Kawi language, or the Ancient Javanese, we can find terms that were related with painting technology, such as daluwang, dalancang, mangsi, hatal, laka, kepuh, galuga, and even gumaluga (or "painted red").

The skills of making pigments from natural substances (stones, soil, plants, and soot) and processing barks into jeluang are still known among communities that have been relatively isolated and untouched by the Hindu culture in the Indonesian archipelago. This shows that these techniques have a very long history and even predate the Hindu influences. In the beginning of the fifteenth century, a Chinese, Ma Huan, stopped by at Majapahit and watched a peculiar painting exhibition, which he recorded in his travelogue, Ying-yai Sheng lan (1416). "There was a group of people who made drawings on paper, depicting humans, birds, animals, insects, and many

到满者伯夷，他看到了一场别开生面的绘画展。在他的游记《瀛涯胜览》(1416)中他是这样记载的：“一群人在纸上画画，描绘出人类、飞禽、走兽和昆虫的形象。纸张由木棍撑起，约有3英尺高。一端的木棍与纸同宽，另一端的木棍突起。有人蹲坐在地，将面前的画作一点一点向观众展开，并用本地语言响亮地跟大家解释画作的每一个部分。观众围坐在他身边，专心地聆听，跟着故事的跌宕起伏或欢笑、或哭泣。”(此处中文从英文转译而来)显然，马欢所看到的是一场贝柏戏表演，不过文中马欢并没有提到甘美兰音乐伴奏。

19世纪末，在日惹古弄辛度地区贝柏戏表演是没有甘美兰伴奏的。马欢所记载的贝柏戏风格绘画就是画在树皮纸上，画家甚至连微小的细节都勾勒了出来(飞禽、昆虫)。根据他的记载，我们可以了解到观众与表演者的关系非常亲近，从大家投入的程度来看，贝柏戏在满者伯夷王朝是非常受欢迎的表演形式。

我们可以把贝柏戏看作一种戏剧表演。然而，图像和表演在激发观众的想象力方面发挥了非常大的作用。那么，我们是不是应该把贝柏戏看作一种有图释的口头文学呢？“图释”是表演的核心、观众关注的焦点。从某种程度上，贝柏戏可以看作绘画与口头叙事的结合。

巽他歌(Kidung Sunda)可谓公元6世纪中叶古爪哇文学的一朵奇葩。跟其他文学作品一样，巽他歌也不能被当作客观的历史记载。而值得我们仔细分析的是作者创作的理念，在下文中我们会进行更深入的探讨。

国王哈亚·乌鲁克(Hayam Wuruk)准备选妃立后，命几位画家到印尼群岛各处为美丽的公主们画像。画家带回来了一批画像，但是国王一个也没有看上。后来，哈亚·乌鲁克听说顺塔(Sunda)国王有一个非常漂亮的女儿，为此他专门派出一名宫廷画师。过了很长一段时间，画师终于带回了顺塔公主的画像。作品

others. The paper seemed to have been rolled and installed between to wooden rolls that were three feet high. On one end, the wooden roll was as wide as the paper, and on the other end, the roll protruded. The person was squatting and presented the drawings in front of him, opening part by part and showing it to the audience, while loudly explaining each part in the local language. The audience sat around him, listening, laughing, and crying in harmony with the story that he was narrating." It was obvious that what the Chinese man was observing was a wayang beber performance. Ma Huan did not say anything about musical accompaniment of gamelan.

In Gunungkidul, Yogyakarta, at the end of the nineteenth century, wayang beber was also performed without gamelan accompaniment. The wayang beber recorded by Ma Huan was made on daluang paper, and the painter drew even the small details (birds, insects). The relation between the audience and the performer was reported as very intimate, full of emotions, indicating that wayang beber performance had been a popular show in Majapahit.

One can perhaps consider wayang beber as a kind of theatrical performance. The actions, however, arose in the audience's imagination, thanks to the images and the presentation. Or should we consider wayang beber as a spoken literature accompanied with illustrations? The "illustrations", however, served as the center of the spectacle, the focus of the audience's attention. Wayang beber could also be considered as a painting presented alongside spoken narratives.

Kidung Sunda or the Sundanese traditional songs, a fruit of the Kawi literature of mid-sixteenth century, like any other work of literature, could not be taken as historical records. What is interesting in relation to our analyses here is the author's idea, which we will study further below.

King Hayam Wuruk, in his effort to find a wife, ordered several painters to make pictures of beautiful princesses all across the archipelago. The painters came home with portraits, but none of them suited the king. When he heard of the news that the king of Sunda had a very beautiful daughter, he sent a pra-

画在一块黄色丝绸上。"Tininghalan punang peta... kaya kalapan urip, dadi sirawuru gadung"。(国王仔细端详着画像……画面中的女子仿若天仙下凡、栩栩如生，国王立即坠入了爱河)。

如果我们把这个故事视为作者的想象与文艺创作，我们还是可以提出这样一个问题：作者的灵感从何而来呢？显然，这与作者熟悉的或者听说过的绘画实践有着密不可分的关系，他的信息可能来自于自己的同时代人，也可能来自于前辈(巽他歌出现的时候，满者伯夷王朝已然瓦解)。还有一点也很值得注意：歌中将画师们称为"duta kang anulis"(书画使节)。在巽他歌作者和其他同时代的人看来，绘画与写作(anulis，"nulis"表"写作")以及用尖锐的工具勾画与线条的行动是共通的。这次，我们再次回到了本文开头提出的一个观点，即线条在满者伯夷时期的绘画中扮演了非常关键的角色。

在古爪哇语中，也有许多指代画家的词，包括：prabhangkara、citrakara、ranggajiwa等。而表示绘画作品的词也相当丰富，包括tulis、surat、peta、wimba、warnana、rupaka、citraleka、hastaleka等。当然，更多关于古代绘画技巧的发现仍有待进一步的研究。

bhangkara widagdha (an expert painter). After a long while, the painter finally came home presenting to the king the portrait of the Sudanese princess, painted on a piece of yellow silk. "Tininghalan punang peta... kaya kalapan urip, dadi sirawuru gadung" (As he looks at the portrait... the picture seems alive, and he falls head over heels in love).

If we accept such story as the fruit of an author's imagination, we can still ask: Where did the author's idea come from? Certainly it originated from the practices of painting that the author had been familiar with or heard about, either from his contemporaries or predecessors (when Kidung Sunda was created, Majapahit was falling apart). There is another noteworthy thing: the song calls the painting envoys "duta kang anulis". To the author of Kidung Sunda, and certainly to his contemporaries as well, painting was essentially the same as writing (anulis, "nulis" is "to write"), or the act of drawing lines with sharp tools. Again, we encounter the idea that has been presented in the beginning of this essay, namely that in Majapahit paintings, lines play a key role.

In the Kawi language, there are several terms used to refer to painters: prabhangkara, citrakara, and ranggajiwa. For the painting itself, there are such words as tulis, surat, peta, wimba, warnana, rupaka, citraleka, and hastaleka. Further studies are still needed to find out whether these terms refer to different specific skills in the painting realm.

Artists | 艺术家

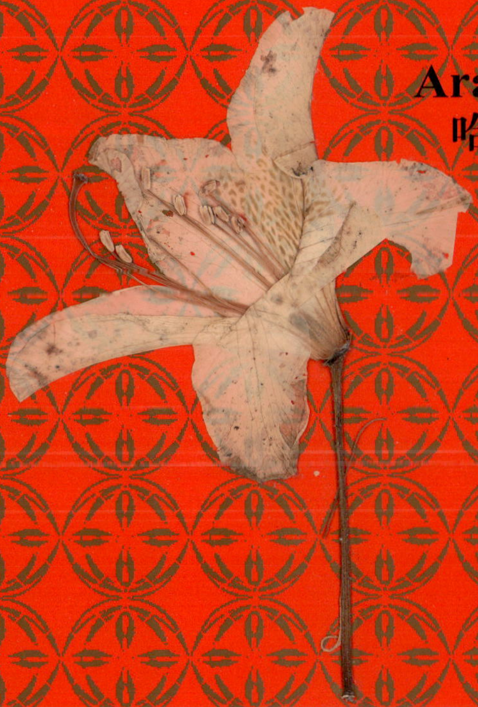

Arahmaiani

哈拉海麦尼

Interview with Arahmaiani

Yogyakarta, over coffee
June 2010

Arahmaiani: **A**

Biljana Ciric: **B**

B: How do you choose the community that you wish to work with?

A: As I said, I tend to lean towards the weak and unfortunate, and they could be all different kinds of people with different professions, with different beliefs and cultures. It doesn't really matter to me. In every culture you have certain ways of looking at other people. For my research it may be important, but also as a way of dealing with people. In my mind, people are the same; the only thing different is how fortunate or unfortunate they are, their position of weakness or strength, and the relation between these two poles. I am simplifying this now, however. This power relation is very interesting and an important subject matter in my work, and for my approach. If you are starting from this idea, it could be anything that has that kind of structure. I can work with any community and anywhere. This kind of relation always exists, from the smallest community like a family, to the society at large; we all share this pattern. As an artist you can al-

哈拉海麦尼访谈

日惹咖啡馆
2010年6月

哈拉海麦尼：**A**

比利安娜：**B**

B: 你如何选择作品中要表现的族群?

A: 正如我一直所说的，我倾向于选择不幸的弱势群体，他们来自各行各业，信仰与文化也各异，这些差异对我并不重要。在每一种文化中，人们以特定的方式对待他人，这可能对我的研究很重要，但却不能告诉我们如何与人相处。因为在我看来，人都是平等的，唯一的区别是幸运与不幸，以及身体的强与弱，而且两者之间有着特定联系。我正在试图将其简化。这种权力关系很有趣，也是我的作品的重要主题。如果你以这种思想为起点，任何事物都可以用这种结构来解释。无论身处何地，我可以与任何族群相处。从最小的族群(如家庭)到更大的社会，这种权力关系始终存在，这就是我们的模式。作为一名艺术家，你通常需要选择你想要走的路，你所感兴趣的事物或者你能做的事。可能听起来像是我把他人的生

ways choose in which direction you would like to go, the things that you are interested in or things you are able to do. Maybe it sounds like I am playing with the lives of other people. Of course it is not like that. As you are dealing with the lives of other people it is not up to us anymore; you have been absorbed into their life. You try to go and see what they see or understand their logic, and up until a certain point you have to be careful, because you can become one of them, and then you loose the awareness of difference that you need. That is the art.

B: You mentioned that you want to write more books in the future.

A: Yes, as you know I have been working with different groups of people, with different cultural backgrounds, under different conditions, and I have been traveling from one place to another. So I feel I have a lot to say actually. I want to write for myself as well, because if you gather a great amount of information in a short period of time, you need the time to reflect and to really think about what has transpired. What did I witness and experience? Because it can continue on like that, and you can go through these things and then they disappear, people forget. I don't want to forget it. You need to understand that life has a meaning. Because if you try to imagine that it's meaningless, then I think there is a problem.

B: Are you writing anything in particular at the moment?

A: I already wrote a lot of things that I have had on my mind in essay form, and I also have a column in the largest newspaper in Central Java, called the Voice of Freedom. This is also a way for me to channel my thoughts, and that is something that I also consider as material for my books in the future.

B: Your practice has been developing in a number of parallel ways; you started writing poetry very early on and you are still writing; you have been doing performances and you are still developing this practice through different approaches; and then there is also something that I found very

活当成儿戏，事实当然并非如此。当你面对他人生活的时候，我们不再重要，你已经被他们的生活所吸纳。你想要去发现他们看到了什么以及他们的逻辑，而到了特定的阶段，你必须小心，因为你已经成为他们其中的一员，然后你放松了警觉，这就是艺术。

B: 你提到将来想要再多写几本书。

A: 你知道我与不同族群的人一起工作，他们的文化背景不同，条件也各异。从一个地方到另外一个地方，我有许多需要表达。我想要为自己写作，因为如果你在一段时间内收集了许多信息，你就需要去反思，去思考这是什么，也就是你的所见所闻。应该将经历的事情记录下来，否则这些事会消失，最终被人们所遗忘。我不想忘记它们。你要意识到生活是有意义的。想像一下，如果生活是无意义的，我想我可能出问题了。

B: 你现在手头有具体的写作项目吗?

A: 在我的散文中我已经写了很多我所经历的事情，我还在中爪哇最大的报纸上开设名为“自由之声”的专栏，这些也是我打通思想的方式。我认为，它们可以成为我将来写书的参考。

B: 你的创作实践经历了几种平行的发展方式。刚开始你主要写诗，现在仍然在写。你也做过行为艺术，现在依然也在继续，而且以不同的方式来呈现。我还发现一系列有趣的自画像，这些自画像与你那些广受好评的大多数作品很不一样。这些不同的体类作品是如何启发你的? 你在艺术界以积极参与社会与政治活动著称。你是否想过，这些经历是如何附加于你生活的不同方面的?

A: 想过，事实上我想了很多。我首先想了解我自己，这也是我创作活动的最基本方面。如果我能

interesting which was the series of self-portraits. These were something very different when compared to the rest of your body of work that you have gained recognition from. How do these different bodies of work reflect who you are? There is a certain reputation that you have in the art world as a socially and politically engaged figure. Did you ever think about how these things are attached to different aspects of your life?

A: Sure. I think about it a lot actually. I think I basically try and understand myself, and that is a fundamental aspect of all of my activities. If I am able to understand something about myself, then I am able to understand something about life. Again, I am not detached from others, and, again, it becomes a very complex thing. In this whole complexity, I come to a simple understanding. Ok, there is this part of myself that has to deal with the outside world, whether it is socially, politically, or environmentally. And there is another in which I basically deal with myself, and the things deep inside of me. They are related one to another. In a way, we are dealing with things, organizing things in an attempt to separate the private and the public. I don't know if is this a good way to try and understand our lives. Because when I work with communities I start to also see another way of looking: there is the private, the public, and the communal, as the community is different from the public. In a community you are an integral part of the larger whole, while in the public you could be there but acting as an individual. This is very interesting. So I agree that this kind of private area needs to somehow be nurtured as well, aside from my public life. But this awareness of my private life came rather late.

B: When did you start thinking about it?

A: Just recently, not so long ago. Three, four, five years ago. I realized that it is a part of reality, and that I should deal with it. So I tried turning into myself, and to express ideas through paintings because it offers such a direct encounter. Also, my life is going through a change. I spend more time on my own. It became something that I needed. Before, my life was very public. I still

对自身有一定理解，我就能对生活有所理解。我要再次声明我并没有离群索居，而这样一来，事情就变得很复杂。从这种复杂性中，我得出了一个简单的结论。没错，我被分成了两部分，一个我去应对外部世界(社会、政治、环境)；另一个我应对自身和深藏于自我之中事物。两个“我”相互联系。在我们应对和安排事物时，倾向于公私分明。我以前不懂这种理解生活的好方法。因为在我与不同族群的人相处时，我看到了另外一种应对问题的方式：除了私人的和公共的，我们还有族群。因为族群与公共领域不同。你是族群中不可分割的一部分，而在公共领域中，你可以身处其中，但仍然在做自己的事。这很有趣，所以我认为，除了我的公共生活，这种私领域(社群)在某种程度上需要得到培养。但是我对私领域的这种认识出现得较晚。

B: 你什么时候开始思考这个问题的?

A: 时间不长，大概3、5年前吧。我认识到它是现实的一部分，我应该去面对。所以我试图深入自我，通过绘画来表达思想，因为这样更直接。我的生活也发生了变化。我花更多的时间独处，这逐渐变成了我的一种需要。以前我每天都要应对很多事情，过着公众人物的生活。现在依然如此，我觉得这其实也很重要。但是我会试图在两者中间取得平衡。

B: 你感觉孤独吗?

A: 有时会。我的问题是，我基本上会对生活中的一切产生疑问。这会造成某些人的孤独。如果你没有疑问，你就会轻易地说：我同意你的看法或者大多数人的看法。你就不再孤独。但是，如果你等待一分钟，问自己这是什么或者那是什么，你就会感觉孤独。

have that. I think it is also important, but now I try to find a balance.

B: Do you feel lonely?

A: Sometimes. My problem is that I am basically questioning everything in life. That is what makes somebody lonely. If you don't question things, you would easily say that I am with you or I am with the group, and you are not alone anymore. But if you are like: Wait a minute. What is this? Or, what is that? Then you have to be alone.

B: What about poetry? That was present in your life all the time?

A: Yes. It was always there. Another writing outlet for me are the essays. The text is becoming a very important thing for me. Sometimes if I want to clear my mind and clarify some conceptual ideas, I need to write it down; but sometimes what the text can't reveal, the form can. So I try to combine these two things. My art is not separated from my writing and my poetry. It all has to do with my experiences, even my texts as well. In a way, it's actually quite subjective, what I try to offer to people. But everyone needs that kind of subjectivity, and maybe it's actually stronger than objectivity.

B: How do you imagine yourself in ten years?

A: I will be getting old. I will keep working on my art and the things I believe in. That's something I must do.

B: Is that driving force for you to keep momentum, to keep working?

A: Yes, because that's what I have been doing and that is my life. I think in ten years time we will face a lot of problems here in Indonesia and maybe also in the world. So we will have a lot of things to do. When I was younger I thought after 50 I would want to settle down a bit, work less and enjoy my life. But when I see what is happening in Indonesia and where I travel, I realize that maybe I need to work even harder.

B: 诗歌呢？诗歌是最鲜活的。

A: 是的，我一直都有在创作诗歌。我的另外一项写作活动是散文。文字对我很重要。有时，如果我想阐述我的思维方式与厘清某些概念性思想，我需要把它们落成文字。但有时文字不能展现的却可以通过艺术的形式来表现。所以我尝试将两者结合起来。我的艺术是不能和我的散文与诗歌分开的。这与我的经历有关。以这种方式展现我的意图，实际上相当主观。但事实上每个人都需要这种主观性，这种主观性或许比客观性还强大。

B: 你对自己未来十年是如何规划的？

A: 我的年龄越来越大了。我将继续工作，坚持做我自己的艺术。这是我必须做的。

B: 这是你继续前进、继续工作的动力吗？

A: 是的。因为这是我一直做的，是我的生命。我想10年后的印度尼西亚，甚至世界各地都将面临许多问题，因此我们有许多事要做。我年轻时想过，等过了50岁，我将逐渐安定下来，减少工作，享受生活。但是，当我看到印尼所发生一切，我意识到我可能需要更加努力地工作。

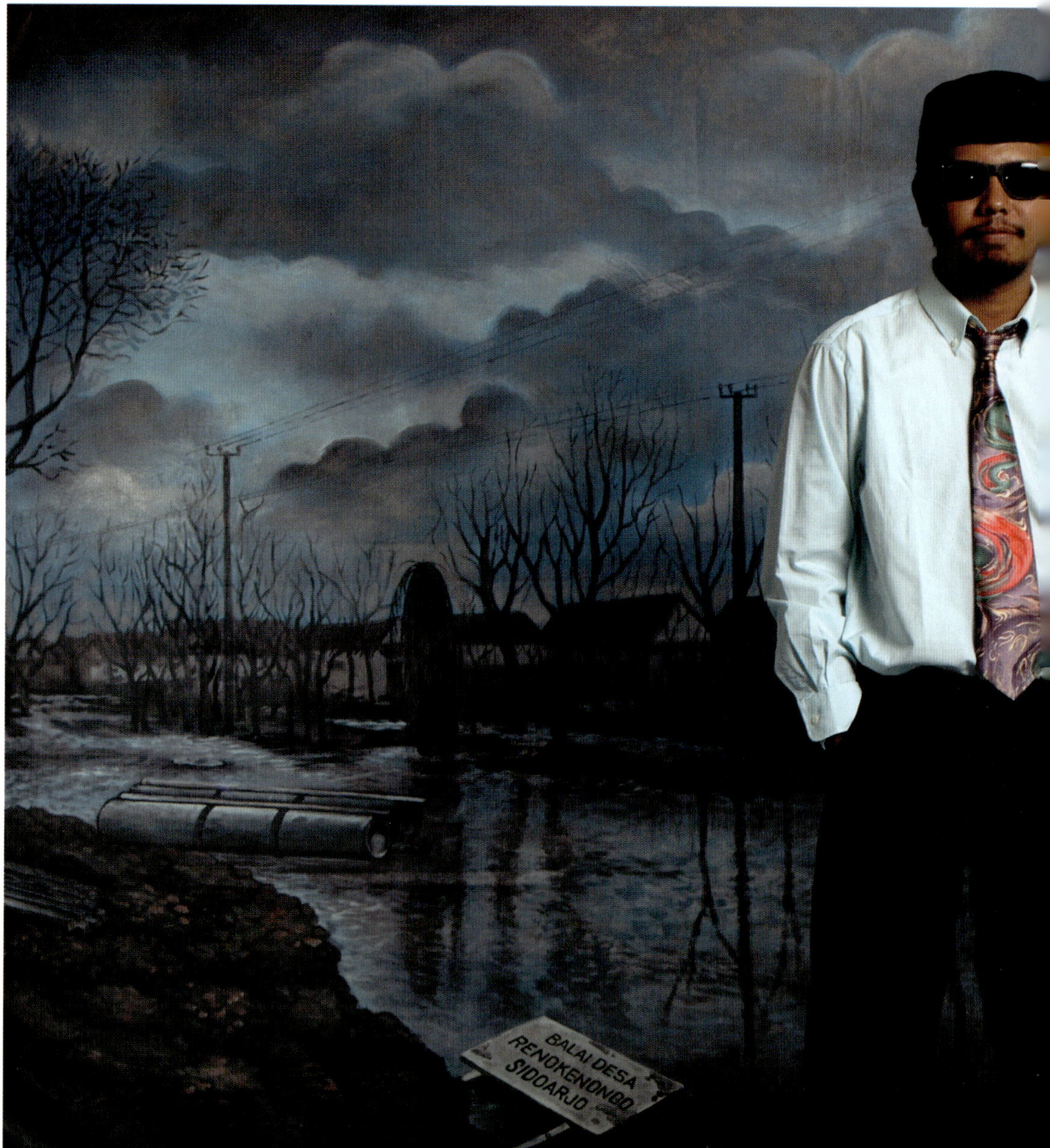
BALAI DESA
RENOKENONGO
SIDOARJO

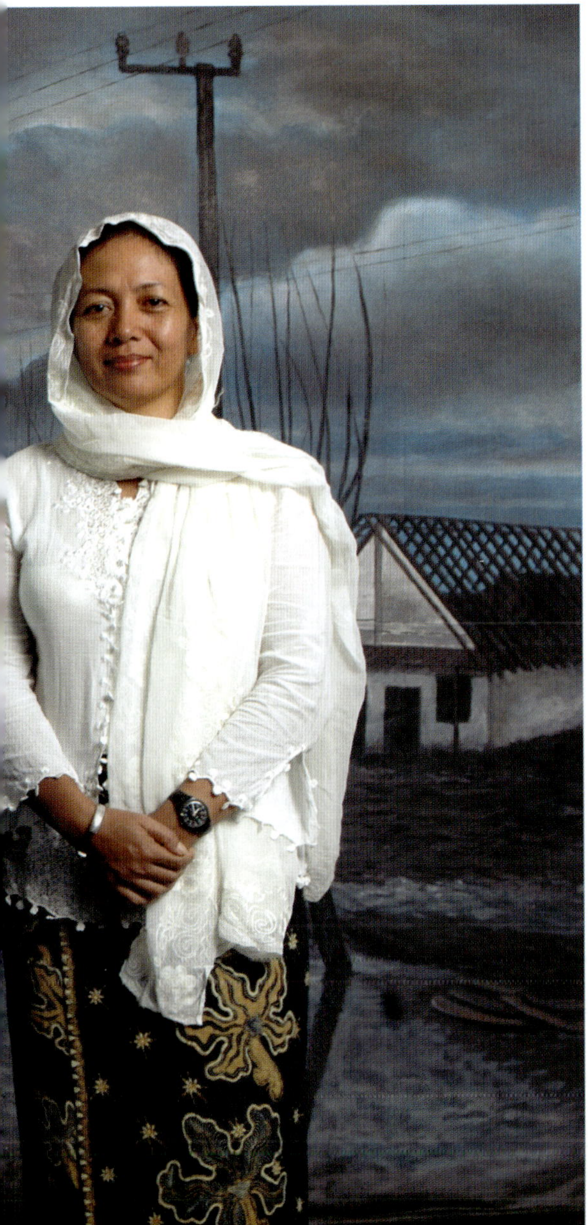

From: Arahmaiani Feisal
To: Biljana Ciric
Date: Mon, Jun 28, 2010 at 5:56 PM
Subject: Re: Archive part

Hi Biljana,

Why the suitcase & costume from my performances?

Because I've been living nomadically for at least the last 25 years. And aside from the basic needs that I must carry around in my suitcase ands bags, since I'm a performance artist, I also almost always need to carry my performance costumes. These costumes have symbolic meaning for they reveal something of my understanding and the development of my role as an artist in society.

I hope this is clear and short enough, but if you think I need to elaborate it further just let me know, ok?

Best,
Iani

- Show quoted text -

On Fri, Jun 25, 2010 at 6:31 PM, Biljana Ciric wrote:

Hi Arahmaiani,

I need a very short statement about your idea for the archive portion of the exhibition... Why the suitcase and why costumes?

Hope you can send it to me by Monday.

Thank you!

--
Biljana Ciric
Curator

发件人：哈拉海麦尼·费舍尔
收件人：比利安娜·思瑞克
日期：2010年6月28日星期一，5:56 PM
主题：回复：档案部分

比利安娜，你好：

为什么要选我表演时用的箱子和服装呢？

因为我在过去的25年多来一直过着流浪的生活。自从我成为一名行为艺术家后，除了我必须在箱子和包里四处游走时摆放的生活必需品外，我还常常必须带上我的戏服。这些服装有象征性意义，因为它们显示了我的一部分理解并表明我作为一名艺术家如何在社会中发展我的角色。

我希望这足够清晰和简短，但如果你希望我进一步详细地描述它们，只要告诉我一声就好了，可以吗？

祝好！
Iani

--显示引用文本--

在2010年6月25日，星期五，6:31 PM，比利安娜·思瑞克写道：
哈拉海麦尼，你好：
我希望对你对展出中的档案部分给出一段简短的说明文字……为什么是箱子和服装呢？

希望你能在周一之前回复给我。

谢谢！

--
比利安娜·思瑞克
策展人

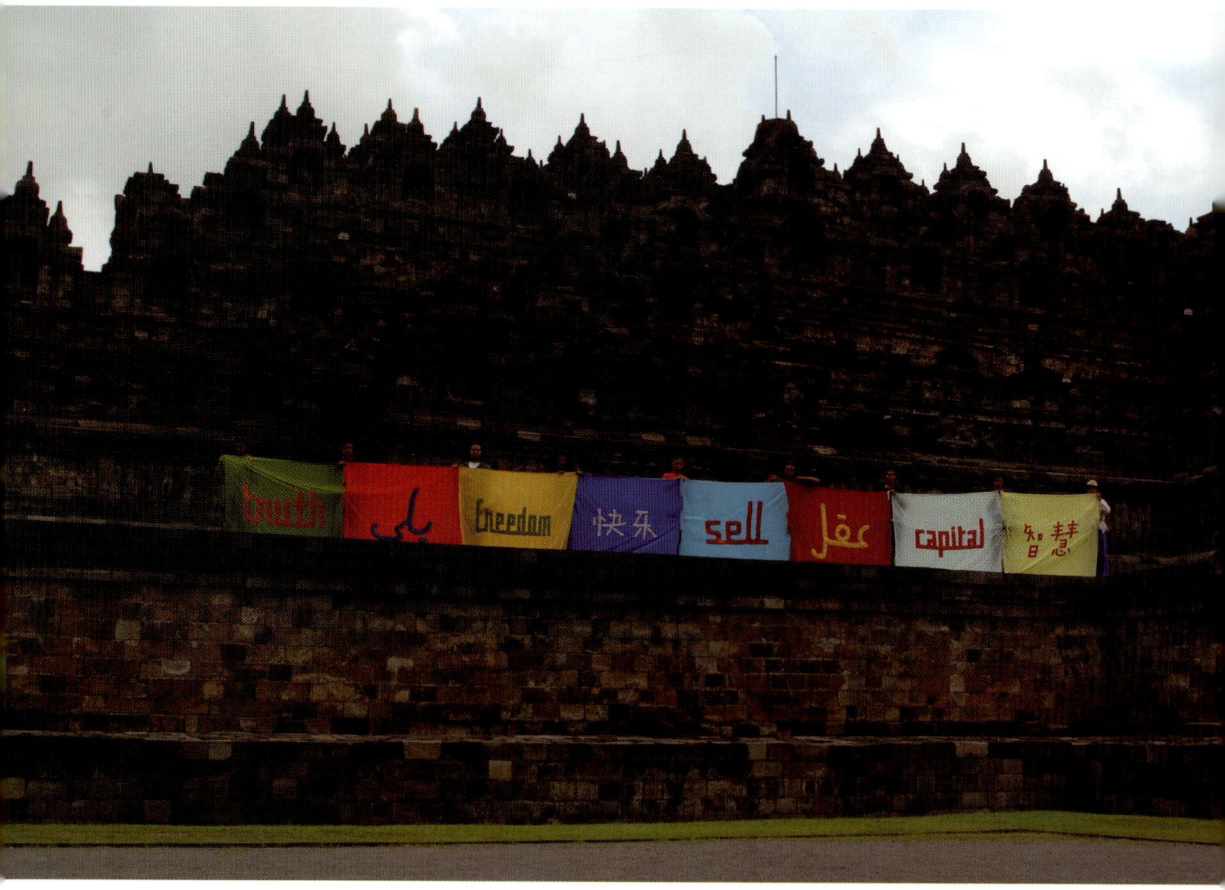

Flag Project
Community based art project in various countries

旗帜项目
在不同国家持续开展的公众艺术项目

2006-2010

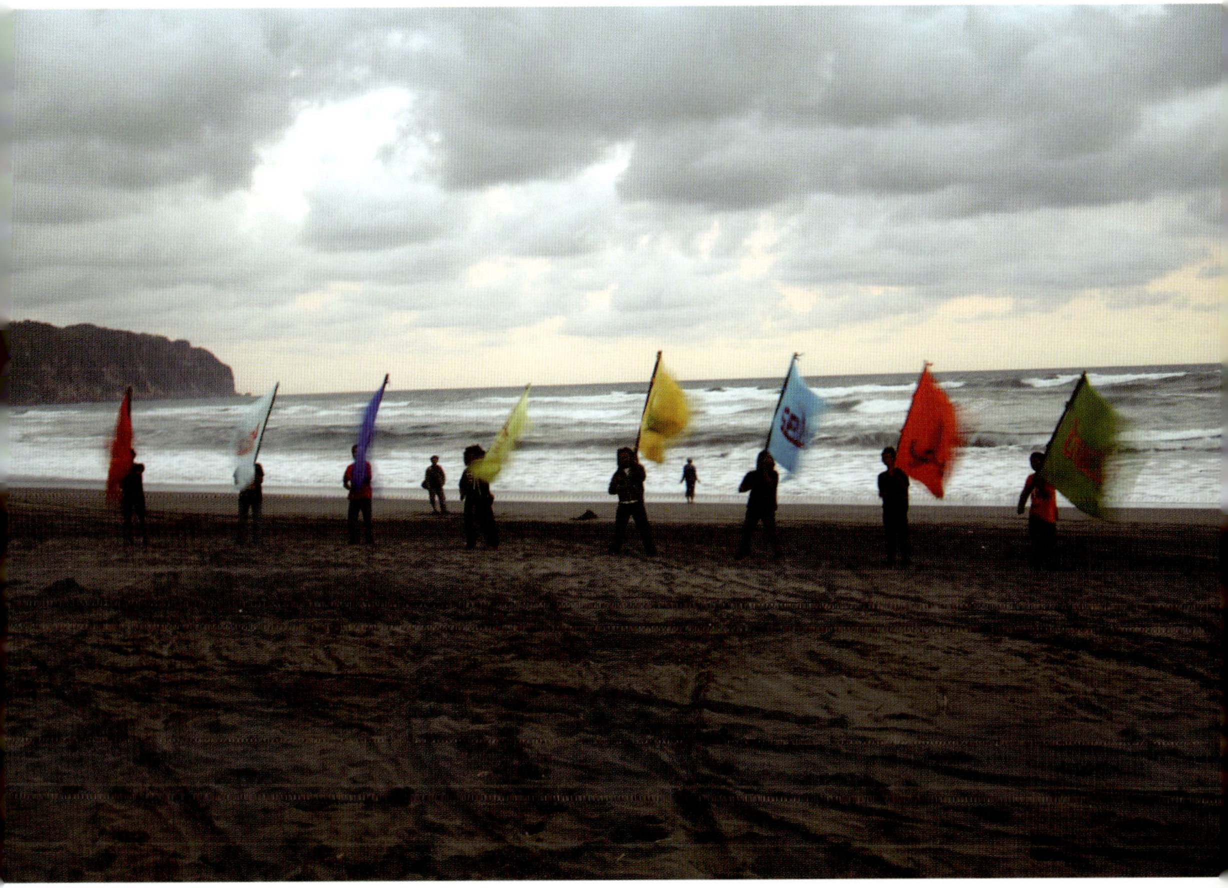

Wimo Ambala Bayang
维莫·安巴拉·巴扬

Interview with Wimo Ambala Bayang

MES 56, Yogyakarta
June 2010

Wimo Ambala Bayang: **W**
Biljana Ciric: **B**

B: Did you study in the photography department?

W: Yes, beginning in 1996 for fourteen years.

B: Why did it take you so long?

W: I was very busy outside of school, busy with non-academic projects. I have been making exhibitions since 1999.

B: What did you do between 1995 and 1999, aside from studying?

W: I studied up until 1999, and by then I already knew how to put together an exhibition, and to identify opportunities for exhibition. So in this way I got busy doing things outside of school.

B: Did you finish school?

W: Yes, in 2006.

维莫·安巴拉·巴扬访谈

MES 56，日惹
2010年6月

维莫·安巴拉·巴扬：**W**
比利安娜：**B**

B: 你读的是摄影系对吗?

W: 对，从1996年开始，已经有14年了。

B: 为什么你学了那么久?

W: 因为当时校外活动频繁，我要顾及许多与学业无关的项目，比如我从1999年起就开始做展览策划。

B: 从1995年到1999年，你除了学习还做了些什么?

W: 挣钱。我的校园生活一直持续到1999年，那时我已经了解如何策划展览以及如何争取展览机会，于是我在校园之外的生活日渐忙碌。

B: 你最后毕业了吗?

B: Did you ever really choose photography specifically?

W: Yes, I guess I did choose of photography, but really I just love art. I also really liked to paint and draw. At that time, I was scared that I wouldn't be accepted into the painting department, because at that time it was very competitive at the Institute of Art.

B: And that's why you chose photography?

W: Yes, it was much easier to get accepted to the photography department.

B: It wasn't because you love photography?

W: No. As one scientist said: If there is a group of women, don't choose the most beautiful one, just choose the second most beautiful one. Then you will get her, because most of the boys will chase the most beautiful one.

B: Are you working on any long-term projects?

W: I made an archive of photographs of sculptures.

B: What kind of sculptures?

W: Every sculpture. Since 2006, after I bought my plastic camera, I have been trying to capture images of realistic sculptures all the time. I always take my camera with me to every place I go, and if I see a nice sculpture, I will shoot it.

B: What do you mean by a nice sculpture? So you don't take photos of every sculpture? Is there a specific framework?

W: Like a tiger sculpture in a park, a realistic sculpture, but not too realistic because it's surrounded by other things. So for me it's nice; it's funny in a way. I have a lot of tiger sculptures, a lot of

W: 我是2006年毕业的。

B: 选择摄影是你当初的真实意愿吗?

W: 可以这么说。我那时热爱艺术，非常喜欢绘画，但又害怕考不上绘画系，因为它是艺术院校里录取竞争最激烈的。

B: 于是你才转向了摄影。

W: 是的，录取难度小很多。

B: 所以你的选择并不是基于你对摄影的热爱。

W: 不能这么理解。正如一个科学家所说，当大多数男孩都在追求最漂亮的姑娘的时候，你改变策略，追求容貌第二漂亮的那个，这样不仅少了许多竞争者，而且更有可能抱得美人归。

B: 你手上有正在进行的长期项目吗?

W: 我在做一个雕塑摄影档案。

B: 是什么样的雕塑?

W: 各种各样的。自从2006年我有了塑料相机后，我总是用镜头记录下各式各样的雕塑，不论走到哪里我都带着相机，伺机捕捉好的雕塑作品。

B: 这么说来你有一定的筛选准则，不会随意按下快门。你认为什么是好的雕塑作品呢?

W: 例如公园里的老虎雕塑，作品很写实，但在周围环境的衬托下又显得不够逼真。我很欣赏它，于是拍了很多张。我还有许多以恐龙、人或上帝为主题的雕塑摄影作品。

B: 你积累了那么多作品，是想为自己建一座雕塑博物馆，或者摄影档案馆吗?

dinosaurs, humans, and pictures of Jesus.

B: So you are building your own sculpture museum as a photo archive.

W: No, I don't have the desire to make a museum. If I have enough money, I will make a book. I have made two books so far, but they are not so perfect. They are about the sculptures. Last time I showed the work in Nadi Gallery, the project was called "I shot." So it says: "I shot dinosaur," or "I shot Jesus."

B: How do you see yourself in ten years?

W: It's a little difficult to see myself in ten years, because I still sleep on the floor. It's still the same as it was in 1995 when I began my studies.

B: Has anything changed?

W: Yes.

B: What has changed?

W: The change is that now I have a good computer.

W: 我没有这么宏大的目标，但如果有充裕的资金，我会出一本书。我已经出版了两本关于雕塑的书，但是还是有很多可以补充和提高的空间。上次我参加了Nadi画廊举办的“我拍”(I Shot)展览，当时展出了一些我所拍摄的以恐龙和上帝为主题的雕塑的照片。

B: 你能展望一下未来十年的自己吗?

B: 这挺难的。比如我现在仍睡在地板上，和1995年我刚上大学时的情形一模一样。

B: 生活有变化吗?

W: 有。

B: 哪里不一样?

W: 区别在于我现在有一台不错的电脑。

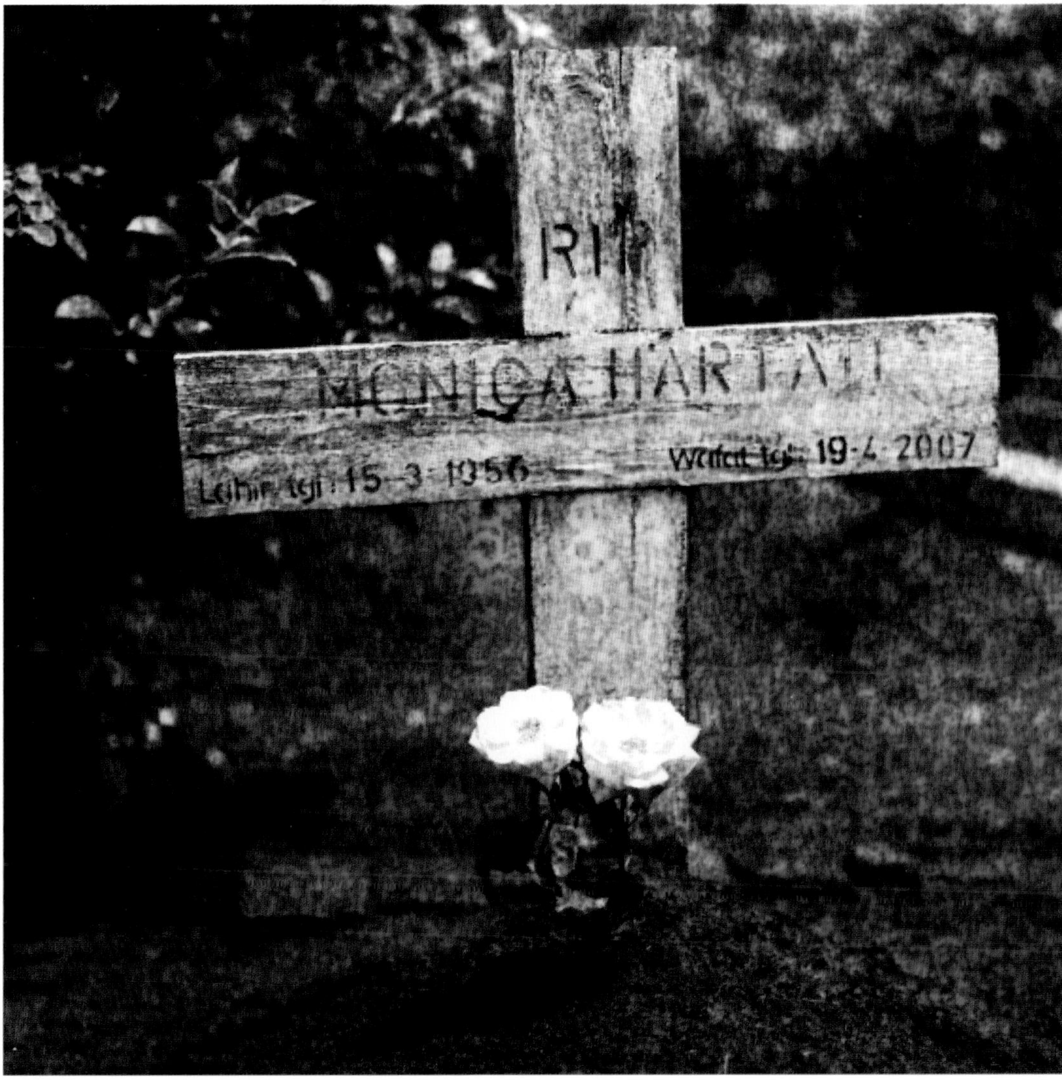
RIP
MONICA HARTATI
Lahir tgl: 15-3-1956
Wafat tgl: 19-4-2007

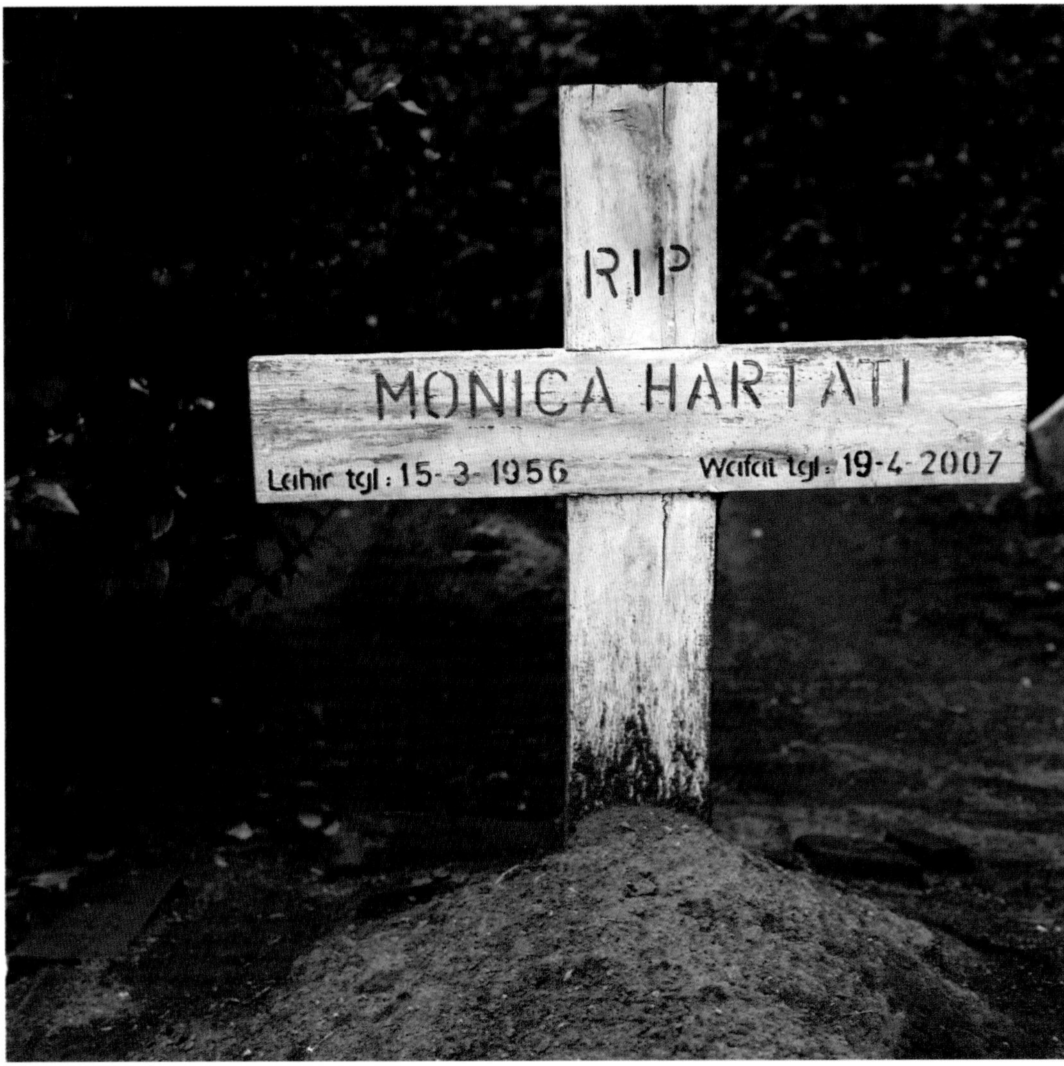

About Pilgrimage to my Mother's grave

This pilgrimage is my way to keep remembering her in my memory and as a cure whenever I miss her. I have disappointed my Mom a lot when she was still alive.

I was rarely back home at that time, because I'm too busy with my art career which I thought it can make her proud.

This pilgrimage is my forfait for all the bad things I made to my mother, and keeping my spirit to make her proud.

关于去我母亲的墓地朝圣……

这次朝圣是我以自己的方式继续在我的记忆中缅怀她、崇敬她，也是我每次想念她的解药。当母亲还在世时，很多次我都对她感到很失望。那时，我很少回家，因为我忙于自己的艺术事业，我以为这一事业会使她感到很骄傲。这次朝圣是我以自己的方式补偿所有我给母亲造成的遗憾，我以这种方式来振奋自己的精神使她感到骄傲。

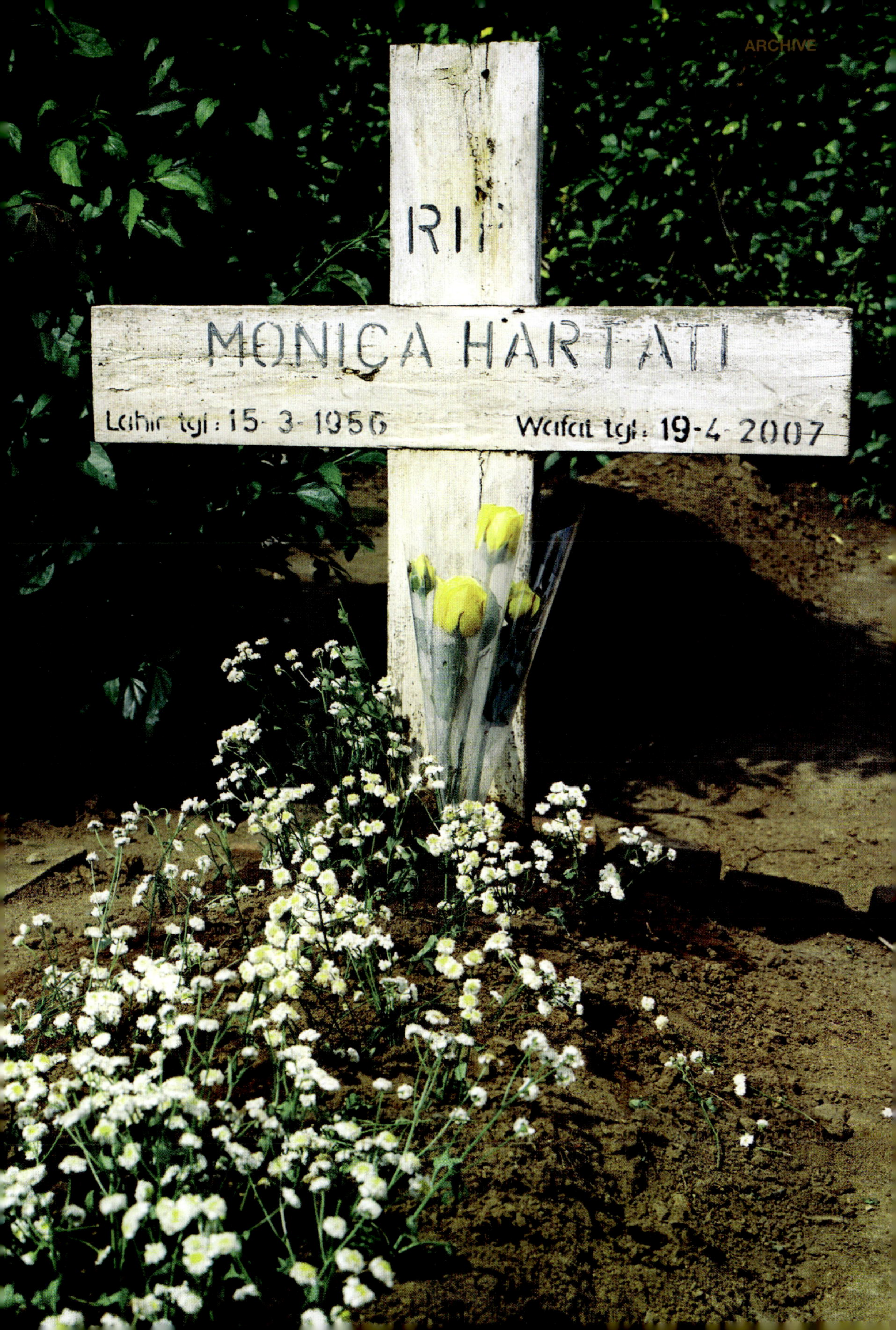

ARCHIVE

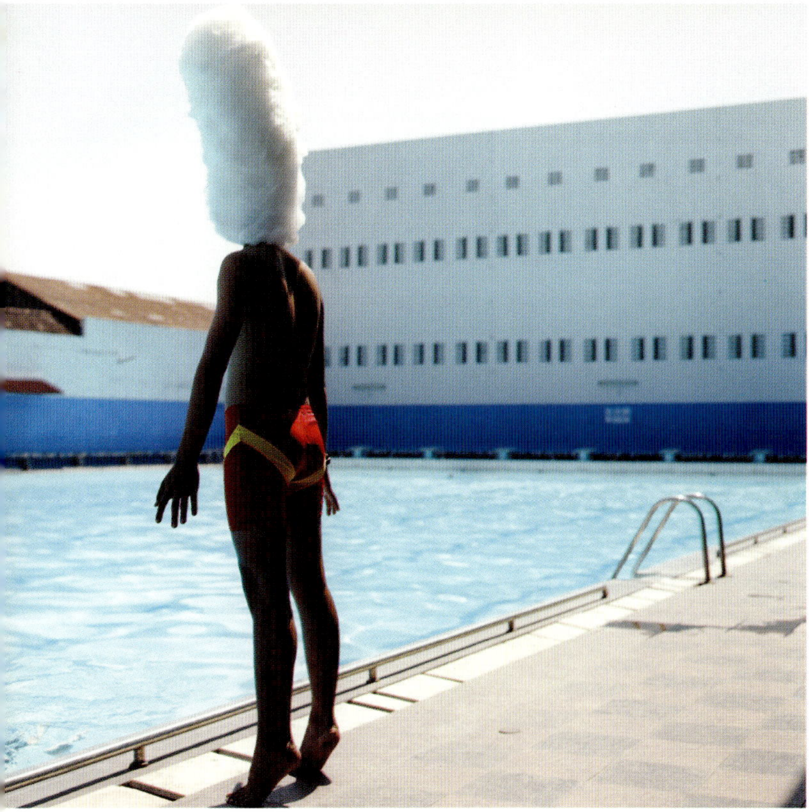

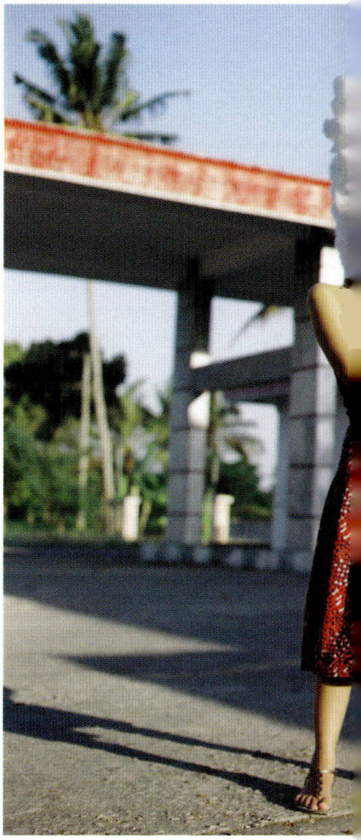

Hope
Series of 3 photographs

希望
三张系列照片

120×120cm
2009

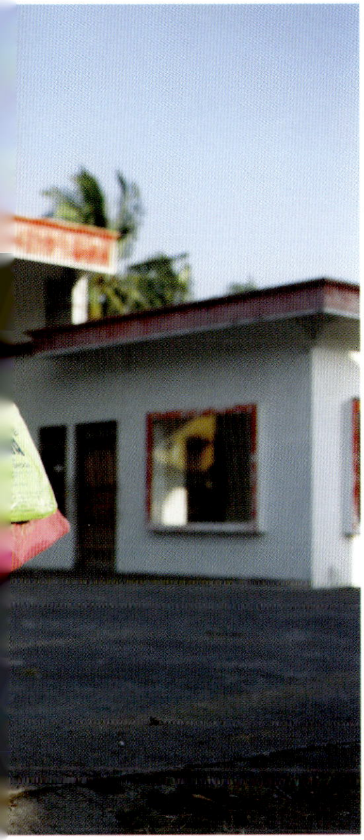

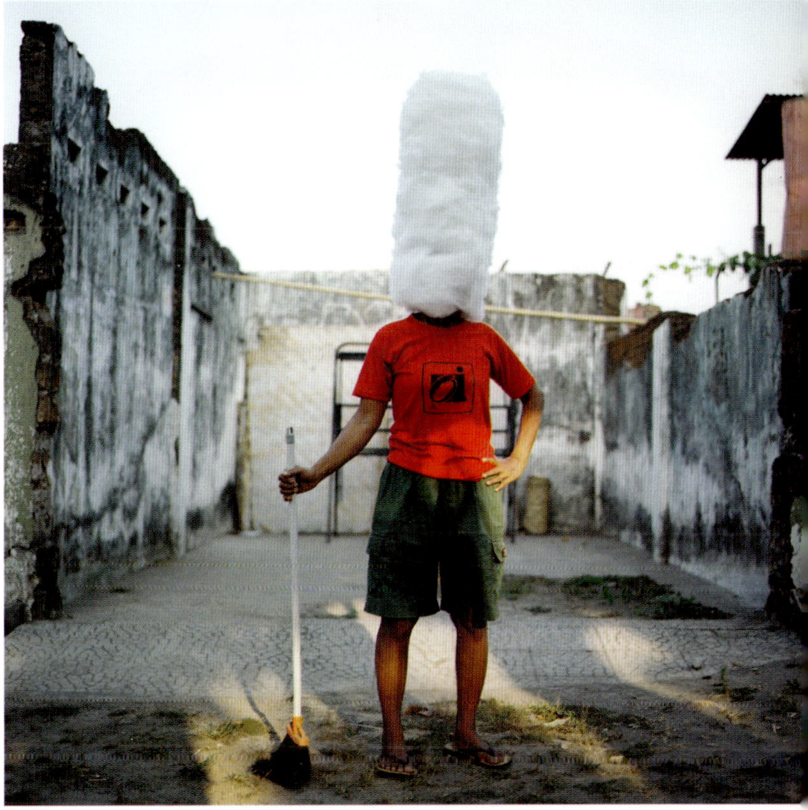

Edwin
艾德文

Interview with Edwin

Jakarta Zoo: Hippo Cage
Shooting location of "Postcard from Zoo"
June 2010

Edwin: **E**

Biljana Ciric: **B**

B: So, you are preparing to make a new film that will be shot in the zoo, called "Postard from the Zoo." Is there any relation between this shoot and your first feature film: "Blind Pig Who Wants to Fly"?

E: No, it's totally different. It's more narrative. It's more entertaining. We will have to see though.

B: Why?

E: Because we will follow the journey of this little girl living in the zoo.

B: So this a fictional account, right?

E: It's a fiction, yes.

B: How did you come up with the idea for this film? You have the idea, and then you write a sort of script? How do you usually work?

艾德文访谈

雅加达动物园河马笼
(影片《来自动物园的明信片》拍摄地)
2010年6月

艾德文：**E**

比利安娜：**B**

B: 你正在筹拍的新片《来自动物园的明信片》(Postard from Zoo)将在动物园取景拍摄，这与你的第一部剧情片《失明的猪也想飞》(Blind Pig Who Wants to Fly)之间有何关联?

E: 不，两者完全不同，这部新片更注重叙事，也更具有娱乐性。

B: 为什么这么说?

E: 故事的主人公是一个住在动物园里的小女孩，我们将跟随她的脚步开始一段奇妙的旅途。

B: 所以这是一部小说，对吗?

E: 是的。

B: 你是如何想到筹拍这部电影的? 是先有了想法，然后将想法落实为剧本吗? 你通常是如何创作的?

E: I wrote this script myself, and I have a friend who is also a scriptwriter. He helps with the structure. I always enjoy spending time here, in the zoo; it's a very personal thing, it's can be so stressful living in the city. Why am I interested in the zoo? There are some similarities between the zoo and us, the people who live in cities, like Jakarta. I look at the connection between these people and the animals, and at times they seem the same. We are all living in a zoo. The zoo system, with its fences, is similar to the one of us living in the city. We also have our rules and things like that. I just want to portray this situation, of how we are actually the same as the animals in the zoo.

B: In the beginning did you make more short films?

E: Yes, short films, they were from some small idea I would have. I could shoot them in only one or two days. For a larger idea, like this one, I have to wait.

The short films are more impulsive, spontaneous. I'm not trying to prepare like I would for a short film, since it will be for like a year or so. Usually, I challenge myself to do things spontaneously; it's like a learning process in preparation for the big feature film.

B: Did you make any short films in between "Blind Pig Who Wants to Fly" and "Postcard from the Zoo"?

E: I made a few short films after "Blind Pig Who Wants to Fly." One was a project for the Rotterdam Film Festival. It was a documentary made in Kenya, Africa. We screened the film just last January of this year, and I shot it in either August or July of last year. Just two month ago I shot another short film in Jakarta. It's also a fiction. It's about two best friends who are trying to explore

E: 这个剧本主要是我自己完成的，我的一个编剧朋友，他在剧本的结构上给我提供了帮助。我通常会花很多时间在动物园，面对着(动物园外)大都市所带来的压力，能够有这样独处的时光是非常愉快的。因此我至少会每天花半天的时间待在动物园，观察这里的人。我为什么会对动物园感兴趣呢？因为动物与生活在雅加达这样的大都市的居民有很多相似之处，我看到了这种联系。人与动物一样，生活为藩篱所限制。动物园的围墙就像城市的各种规则。我想要在作品中表现这种相似性，我们与生活在动物园中的动物并无不同。

B: 起初你更多地是选择拍摄短片，对吗?

E: 是的，一些小的想法往往以短片的形式呈现，一两天就可以拍摄完成。而像这样大的构思，我得耐心等待适当的时机。

B: 在拍摄剧情长片的时候，你心中是不是还保持着一些“小的想法”？

E: 拍摄短片更多的是一种冲动，其过程往往是一气呵成的。我不会为短片特意安排筹备期。我希望在自然自发的状态下完成拍摄，这是我对自己的一种挑战，也是着手拍摄长片前的学习过程。

B: 《失明的猪也想飞》之后你还拍过其它的短片作品吗?

E: 有。我为鹿特丹电影节拍过一部记录片，是在非洲的肯尼亚拍摄的。电影拍摄于去年7、8月间，并已于今年1月上映。两个月前，我还在雅加达拍摄了一部短片。故事是虚构的：(影片中)两个最要好的朋友试图通过挑战自我来探究性以及他们之间的关系。裸露的身体在影片中成为真实与坦率的象征。通过对于身体的探索，我试图呈现的是对于真诚与真实的追寻。

their relationship by challenging each other and exploring their sexuality. This young couple talks about being naked as a metaphor for truth. They talk about honesty. I tried to draw a metaphor between honesty and nakedness through the exploration of physical bodies.

B: What's that one called?

E: "Rollercoaster."

B: In the selection of your short films that you gave me I noticed that in many of them there is this underlining interest in sex and sexuality.

E: Yes, I'm interested in exploring sexuality. As you know, we are living in a country that is not very open to discussions about sexuality and nudity. It's taboo to talk about these things, but it's everywhere, and people do it. We love it. Even if only subconsciously. There is always sexuality in the films that I do. Maybe you can see this in my latest works as well; exposing one's sexuality is like opening your personal barrier, your door so to speak, which makes you more vulnerable, more pure. For me a film has to talk about something pure. Sensuality, nakedness… these things for me are always pure things.

B: Maybe it delves into the core of human experience.

E: Yes, that's true.

B: What are some other issues, for instance in "Blind Pig Who Wants to Fly"? How did this movie come about? Do you always write the script on your own for the different scenes?

E: Most of them I write by myself. I have a lot of different writings and short stories, short sequences. I use a lot of them like that, in pieces. I start

B: 那部影片叫什么?

E: 《过山车》(Rollercoaster)

B: 我看过你的几部短片，发现大都涉及性这个主题。

E: 是的。我对性的探索很有兴趣。我们生活在一个不能公开谈论性与裸体的国家，谈论它们是一种禁忌。但是性无处不在，每个人都需要它。我们的潜意识里喜欢性。因此我的电影中经常会讨论性。你可能已经在我最近的作品中看到，对性的探讨也是一次心灵的涤荡，会让人变得更加纯洁。我相信电影是需要表现一些纯洁的东西的，而性和裸体都是纯洁的事物。

B: 它触及到了人的本性。

E: 是的，没错。

B: 其它的主题呢? 比如《失明的猪也想飞》想告诉我们什么? 这部影片的是如何产生的? 也是你自己创作的剧本吗?

E: 大部分是我自己写的。我写过许多小故事和短剧，我很喜欢写作。在我动笔之前，脑海中会先有画面。以《失明的猪也想飞》为例，当时出现在我脑中的画面是一个想要吃爆竹的女孩的形象。

B: 这画面从何而来?

E: 我也不知道，但是这画面在我的头脑中挥之不去。我想把它拍成电影，所以我围绕这个画面创作了一个关于身份性的故事。故事里包含了我非常个人化的感受与想法。我一直关注印尼华人的身份性问题，这些华人不会说中文，与中国文化也没有实质性的联系。年轻时我常常对自己的华人身份感到困惑，也因此受到过歧视。华人与印

with an image, for example, in "Blind Pig," before I wrote the script. I work with an image first, I had a very strong image of a girl who is trying to eat a firecracker.

B: Where does the image come from?

E: I don't know. I don't know why, but for me it's a strong image. I want to have it in a film, so I try to make a story around it. In this way the image grows into a larger idea about identity. It's always a very personal idea; it's always about my questioning of being Chinese and living in Indonesia, and how people like myself really don't know how to speak Chinese, and who really have no connection with Chinese culture. When I was younger, it felt strange being Chinese in Indonesia, because of all of the discrimination. I feel it's like a collective question as to whether you are Chinese or Indonesian. I believe that film is a perfect medium through which to try and answer this question, the people's question about the reality of their lives. I learned a lot from the film through the process of making it, about being Chinese Indonesian.

B: Why is it called "Blind Pig Who Wants to Fly"?

E: I don't have any specific reasons. I think because it was something that was impossible. A blind pig who wants to fly… it is the desire to do something that really isn't possible.

B: I want to go back to your working process. Sometimes you have an image in you head, then you work out the story around the image, and sometimes you work on a short story. Do you have a working structure that you develop every day?

E: There is no routine to the process. I guess if something like either the story or the image has

尼人这两种身份的融合成了摆在很多人面前的一个问题。我相信这部电影为解决这一问题提供了一些启迪。在拍摄过程中我也对印尼华人的历史与现状有了更深入的了解。

B: 影片为什么取名《失明的猪也想飞》？

E: 其实并没有什么特别的原因。如果一定要说的话，"失明的猪想要飞"本身是一件不可能发生的事，这个标题承载了我的一些理性主义的愿望吧。

B: 我们还是回到创作过程这一话题。有时候你是脑海中先有画面，然后再开始构思故事；而有时候你会进行短片剧本创作。你有系统的渐进式的创作架构吗?

E: 创作的过程并没有固定的模式，如果某个故事或画面在我的头脑中挥之不去，我就会着手把它们落实成剧本。

B: 哪些人真正对您的创作产生过影响?

E: 你是指其他的电影人吗?

B: 对，也包括其他艺术家、或对您现在的创作产生过影响的人事物。

E: 我看过许多电影，不过我不太喜欢读书，我读的书很少。

B: 但是您看过许多电影。

E: 是的，在某种程度上，所有我看过的电影对我都有潜移默化的影响。我看电影并不是光看情节，我可能会对某一组或一个镜头特别感兴趣。这些镜头会牢牢印在我的脑海中，我从中创造出新故事。

不过我不喜欢反复看同一部电影，我通常只看一遍，有时甚至不会完整地看完。我会盯着我喜欢

a strong presence in my mind, then I will do it.

B: Is there anyone who has really influenced your work?

E: Another filmmaker?

B: I don't know, like other artists or filmmakers, or someone that you think that has kind of influenced what you do today?

E: Yes, I watch a lot of films, but I'm not a book lover. I read very few books.

B: But you watch a lot of films?

E: Yes, I don't know. I think all of the films that I see maybe they subconsciously influence me, in some aspect. I'm thinking how I watch a film, actually; I don't get the whole story. I really get into one sequence, one scene, and it can be very powerful. I just recreate it in my own mind; I make a new story out of it. I don't like to watch one film again and again. Usually I just watch a film once. Sometimes I don't even finish the film, because I'm enjoying this one sequence so much. I think I lose the whole idea of the film, but I get something from that sequence. So sometimes I forget the title when people ask me: Did you see this film? And I would say no, and they would give me the DVD and I would realize that I have already seen it.

的场景看，为此我可能会错过一个完整的故事，但是却从片段中得到了收获。不过有时我记不住影片的名字。当别人给我DVD时，我才意识到自己已经看过了。

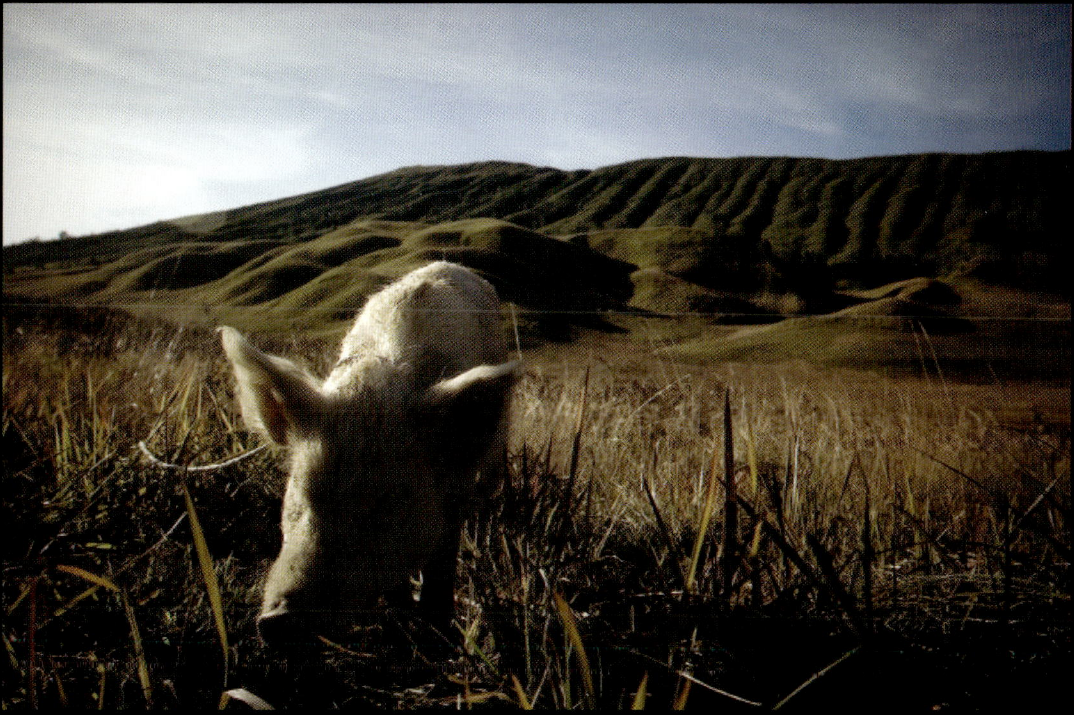

Blind Pig Who Wants to Fly
Scene Description: The Pig. Is it free?
Cast: the pig
Location: Mount Bromo, Indonesia
Photo by: erieknjuragan

失明的猪也想飞
场景描述：盲猪，它自由吗？
演员：盲猪
地点：婆罗摩火山，印尼
照片提供：erieknjuragan

2009

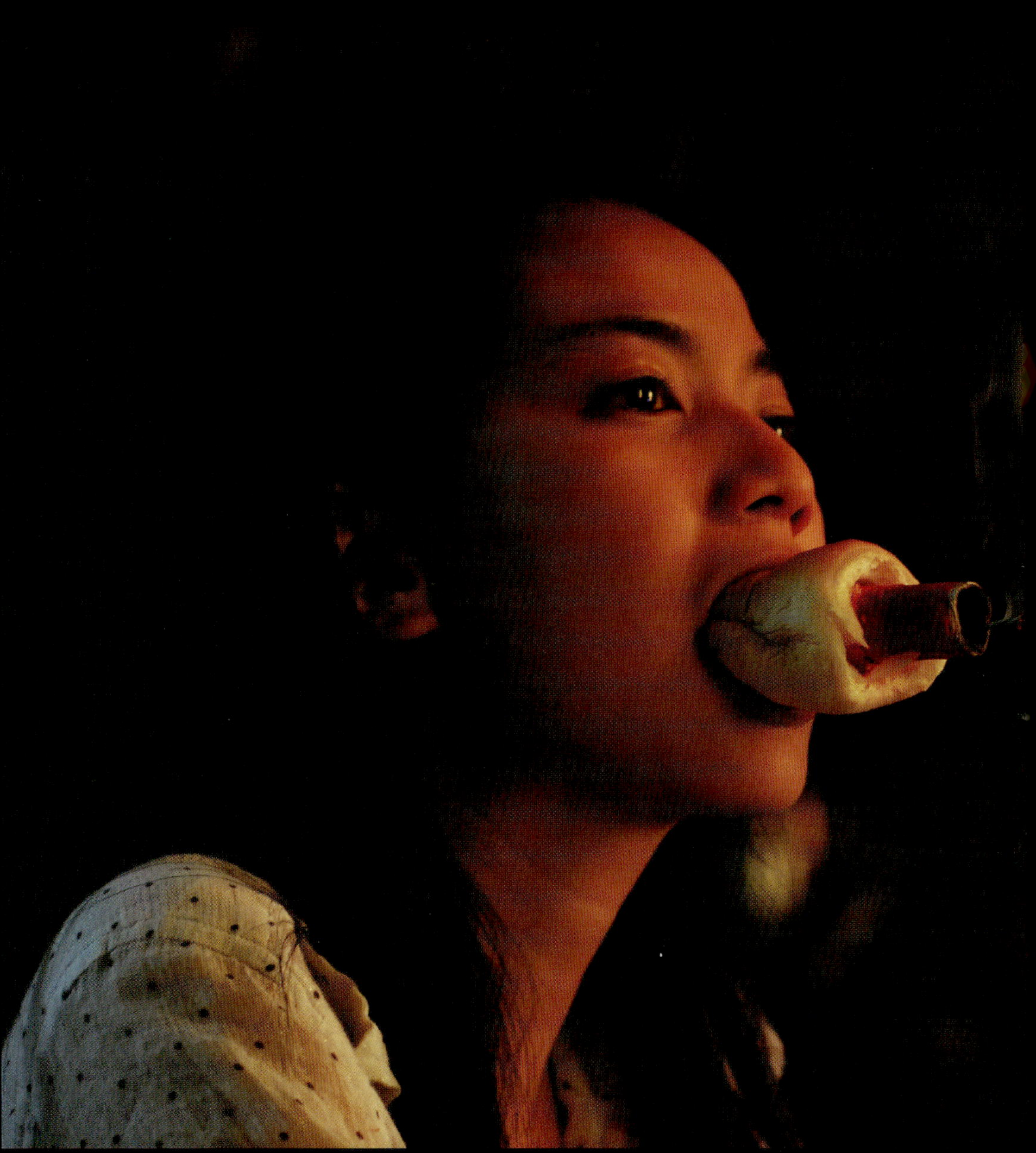

Blind Pig Who Wants to Fly
Director: Edwin
Scene Description: Linda, the girl who eats firecracker
Cast: Linda by Ladya Cheryl
Location: Jakarta, Indonesia
Photo by: erieknjuragan

失明的猪也想飞
导演：Edwin
场景描述：Linda，吃鞭炮的女孩
演员：Ladya Cheryl
地点：雅加达，印尼
照片提供：Erik Njuragan

77'
2008

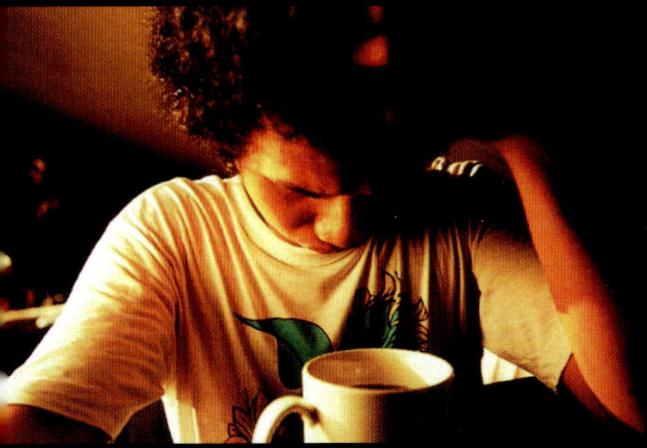

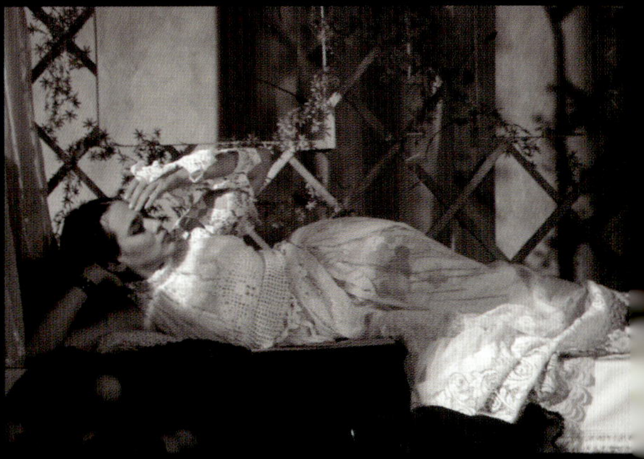

A Very Slow Breakfast (2003) , 5'
The film that explore feelings about individuality and the loss of family values. An attempt to redefine the meaning of family in the changing realm of modernity.
Produced by: Kotak Hitam, with Institut Kesenian Jakarta, and Aksara Bookstore.

一次缓慢的早餐 (2003)，5分钟
该片试图对个体与家庭价值衰落的感受进行探索，是一次对变动中的现代性语境中的家庭的重新定义。
制片：黑盒电影公司、雅加达艺术学院、Aksara书店

Dajang Soembi: Perempoean Jang Dikawini Andjing (2004) , 7'
An absurd folk tale, inventively told in the form of a silent movie.
Production: Kotak Hitam Film, Renate Tombokan

嫁给狗的女人 (2004)，7分钟
以默片的形式创造性地讲述了一个荒诞的民间故事。
制片：黑盒电影公司、Renate Tombokan

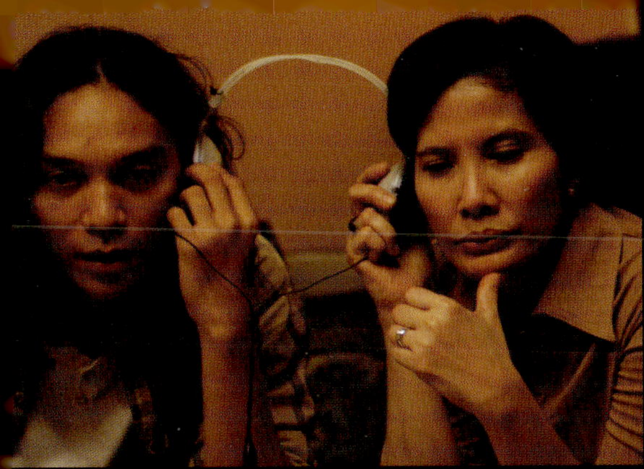

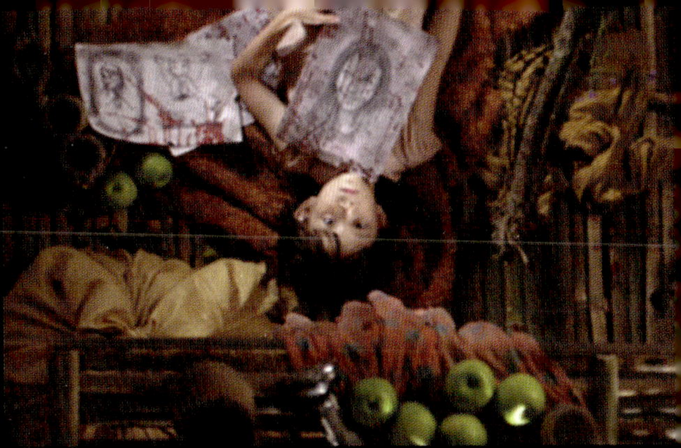

A Very Boring Conversation (2006), 9minutes
The conversation starts from coments about music and internet emails, then slowly moved to unlogical things that could possibly change a 'mother-son relationship' to a 'man-woman relationship'.
Produced, Written and Directed by Edwin.

一场非常无聊的谈话 (2006)，9分钟
这场谈话以音乐和电子邮件开始，逐渐转向了非逻辑性事物，这种转变可能使"母子关系"变为"男女关系"。
制片、编剧、导演：艾德文

Kara, Anak Sebatang Pohon (2005), 9 minutes
Hit by fate. A statue falling from the sky kills the mother of the newly born Kara. As a little girl, she goes to get her own back.
Kara is a little girl living in an isolated place. Her father disappeared after Ronald killed her mother. A journalist's invasion of her life makes her decide to seek out Ronald and ask him the ultimate question. Ronald is Ronald MacDonald, and that doesn't give everything away. An exercise in absurdist globalism.
Production: Kotak Hitam Film, Renate Tombokan

卡拉，树的女儿 (2005)，9分钟
命运致命的一击！一尊从天而降的塑像卡拉的妈妈，而当时，卡拉还是个刚出生的婴儿。小女孩则试图寻找自我的道路。
小女孩卡拉独自住在一个与世隔绝的地方，她的爸爸在妈妈被罗纳德砸死后失踪了。一个记者闯进了小女孩的生活，这使她决定寻找罗纳德来解答她的终极疑问。罗纳德就是罗纳德・麦克唐纳，而这并不能解答小女孩的所有问题。影片是可以视作一个荒诞主义者的全球主义演习。
制片：黑盒电影公司、Renate Tombokan

F.X Harsono
方济各・沙勿略・哈索诺

Interview with F.X Harsono

Sultan Hotel Jakarta
June 4, 2010

F.X Harsono: **F**

Biljana Ciric: **B**

B: How has your work evolved since the beginning of the new art movement?

F: During the Suharto era, and between 2000 and 2002, I was still working on the same issues; these were social and political issues. After the Suharto era, around 2002 and 2003, when I had my first solo exhibition, my concerns started to shift from dealing with social and political issues, and I started working around my own identity. I just started to ask questions about myself as an Chinese Indonesian, and I wanted to see things more clearly.

B: Why did this start around 2002 or 2003? Was there any specific movement that this shift was attached to?

F: Yes, this was when Suharto's power began to diminish as president. In 1998, there was a big

方济各·沙勿略·哈索诺访谈

苏丹酒店，雅加达
2010年6月4日

方济各·沙勿略·哈索诺：**F**

比利安娜：**B**

B: 从“新艺术运动”至今，你的作品经历了哪些新的发展？

F: 在苏哈托时代以及2000-2002年间，我的作品大多围绕着相同的社会政治问题。在苏哈托时代结束后，也就是2002-2003年间，我举办了首次个人展。其时我的关注点开始从社会和政治事务转向寻求自我认同。我开始追问自己作为印尼华人的身份性。我想把问题看清楚。

B: 为什么开始于2002年或者2003年呢？那时有什么特别的运动吗？

F: 是的，苏哈托的下台标志着苏哈托时代的终结。1998年，印尼发生了大暴动，许多华人在暴动中成了受害者。在那场暴动后，局势完全转变了，苏哈托下台，我们有了新总统。从那以后，政局完全改变了，所有的人可以批评政府。我们

riot in Indonesia, and most of the Chinese people were victims in the riot. After that, things totally changed: Suharto was removed, we got a new president, and so after, the political situation was completely different and all of the people could criticize the government. It appeared that we had obtained the freedom to speak, to criticize the government, and so I started to wonder in that moment—when everybody could criticize the government—does my art work need to do the same, or is it time to pursue another direction? I saw the changes, all the people could criticize the government, and so I thought that the cultural needs would also change. So from then on I started looking to develop another direction for my work. So that's how I began questioning myself about who I am, and for what reasons I am questioning the direction of my art making and it's connection to social and political issues.

Suddenly, I realized that I'm Chinese, I'm Chinese Indonesian, and then I started questioning myself again: does that mean I am a real Indonesian? Then I was thinking: Oh no, I don't know anything about Indonesian cultural, so I must be Chinese; but I don't know anything about Chinese culture as well. So at that time I was very confused about who I was. I had a lot questions for myself, and I got a lot of ideas to make artworks about these questions. After that I found out that throughout Chinese history there was a lot of discrimination, so I started to talk through my personal history as a Chinese Indonesian. I started reading books about the history of Chinese Indonesians. I started talking to people, doing research, asking my parents and other older people living in Blitar.

B: Blitar is you hometown?

F: Yes, Blitar is my hometown. At that time it seems I wanted to look back, deeper into my past.

拥有了言论自由、能够对政府进行批评。因此我开始思考，在这场运动中，当每个人都可以批评政府时，我的艺术作品是应该顺应这种转变，还是应该从另一个角度去思考问题。既然大家都可以批评政府，那么我认为文化也需要改变。从那以后，我开始考虑如何从另一个角度进行艺术创作。

我开始对自己的身份性提出诘问，开始质疑自己的艺术创作方向与社会、政治事务之间的关系。

突然之间，我意识到自己是华人、是印尼华人。接着，我再次追问，我真的是一个印尼人吗?不，我对印尼文化一无所知。那么，我是一个真正的华人吗? 但我也不了解中国文化。我很迷惘，我究竟是谁。我对自己提了很多问题，并从这些问题中获得许多灵感来创作艺术作品。我发现华人在印尼历史上遭受了很多歧视，因此我开始讲述我作为印尼华人亲历的故事。我开始阅读关于印尼华人的历史资料。我开展了一些采访和研究，向我的父母和其他住在布里塔(Blitar)的老人了解情况。

B: 布里塔是你的故乡?

F: 是的，布里塔是我的故乡。借此机会我也回顾了一下自己的过去。

B: 你在什么时候发现了你父亲的照片?

F: 那些照片很早之前就属于我，那时我开始思考关于自己的身份性的问题。我意识到这些照片对我来说很重要，对我的家庭、对华人社区来说也是。我重新把照片找出来，发现了上面的题字，接着我开始研究1948年的局势。小时候我就看到过这些照片，它们一直放在家庭相册中。但直到2000年，我才意识到这些照片对我具有重大的意

B: When did you discover you father's photographs?

F: Those photographs belonged to me for a long time, even before I started to think about my identity. Then I realized that these photographs were very important to me, and also for my family, and also for Chinese people in general. I started to look again at the photographs, and I found the captions, and then I started to investigate the situation during 1948. I had been looking at those photographs since I was a child, because those photographs were always in my family's album. But until 2000, I never thought that photographs were a very important part of my life. So after that, when I started to question my life and my identity, I realized that photographs are very important to me.

B: You told me last time that you're not only an artist, but also very socially engaged, doing a lot of volunteer work. How is this related to your practice as an artist?

F: At the art school we realized that we weren't getting a lot of socially and politically related subject matters in our education. So if I wanted to talk about social and political issues in my artwork, it meant I had to understand them and also how these things change. How to understand these things clearly, that was the first problem. And second, if my artwork doesn't have a root structure, then I am just seeing the social and political issues from the outside, so I felt that this was not the right way. Starting in 1985, I began to participate in some NGOs in Indonesia, those NGOs that were socially and politically active in Indonesia. When I was active in these NGOs, those experiences helped to teach me a lot about social and political problems in real terms. Around then I also started to read a book about social and political subjects to help me understand both

义。从那以后，我开始对生活、对身份性提出质问，开始意识到这些照片对我来说很重要。

B: 你上次曾对我说过，你不只是一位艺术家，你还积极参与社会活动，做了很多志愿者工作。这些与你作为艺术家的实践有什么关联?

F: 作为艺术家，我意识到在艺术学校内，我们的教育很少涉及到社会政治话题。而如果我要在作品中谈论社会政治问题，我就必须先去理解这些问题，理解它们的发展变化。清楚地理解这些问题，这是最重要的。其次，如果我的艺术作品没有根基，那么我仅仅是从外部观察社会政治、我看到的只是问题本身，而这恰恰是不正确的。从1985年开始，我参加了印尼的一些非政府组织，尤其是活跃于印尼社会和政治舞台的非政府组织。参加这些组织的活动帮助我更深入地了解了现实的社会政治问题。同时，我开始阅读关于社会政治问题的书籍，这让我更清晰地了解到变化和问题出现在哪里。

在1998年的暴动中，据说许多华人妇女遭到强暴。为了了解真相，我成为了印尼反对对妇女施暴组织的志愿者。这个组织专门为1998年暴动中的女性受害者提供帮助。在志愿服务期间，我了解到之前的传言是真实发生过的。

我的作品都是以自己的社会体验为基础，我不希望仅仅从旁观者的角度来看问题。

B: 我另外还有一个问题。请你展望一下10年后的自己好吗?

F: 10年后？实在不好说，但有些东西是不会改变的，那就是我对人性的关注，包括人权问题，人性的意义以及人们互相的关爱等。爱是很重要的。如果没有爱，你就无法理解人性，也不会去

the changes and also the problems.

During the riots in 1998 it was said that many Chinese women were raped, so I wanted to know the truth about this matter, and I became a volunteer in an organization that dealt with violence against women in Indonesia, specifically women who were victims of violence during 1998. Working there I came to understand that these things truly did occur. I think that all of my work is based on my experiences in society, and reflective of how I don't want to just look from the outside at these problems.

B: I have one more question. How do you see F.X Harsono in ten years?

F: In the next ten years? I don't know yet, but there is something that I cannot change and that is my interest in humanity, mainly as to human rights' issues. Humanity means the way that one person loves and relates to another person. Love is very important, because without love, you cannot understand humanity, and also we cannot take care of or pay attention to other people's lives. Through love we can see other people's lives, and we can see the problems within humanity. That's very important.

关心或关注别人的生活。而如果有爱，我们就会真正付出关心、真正发现问题。这一点很重要。

中華人民共和國許可出籍證書

雅總（出）字第 013005 號

申請退出中華人民共和國國籍，經審查准予出籍。特發給許可出籍證書，以資證明。

出籍人：姓名 林宣娘 性別 女

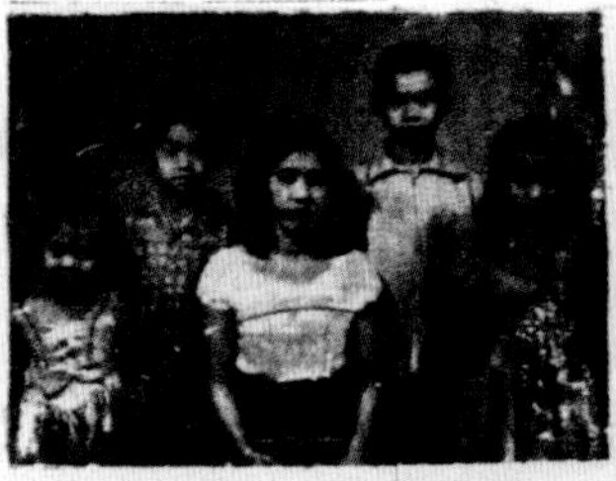

出生時間 1925 年 12 月 1 日

出生地 印度尼西亞

現住地 勿里达

職業 家务

隨同出籍子女： 胡丰文（男）

胡丰梅（女）

胡丰良（男）

胡美兰（女）

中華人民共和國
駐雅加達總領事 关宗周

1963 年 3 月 16 日

Formulir : VIA.

No.: 4 /1966/W.N.I.

SURAT TJATATAN

Pernjataan keterangan melepaskan kewarganegaraan Republik Rakjat Tiongkok untuk kembali mendjadi: WARGANEGARA REPUBLIK INDONESIA.

Jang bertanda tangan dibawah ini saja, M. MISBACH, berdjabat HAKIM/PD. KEPALA PENGADILAN NEGERI DI BLITAR, menerangkan, bahwa pada hari : SENIN, tanggal : 31 DJANUARI 1966, datang pada saja seorang bernama:

OH HONG BOEN,

jang, sekarang setelah mendjadi dewasa, menjatakan keterangan:

MELEPASKAN KEWARGANEGARAAN REPUBLIK RAKJAT TIONGKOK UNTUK KEMBALI MENDJADI WARGANEGARA REPUBLIK INDONESIA.

Orang jang menjatakan keterangan ialah:

laki-laki, lahir di Blitar

pada tanggal : 22 Djanuari 1948;

anak sah dari Bapak bernama : OH HOK TJOE, jang menurut surat-tjatatan penolakan kewarganegaraan Indonesia jang dibuat pada tanggal 7 Desember 1951 bernomor: 233/1951 dimuka Hakim Pengadilan Negeri di Blitar, telah menjatakan keterangan menolak kewarganegaraan Indonesia untuknja sendiri/selaku wakil sah untuk anak-anaknja;

oleh karena itu telah kehilangan kewarganegaraan Indonesia;

dan selama belum dewasa hanja mempunjai kewarganegaraan Republik Rakjat Tiongkok, karena penolakan dari orang tuanja;

Sekarang bertempat tinggal di Djalan Kawi No.10, BLITAR;

Menerangkan dengan sungguh senondjak penolakan dari orang tuanja belum pernah meninggalkan wilajah Republik Indonesia tanpa idzin-kembali (reentry-permit) atau belum pernah meninggalkan wilajah Republik Indonesia selama waktu jang melebihi djangka waktu idzin kembalinja. -

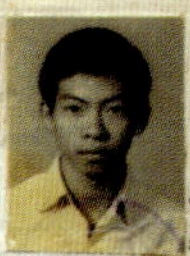

Tanda tangan atau tjap (empu)djari orang jang menjatakan keterangan.

(Oh Hong Boen).

Dibuat di Blitar pada tanggal:

31 Djanuari 1966.

(Tanda tangan petugas)

(M. MISBACH).

Lembar ke : III

Lembar ke 1 : Departemen Kehakiman

Lembar ke 2 : Pemohon.

Lembar ke 3 : Walikota Kepala Daerah.

WALIKOTA KEPALA DAERAH KOTAMADYA DI BLITAR

No. Daftar : I.22/ 322 /68.

Surat pernjataan ganti nama

Berdasarkan Keputusan Presidium Kabinet No. 127 / U / Kep / 12 / 1966.

Jang bertanda tangan / Jang tjap (empu) djarinja tertera : dibawah ini, saja OH HONG BOEN [L./P. x]

a. Warganegara Indonesia berdasarkan : Form. VIA No. 4/1966/WNI.P.N. Blitar tg. 31-1-1966.

b. Pekerdjaan : PELADJAR.

c. Lahir di : Blitar, tgl. 22-1-1948.

d. Bertempat tinggal di : djl. Kawi No. 10 Blitar.

e. x) kawin sah dengan —— pada tanggal : —— di —— Warganegara Indonesia berdasarkan —— atau asing —— pekerdjaan —— lahir di —— bertempat tinggal di ——

f. x) mempunjai anak jang sekarang belum genap berumur 18 tahun dan belum kawin bernama :

1. —— lahir di —— pada tanggal —— pekerdjaan —— Warganegara —— bertempat tinggal di ——
2. —— lahir di —— pada tanggal —— pekerdjaan —— Warganegara —— bertempat tinggal di ——
3. —— lahir di —— pada tanggal —— pekerdjaan —— Warganegara —— bertempat tinggal di ——
4. —— lahir di —— pada tanggal —— pekerdjaan —— Warganegara —— bertempat tinggal di ——
5. —— lahir di —— pada tanggal —— pekerdjaan —— Warganegara —— bertempat tinggal di ——

MENJATAKAN KEINGINAN MENGGANTI NAMA

Untuk	Nama sekarang		Diganti mendjadi	
	Nama ketjil	Nama keluarga	Nama ketjil	Nama keluarga
Pemohon	Hong Boen	OH	——	HARSONO, Franciscus
Isteri	——	——	——	——
Anak	——	——	——	——

MENGESAHKAN / Potret / Foto copy sesuai dengan aslinya

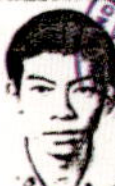

Kepala SMA I Blitar,

ABDULLAH UKI

NIP. 130220049

BLITAR, tgl. 7 Maret 1967.

Jang menjatakan keterangan :

[Tanda tangan atau tjap empu djari]

[OH Hong Boen]

Atas nama Menteri Kehakiman :

Menerima dan mengesahkan Surat Pernjataan Ganti Nama ini :

DI BLITAR pada tgl. —— 1967.

Petugas

Walikota Kepala Daerah Kotamadya Blitar,

[R. PRAWIROKOESOEMO].

x) Jang tidak perlu dicoret.

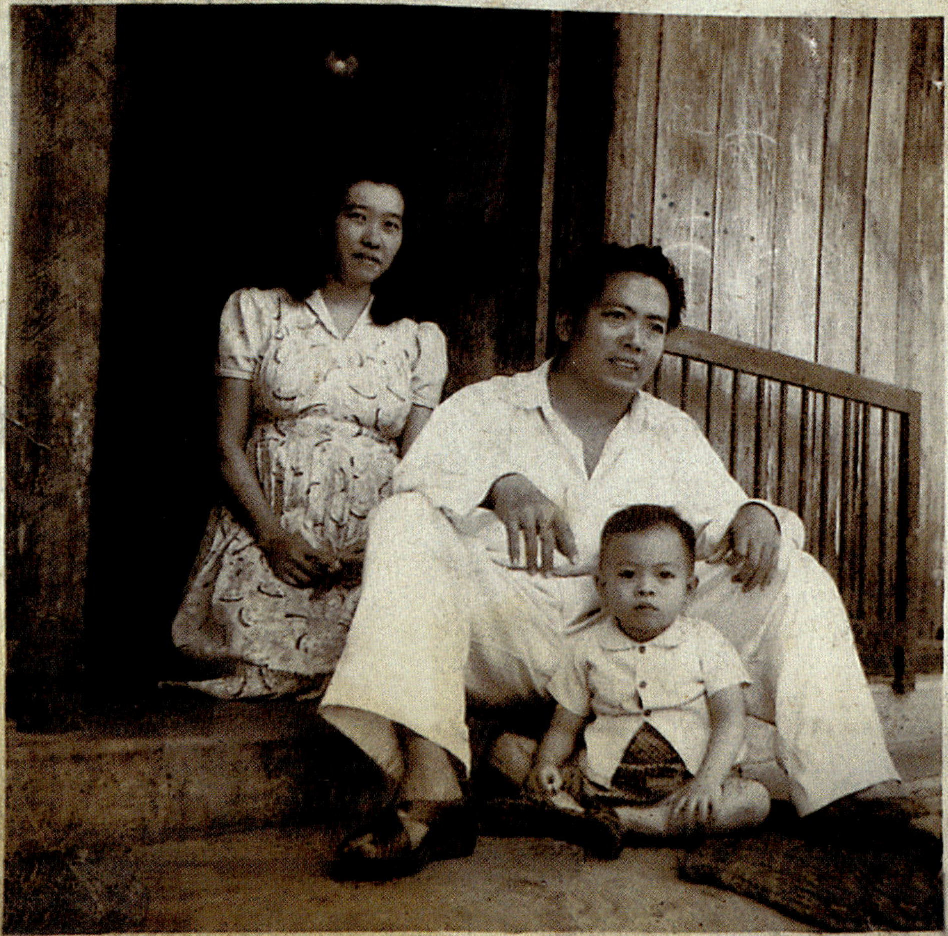

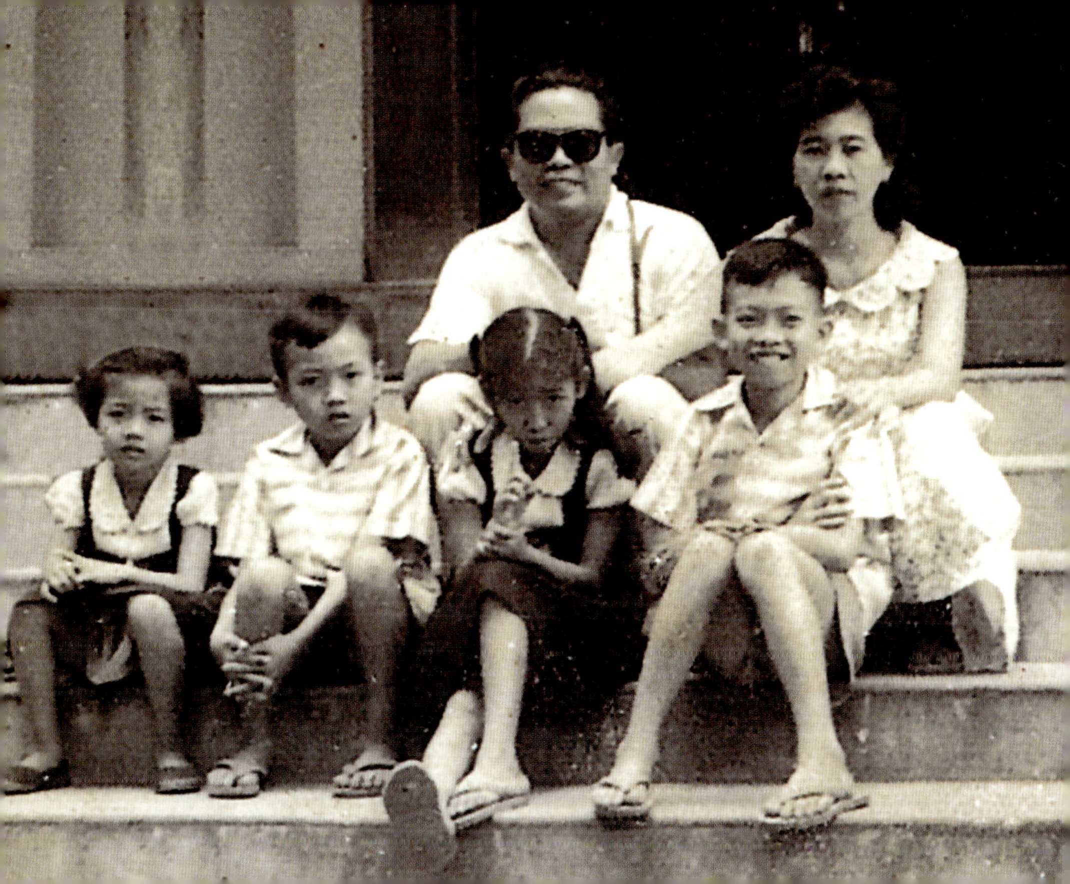

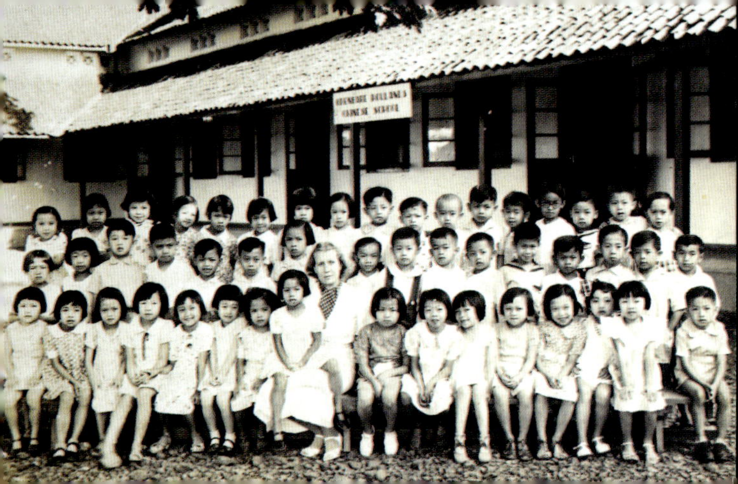

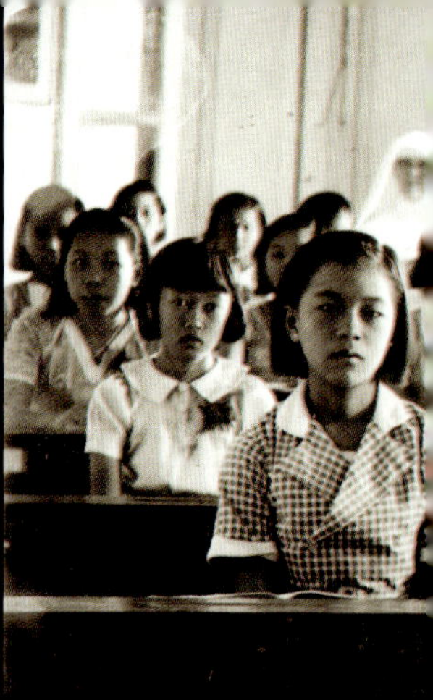

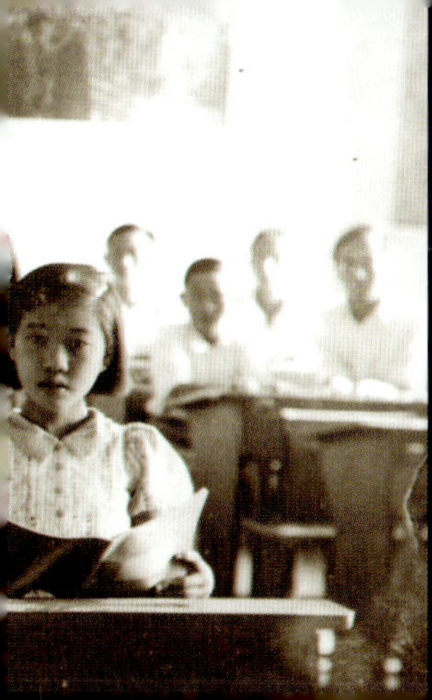
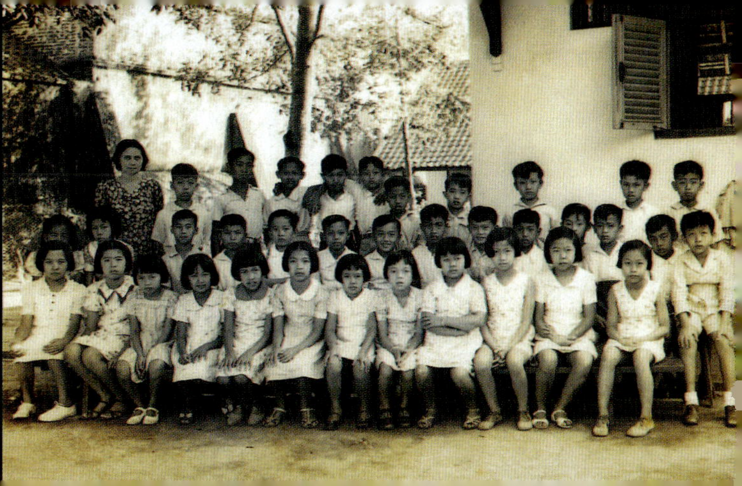

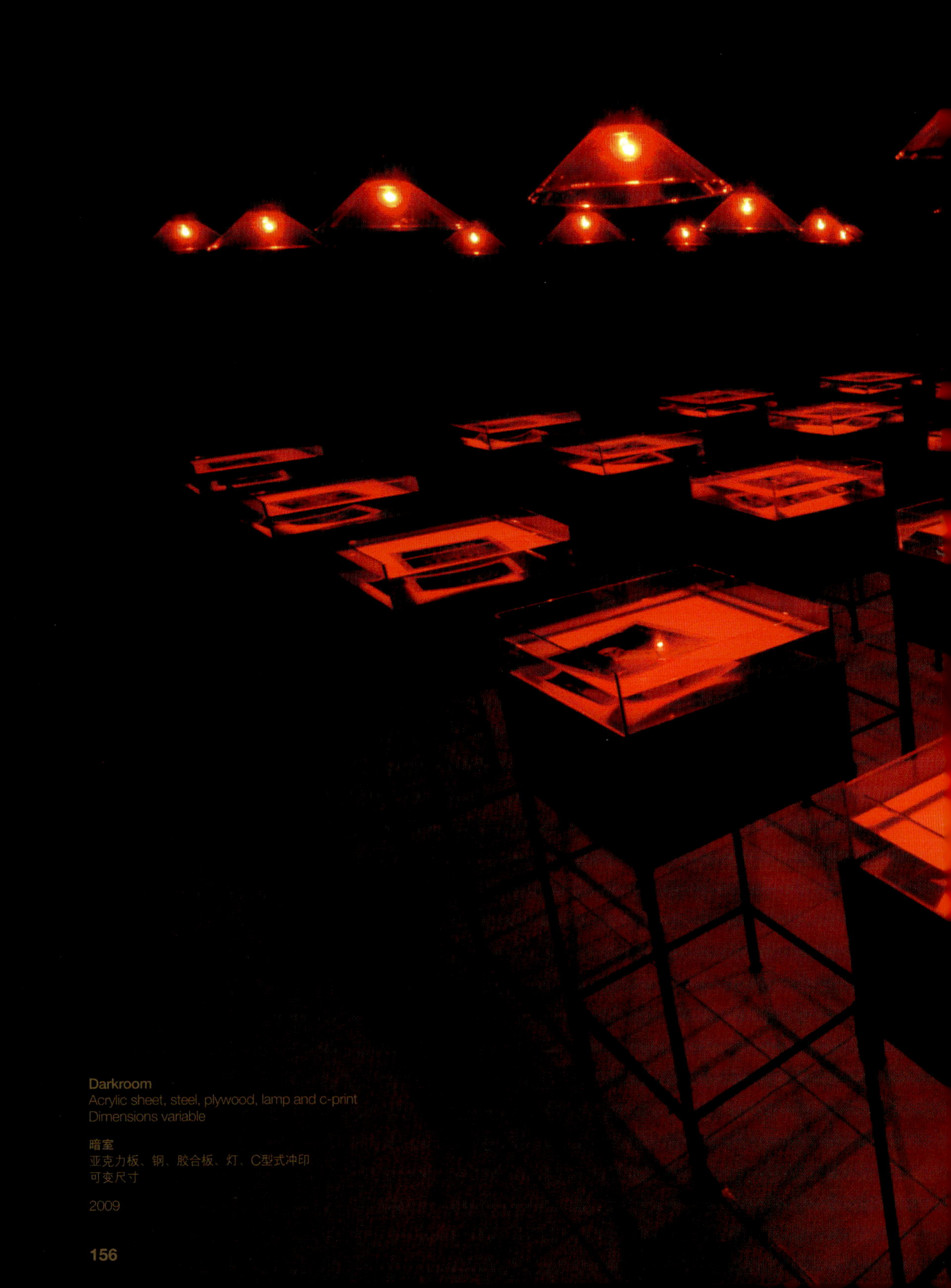

Darkroom
Acrylic sheet, steel, plywood, lamp and c-print
Dimensions variable

暗室
亚克力板、钢、胶合板、灯、C型式冲印
可变尺寸

2009

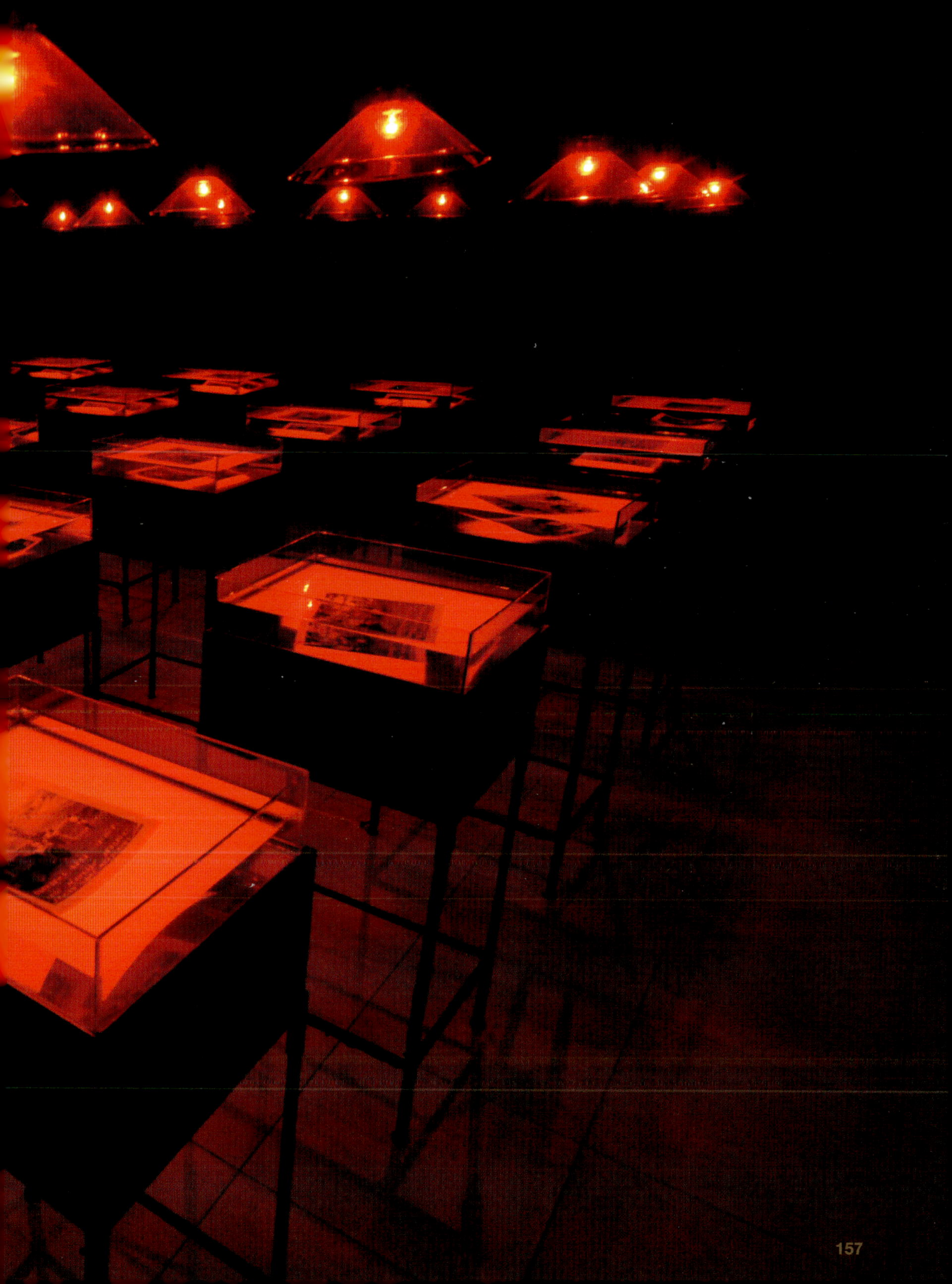

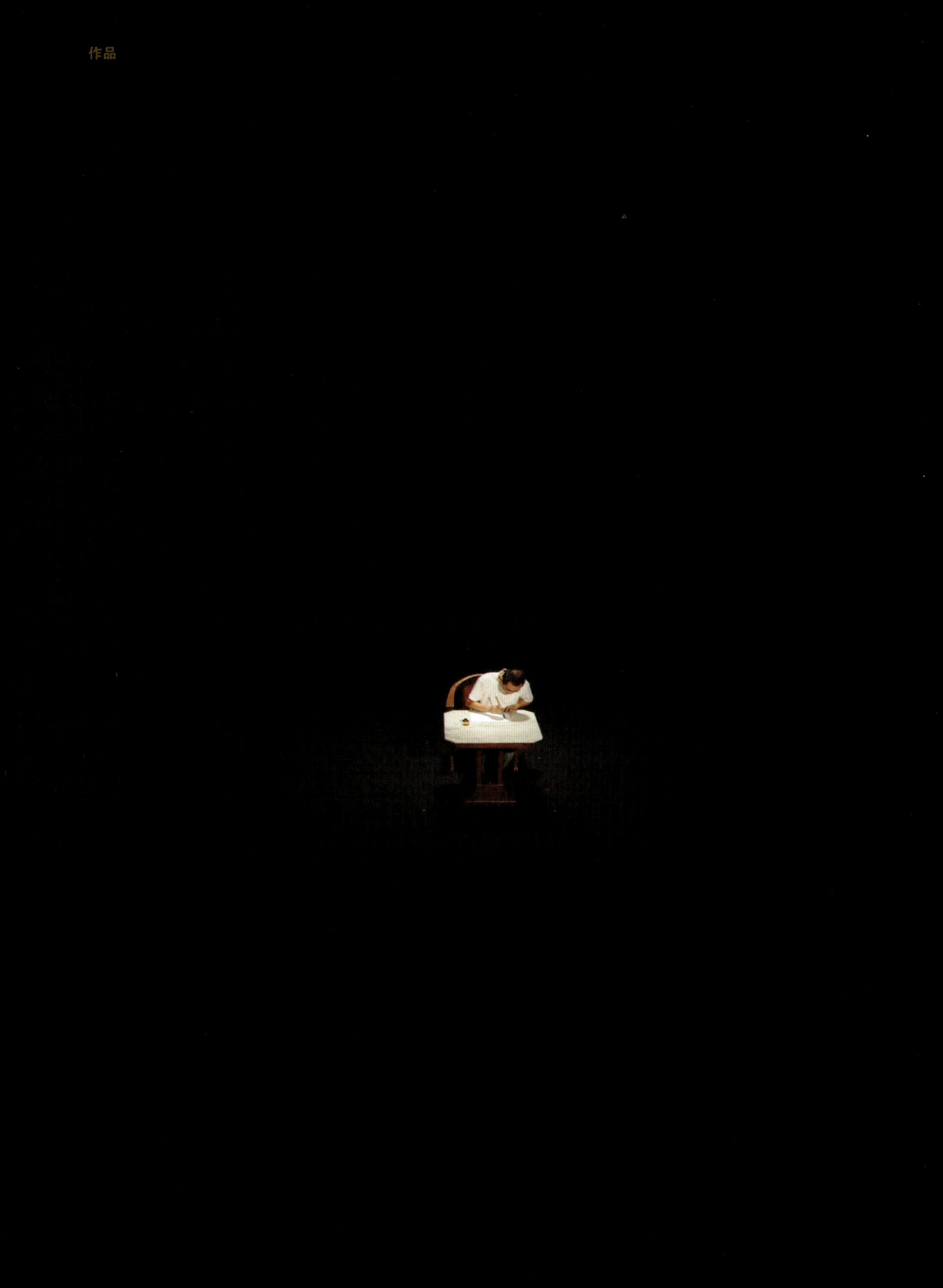

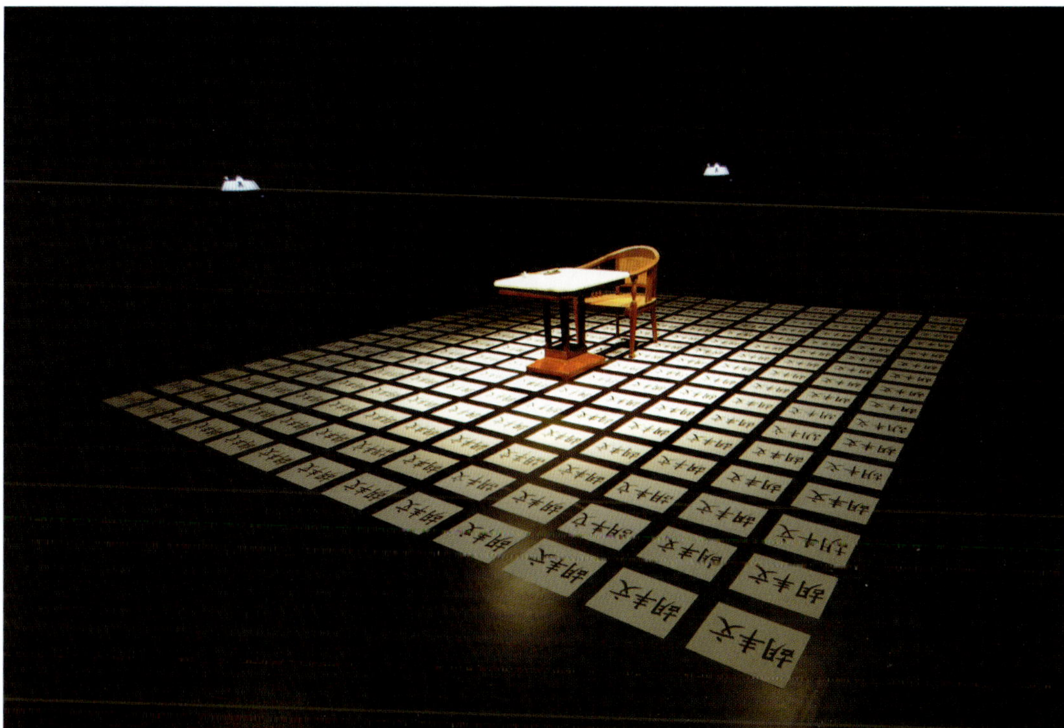

Rewriting The Erased
Video Performance / Installation
3 channels video, paper, Chinese ink, wooden chair and table, marble
Dimensions variable

擦掉重写
录像行为 / 装置
3频录像、纸、墨、木椅、木桌、大理石
可变尺寸

2009

Ndudah/Digging
Documentary video

挖
纪录片

21'20"
2009

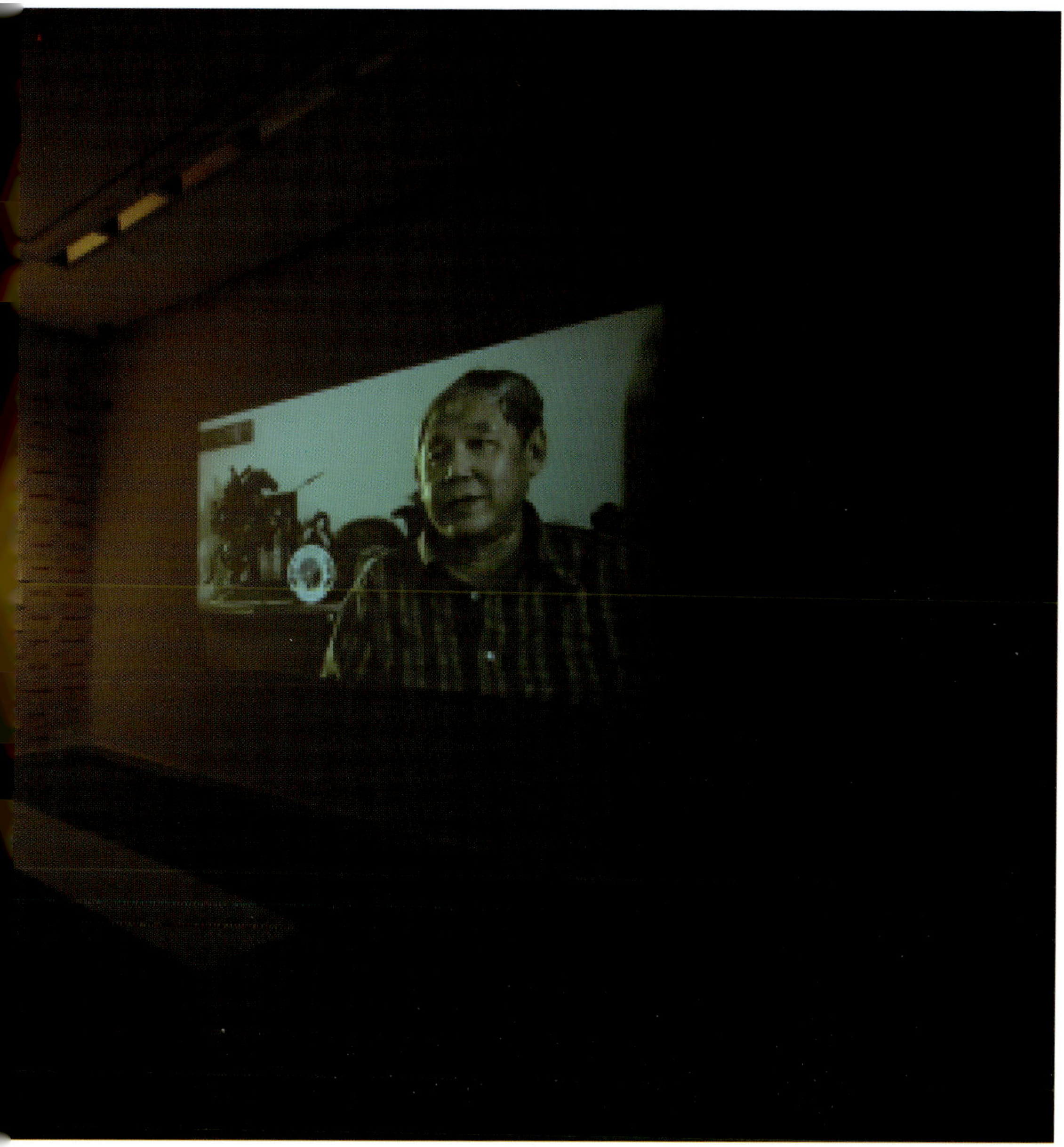

Budi Kustarto

布迪·库斯塔图

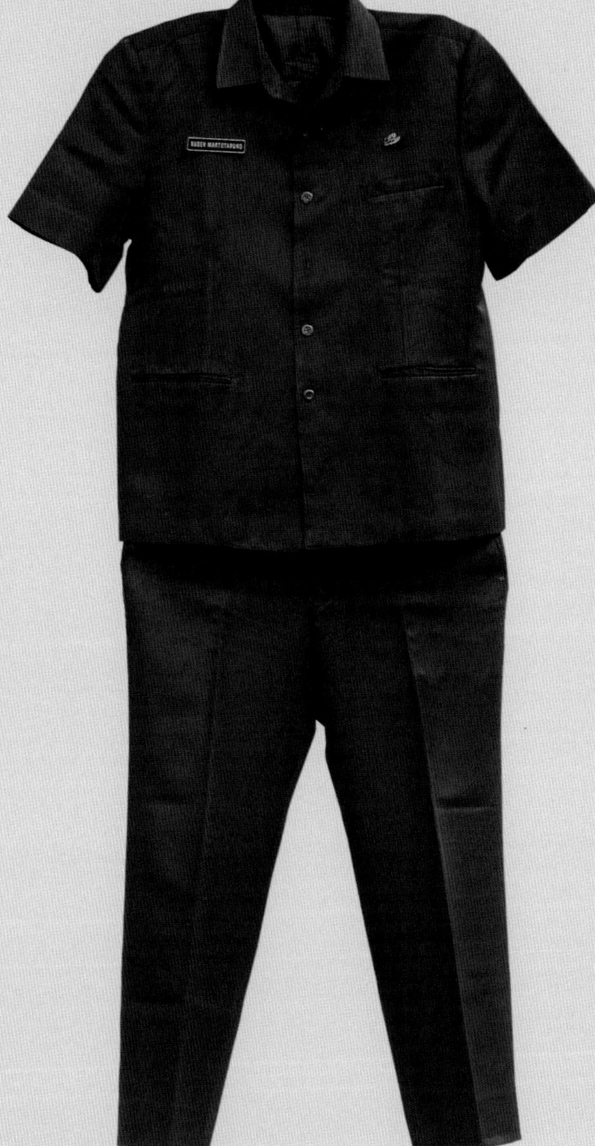

During the Suharto era, my parents were teachers in a government-run elementary school for which they were paid a minimum wage. They struggled to make a living for their four kids. My father was a fighter; a hard working headmaster moving from one place to another in order to develop different schools, and so too was my mother. They sacrificed a lot for us.
Growing up, I looked up to them as they were going through these difficult times. Their determination, honesty, goodness and loyalty has touched me, and the virtue of which has become an important part of my life since birth.

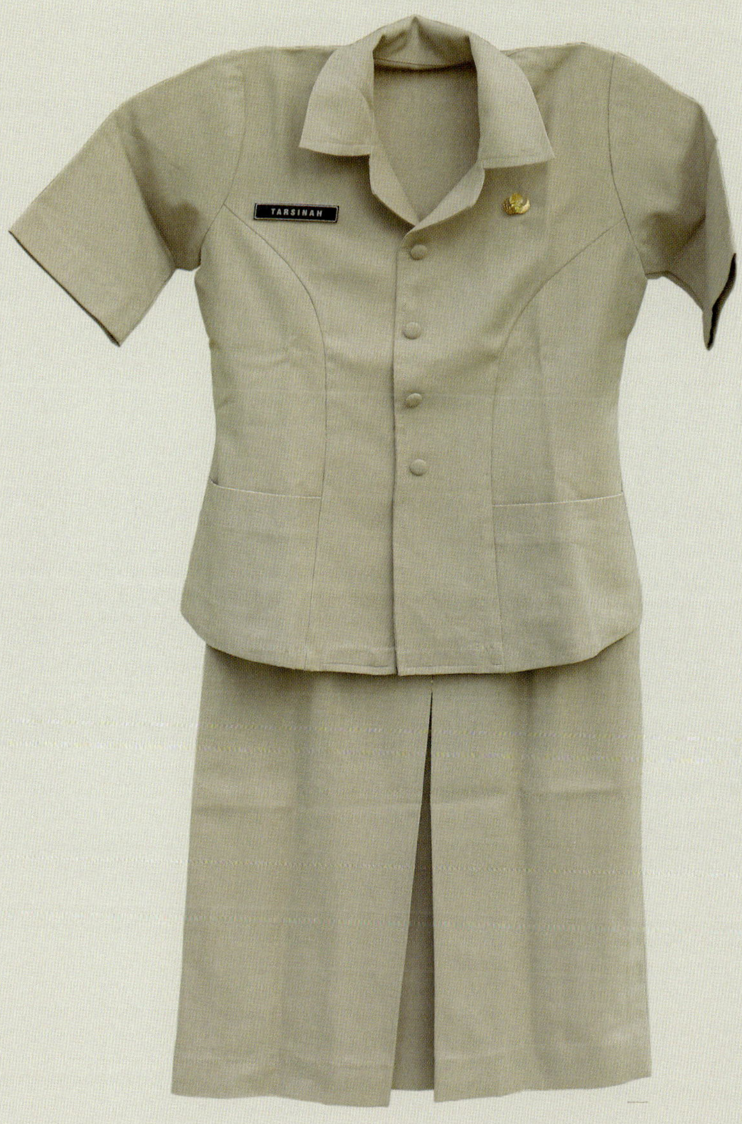

在苏哈托时代，我的父母在政府创办的小学里担任教师，当时他们的工资是按照最低标准支付的，非常有限。他们努力工作养活四个孩子。我的父亲是一个工作狂，他是一个努力工作的校长，从一个职位调度到另一个职位以发展不同的学校，而我的母亲也是如此。他们为我们牺牲了很多。
随着年龄的增长，我看着他们如何经过了不同的困难时期。他们的决心、他们的正直、他们的善良和忠诚感动着我，这些美德从我出生以来就成为我生命中重要的一部分。

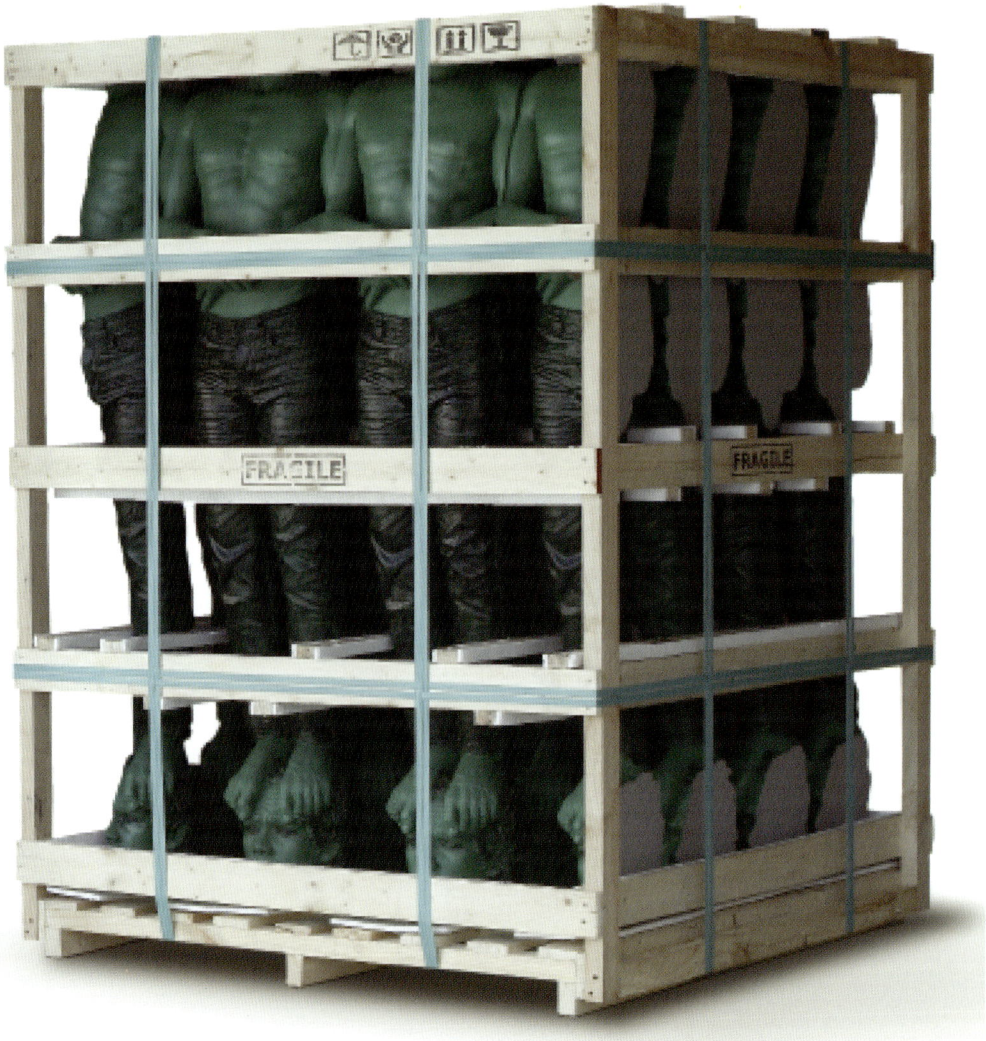

On The Move
Fiberglass, wood

行进中
玻璃纤维、木材

183×135×133cm
2010

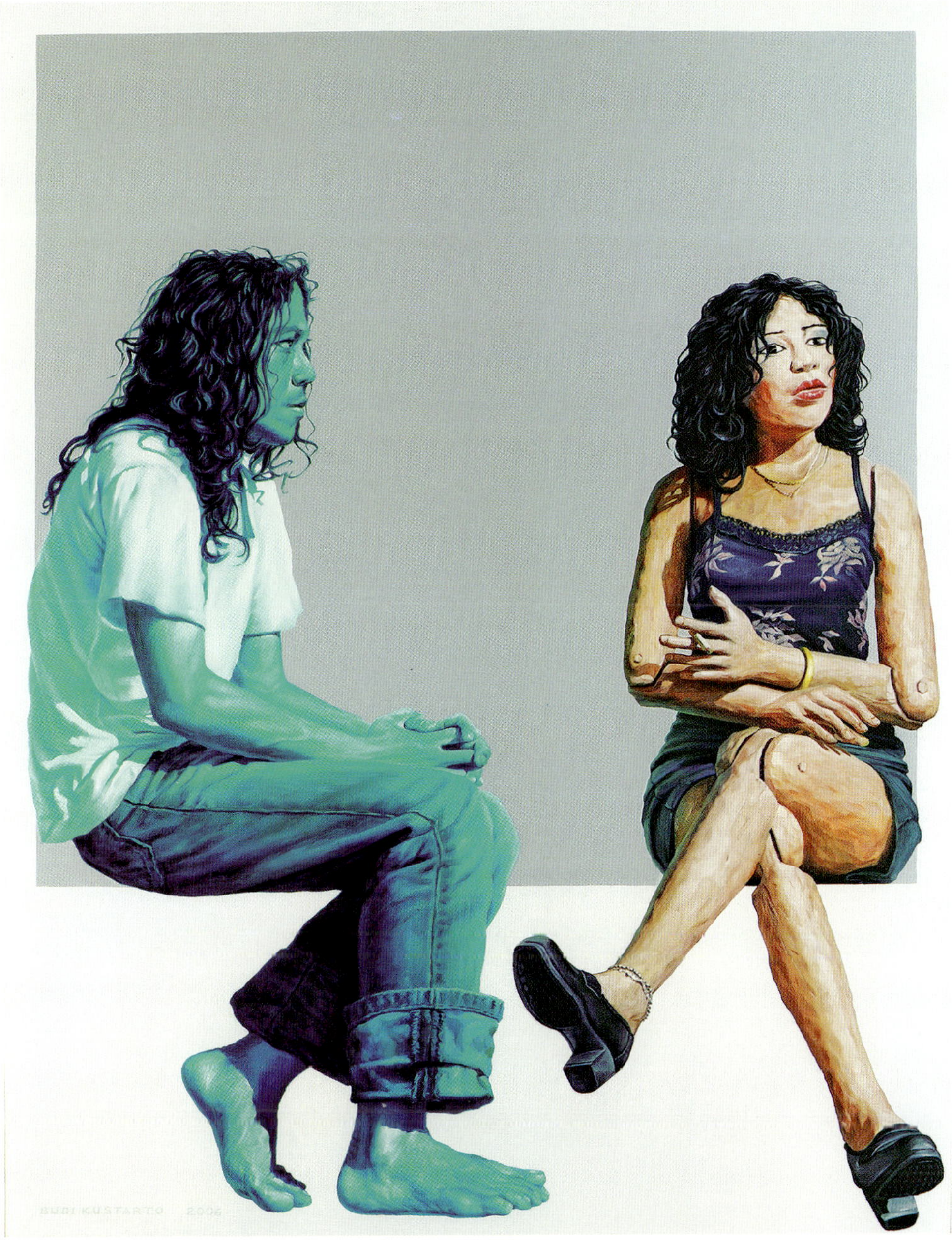

Married Me
Oil and acrylic on canvas
OHD Museum collection, Magelang

嫁给我
布面丙烯油画
印尼马格朗OHD博物馆馆藏

200×150cm
2006

Jompet Kuswidananto
琼佩特・库斯伟达纳托

Interview with Jompet Kuswidananto

Garasi Theatre Stage, Yogyakarta
June 2010

Jompet Kuswidananto: **J**

Biljana Ciric: **B**

B: When did you start getting involved in the art scene?

J: After I finished my diploma in 1999. Around that time I also started getting a bit bored with my music because I lost my platform, I lost my audiences, and I was exiled from my environment. So I started to think about how to make a new platform, to develop new audiences. And I started to make sound performances. I worked with Wenza for 2 years and we made sound and video performances together. Then one day, a visual arts gallery in Singapore, Plastic Kinetic Worm, invited me to join an exhibition and that was the first time my work was curated in the context of the visual arts.

B: Why has the artifact had such a big impact on your work?

J: My reading of Javanese history is more focused on the ways that Javanese culture negotiated

琼佩特 库斯伟达纳托 访谈

Garasi剧团舞台，日惹
2010年6月

琼佩特・库斯伟达纳托：**J**

比利安娜：**B**

B: 什么时候开始涉足艺术领域?

J: 在1999年毕业后，我当时开始觉得再这样做音乐有点无聊，因为离开了学校就意味着失去了自己的舞台、自己的观众，感觉自己已被排除在外。所以自然而然的我开始寻找新的舞台，新的观众。我开始做声音表演。跟Wenza合作了两年，一起做声音和录像表演。有一天一个叫做“活动的塑料虫”的新加坡空间邀请我参加一个展览，这是第一次我的声音表演出现在视觉艺术领域。

B: 为什么手工制品对你的作品影响这么大?

J: 我对爪哇历史的阅读主要集中在爪哇文化与各种不同的外来文化的碰撞与结合。我们有悠久的与外部世界交流的历史。这个现实改变了今天的爪哇文化，所以与其它外来文化碰撞、融合的结果在很大程度上构造了今天的印尼。对我而言这个

the various incoming cultures. We have a very long history of being connected worldwide. It has changed the shape of Javanese culture today, and the way that Javanese culture negotiated the incoming cultures also really shaped Indonesia today. For me it's really important. I found that the idea behind this, or one of the basic methods for negotiating incoming cultures, was especially present in the uniforms of the royal army. And not only in the uniform, but in the roles, the music, the way they hold their ceremonies. I mean, these are excerpts of this larger negotiation.

B: Are you still working on the Java project?

J: Yes, Java Machine, the piece with the royal army uniforms. It addresses the beginning of the modern era in Java, the social and political background at the beginning of the 19th century. I work a lot with that time period, but now I'm trying to see it in perspective of today. Not only in Java but also in Indonesia.

B: What's your vantage point on at history today?

J: I think I have many vantage points, because I try to conduct research in many different places. Different places have different vantage points.

B: Can you tell me about your recent research for example?

J: I am conducting research for a theater Garasi production. It's deeply connected with my visual art project. It's about the production of the third reality. If you remember the title of my work for the Asia Art Award in Seoul, it was "Cortege of the Third Realm." So the idea is to look at how the Indonesian community survived in their existence, in light of the interference of many different cultures since the world has become so open. What the community does is create a new reality, and that's what I call the third reality. The history of Indonesia is a history of transi-

很重要。我找到一个最基本的由碰撞融合带来的结果，这一结果最好的表现在了皇家军队的制服上。而这些现象不仅只在制服(的演变)中可以找到，并且在音乐、举行仪式的方式等等都可以发现。而这些都只是文化碰撞融合的局部案例。

B: 你还在延续爪哇的项目吗?

J: 对。爪哇机器，皇家军队的制服。其实它标志着19世纪初现代爪哇的形成，它的社会和政治背景的建立。我研究这段时期很久了，但是我在考虑从今天的社会框架去重新看待它。不仅仅是爪哇，而是整个印尼。

B: 那么今天看待的历史，你的出发点在哪儿?

J: 我想我的出发点很多，因为我一直在想办法去很多地方作考察。不同的地域肯定有不一样的出发点。

B: 能否谈一下你最近的研究项目?

J: 我在做一个研究，关于Garasi剧场的制作。这与我的视觉艺术作品密切相关。尝试探讨制造第三种现实。如果你记得我在首尔参加亚洲艺术大奖时的那件作品，叫做《第三领域的行列》。整个想法是在试图审视印尼的社群在如此开放的全球化大环境中如何在各种不同的文化的干扰和冲击下继续生存。而群体在做的正制造着一个新的现实，这个新的现实被我称做“第三现实”。印尼的现代史是一部从殖民到后殖民、从传统到现代、从农业化到工业化的历史。

这个长长的转变的过程一直在持续，而且我可以说印尼总是在转变中。正是这样的一种状态我认为印尼在塑造一种新的现实。

B: 在印尼作为艺术家意味着什么?

tions from colonial to post-colonial, tradition to modern, from agricultural to industrial. It is a long transition that goes on and on, and I can say that Indonesia is always in transition. From this kind of situation I think that Indonesia has created a new reality.

B: What does it mean to be an artist in Indonesia?

J: Being an artist in Indonesia is a kind of privileged position. Almost whatever you do is right, because if you look back at the traditional art in Indonesia, the artist is more like a priest. For example, the shadow puppet master, he is the highest level of priest. From that kind of tradition, being an artist now in Indonesia is a privilege. Whatever you do is right. People give you more space. People give you more time to understand what you say.

Being in this kind of third reality, for me, it's not only an artist's problem. It's a natural problem for all people. I'm an artist, so I try to express it through art. I think that it is as simple as this. This kind of situation, in the gray area of production and the third reality, is becoming the situation for most of the Indonesian people, and is actually shaping the identity of Indonesia.

B: Can you talk about the third reality project more?

J: My project related to the third reality is also the project for the theater group that I am collaborating on with Garasi. It was actually inspired by the theory about the Third Body, a discussion about small-scale cultural negotiations… I am not good at quoting theory.

J: 在印尼，艺术家是处于一个特权的位置。差不多就是你做什么都是对的。如果你回头看看印尼的传统艺术，印尼的艺术家就如同祭司。比如，以前表演皮影戏的艺术家就是最高等级的祭司。因为有这样的传统，今天的艺术家就是有特权。你做什么都是对的。人会跟你更大的空间。人们会花跟多的时间听你说的话。

B: 你能再聊一下“第三现实”的项目吗?

J: 我与Garasi剧团的合作与我的“第三现实”也有关。是从“第三身体”的理论得到了启发，探讨在小范围内的文化碰撞与融合……我并不是一位好的理论引用者。

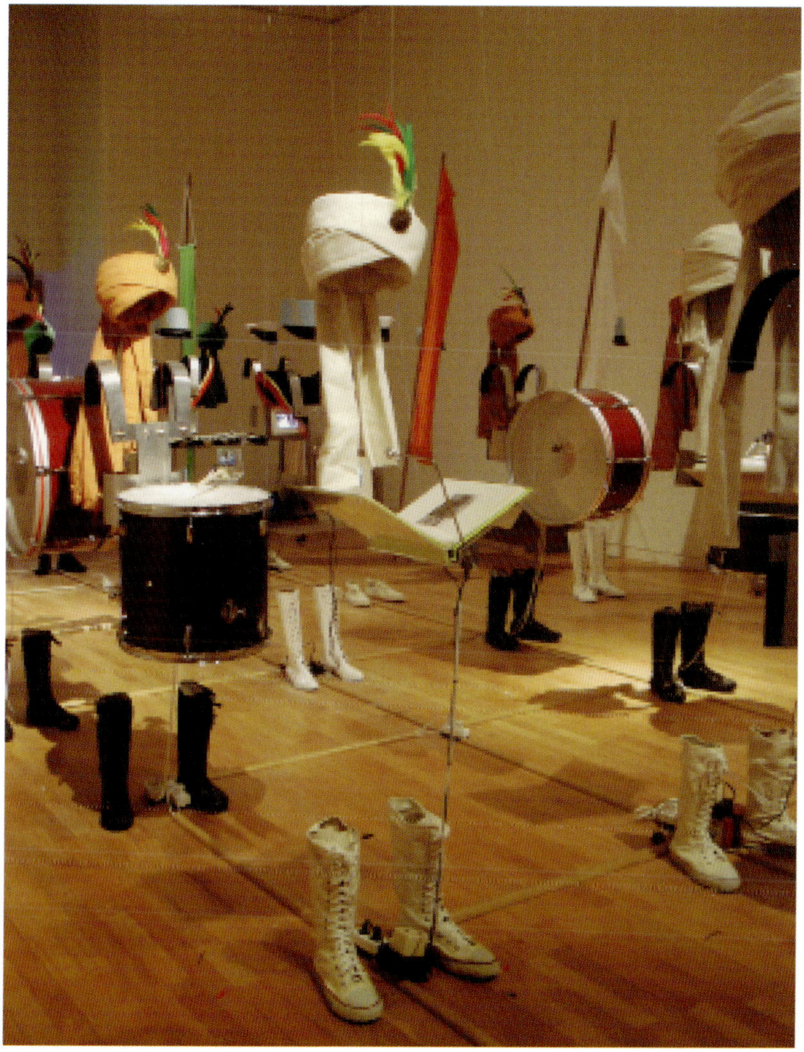

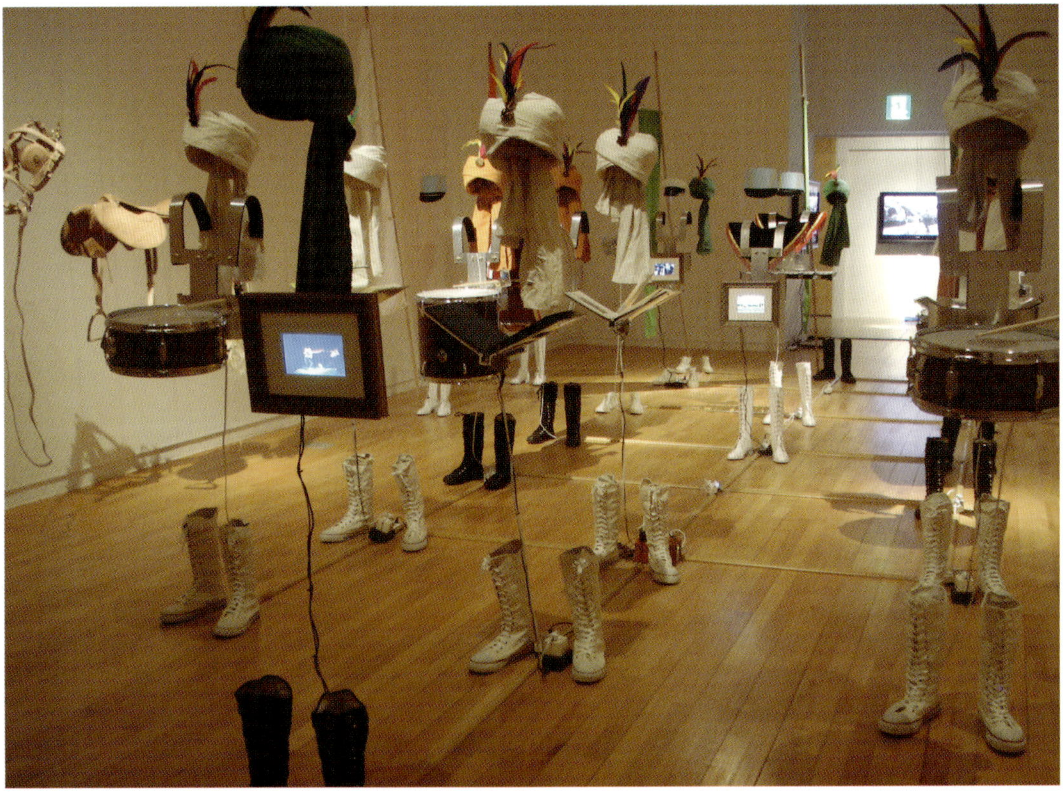

Cortege Of The Third Realm
Installation, 24 lifesize figures

第三领域的行列
装置，24个真人尺寸形象

2010

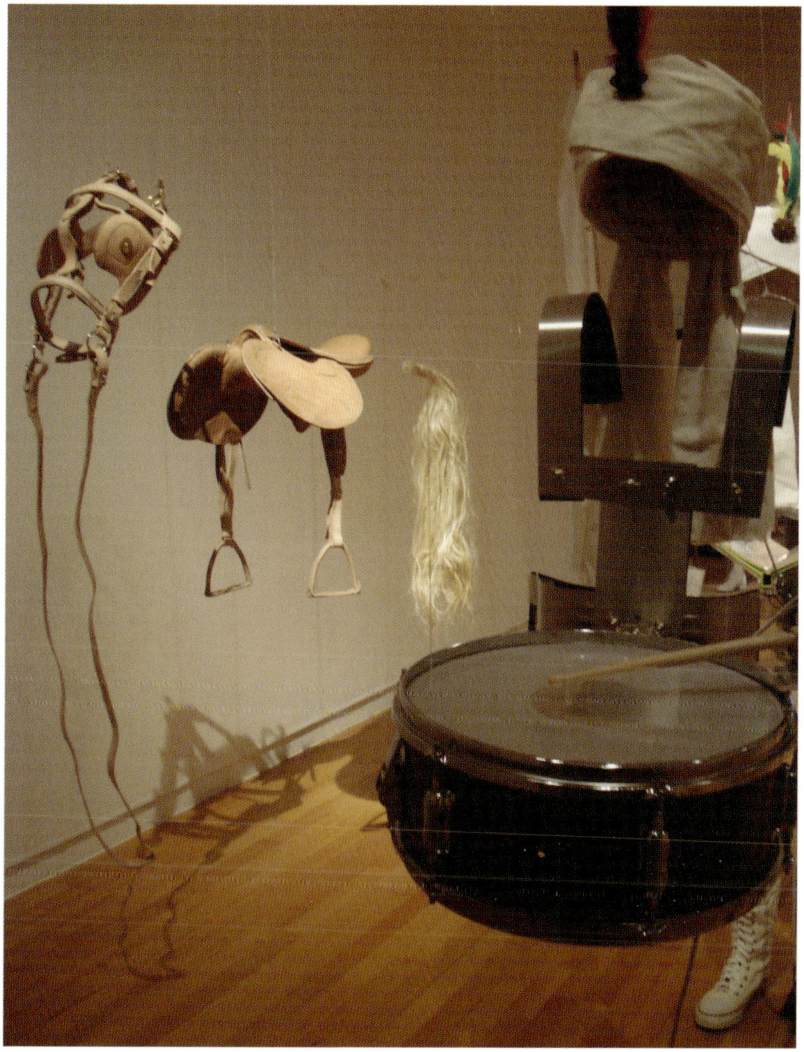

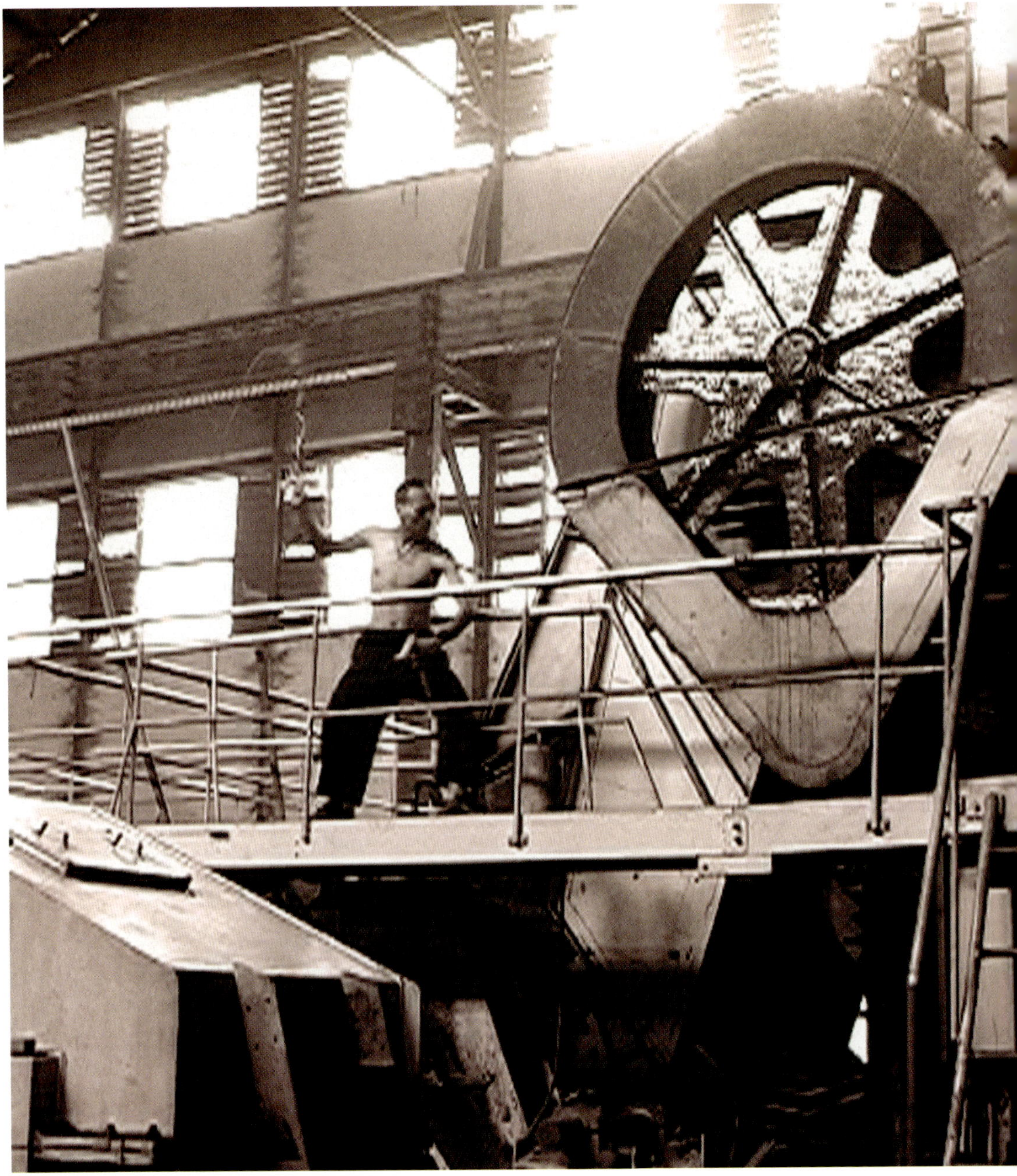

War Of Java, Do You Remember? #2
Single channel video

你记得爪哇战争吗？#2
单视频录像

5.48', loop/循环播放
2008

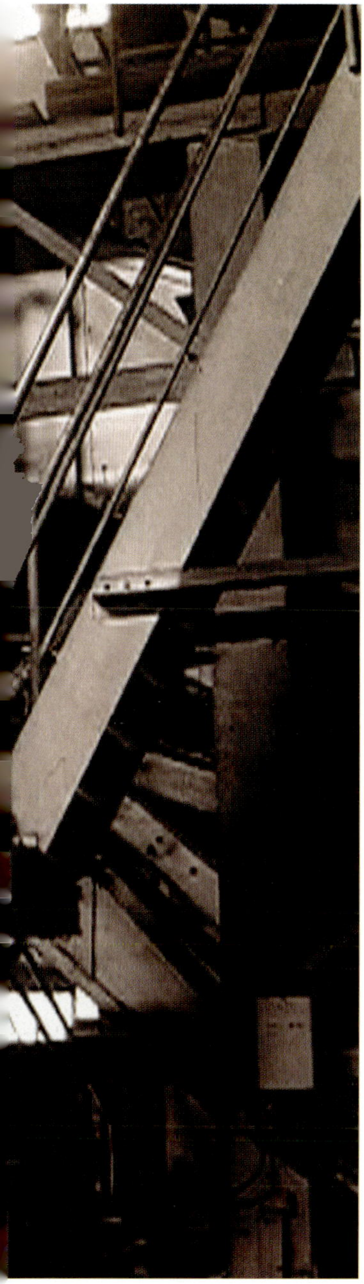

Rudi Mantofani
鲁迪·曼度凡尼

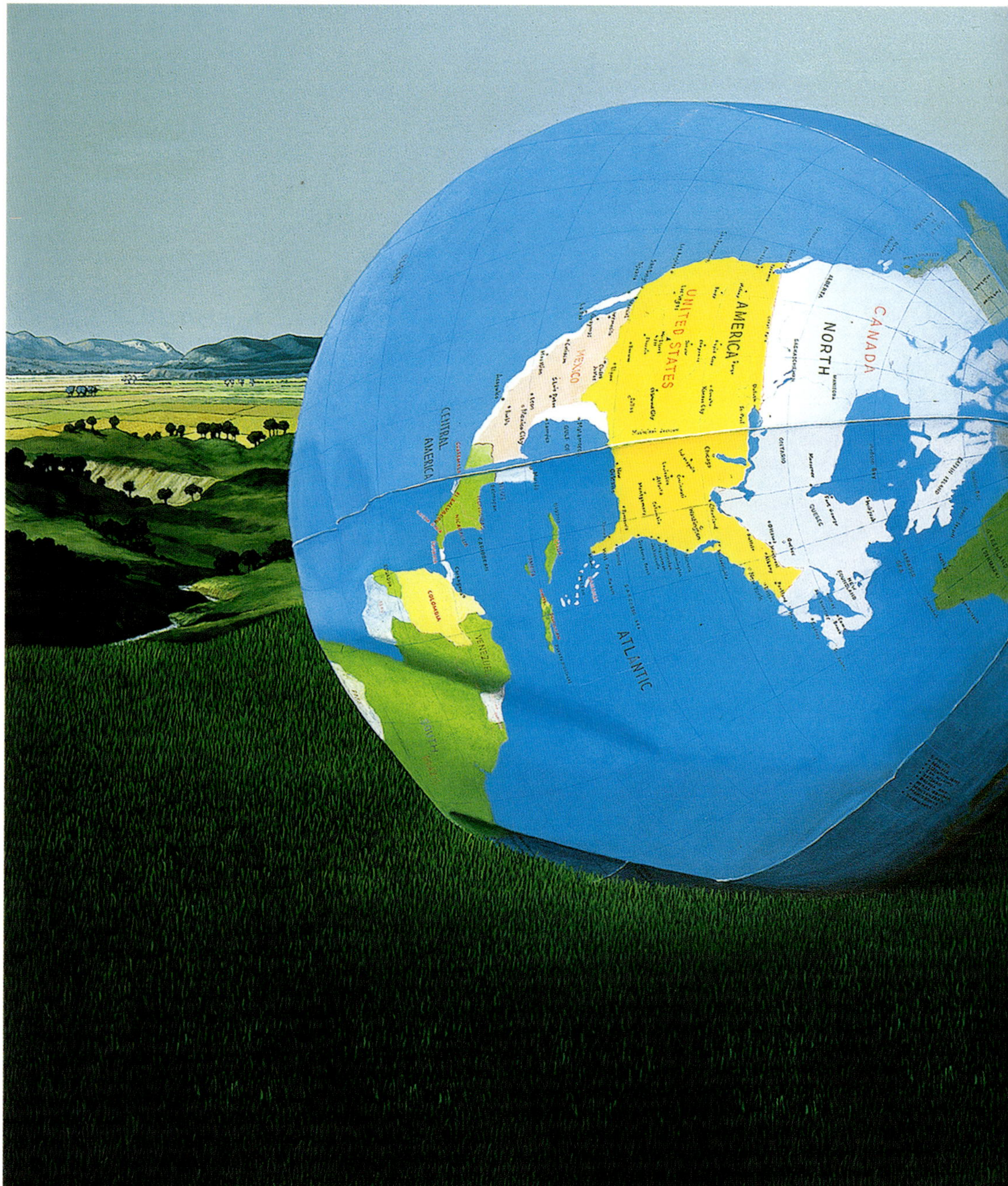
AMERICA
UNITED STATES
NORTH
CANADA
MEXICO
CENTRAL AMERICA
ATLANTIC

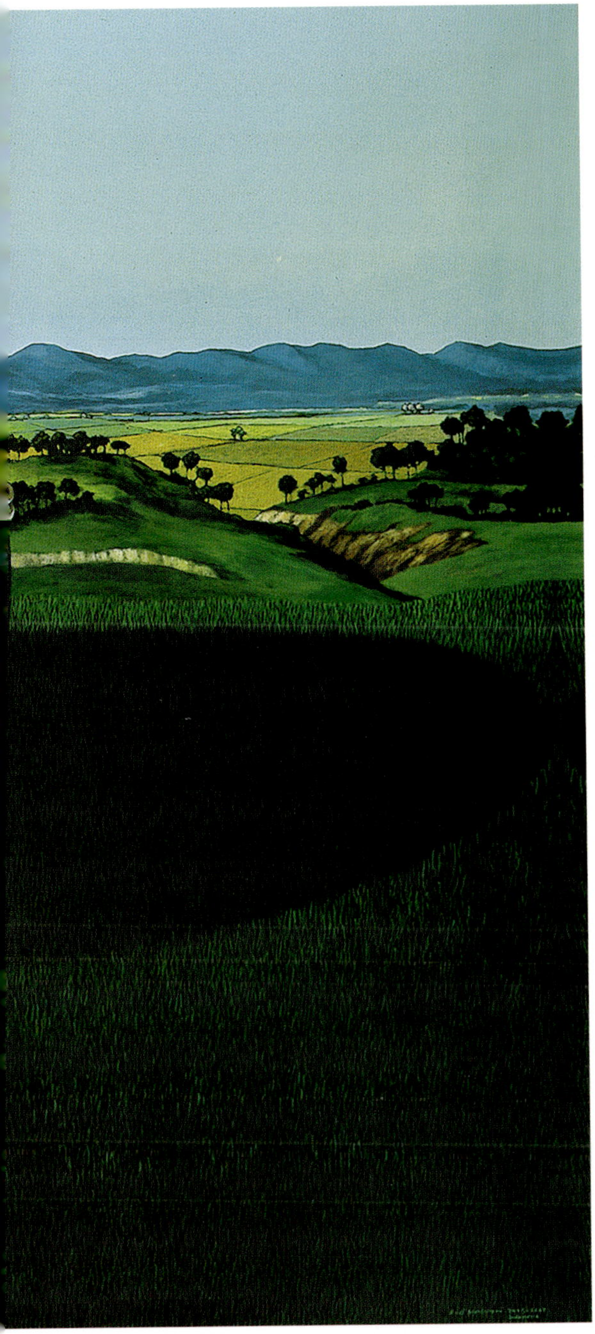

Globe Falls Down onto Earth
Acrylic on canvas
Collection of Mrs. Poppy H. Setiawan, Jakarta

全球倒在地球上
布面丙烯
雅加达Poppy H. Setiawan女士私人藏品

145 x 195cm
2005

The World Falling onto Earth
Mixed media

世界掉到了地上
综合材料

290×240×150cm
2009

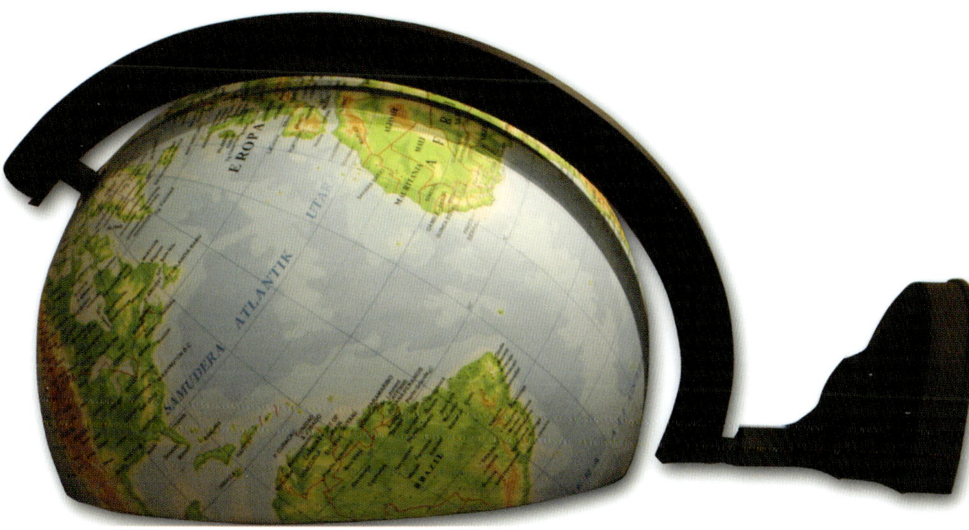
EROPA
SAMUDERA
ATLANTIK
UTAR

I Nyoman Masriadi
米斯尼亚迪

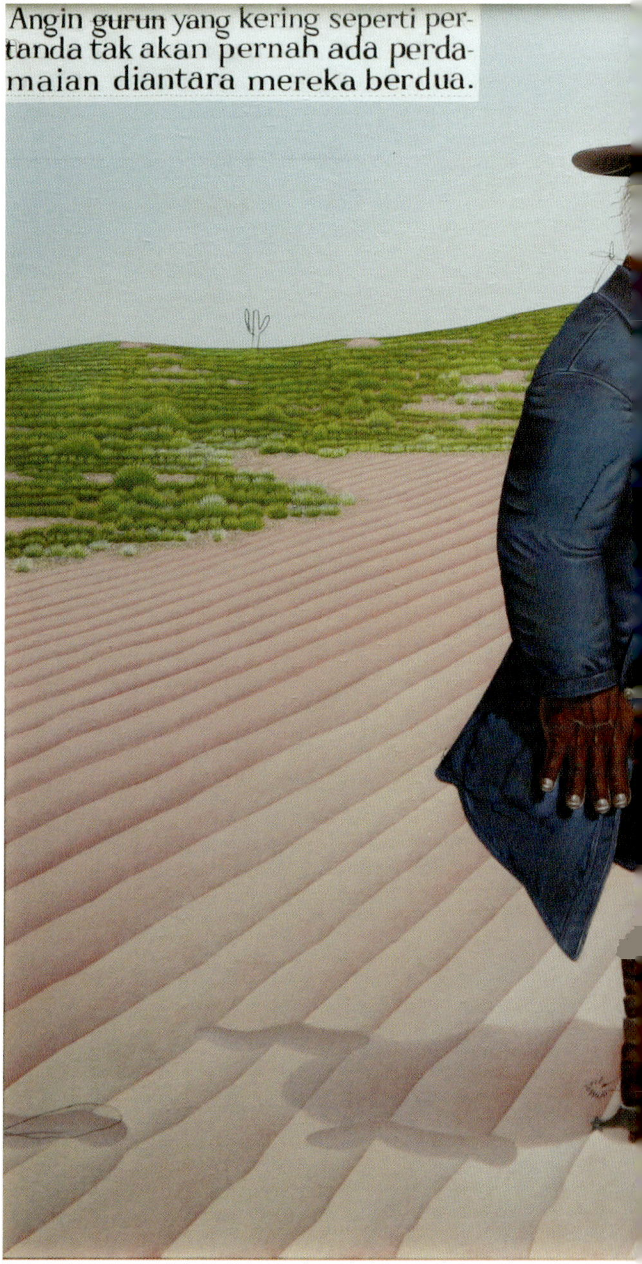

Negotiation
Oil on Canvas

协商
布面油画

300×200cm
2008

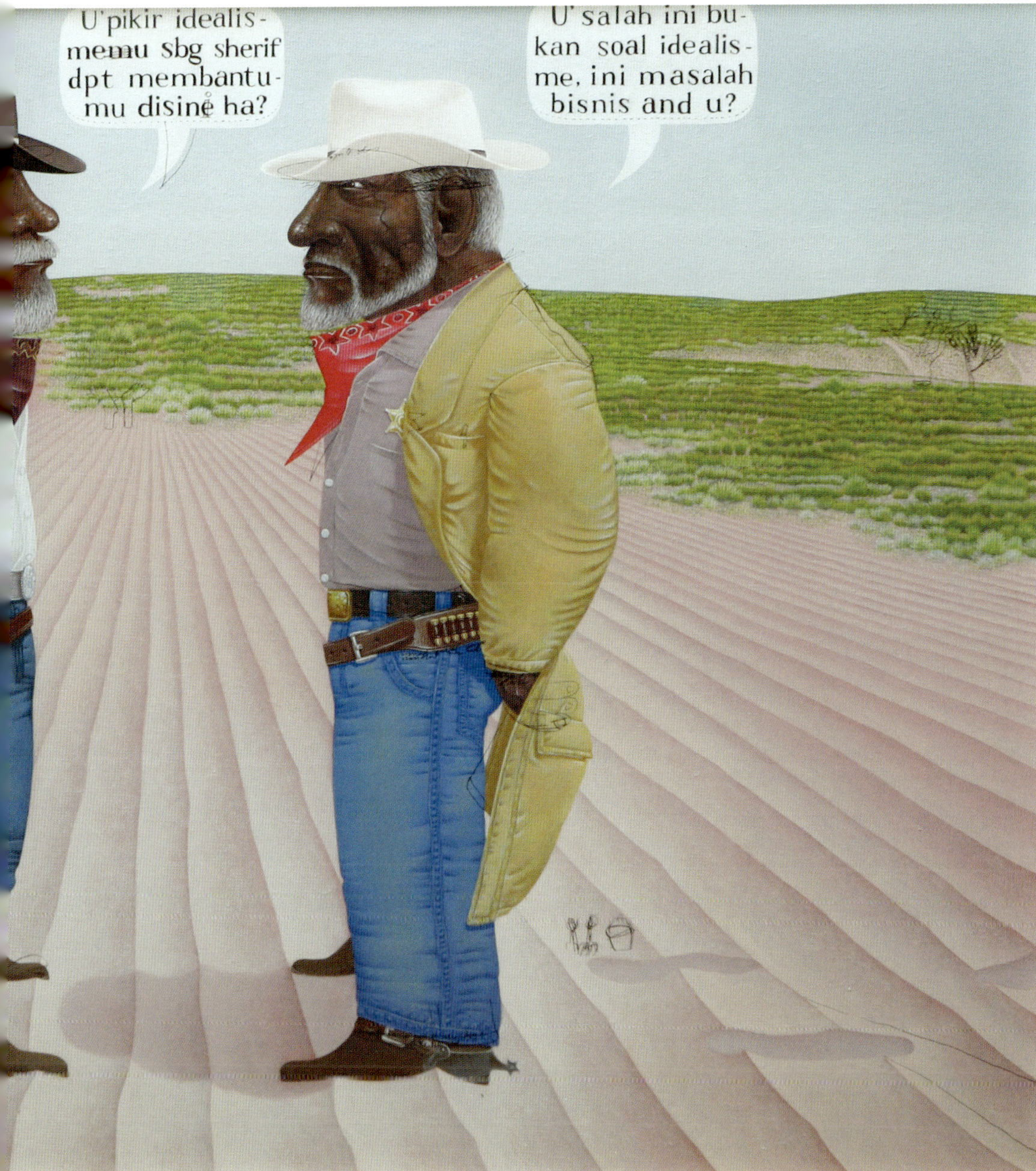
U'pikir idealis-memu sbg sherif dpt membantu-mu disine ha?
U'salah ini bu-kan soal idealis-me, ini masalah bisnis and u?

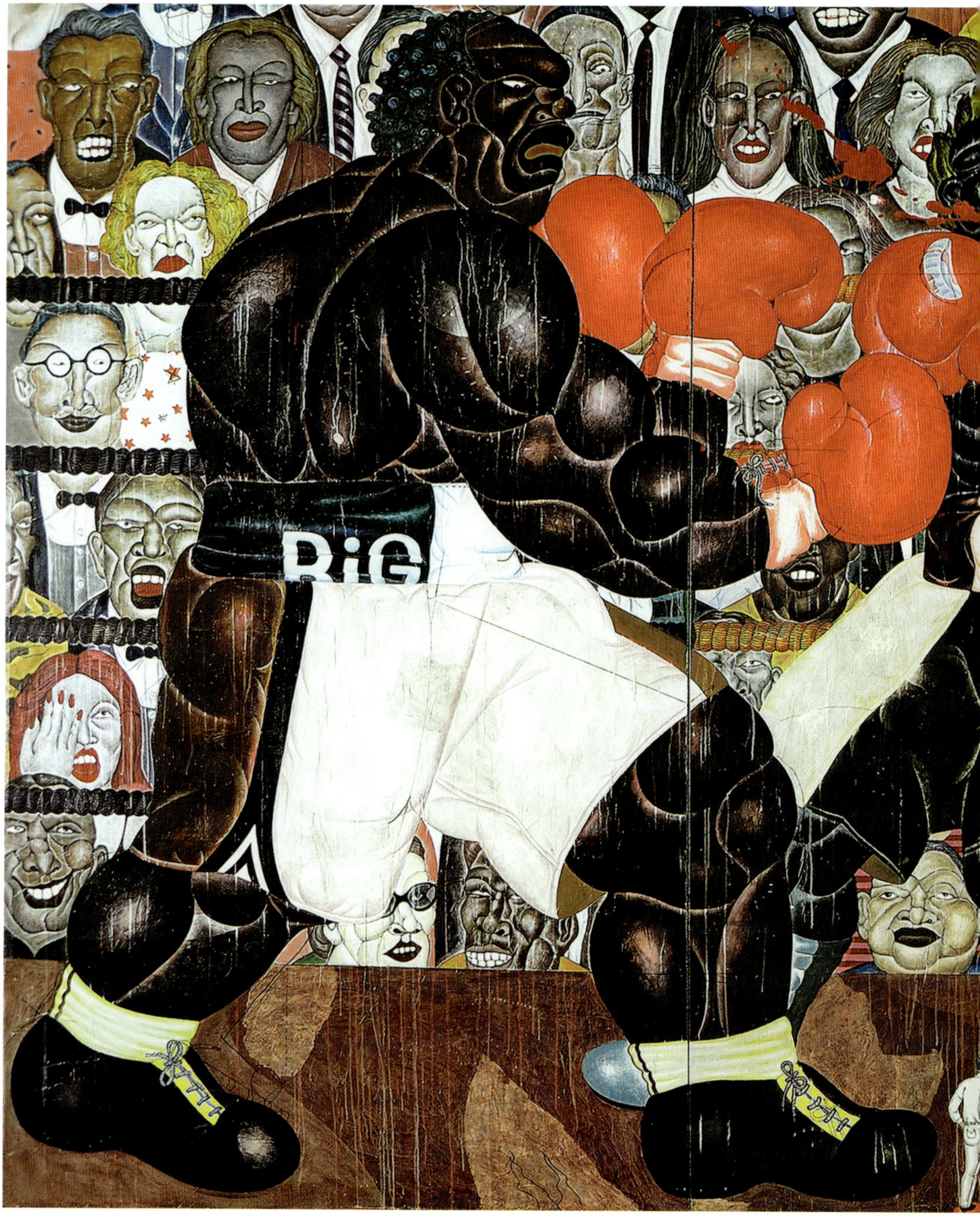

The Man from Bantul: The Final Round
Mixed media on canvas
Private collection

来自班图的人：最终回
布面综合材料
私人藏品

250×435cm (triptych / 三联)
2000

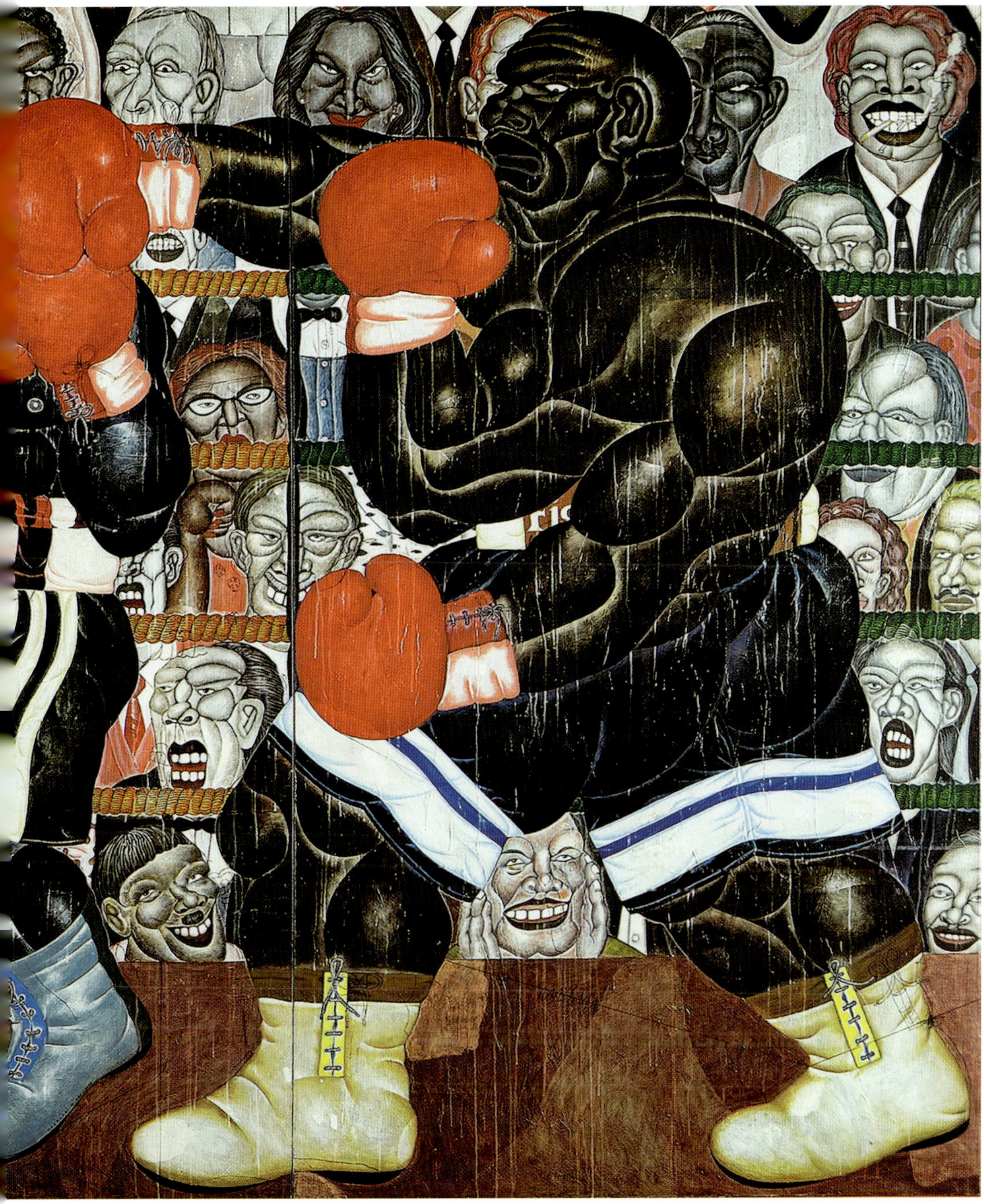

Nasirun S.Sn
那室兰 S.Sn

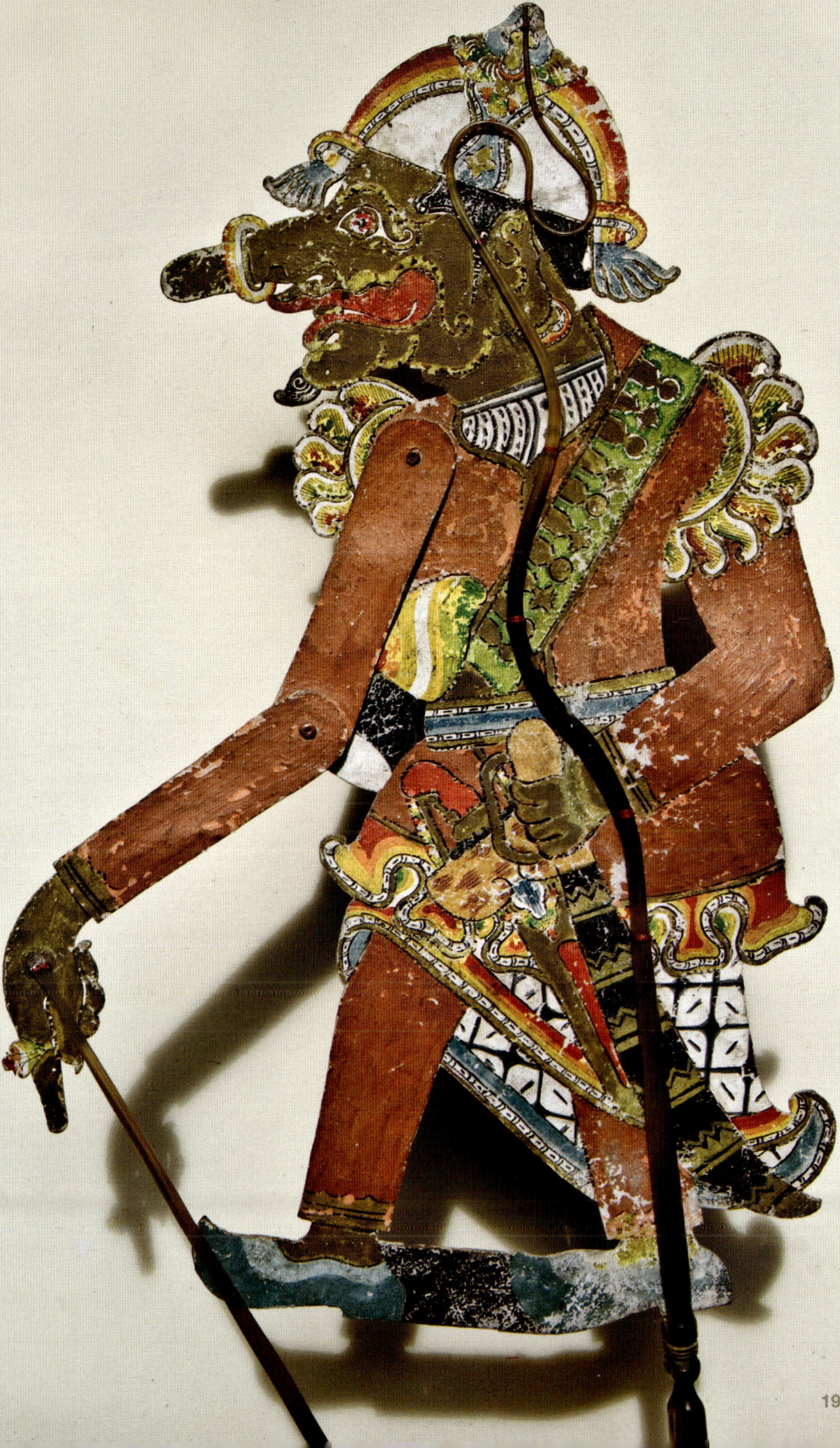

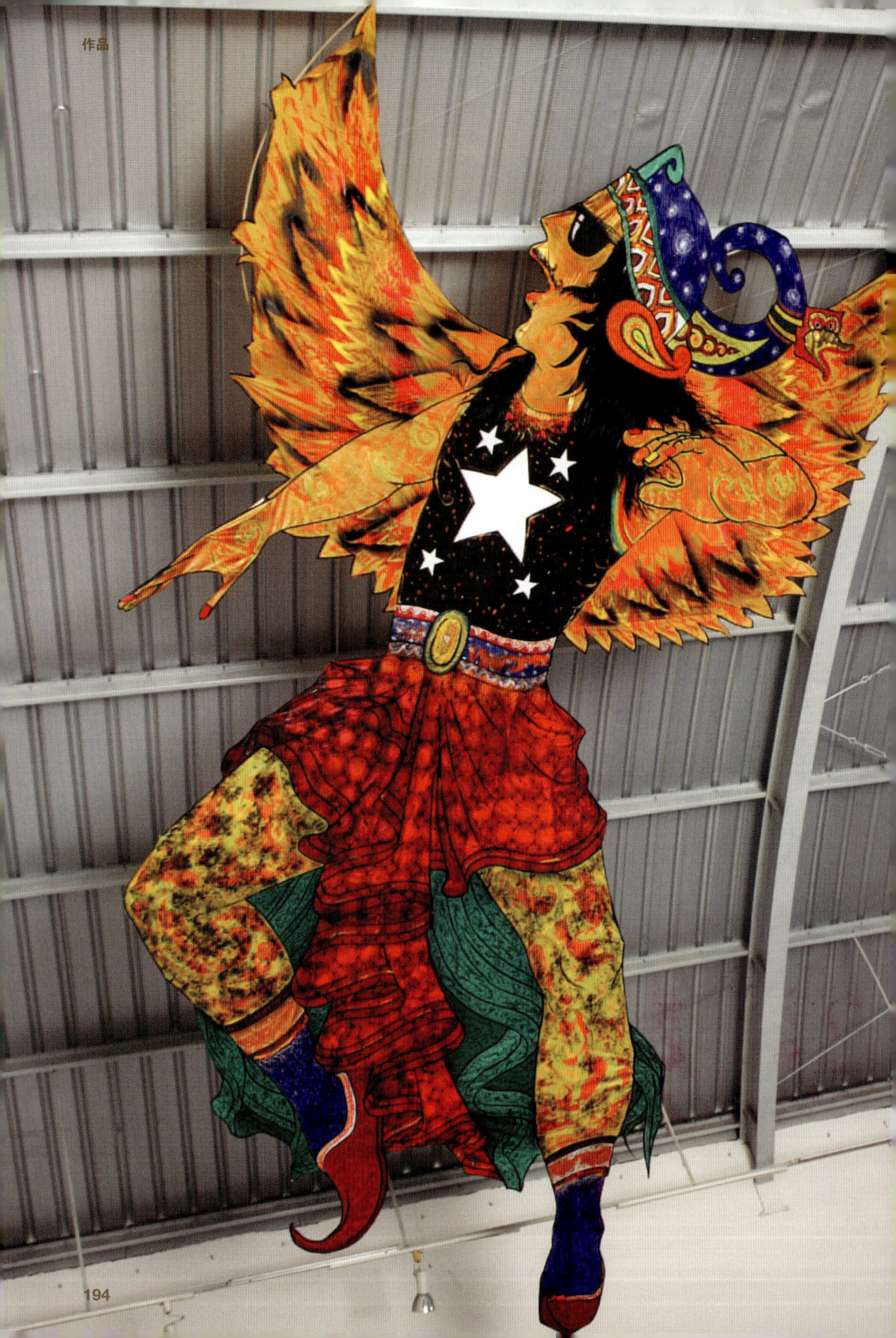

Wayang Republik

木偶共和国

200×800cm
2009

Garin Nugroho
加林・努格罗

Interview with Garin Nugroho

Sultan Hotel, Jakarta
June 2010

Garin Nugroho: **G**

Biljana Ciric: **B**

B: I read that you started working on documentaries.

G: I started making documentaries in the beginning, and writing film criticism as well. While I was still a student at the Jakarta Institute of the Art I made documentaries for UNICEF and many other foreign organizations working on environmental and social issues. I started making documentaries in 1983, and step-by-step started working on my own documentaries.

B: And you were in school at that time?

G: Yes, I was studying for two different majors: in the law school, and at the Jakarta Institute of Art as a cinema major. At that time my family only gave me money for one of the schools so I had to find money to support my cinema studies.

B: How did you pay for cinema school?

加林·努格罗访谈

苏丹酒店，雅加达
2010年6

加林·努格罗访：**G**

比利安娜：**B**

B: 你是做纪录片入行的对吗?

G: 我最初做纪录片，也写些影评。在雅加达艺术学院念书时，我为联合国儿童基金会和许多境外机构制作了环境和社会题材的纪录片。1983年的片子是我的处女作，然后我开始逐步创作自己的纪录片。

B: 那时你还在上学吗?

G: 是的，我修读了两个专业，一个是法律，另一个是雅加达艺术学院的电影学，但家人只能负担一个专业的学费，所以我只有挣钱才能继续学习电影。

B: 那么你是怎么挣学费的呢?

G: 我自己找了些工作，比如为联合国儿童基金会或

G: I was looking for jobs, like the one to make the documentary for UNICEF or some other agricultural organization, so I could go to many of the islands of Indonesia. For example, I did one about Komodo Island—that was my first job—and had a column in Kompas, the best newspaper in Indonesia for writing on film.

B: So since the early 80s you started getting involved in the art and film scene in Indonesia?

G: Yes, but I made my first feature film in 1990. But ten years before, I was active in film criticism and the film industry.

B: How were the films in Indonesia in the 80s?

G: I think this was the era when the economy and military were working closely together—how do you call it—it means something like the era of oil, when the price of oil was very high, and the economy of Indonesia rested on the oil industry with very strong government control. Each time when the military was strong and the economy was strong, then the country looked very strong. But that was the time of the golden era of cinema. There was production of over a hundred films per year, however, the censorship was also very strong. I think that time was one of the best for cinema, and the distribution wasn't yet monopolized. Every island had its own distribution, like Kalimantan, Sumatra, and Java. That was the golden era of cinema in the 1980s. The popular culture was very different then. We had very famous novelists, local comics; we had so many icons of popular culture; we had a new species of art centers, and this was the first era of what I call the new transition in art.

The cinema, art, performance art, and popular culture developed as a result of the good economic conditions. But you saw the content of the art, how they criticized the government indirectly, not directly. I started making a feature film in the time of crisis, when the oil prices fell and

者农业机构制作纪录片。为了拍片我还有机会去了许多印尼的小岛，制作科莫多岛的纪录片是我得到的第一份工作。我还为印尼发行量最大的报纸《罗盘报》撰写电影专栏。

B: 也就是说80年代初你就开始踏入印尼的电影界了？

G: 是的，但我直到1990年才完成了第一部故事片，那之前的十年我活跃于影评界，专注于电影产业的发展。

B: 那是反映80年代印尼的电影吗？

G: 80年代是中心话题是经济和军权。那是石油的时代，石油产业被军政府牢牢掌控，高昂的油价推动了印尼经济的发展。强硬的政府、繁荣的经济、富强的国家，那是电影业的黄金时期，每年能出品100部电影，但都要经过严格的审查才能上线。当时电影的发行渠道尚未为被垄断，每个岛的发行运作都很独立，比如加里曼丹、苏门答腊和爪哇，那的确是电影业行情最好的时候之一。流行文化产业的模式和现在大不相同，我们有自己的畅销小说和本地喜剧，流行明星和新艺术中心层出不穷，那是被我称为新艺术转型期的第一阶段。

电影、艺术、行为艺术和流行文化都因经济繁荣而得以发展，但艺术却在含沙射影批评政府。我是在危机年代开始制作故事片的，当时油价下跌，苏哈托政权动荡，新技术涌入印尼，全球化浪潮袭来，电视产业私有化逐渐普及。全球化使得印尼的电影发行出现垄断局面，本地的流行明星渐渐被淘汰。于是我们也加入了全球化的大军，迎来了咖啡、百货商店还有互联网。这时电影业开始遭遇危机，90年代只有我和我的朋友还在制作电影，有一年只出品了四部电影作品。

the Suharto regime started losing power. New technologies came to Indonesia, new forms of globalism, and privatized television networks. Globalization brought about a monopolized system in the distribution of cinema works, and local popular cultures began to die off. Then started a kind of franchised globalization with new public spaces where we discovered coffee, malls and the internet. Film fell into a crisis during this time too. Only a friend of mine and myself made films in the 90s. There were only four films made in those years. I produced the film "Letter to an Angel" (1993), and "And the Moon Dances" (1995), which talked about decentralization. In 1998, when Suharto fell, it was the first moment of change at the highest level of power since the regime had begun in 1985, with the fall of oil prices and the presence of new technologies that were difficult to control.

B: Did you finish your law degree?

G: Yes, I was a lawyer for one year, but there was so much corruption, and this is why I closed my law office and started making art.

B: How do you develop your ideas for your films?

G: I develop them from poems. I develop them from books, from the paintings that I saw in Australia, and then I develop the situation from the actual sociopolitical circumstances. But the majority of my films I made because I was angry, angry at a particular situation. For example, in "Letter to an Angel" I was angry about the political centralism in Indonesia, and in "And the Moon Dances" I was angry at the prevalent feudalism. In "Opera Java" I was angry at the extremism in politics and religion at the time. In "Of Love and Eggs" I was angry with the symbolic religious beliefs in Indonesia, at how so many people use religion to different ends. I was angry with all of these situations, and every time I am angry I get an idea. I want to say something in response to the situation, but the anger must have some roots.

我1993年制作了《致天使的信》(Letter to an Angel)，1995年制作了《月亮舞》(The Moon Dances)探讨地方分权。1998年苏哈托政权的垮台不过是1985年起一系列危机积蓄以及油价大幅下滑和新技术逐渐走向失控等问题的最终爆发。

B: 你最后完成法律专业的学习了吗?

G: 我毕业了，之后还当了一年律师。但那真是个腐败横生、金钱至上的行业，于是我放弃经营自己的律师事务所，踏上了艺术之路。

B: 你是如何构思电影的?

G: 我的灵感来源很广，可以是一首诗、一本书、一幅我在澳大利亚看到的画或者是民生政局，但大多数情况下，是我的愤怒激发了我的创作欲望。比如我对印尼的中央集权制感到愤怒，于是创作了《致天使的信》；我对封建制度感到愤怒，于是创作了《月亮舞》；我对政治和宗教极端主义感到愤怒，于是创作了《爪哇歌剧》(Opera Java)；我对印尼的象征宗教感到愤怒，觉得很多人在利用宗教，于是创作了《甜心鸡蛋》(Of Love and Eggs)。每当我对现状有强烈不满时，我就会获得灵感，想要对问题做出回应。愤怒的情绪一定有源头，它可能在诗中、在画里，在任何可以给我带来创作动力和灵感的地方。

B: 你写诗吗?

G: 写，不过只是随便涂几笔。我自己写剧本，有时纯粹靠直觉。有次我在巴布亚拉岛的飞机场里遇见了当地的游击队领袖，我突然有种不祥的预感这里会发生流血事件。于是我打电话回办公室告诉员工我想要在巴布亚拉岛拍片，大家都以资金匮乏为由否定了我的想法。每当我产生一个坚定的想法，我都不会在意资金问题，因为我相信“

The roots can develop from a poem, from a painting, from anything that gives me renewed energy and a new idea.

B: Do you write poems?

G: Yes, but not formally. I write out my scenarios, but sometimes I work from instinct. When I was in the airport in Papua, I met with one of the Papua guerrilla leaders. I had an instinctual feeling that this was not a good situation; that many people would die. So I phoned my office and told them that I wanted to make a film in Papua, and all my staff said: "But Garin, we don't have the money." Every time I say something that I believe in, I don't know where the money will come from, but I believe in it. I will never believe that; the world is so beautiful, it gives you everything if you believe in it.

Being a director is like a gallery space: you have many rooms, one's with concepts, issues, and visions; you can open your gallery very fast, and you know very well how you can put all the Heri Dono's in place to fill the room with his works. The director is more like a gallery, but with a vision that introduces different issues. It's like the leader of a ceremony; it's like an art happening that people can come and take part in. You make the flour, you do the cooking, you dance, you sing, you install everything and invite the best group of artists; it's like that. Just give them room to make the ceremony. That's why many Asian directors never had such scenarios as Hou Xiaoxian from Taiwan, or even Wang Jiawei. The scenario is a formal thing. We Asian people combine oral tradition and a window to the world that is lead by the American way. The kitchen exists in oral tradition, but because we need to have a guest room for the global, we adapt the methods of globalization. The kitchen is the same, the Warung (a small street restaurant), and the guestroom is global. The Indonesian kitchen is China.

莫愁前路无知己”，即使自己的想法被人视作荒唐，我也想坚持下去。只要有信念，问题总会迎刃而解，世界就是如此奇妙。

导演电影好比布置画廊，有那么多房间等着你用概念、议题和眼光去装点。你在房间里挂满赫利·多诺的作品，你的这家画廊就可以开门迎客了，这时你呈现给大家是各种议题。不同的视野和眼光会带来不一样的呈现议题。导演的角色更多的像是庆典的筹办方，你备好鲜花、佳肴和歌舞，一切安排妥当，只等嘉宾入席你就退居幕后，因为他们才是主角。所以很多亚洲导演不会预先准备剧本，比如台湾的侯孝贤，甚至香港的王家卫，因为按照剧本拍戏太刻板。我们亚洲导演喜欢把口头传统和美国式的文化传播结合在一起，好比厨房是我们保留传统的地方，但我们也需要一间客厅来招待全世界的观众。我们正在融入电影全球化的发展，既保留充满风土人情的厨房和街边小店，也有顺应国际品味的客厅。印尼的传统和中国的很相似。

B: 你用什么样的标准去挑选演员？倾向业余的还是专业的？

G: 我挑的95%是业余演员的。

B: 你是怎么找到这些演员的？

G: 一般我会去影片的拍摄地点当场招人。

B: 所以你是确定地点后才开始构思角色。

G: 是的，因为人都有表达和交流的诉求。你可以让他们来布置画廊，他们需要自我表现的空间，就像树需要生长的土地。你必须充分了解人的这种本性。

B: 一旦你脑海里有了电影的雏形，你会去拍摄地点

B: How do you choose actors? Between using non-professionals or professionals?

G: 95 percent are non-professional.

B: How do you find these people?

G: I usually travel to the location, and find them there in the location.

B: So when you choose the location, you also choose the characters?

G: Yes, because every human being needs a form of expression and communication. You just give the gallery over to them, the room and the place where they can express themselves. Like you give the land to the tree; every one is like that, every human being is like that. You must know this very well.

B: So you have an idea for a film, and then you go to the location, and usually you spend a long time at the location?

G: Yes. Many directors send their crews first, but I go to the location before my crew, alone. For example, while I was working in Papua, in the conflict area, I would sit down in a cafe and the guerillas and the military would see you, and this would be in a neutral, protected border area. Then after two weeks they would come to me and ask me: "What are you doing here Garin?" You must gain their trust and it is not easy. To go and meet the guerilla leaders in the forest you must be an anthropologist, sociologist and psychologist.

B: Are you developing anything else at this moment?

G: Yes, at this moment I am making a new musical drama for the 45-year anniversary of Kompas, the Indonesian newspaper. Also there are a lot of films about religion nowadays, for example,

考察，然后在那里待上很久，对吗?

G: 是的。很多导演会派剧组成员做先行部队，但我喜欢一个人先去。比如有次我在巴布亚拉冲突地带拍片，要知道你光坐在咖啡馆里就可能被游击队或者政府军盯上，然后他们会把你赶到中立保护区里。但两个星期后，他们会问，"加林你来这里究竟做什么？"你必须要赢得他们的信任，但这非常困难。想要去丛林里见游击队的领袖，你必须同时具备人类文化学、社会学和心理学方面的知识。

B: 你手上有正在进行的项目吗?

G: 有，我正在为《罗盘报》制作纪念创刊45周年的歌舞片，另外还有许多关于宗教的电影，比如穆斯林的领袖，但我想尝试自己信仰以外的宗教题材。人们一直对此持有偏见，例如伊斯兰教电影的剧组应该多数是穆斯林，而导演更是必须是穆斯林。我想打破这种陈规，比如制作一部以天主教英雄为主角的电影。

B: 谁是你心目中的英雄?

G: 我崇拜很多英雄，比如毛泽东。

B: 你觉得目前电影和视觉艺术界存在批判性的讨论吗?

G: 没有。印尼的发展问题在于从直接从军政府独裁跨越到市场经济，中间没有过渡。我们从前的敌人是军政府，而现在则需要为票房而战。印尼的电影市场正在变得乏味，制作数量庞大，却鲜有艺术内涵。我们的电影产业只有高产，却没有长久的生命力。但发起电影界的批判性讨论无法一蹴而就，需要开启艺术家之间共谋长远发展的对话。而一旦电影界只剩下制作和票房，那势必是一场你死我活的内斗。

like about the leaders of the Muslim faith, but I want to create a character that is not of my own religion. If you make a film about Islam, the majority of the crew must be Islamic, the director must be Islamic, and so on. I don't agree with these stereotypes. Although I am Muslim I want to make a film about a Catholic hero, for example.

B: Do you have your own heroes?

G: Many. Mao Zedong is one of them.

B: Do you think there is a critical discourse in cinema and the visual arts?

G: No. The problem with Indonesia is that it went from militarism straight to a market economy. We used to fight the military and now we fight the market. The market has become banal. The problem is that the production of art is large in quantity, but the analysis and intellectual value is lost. And what is the purpose of this productivity and the market if these life cycles are so short. If you want to develop a critical discourse you need time to meet and discuss and give artists a chance to develop their work over longer periods of time. But if there is only production and the market, it becomes a game of life or death.

B: And how do you deal with this issue?

G: I still believe there is a hospital for crazy people.

B: 那你会如何应对这个问题?

G: 还是那句话：莫愁前路无知己。

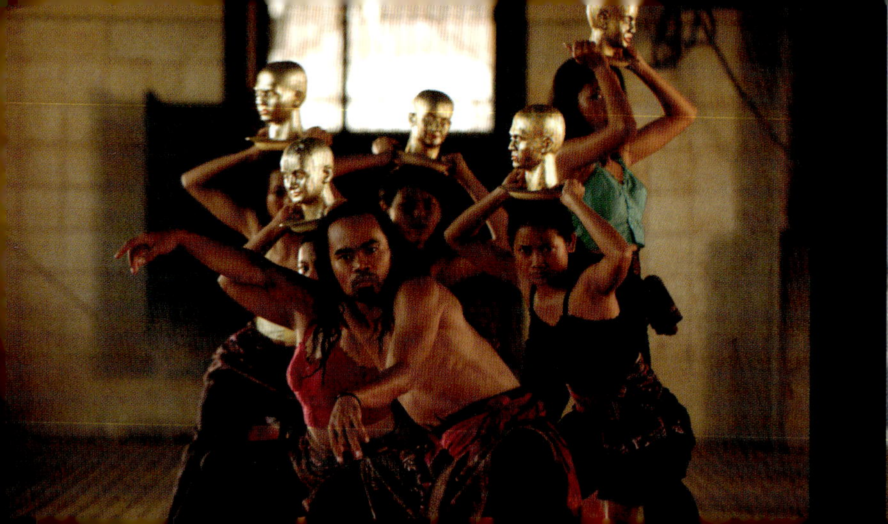
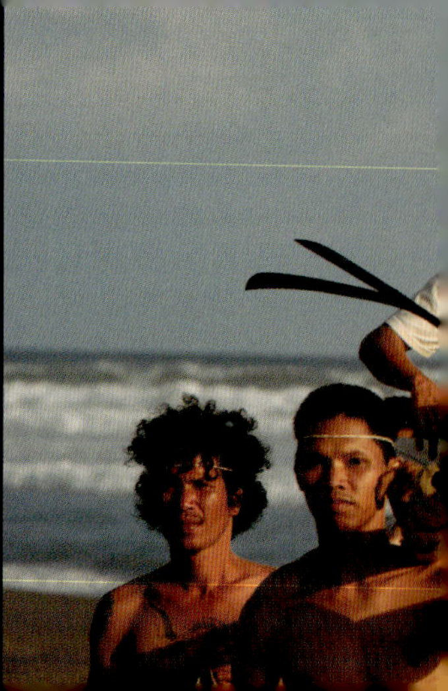

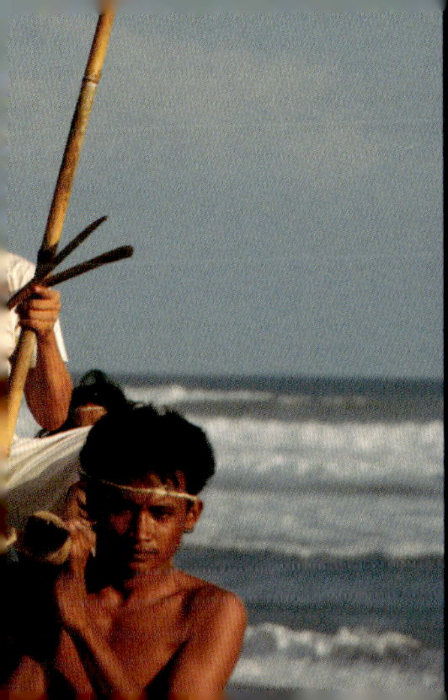
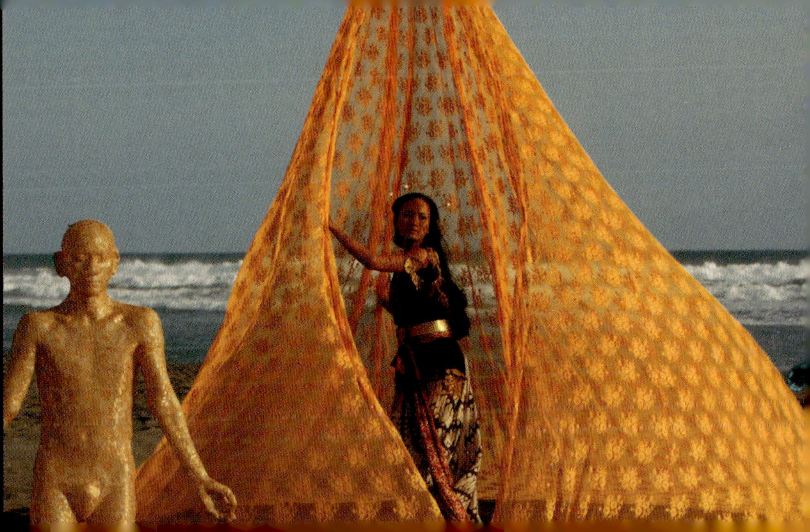

Opera Java
Part of the commissioned New Crowned Hope project, the film combines gamelan music, ballet, and eye-feasting visual pageantry in a tale of a village potter's unfaithful wife and his vengeance against her seducer. Film is based on "The Abduction of Sita," from the Hindu epic The Ramayana.
Produced with financial support of: New Crowned Hope Festival Vienna 2006, SET Film Workshop, Goteborg Film Festival Fund, Hubert Bals Fund of The International Film Festival Rotterdam
Screenplay by: Garin Nugroho, Armantono
Director of Photography: Teoh Gay Hian
Art Director: Nanang Rakhmat Hidayat

爪哇安魂曲
影片作为"新冠希望计划"(New Crowned Hope project) 的一部分，是一部结合甘美兰音乐、芭蕾等元素视觉盛宴，影片讲述了一位农村陶匠因不满妻子 的不忠愤而复仇的故事。影片改编自印度著名史诗《罗摩衍那》的"绑架西塔"一节。
制片与资金支持：2006年维也纳新冠希望电影节、SET电影工作室、哥德堡电影节基金、鹿特丹国际电影节休伯特巴尔斯基金
编剧：加林・努格罗、 Armantono
摄影指导：Teoh Gay Hian
艺术指导：Nanang Rakhmat Hidayat

120'
2006

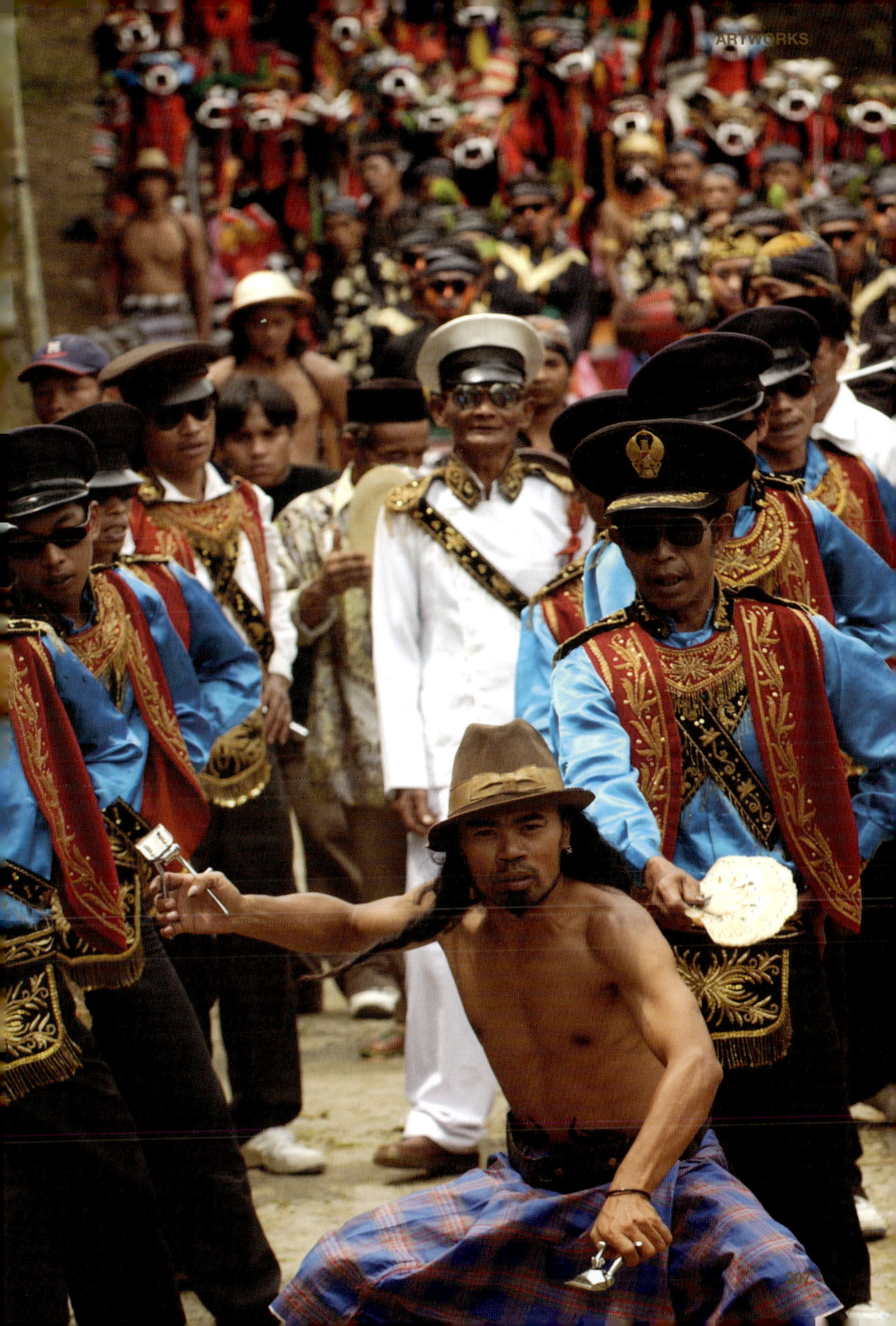

Eko Nugroho
艾柯・努格罗荷

Interview with Eko Nugroho

The Artist's Studio, Yogyakarta
June 2010

Eko Nugroho: **E**

Biljana Ciric: **B**

B: I read something on your website that drew my attention, you said: "people are lost in freedom, and I have become interested in this situation, there is kind of political and social setting in art…"

E: This is a simple thing that I would like to do, to produce a kind of setting through my work around this idea. I find the daily life around me interesting, and so I include smaller situations in the setting of my artworks, like things from the daily life, the political situation, or whatever.

B: Why do you say that "people are lost in freedom"?

E: It's quite interesting, after 1998, everything became free; people absorbed the freedom, democracy, and a freedom of the mind. It became a problem though because the majority would decide what was right or wrong. Everything was decided by the majority. The majority made new rules. They could do anything, they could control you; they were strong and powerful. If they

艾柯·努格罗荷访谈

艺术家工作室，日惹
2010年6月

艾柯·努格罗荷：**E**

比利安娜：**B**

B: 我在你的个人网站读到一段话引起了我的注意，“人们已经在自由中迷失，所以我开始对这样的状况产生兴趣，在艺术内部去建立政治和社会的框架……”

E: 这是我想要做的一件简单的事儿。用自己的作品来建构一些框架。每天围绕在我身边的日常生活不断吸引着我，于是我便试图把这些细微的情境纳入我的作品：日常生活、政治局势抑或更为琐碎的事件……

B: 为什么认为人们已经迷失于自由?

E: 这个说来很有意思，1998年之后似乎什么都“自由”了，自由、民主变成了我们脑子里边美好的想象。一切都听从大多数人的，他们决定什么是对什么是错，而什么都只是由多数人来决定肯定会出现问题。多数人制定了新的规则。他们为所

say it's wrong, then it becomes wrong, because they can put you in the wrong, you know, and this is the majority and you can't do anything, because they have the power of violence. This is a big problem in today's concept of freedom. So I have been actually questioning: what is freedom?

B: Are there any artists that inspire you, or people that surround you?

E: The idea of the neighbour is important to me. I used to live in a small district. Now, here I live in a small village, and we all live together. An important point of my work concerns communication, and I always initiate communication before I start to do anything else. The most interesting things come about from talking with people, or trying to communicate with the issues and the space, these are things I want to connect to in order to understand it first. For example, to live in the village is very beautiful, your life is full of people, and we are helping each other, we are supporting each other. From that kind of situation we develop communication. My daily life is in the village. I talk with the neighbours, and they give me a lot of inspiration. We talk about issues, we talk about politics, we talk about how to plant rice, how to protect the village from thieves, and so it's a simple way that is yet a big influence on me. Then for me the most interesting thing is how we are living in this small village, far away from the centralized Jakarta. It is a lot of fun, and it is these situations that I try to capture.

B: You also have a shop here. Where did that idea come from?

E: The name of the shop is "Fight for Rice." It's a simple idea for the shop project; it's the same idea as the book "Daging Tumbuh." I'm creating a space. I'm creating place. I'm creating a medium for the people who need space and a place to express themselves. I don't need them to make some beautiful painting, drawing or text. I just want to put the different works together from different people, and then we experience something different, because your work is next to different people's work, and it is something

欲为，有权有势，他们可以控制你。

他们说是错的那就是错的，因为他们可以让它变成错的，要知道你面对的是多数人，他们可以使用暴力，你无可奈何。 这就是今天“自由”最大的问题。所以我一直在质疑什么是自由?

B: 在你周围，有没有什么艺术家或什么人影响了你的艺术创作?

E: 周围的邻居对我很重要。 我过去住在一个不大的社区。而现在住在这个更小的村里，所有人都生活在一起。我作品中很重要的一点就是交流。在做任何事情之前我都要从交流开始。

我最感兴趣的就是与别人交谈，探讨各种问题。有时候你需要先产生关系以便能够进一步了解。比如，住在村里是非常美好的，你的周围总是住着很多邻居，我们相互帮忙、相互支持。在这样的状态下我们不断地产生交流。我每天的生活都在村里度过，跟邻居聊天，他们给了我很多灵感，我们探讨各种问题、谈政治，我们谈论怎么种米，怎么保护村子免受贼害，所以正是这样简单的方式给了我最大的影响，邻居对我来说非常重要，我也一直对他们有着很大的兴趣，我们所居住的小村子离中心雅加达很远。从我们的生活中我获取到很多趣味及各种情况。

B: 你在村子里还开了一个店。这个想法从哪来?

E: 店的名字叫“为大米而战”，很简单的想法，与我那本书《Daging Tumbuh》的想法是一致的。我在创造空间，给想要表达自己的人创造空间和媒介，我不需要他们画精美的油画或写出华丽的辞藻。我只是想把不同的人的作品放一块，于是你马上会有不一样的感受，因为你的作品在别人的作品旁边，所以又有点像“汇编各种想法”。

like a compilation of ideas. Like the book project I started in 2000, with only 150 copies for each edition, which I distribute by hand.

B: What does "Daging Tumbuh" mean?

E: It means something like growing flesh, like a tumor. It is scary, but can also be fun. For the book project, I wanted to make a project that would grow, in which more people could also explore. I rented a small room on the street. It's the same idea. I invited a group, the younger people, or an independent community, and they can put their own merchandise or things that they want to sell to support themselves. Say if you have a band and you have a new record, you can bring it and sell them. What I can do is this: we have a space where we can make our own merchendise, we can make publications, and we also have a website. Then from there it starts to support a small community of people. I hope it's becoming a space that supports independent communities. Because when I was young, when I was studying, there was nothing like this kind of support. Everyone was doing things on their own. For the young people, there is no place for them to express themselves. So that is why I have this space, so they can also sell their merchandise. It's an important thing. They can earn a small amount of money, and they can continue their work. So that's the idea behind "Fight for Rice."

B: How did "Daging Tumbuh" come about in 2000?

E: It's a funny story. I was in a group of people, and most of us were art students from the Art Academy, in the painting or photography departments. We had a plan to do an exhibition, but every gallery that we approached denied our proposal. The group split and that show never happened. Then I was thinking: why do we need a space? Why do we need a white cube? I can create a space. How about doing the exhibition in a book? This is the idea at first, and then I invited more people into the project, and so the book became a building or a space. Then I went back to the galleries again and asked them to put the book in their venue so people could look

那本书的计划是2000开始的，每次发行150本，每一本都是我亲自做发行。

B: Dagung Tumbuh什么意思?

E: 是瘤(不断生长的肉)的意思。有点可怕但是又很有趣。通过书的项目我开始思考去创造更多类似于这样的“生长中”的项目来吸引更多的人参与。我租了一个沿街的小空间。其实想法还是一样，我邀请年轻人、独立社团、不同的小组、他们可以把自己的产品或者其他的东西放在我店里出售，这样可以卖一点东西来支持他们自己的工作。比如你如果有个乐队你可以把自己出的CD拿过来卖。我能做的是我们会有出版物、网站来出售这些作品。我希望整个计划可以变成一个支持独立社区的空间。因为在我读书的时候没有这样的空间。每个人都只是想办法走出自己的路。当时对于年轻人，找不到空间可以表达自己。这是我开空间的原因，他们可以出售自己的想法，这很重要，他们可以通过卖自己的产品赚一点钱以继续他们的工作。这是“为大米而战”背后的想法。

B: 你的出版物《瘤》在2000年是如何产生的?

E: 这也是一件很有意思的事。我们当时有一群人，大部分都是艺术学院的学生，以摄影和绘画专业为主。我们当时想做个展览，去谈了很多画廊但是没有一个愿意让我们做。这群人慢慢就散了，展览的事也就不复存在了。我就开始想，为什么我们一定要有空间？为什么一定是白立方盒子的空间?我自己可以建立一个空间。在书里做一个展览怎么样？所以这个在书里做展览想法就有了雏形，然后我就邀请了更多的人参与这个计划，就这样书成了我们的展出“场地”。之后我又去找当初的那些画廊，把我们的书放在画廊里让别人随便翻阅，观众可以复印喜欢的作品、甚至将作

through it. They can copy from the book themselves, use the images from the book for t-shirts. It is a book free to pirate. Then this project became interesting for me to continue, and it's still going now, ten years on. You don't need to be an artist to do a project in this book. For example an old friend of mine living in the mosque… The books are online and free to download too.

B: Do you have any heroes?

E: My parents. Yeah, it's a personal issue. I was born in a small town. My father was a newspaper deliveryman until he got his pension. I have five brothers and I'm the oldest. We had hard living conditions growing up, but us children could go to school. My father worked hard to get the money, and only I was able to go to the university, while my other brothers only went to high school. My parents gave me a lot of support, a huge amount of support… it's difficult to explain. I'm feeling very strong images in my head. Maybe I'm a family man in some way…

B: Do you have any projects that you would like to do?

E: I would like to combine creativity and business, in each village. I would like to have people earn a living using their own creativity, without any need to think about their work in the factory or the government, because it's really difficult to get a job like that, which you do on your own. It's an important thing that I want to spread in this way.

B: So you would like to make a business model that could help the small communities in the village to continue their creativities?

E: Yes, this is still an idea, but I think it's a very important plan for the future.

品印在T恤上都可以，这是一本“自由盗版”的书。所以这个计划越发引起了我的兴趣，就一直持续做到现在，已经10年了。你不必一定是艺术家才能参与这个项目。比如最近一期就是我的一位住在清真寺里的朋友给了我他的画……所有书都可以在网上下载。

B: 你有没有心目中的英雄。

E: 我父母。这是比较个人的问题。我在小镇出生。我的父亲直到退休一直都是一位送报员。我有五个弟弟，我是年纪最大的。我们生活很艰难，但所有孩子都能够去上学。我的父亲工作很辛苦，只有我上过大学，弟弟们都是高中毕业。父母给了我很大的支持，非常大的支持。很难用一两句话解释，但是心中的感受很深。也许我过于念家……

B: 目前还有哪些想法希望在未来继续发展?

E: 我很想把创作和经营在每一个村里结合起来，我希望人们可以用自己的创意赚钱而不再只是想着为工厂或官方机构打工，因为找到一份工作很难而且很辛苦，但通过自己的想法去创造，对于我来说继续传播是很重要的。

B: 那也就是说你想建立一种经营模式可以帮助村里的小社区来继续他们自身的创造力对吗?

E: 是的，现在只是个想法，但也是未来的一个大计划。

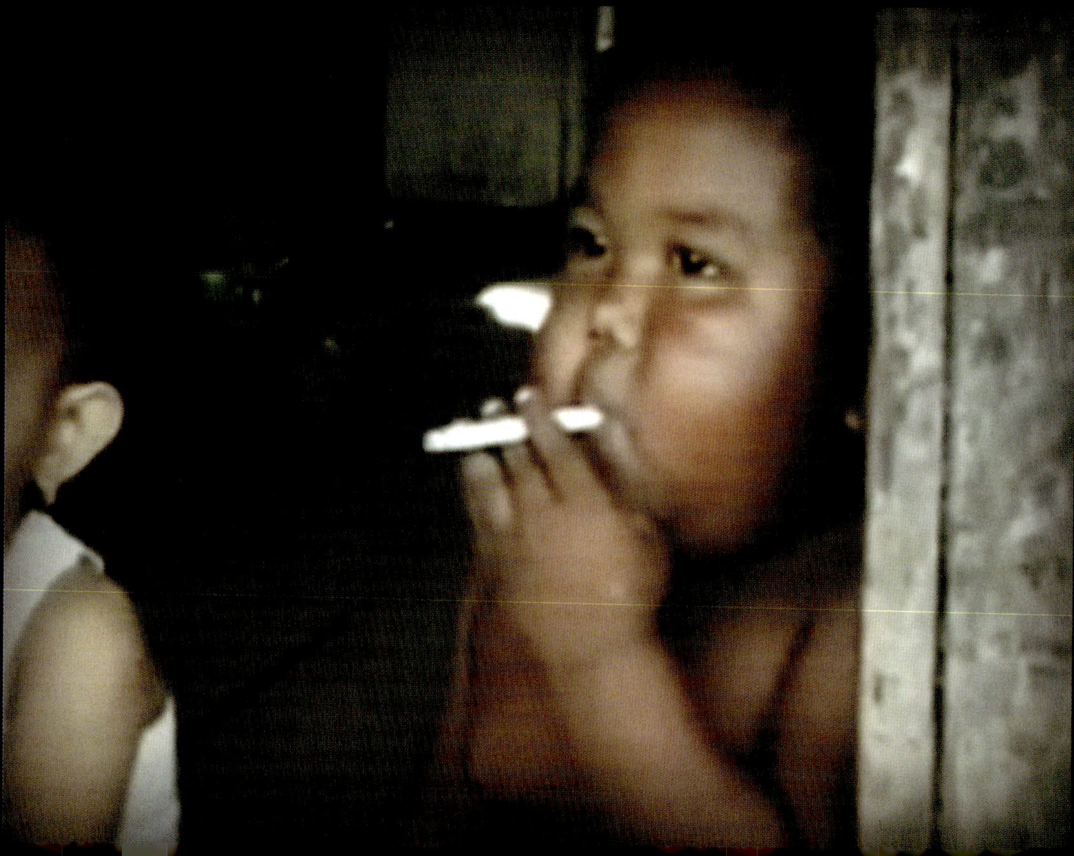

We all have our own satellite,
so our life has universal problems

每个人都有属于自己的卫星围绕，
所以我们的生活中永远充斥着宇宙问题。

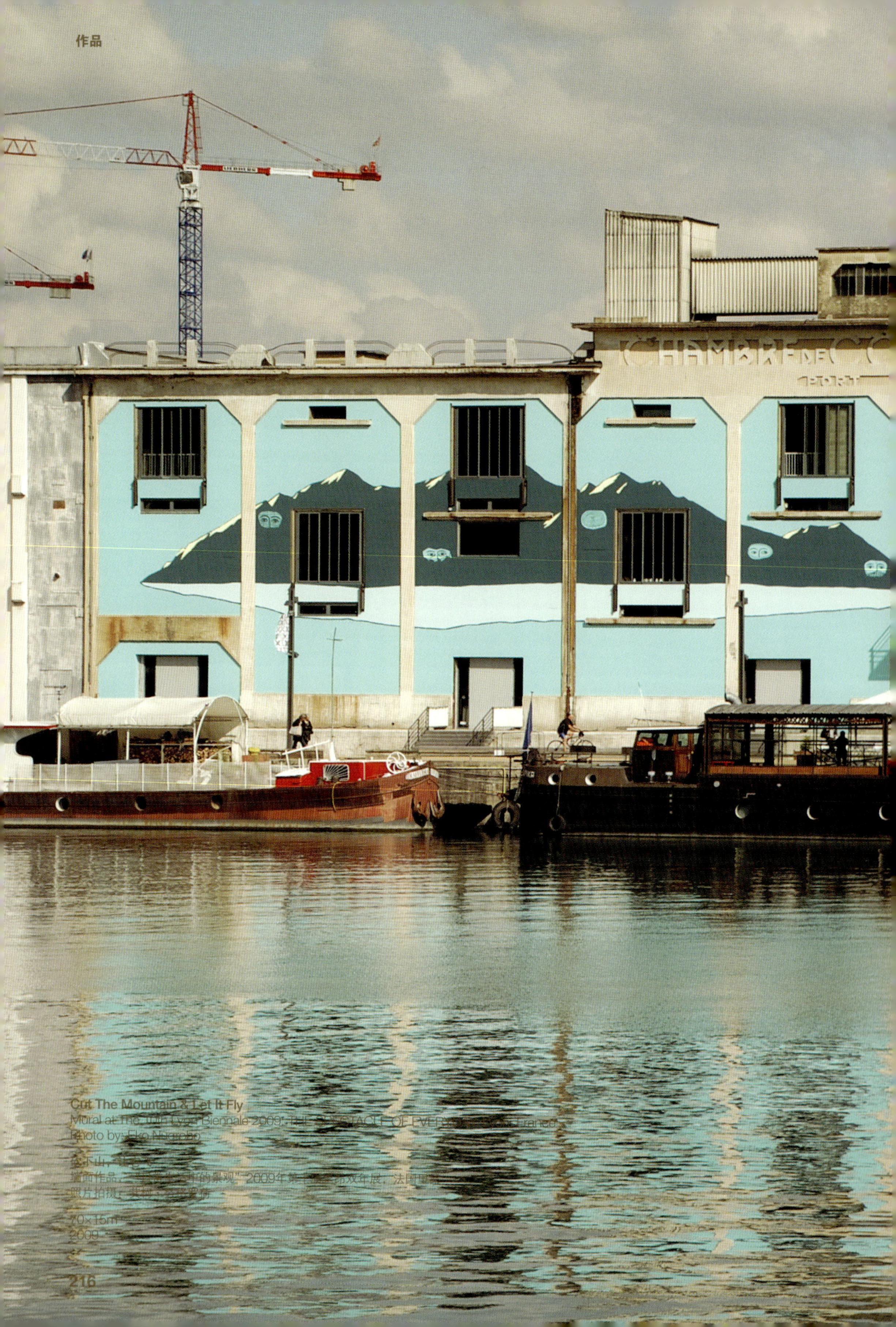

Cut The Mountain & Let It Fly
Mural at The 10th Lyon Biennale 2009: THE SPECTACLE OF EVER[illegible] France
Photo by: Eko Nugroho

砍下山，[illegible]
墙面作品：[illegible]的景观”2009年第[illegible]双年展，法国[illegible]
照片拍摄：[illegible]

70×15m
2009

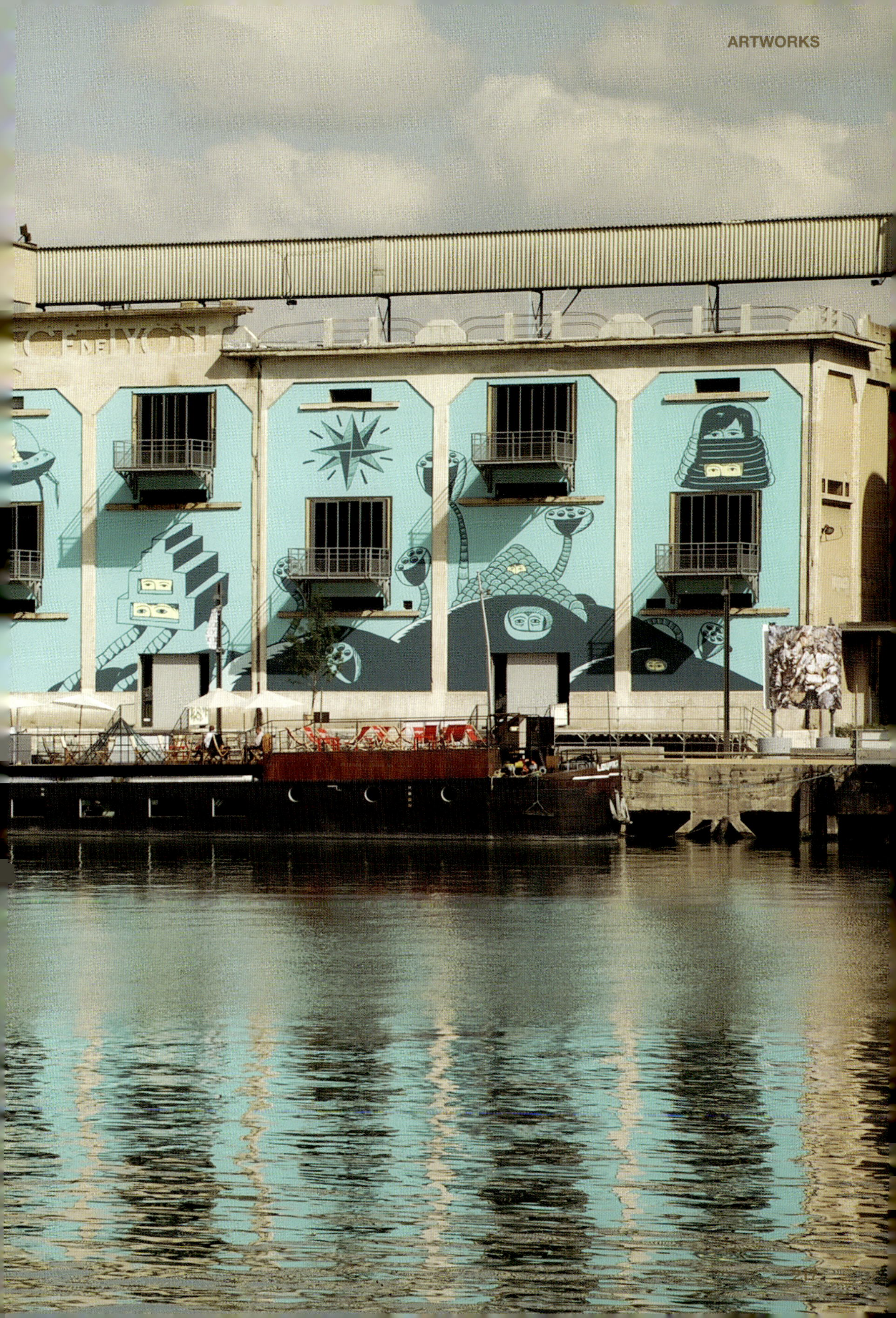

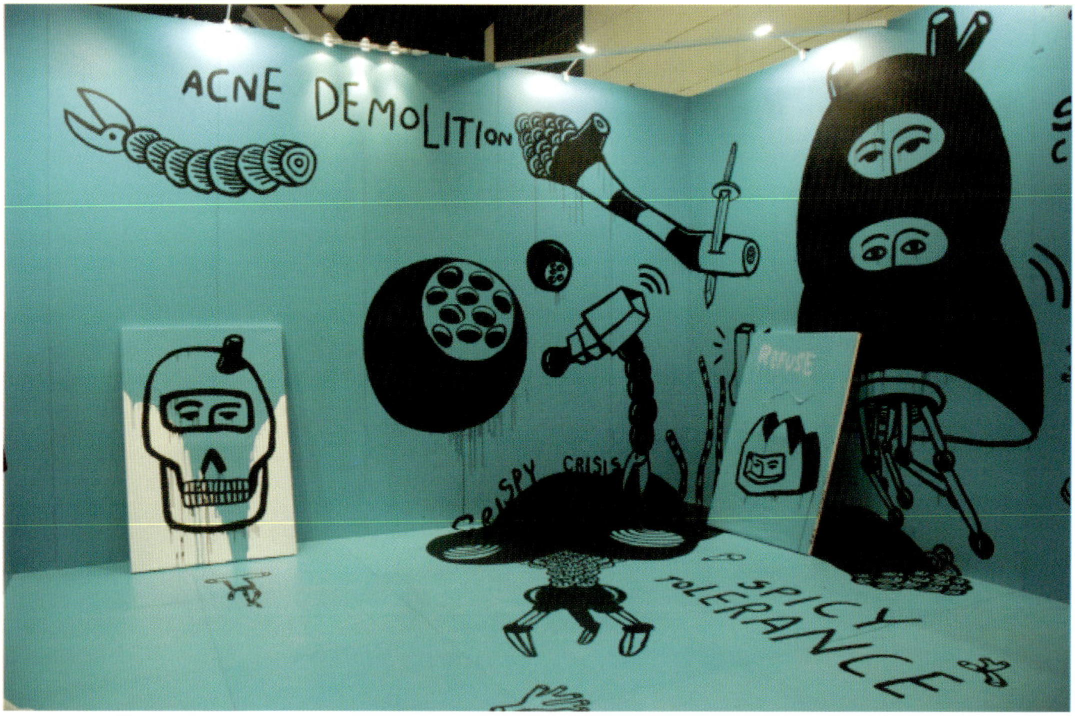

Sticky Conflict
Mural at Hongkong Art Fair 2010
Photo by: Eko Nugroho

粘性斗争
墙面作品，2010年香港艺术博览会
照片拍摄：艾柯・努格罗荷

5×4×3m
2010

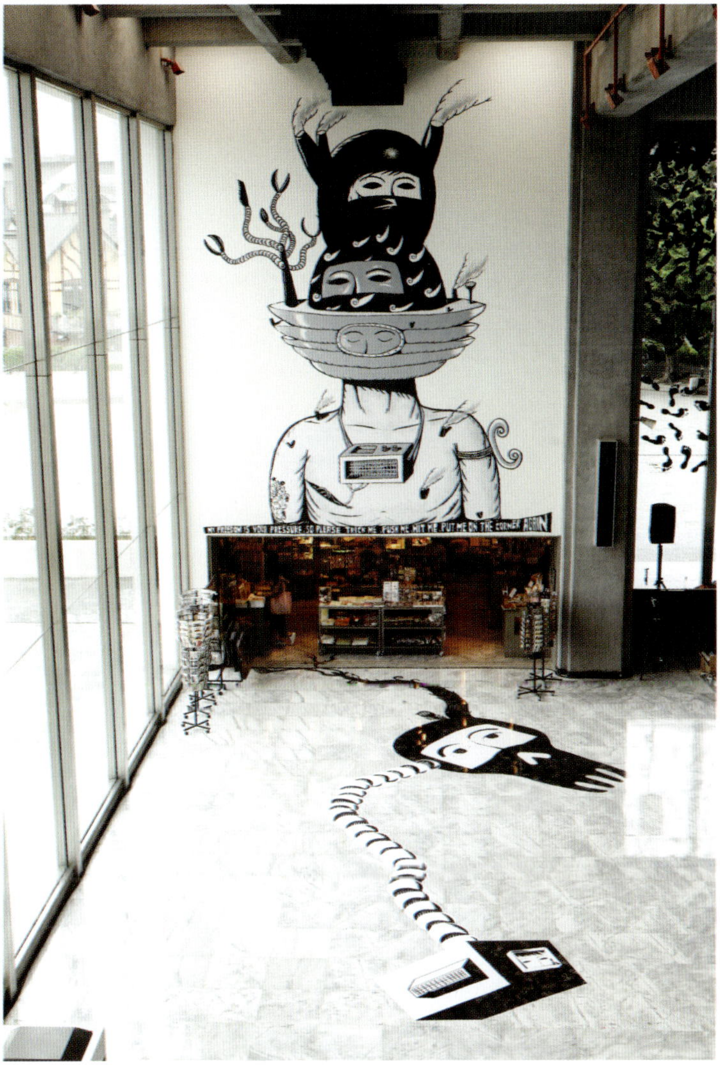

Trick Me, Push Me
Mural at Taipei Biennale 2006
Image courtesy of Taipei Biennale

哄我，推我
墙面作品，2006年台北双年展
照片由台北双年展提供

5×4×3m
2006

Erik Muhammad
埃里克・穆罕穆德

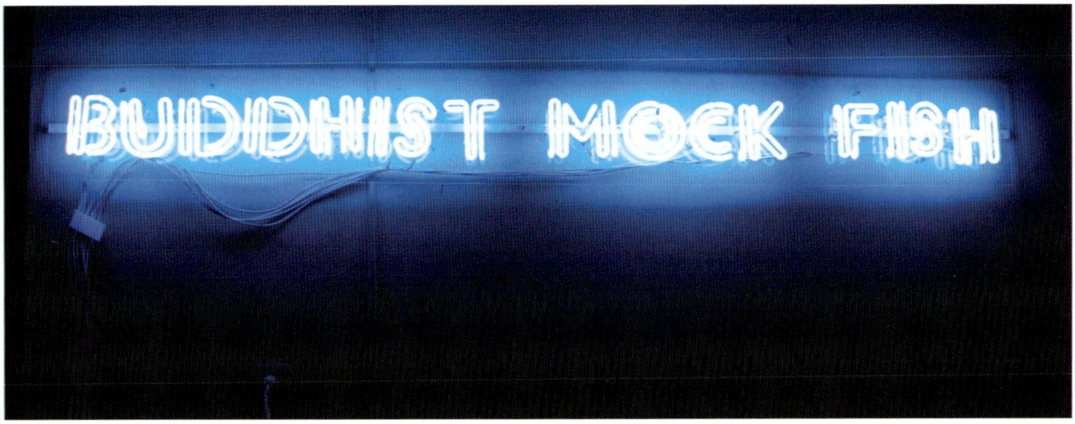

Great White - Buddhist Mock Fish
Embroidery and Neon Sign

大白鲨——佛教徒嘲笑鱼
刺绣与霓虹灯

640×290cm
2010

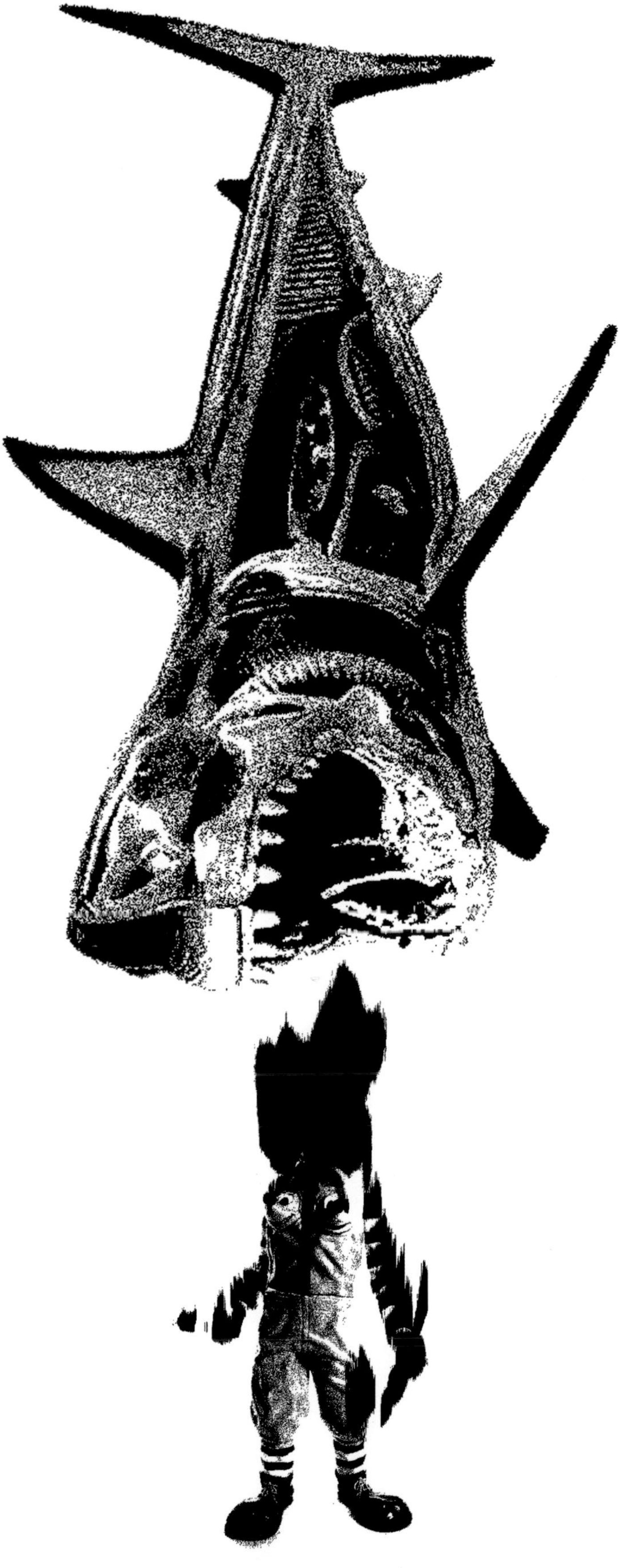

Gotot Prakosa
高托特・普拉考萨

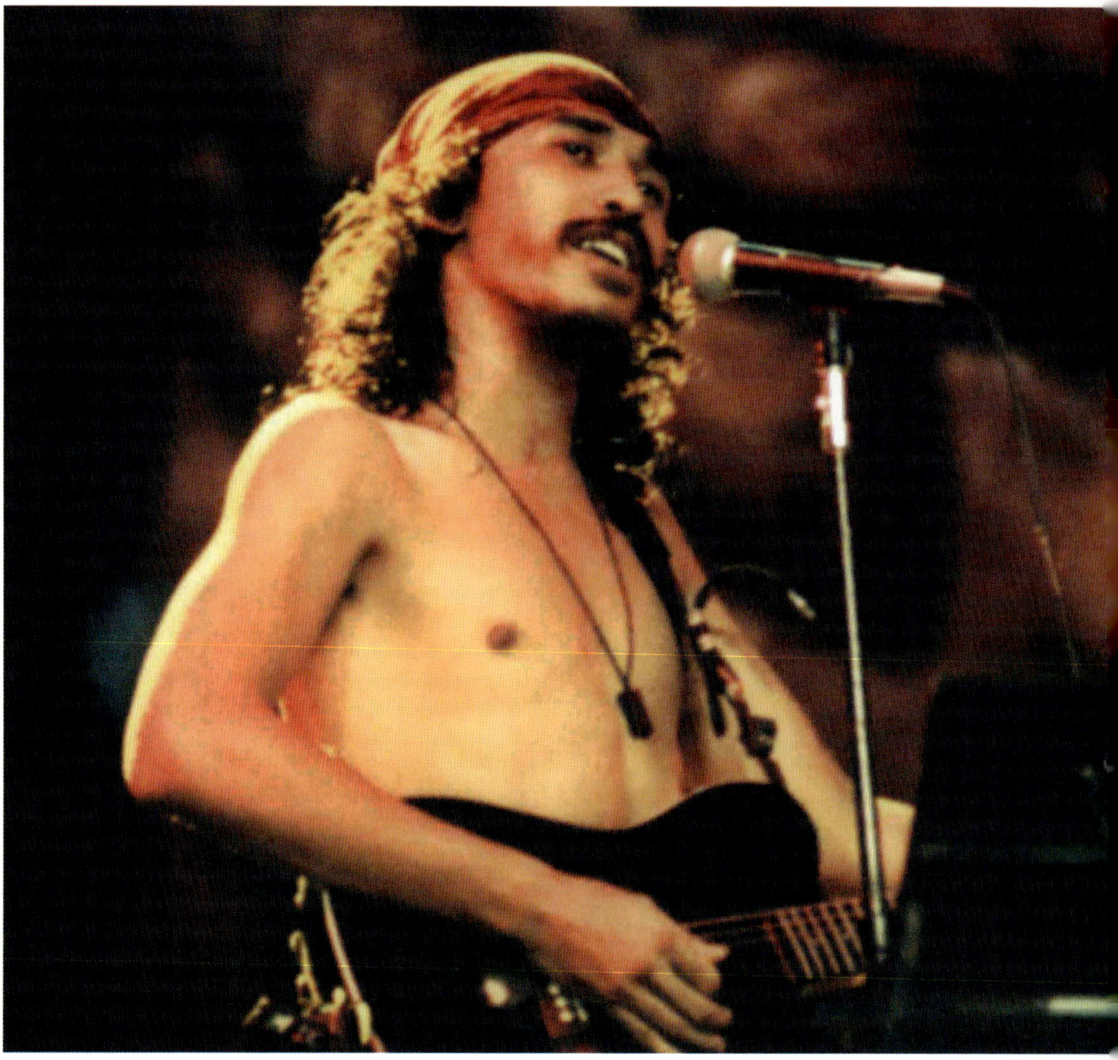

Kantata Takwa
Gatot's recently accomplished work. Named after the legendary Indonesian rock group who take centre stage in the film, Kantata Takwa, a semi-documentary protest against the Suharto regime, is a collaborative effort with Iwan Fals, 'the Bob Dylan of Indonesia', and his band; poet W. S. Rendra and his theatre group; and the filmmakers and artists Eros Djarot, Setiawan Djody, and Gotot Prakosa. Independent and experimental, the film began production in 1990 and includes footage of a Kantata Takwa concert held that year-but was only completed in 2008.

Kantat Takwa乐队
高托特最新力作。影片以印尼具有传奇色彩的摇滚乐团“Kantata Takwa”来命名，并让该乐团在因电影中扮演了重要的角色。《Kantat Takwa乐队》是一部 向苏哈托政权发起抗议的半纪录片式的电影。这部电影是集体努力的结晶，参与者包括：有“印尼鲍勃・迪伦”之称的Iwan Fals与他的乐队、诗人W. S. 伦德拉与他的剧团、以及电影制片人和艺术家Eros Djarot、Setiawan Djody和Gotot Prakosa等。《Kantat Takwa乐队》是一部独立实验电影，开始创作于1990年，Kantata Takwa乐队当年演唱会的片段也出现在影片当中。影片最终于2008年全面完成。

95'
2008

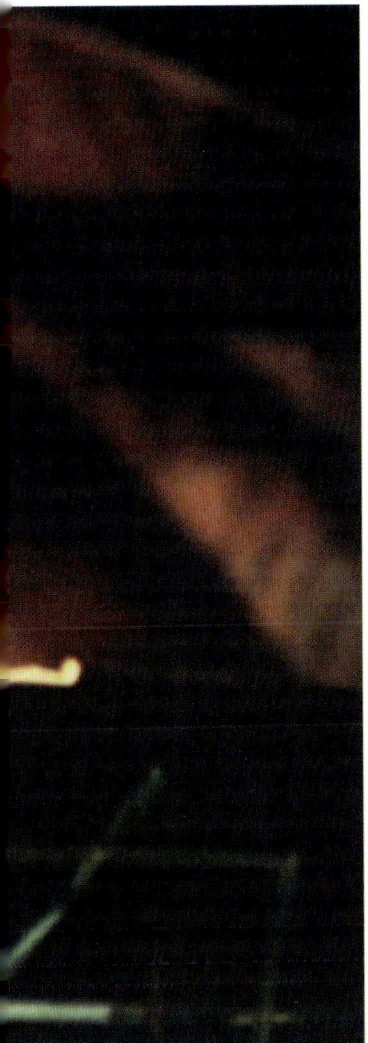

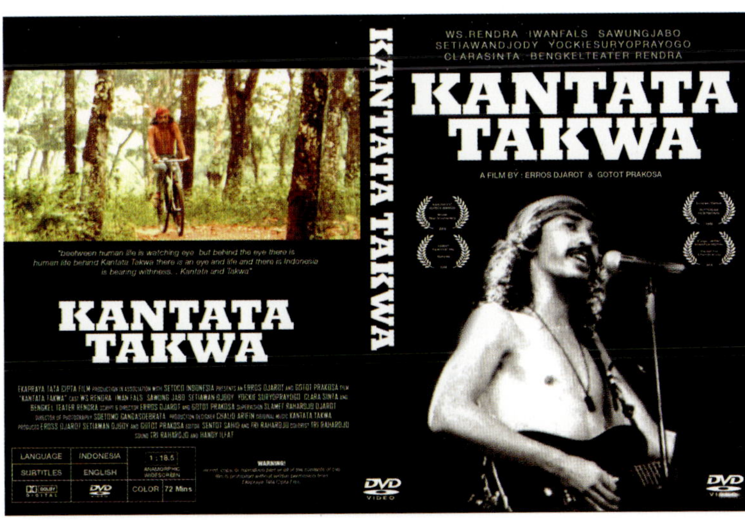
WS.RENDRA IWANFALS SAWUNGJABO
SETIAWANDJODY YOCKIESURYOPRAYOGO
CLARASINTA BENGKELTEATER RENDRA
KANTATA TAKWA
A FILM BY : ERROS DJAROT & GOTOT PRAKOSA
KANTATA TAKWA
"beetween human life is watching eye but behind the eye there is human life behind Kantata Takwa there is an eye and life and there is Indonesia is bearing withness. . Kantata and Takwa"
KANTATA TAKWA
LANGUAGE
INDONESIA
SUBTITLES
ENGLISH
1 : 18.5
ANAMORPHIC WIDESCREEN
COLOR
72 Mins
WARNING!
DVD
VIDEO

Angki Purbandono
安奇·普班度诺

Interview with Angki Purbandono

MES 56, Yogyakarta
June 2010

Angki Purbandono: **A**

Biljana Ciric: **B**

B: Why do you take the year 2000 as a turning point? What kind of work did you do before then?

A: Before 2000, it was more like playing around. Playing with photography in terms of experimenting with the technology, the process of making a photograph, and the narrative in photography. After 2000, it became more serious, especially at that time as I was responsible for the MES 56 as an institution. During that time I barely made any individual work. From 2000 to 2006 my main focus was MES 56. After 2006, I continued my individual practice. In between I did make some work, but I wasn't exhibiting.

B: When did you start showing more frequently?

A: From 2006 on.

安奇・普班度诺访谈

MES56空间，日惹
2010年6月

安奇・普班度诺：**A**

比利安娜：**B**

B: 为什么你把2000年作为自己的转折点？2000年之前你主要做一些怎样的作品呢？

A: 2000年之前还是处于摸索阶段。以比较实验的方式“玩”摄影，从运用不同的技术、冲洗洗照片过程到摄影中的叙事等等。2000年后似乎就变成了更为严肃的一件事情，特别是当我开始负责MES56的整个机构。在这个阶段我几乎没有做什么自己的作品。从2000年到2006年我的所有精力都集中在MES56。2006年后我陆续开始做自己的作品。当然之间也做了一些东西但是几乎没有展出过。

B: 什么时候开始频繁地参与展览呢？

A: 从2006年开始。

B: 你在2006年之后的创作方向有没有产生变化？

B: What was the difference in your approach? And what kind of work did you produce after 2006?

A: During the 90s, photography wasn't considered part of the fine arts, or visual arts. But in 2000 in Indonesia people began discussing video as part of the visual arts. I remember talking with Wimo who had lost his faith in photography and started experimenting with video.

B: So that's why MES 56 is important… as photography became a more accepted medium in the Indonesian visual art scene?

A: I think it was 3 years ago.

B: I need to go back to your work. What kind of work did you begin to make after 2000?

A: I became more focused on the urban landscape. It was easy for me; everyday you find something different in Yogya. I think it is the representative city of Indonesia. So I push myself to capture what goes on in the city, including the animals hit by cars on the street, which was part of my first experience in the narrative. I also continued to learn about contemporary photography throughout the world.

B: This is also when you started making the "Madness" series, during 2004 to 2005. How do you work, what is your process?

A: I just carry my camera around.

B: Do you carry your camera every day?

A: Yes, all the time; I don't care what camera type.

B: Is it a digital camera?

A: Yes.

A: 90年代摄影在印尼根本没有被纳入进当代艺术作为一部分。但是在2000年左右整个印尼开始对录像展开并将其看作当代艺术的一部分。我记得当时维莫(Wimo Ambala Bayang)还有点对摄影失去信心而想开始做录像了呢。

B: 所以MES56就显得十分重要(MES56空间只展出摄影作品)……那么是在何时摄影进入了印尼的当代艺术范畴并开始去讨论它的呢?

A: 大概也就是3年前。

B: 还是回到你的作品。2000年后你做什么作品?

A: 我开始更多地关注城市风景。也许在当时这个对于我最简单;在日惹,每天围绕你的生活都在变化。我就试图让自己不断地去获取城市中发生的事:比如大街上被车撞死的动物,这可以看作是我对于叙事性的初次体验,同样也与当代穆斯林的一些问题有关。我也在不断地通过观察世界来学习当代摄影。

B: 2004、2005年你开始了"疯癫"系列的拍摄。你的工作方式和过程是怎样的?

A: 我只是一直将相机带在身边。

B: 每天都会带相机出去吗?

A: 对。一直带。不管是什么样的相机。

B: 是数码相机吗?

A: 是。

B: 每天会去拍照吗

A: 几乎每天都去。比如我还有一个拍摄橱窗的项目。我拍了很多橱窗照片。这是我工作过程的一

B: Do you take photographs every day?

A: Almost every day. I have a project about window shopping. I have taken a lot of window shopping images. That is part of my process, and it pleases me. After I discovered the scan it became my "masterpiece" in the market arena. Because the market would never pay attention to my "Madness" photographs, or photos of animals killed in the street, or window shopping, they will never like it. But when I make the scans, it all came together. I'm glad, because I have two sides.

B: Isn't that difficult?

A: Yes, I think so. It is more about being attuned to the situation when selecting the artist who will do well in the market. But I'm glad because I have more of a process of experimentation before I get in touch with the market.

B: I was also reading that you are collecting old photographs from the free market.

A: Yes, I bought a lot of photographs from 2006 to 2009.

B: Is it because of your work? Or just a personal interest?

A: Because of my personal interest. I found some old photos about a local student from Yogya. In the free market, there are still a lot of old photos, and most of the buyers are from overseas, from China, Japan, and Europe. They buy a lot of photos, and they always already have had primary contact with the seller. The seller also told me they will use the photos as an archive, or resource, and they will disappear. That's why I try to collect old photos.

B: Do you still collect?

部分，我很享受它。后来当我扫描这些作品的时候我发现了这些“经典之作”，艺术市场的经典。因为市场不会注意到我的“疯癫”系列的照片，或是被撞死的动物和橱窗……他们不会喜欢这种类型的作品。但是当我扫描了所有作品，这一切就不再是问题了。我很高兴我可以做到两面兼顾。

B: 这样不是很难吗?

A: 是很难。这更像是在与挑选适合市场的艺术家时的情况相协调。但是我觉得自己很幸运，因为在我接触到市场之前有了很长一段时间的实验阶段。

B: 我在什么地方读到了你在旧货市场收集老照片。

A: 对，我在2006年到2009年间收了很多。

B: 是个人兴趣吗? 还是作品需要?

A: 是我个人兴趣。我曾经找到过一些日惹本地学生的老照片。在旧货市场，今天仍旧可以找到很多老照片，大部分的买家是海外的，从中国、日本到欧洲等等。他们会买很多老照片，而且与那些收集这些老照片的人都有直接的联系。卖照片的人告诉我他们经常将这些照片作为研究的对象或作为文献收藏。所以我也就慢慢开始收集了。

B: 你现在也在收藏吗?

A: 我跟卖照片的人还保持着联系。他会定期直接来我家，带照片让我挑，挑完了我付钱。

B: 你的收藏有没有去做特别的分类?

A: 刚开始的时候无论他们带什么我都收，但是慢慢地卖家也明白了我要哪一类的照片了，他们会预

A: I still have the relationship with the seller. He comes directly to my house and he brings the photos, and I give him money.

B: Is there any category you collect specifically?

A: First I collected whatever they would bring, but after that the seller already knew what I wanted, and they would pre-select stuff for me, then offer them to me. I am looking at the kind of important poses they display. I have 6 categories: alone, only one person, then as a couple (me and you), then the wedding, family, great day (a lot of people taking the photo together, a celebration), and the rest. I also found families that took photos of funerals and burials. So it's like a life process, you start alone, then couple, wedding, family, great day, and rest in peace.

B: What are you going to do with your collection?

A: Make a small museum in Yogya. I have friends who will help me.

B: You are selecting photos only from Yogya?

A: Almost all the photos are from Yogya, but if I travel I always look for the free market in that area. I brought a lot of photos home from Japan, where I was in residency for 2 months. I send all my clothes by mail, and I bring the photos in my suitcase.

B: So you want to make a museum in Yogya?

A: Yes. It will be called the Anonymous House. That's my plan for the next ten years.

先自己挑选一下然后再带给我。我时常会被老照片中那些人物所展示的重要时刻所吸引。我的收藏目前共分六类：单独照、夫妻(或者“我和你”)、婚礼、家庭、重要的日子(各种很多人的庆祝场面)和亡故。在其中我也发现有些家庭会在葬礼及下葬的时候拍摄合影。所以这一切就像人的一生，你肚子来到这个世界，然后恋爱，结婚，成家，经历各种重大的日子，最后被安葬。

B: 那么对于你的这些收藏在将来有什么打算?

A: 在日惹做个小的博物馆。我有些朋友愿意帮我。

B: 你只挑选日惹的老照片吗?

A: 大部分的照片来自日惹，但是如果我外出旅行我就会去当地的旧货市场转转。我在日本做过两个月的入驻计划，回来的时候带了很多老照片。我把所有的衣物用包裹邮寄回家，随身的旅行箱里则装满了老照片。

B: 所以要在日惹造个博物馆?

A: 对。博物馆的名称是“无名之屋”。这可能是我将来10年的计划。

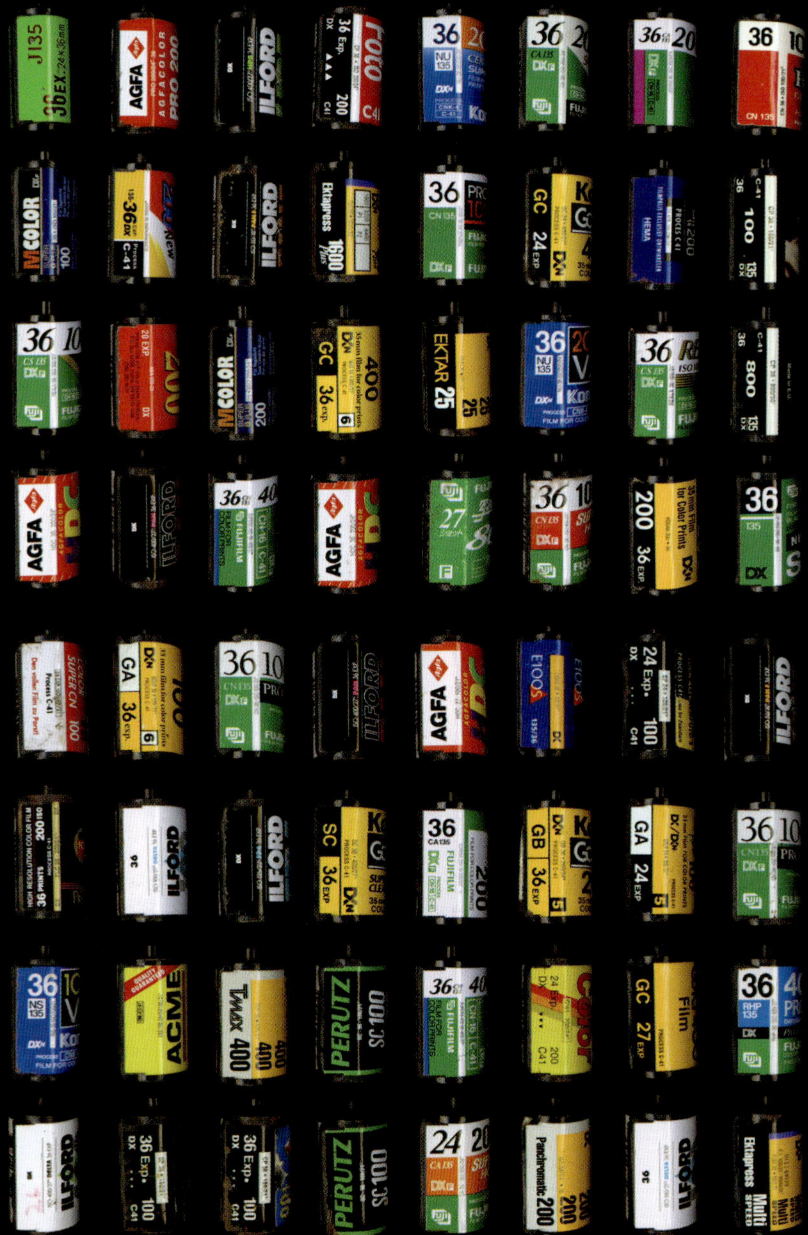

These miniature collections are my favorite because they contain the things that connect me to the history of photography. These empty 35mm film casings have been collected since 1998, and not all of them have I used myself, for sometimes I collect them from waste bins in photo studios in my hometown, Jogja.

The casings were attractive to me because the packaging is ideal and unique. You can find a bunch of secret codes on its packaging that almost no one knows what they mean; only professionals understand what these codes mean. It's a brilliant discovery, to create a mini container that is durable in all weather conditions, easy to carry and to store.

It's probably too early to think that these films are becoming extinct. But for some reason I have already begun to miss them. I'm sure you do too.

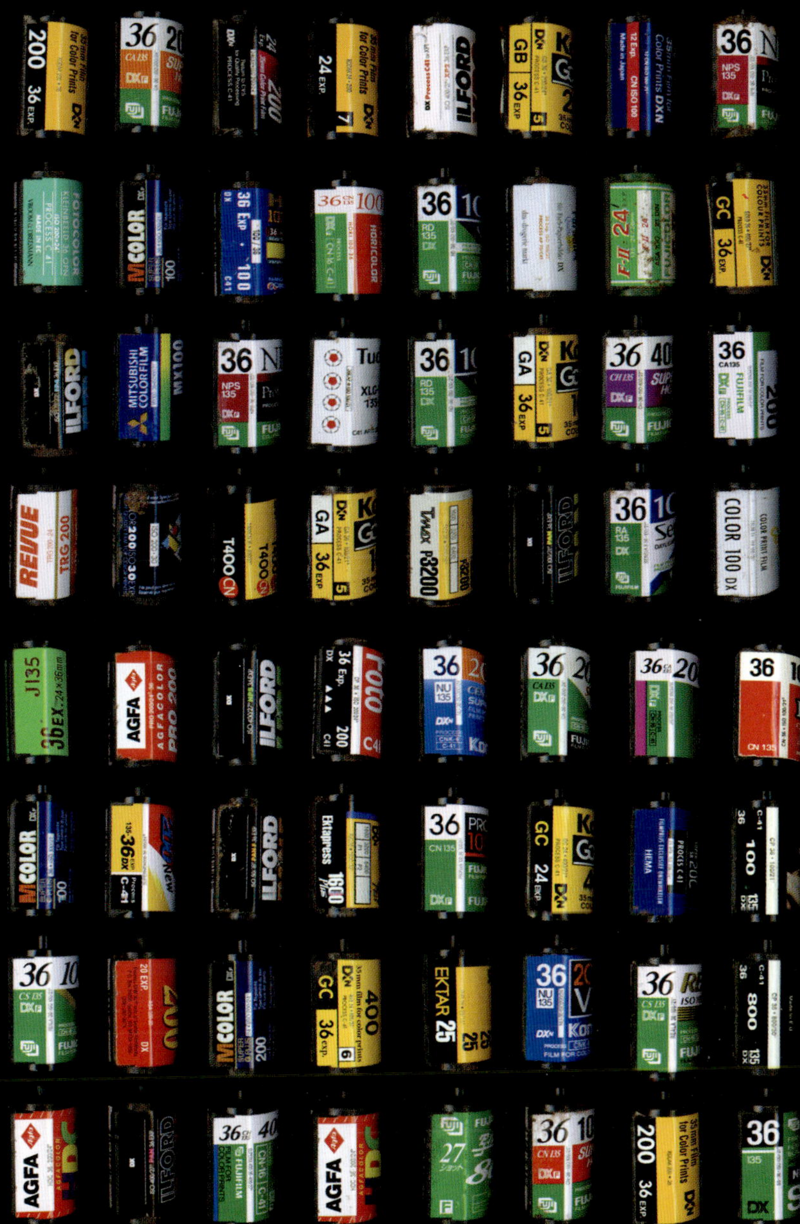

这些是我最中意的收藏品，因为胶片把我与历史和摄影联系在了一起。我从1998年起开始收藏这些35mm胶片空盒，里面的胶片并不完全是我自己用掉的，有时候我也从日本各个摄影工作室的垃圾桶里找出些空的胶片盒子来收藏。

这些盒子之所以吸引了我是因为它们的包装独特而富有美感，包装上的密码形如天书，除了行家，几乎没人能够参悟其中含义。这种小小的盒子可谓是绝妙的发明，便于携带，便于储存，同时又不会受到外界环境因素的影响，经久耐用。

[illegible]

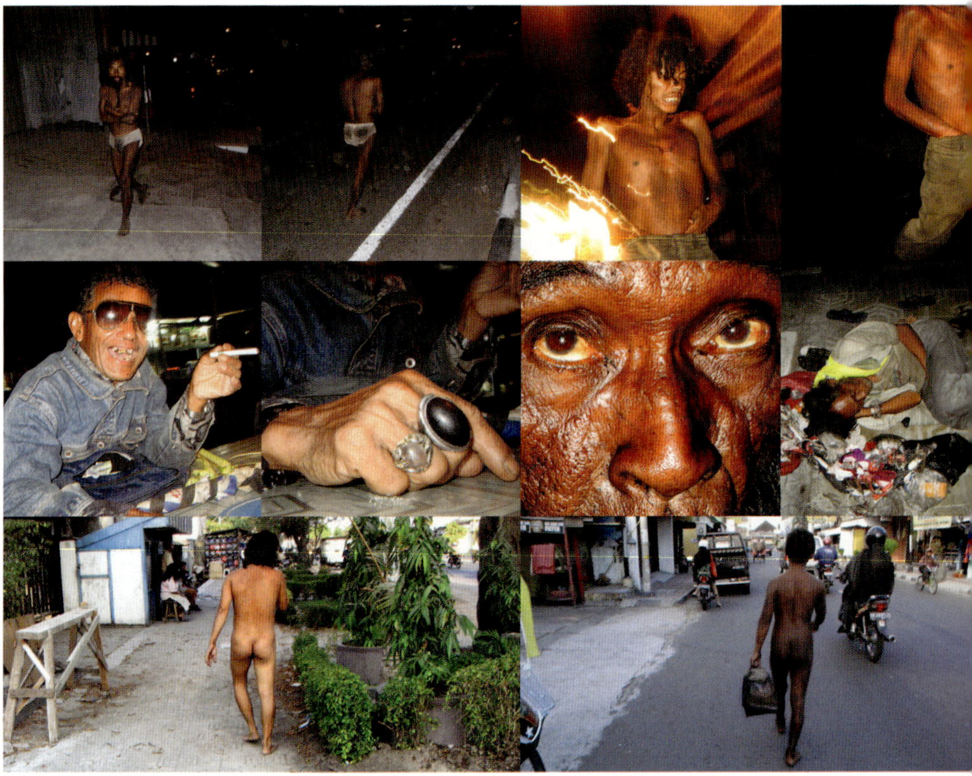

Beyond Versace
Book edition, 1 copy

超越范思哲
图书版，1个拷贝

50×50cm
2004-recent/至今

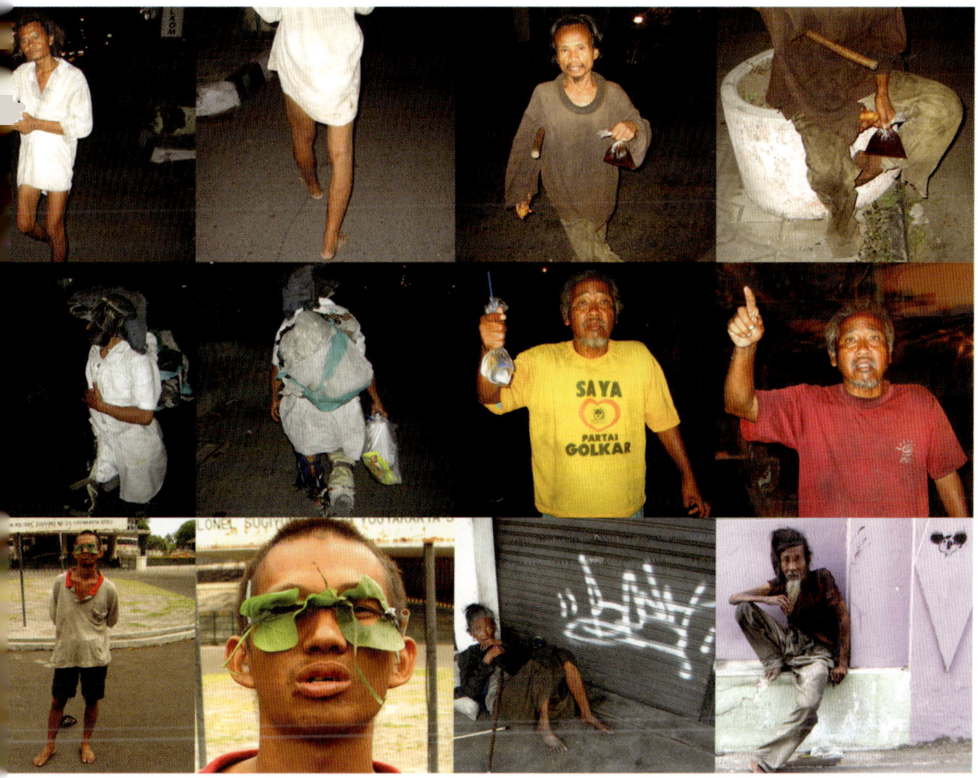
SAYA
PARTAI
GOLKAR

Mangu Putra
曼顾·普川

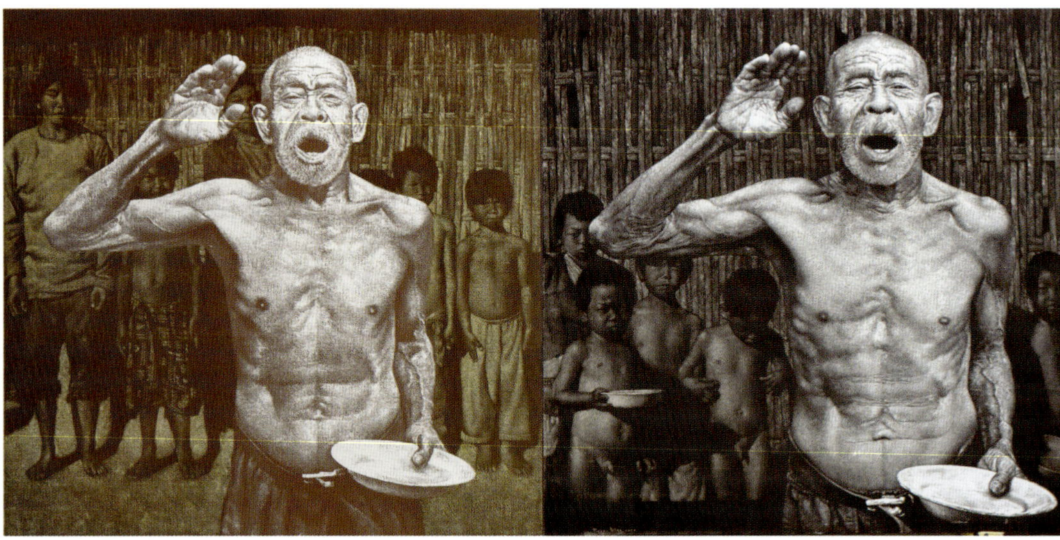

Penantian
Oil on canvas

等候
布面油画

200×200cm (2 panel/两联)
2009

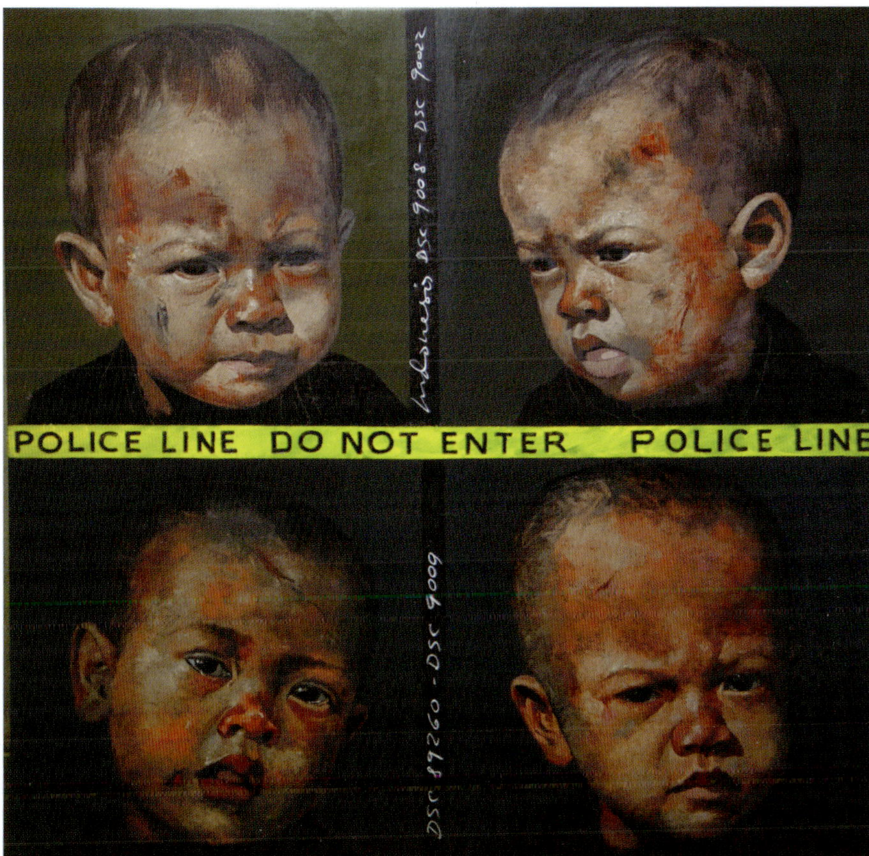

Police Line 5
Oil on linen

警戒线 5
亚麻布油画

200×200cm
2010

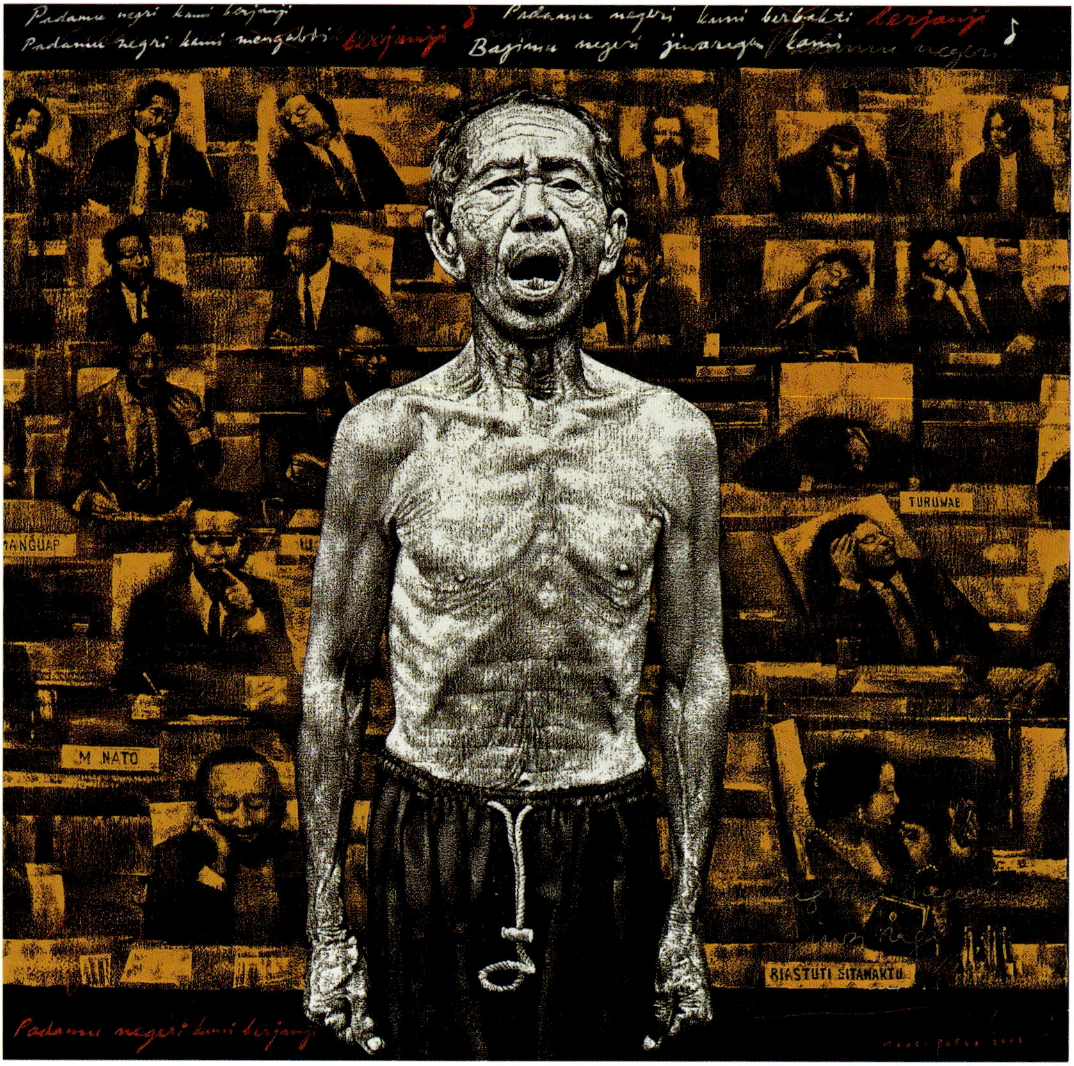

For Your the Country #2
Oil on canvas
Collection of Mr. Frans Mawengkang, Jakarta

致祖国#2
布面油画
雅加达Frans Mawengkang先生私人藏品

200×200cm
2008

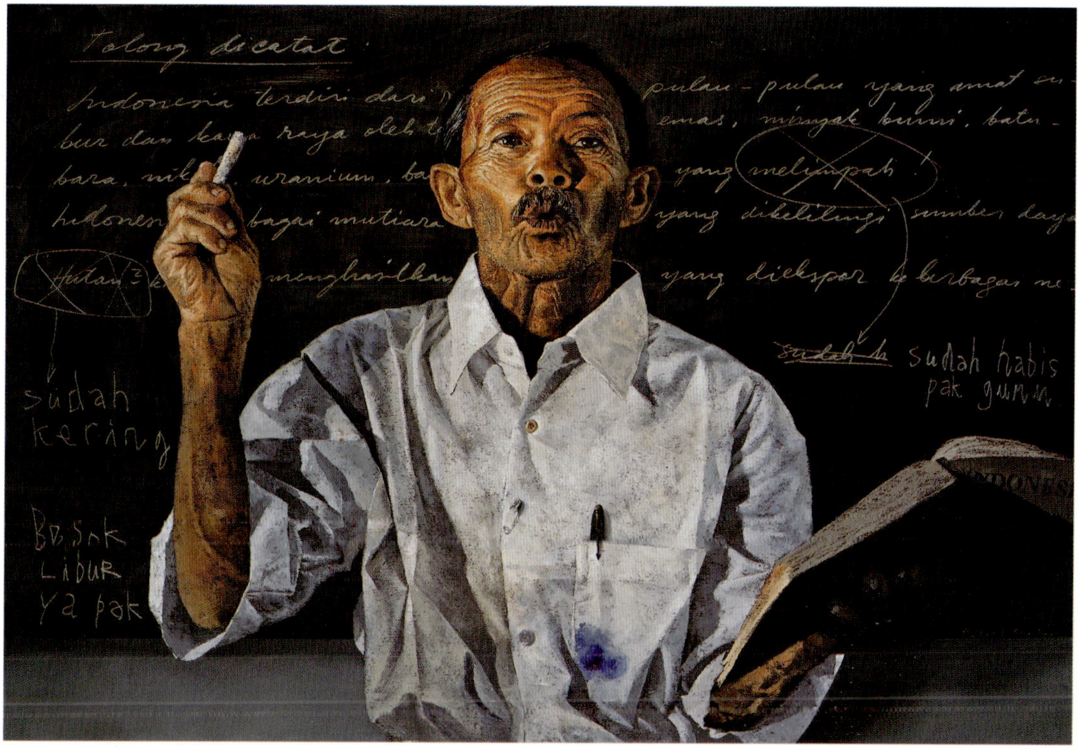

The Teacher
Oil on canvas
Private collection

教师
布面油画
私人藏品

140×200cm
2010

Faozan Rizal
法赞・利泽尔

LE PETIT PRINCE - The Book of Antoine de saint Exupery.

Le petit prince, or The Little Prince, by Antoine de Saint Exupery is the first fictional novel that I ever read when I was ten years old. At that time, the The Little Prince had been translated into the Indonesian language by Balai Pustaka. There were only five books in our elementary school library, because my school was located in a very small village. And The Little Prince was one of the books in the library. So I tried to borrow the book almost every weekend in order to read it over and over again.

The book reminds me of how simple but also how essentially children think, and how easy a language or culture can be understood – or misunderstood. And also of how, when we are grown up, we see the world in all its complexities and lose a sense of what really matters.

The storytelling and the feeling of loneliness and alienation, which I feel when I read The Little Prince, has influenced my own way of creating artwork - in my films, photography and paintings.

For many years now, I have collected The Little Prince from many countries all over the world, where I have been traveling. The story of The Little Prince seems to be beyond words – as, I believe, is my artwork.

《小王子》是安东尼·圣埃克苏佩里的书。

安东尼·圣埃克苏佩里的《小王子》是我十岁时阅读的第一本小说。
那时，《小王子》已经被巴莱·普斯塔卡（Balai Pustaka）翻译成了印尼语。
在我们的小学图书馆里，只有五本书，因为我们的学校坐落于一个非常小的村庄里。
而《小王子》是图书馆中的其中一本书。
因此，我每个周末都试着把它借出来，这样就可以一遍又一遍地阅读了。

这本书让我回想起孩子们的想法是多么单纯但又多么切中本质，
以及一种语言和一种文化如此轻易地就能被理解——或者说是误解。
还有，
我们是怎么样随着长大成人开始看到世界的复杂而却忘了什么才是最本质的东西。

这种讲述故事的方式以及这种孤独感和疏离感是我阅读《小王子》时的感受。
这影响了我创作艺术作品的方式——这体现在我的电影里、照片中以及绘画中。

很多年以后的现在，我已经在旅途中从各个国家收集了很多《小王子》的版本。
《小王子》的故事看来不可言表——我认为这就像我的艺术作品。

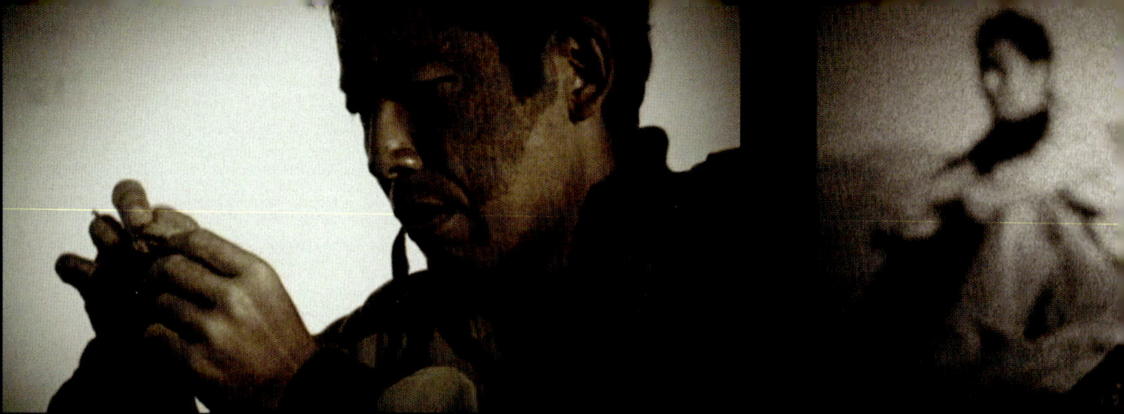

Yasujiro Journey
Super 16 mm
Production: PAOSHAS Film Indonesia

1942 Yasujiro YAMADA a Japanese Zero sentoki pilot fighter crashed in Indonesia on his way to the pacific war. He has never beeen found. In 2002, his grandson, who has the same name as him, came to Indonesia and tried to find his path. His journey in Indonesia's wild nature traces him back into 1942 - he has also never been found.

安二郎之旅
超16mm转录至DVD
制片：印尼PAOSHAS电影公司

1942年，日本战斗机飞行员小津安二郎驾驶的飞机在前往太平洋战场的途中印度尼西亚境内坠毁，小津安二郎失踪。2002年，与他同名的孙子来到印尼，试图追寻爷爷的足迹，他在印尼的野外旅行使他回溯到了1942年——但与此同时，他也失踪了。

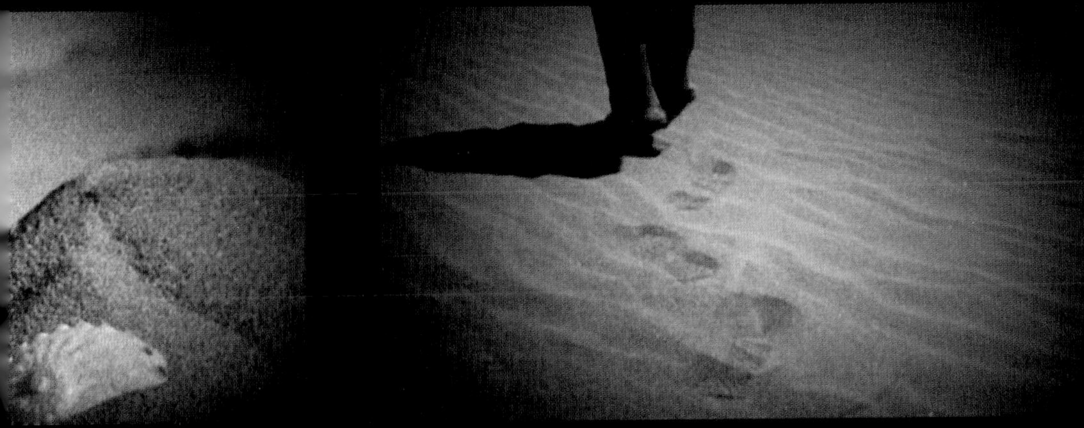

S. TEDDY D.

S. 泰迪 · D.

Interview with S. Teddy D.

Studio/House, Yogyakarta
June 2010

S. Teddy D.: **S**

F.X Harsono: **F**

Biljana Ciric: **B**

B: You mentioned that in 1994 you started making installations?

S: We would do activities sometimes, performing in the street. At that time, performance art was a medium for action. It drew people in as wonder: what are they talking about? What is the message? People would see us as street theater performers.

B: Can you tell me about one of your most important performance projects?

S: I did this performance with a friend. We were talking about human rights issues, it was one human rights day—the 10th of December—and we were talking about racism and violence. Then we made a performance. I painted my body in white, not with acrylic, but with wall

S. 泰迪・D. 访谈

艺术家工作室，日惹
2010年6月

S. 泰迪・D.：**S**

方济各・沙勿略・哈索诺：**F**

比利安娜：**B**

B: 你提到你是从1994年开始作装置作品的？

S: 我们有时会做不同的活动，去街上表演之类的。那个时候"行为/表演"更多的是被我们作为一种行动的工具。人们看到我们会产生疑问：我们在做什么、在说什么？我们要传达的信息是什么？有时候人们会将我们看作为街头剧场的表演者。

B: 能否谈一下你最重要的行为作品？

S: 当时是跟一位朋友一起做的。因为那天正好是世界人权日，12月10日，所以我们就谈人权及其相关的种族与暴力等一些列问题。那么当时我们就决定做行为。我把我的身体全部刷成白色，用的不是丙烯颜料而是刷墙用的涂料。然后我们俩用绳子绕在脖子上并互相连接。我们从学校开始一直这样走到市中心，而且还乘了公共汽车和其它

paint, and we used a rope put around our necks to connect us. We walked from my school to the center of town, and also used the bus and public transportation. My friend started to distribute printed materials to people.

B: So you had a flyer as well?

S: It was just some photocopies. But it was very effective, and became central to the action. It was not just art anymore. The motivation of the performance was not only to make a work of art, but to try and talk with people, to try and communicate with the people and the public.

B: Are you still making performances?

S: Yes, sometimes, I still do with my band.

B: When did you start the band?

S: In 1997, but we are a band that never performs.

F: None of the members can play any instrument. They made a book. The writer told a story about one of the gigs. He said that all of them wear their hair long and have tattoos. When they were on stage, they seemed like professionals. But when they started to sing, they sang a children's song. No one in the public wanted to support or clap for them. After that, they started to sing the student protest song, and all the people stood up because all of them were students; they all knew this song and began to sing along. They received great applause.

B: What's your role in the band?

S: I am a vocalist. But sometimes I also just sit and smoke, and the guitarist sings. Sometimes I just watch. But I am actually the brain behind the band.

交通工具。而我的朋友一路都在向过往的路人发我们的印刷品。

B: 你们还有宣传单吗?

S: 是我们自己复印的。但是这种方式很有效，而且成为了行动的工具。甚至已经不仅仅只是艺术了。做这些行为的动机已不再只是为了做艺术作品，而是试图去跟人产生交流、对话。去尝试着去公众展开交流。

B: 现在还在做行为吗?

S: 当然，有时候做，跟我乐队一起做。

B: 什么时候开始做了乐队?

S: 1997年， 但是我们的乐队从来不演出。

F: 乐队里没有一个成员会使用乐器。他们做了一本书。一位作家在书里描述过他们的演出时，说他们每个人都有一头长发而且满身的纹身，在舞台上他们看上去很专业，但是一开始唱歌就开始唱儿歌。莫名的观众没人愿意给他们支持或掌声。但是儿歌结束之后他们就开始唱是学生抗议的歌，所有的观众都开始站起来并开始跟着唱然后还给予热烈的掌声，因为大部分的观众都是学生。

B: 乐队里你是什么角色?

S: 我是歌手。但是有时候我只是在舞台上坐着抽烟，只有我的吉他在“唱”。有时我只是作为一个旁观者。但其实我是乐队的的大脑。

B: 那你们都唱什么样的歌?

S: 有时候是儿歌、民歌、摇篮曲或者国歌。我们自己只写了一首歌叫“在天上种米”，歌曲在讲我

B: So what kind of songs do you sing?

S: Sometimes a children's song, a folk song, lullaby, or national song. We have only written one song: "To plant (rice) paddies in the sky." The song talks about the land as full of blood and violence, and how we don't have enough land anymore to plant the rice paddies. In Indonesia, the paddies are holy plants, because we consume them. So it's better to plant in them in the sky, because the land is already dirty and full of sin. The song was also written in Indonesian and indigenous languages.

们的土地充满了暴力和血腥，我们已经没有地方种米了。在印尼，我们认为“米”是神圣的植物，因为我们靠它为生。所以把米种到天上更为合适。我们的土地充斥着肮脏和罪恶。歌词同样是用印尼文和土族语言写的。

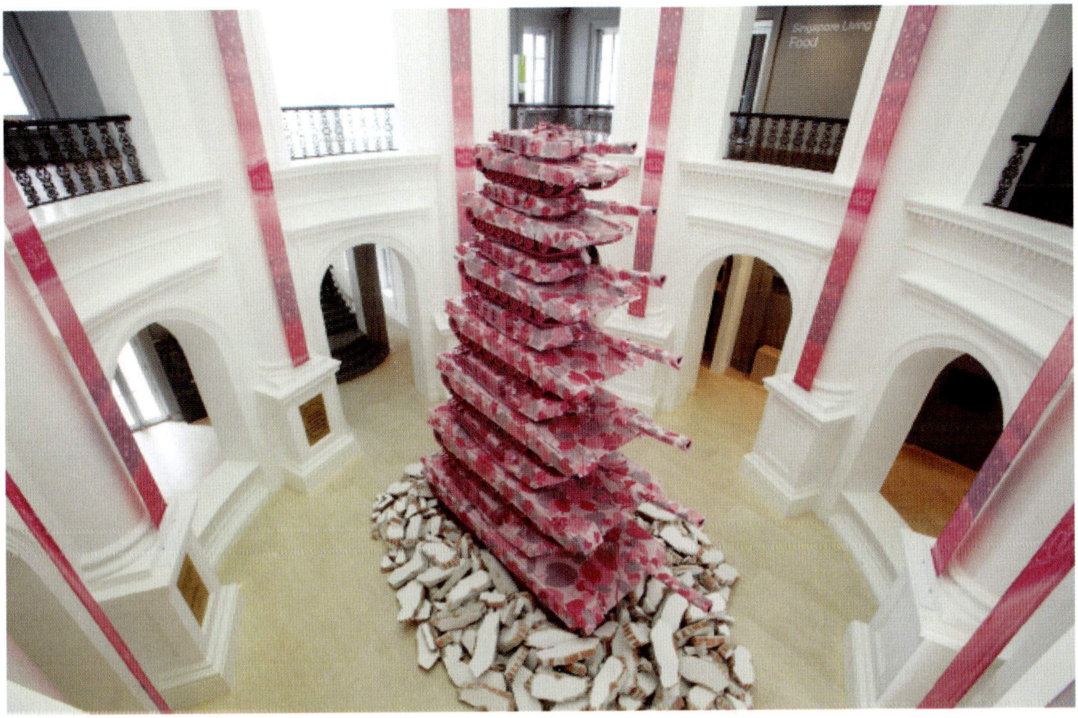

Love Tank
Multiplex, resin, metal structure
Installation View at National Museum of Singapore

爱情坦克
复合材料，合成树脂，金属支架
新加坡国立美术馆

200×500×650cm
2009

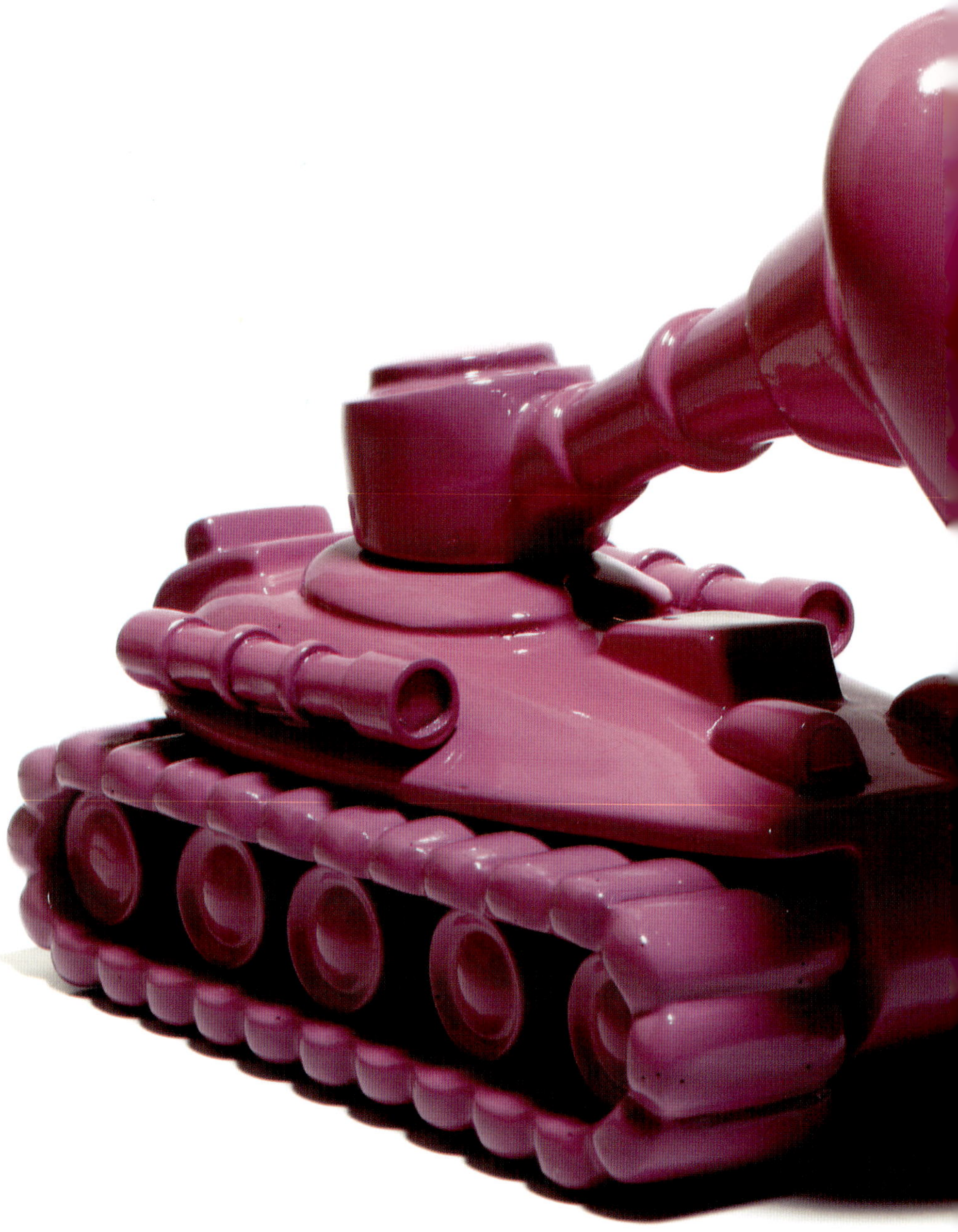

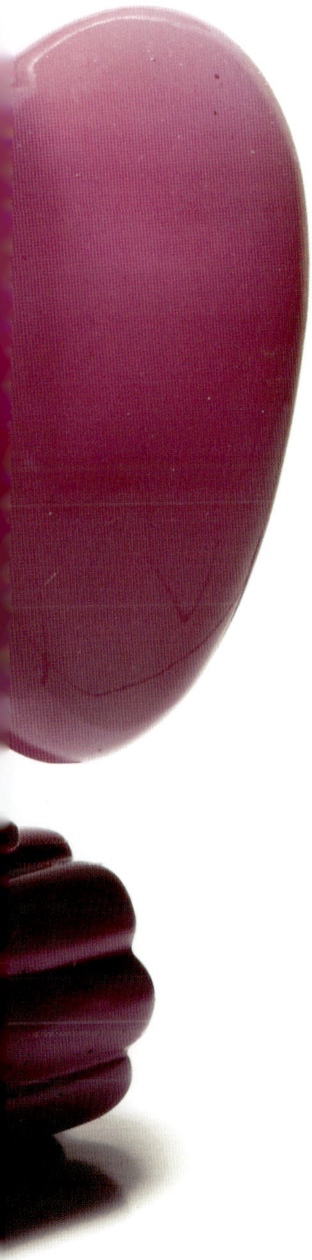

Pink Tank
Polyester

粉色坦克
聚酯纤维

200×140×270cm
2009

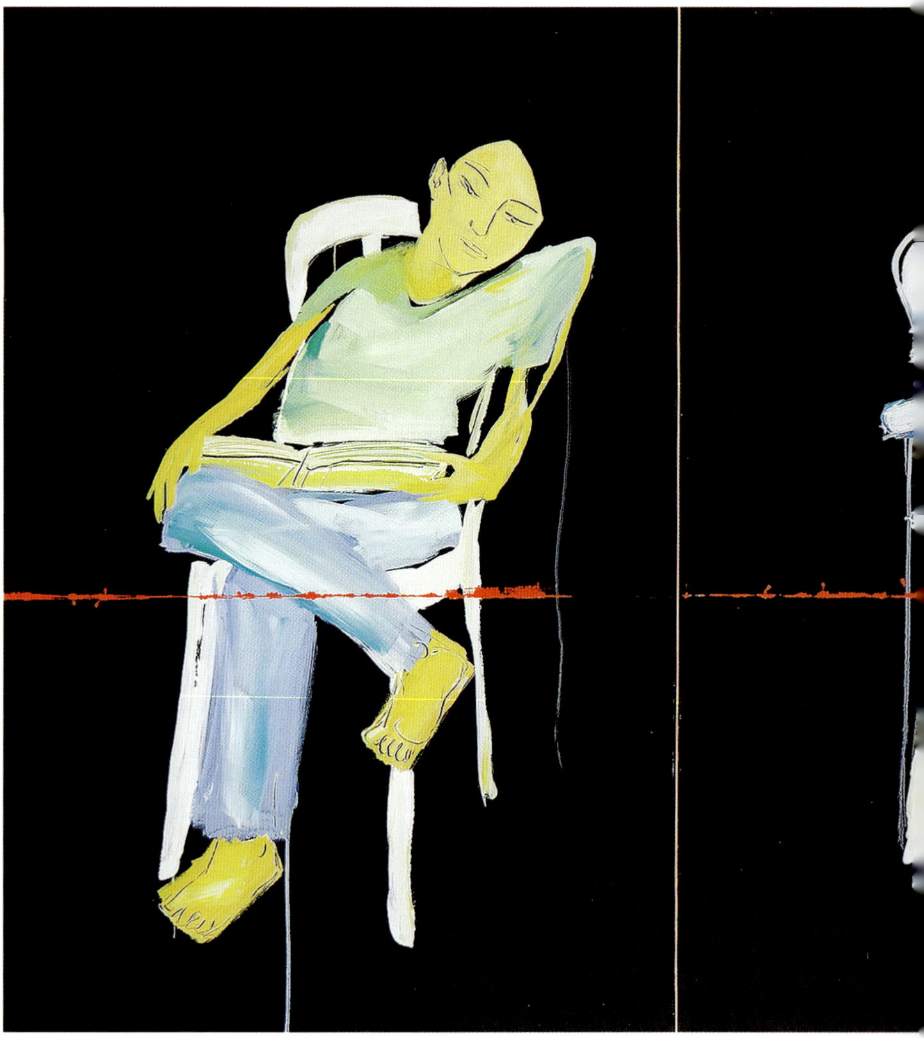

Red String
Acrylic on canvas
OHD Museum collection, Magelang

红弦
布面丙烯
印尼马格朗OHD博物馆馆藏

145×285cm
2005

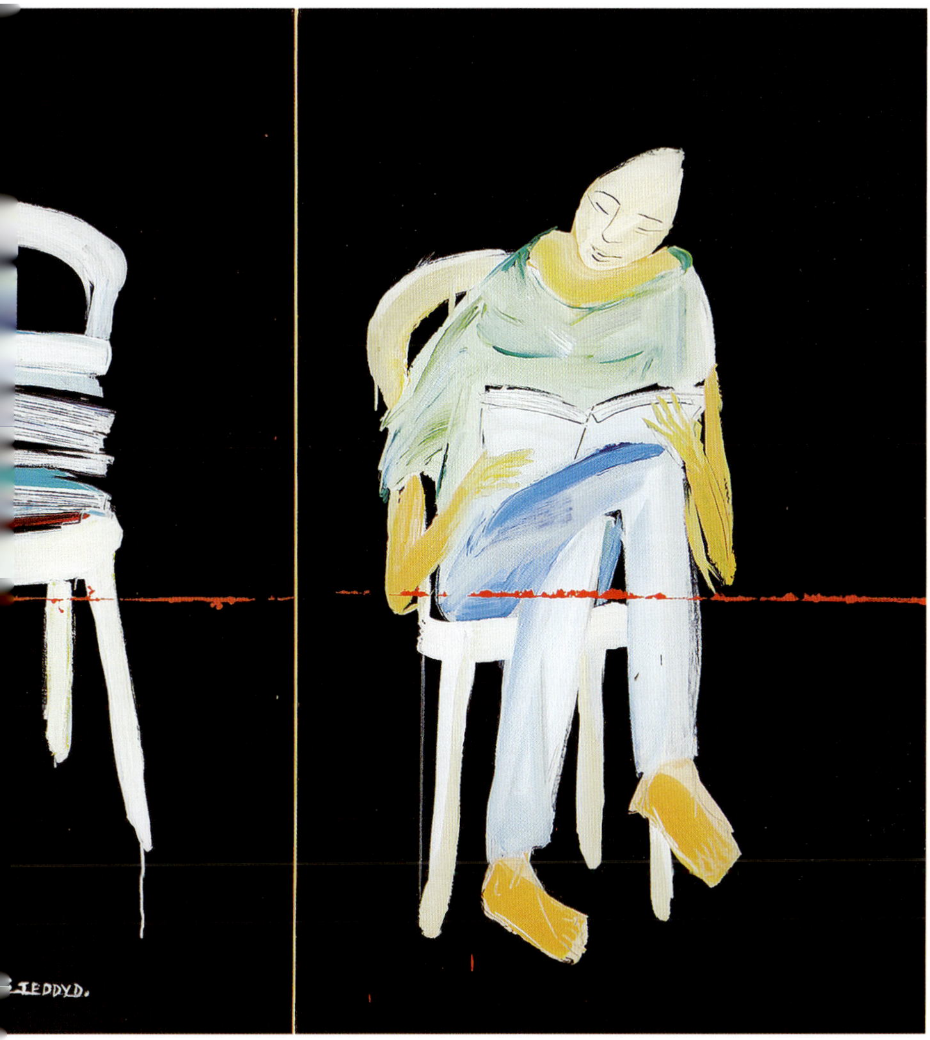
TEDDY D.

Handiwirman Saputra
翰迪怀儿曼·萨普川

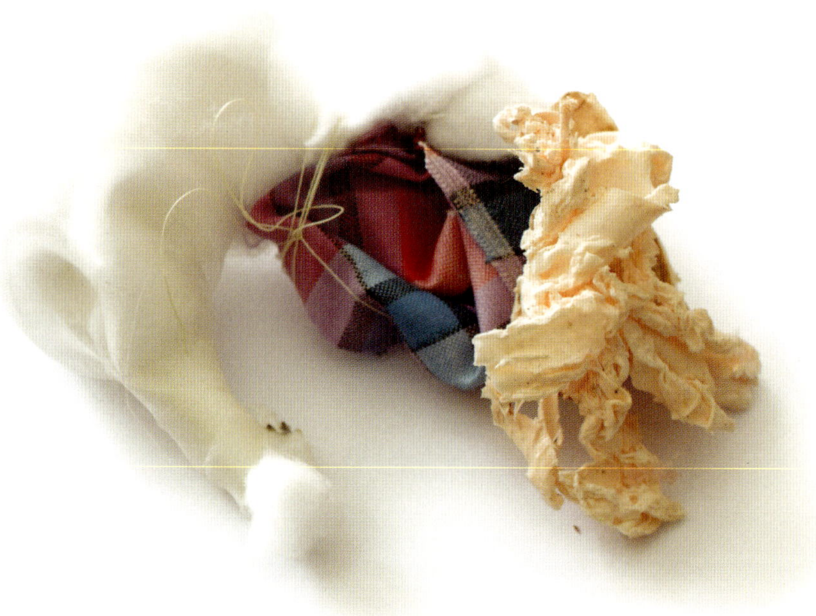

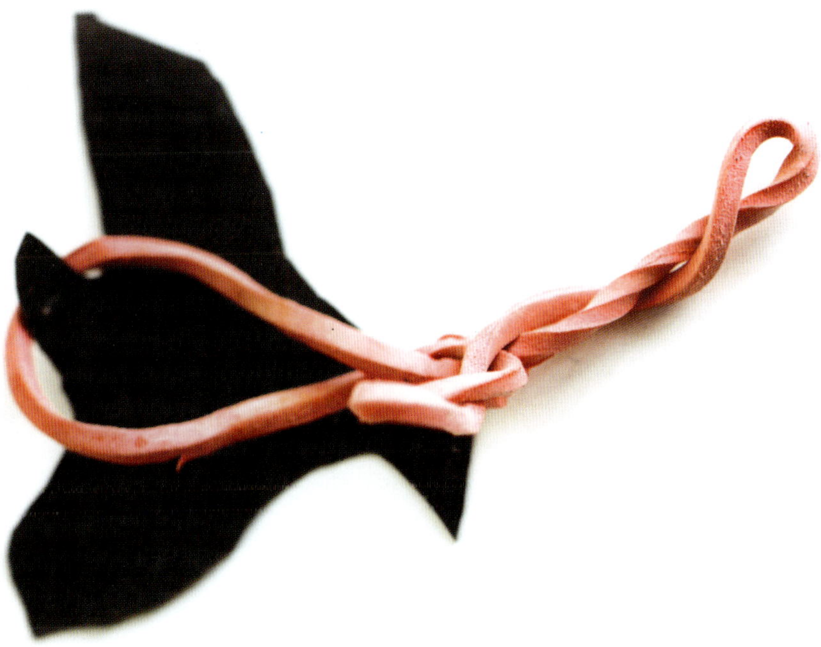

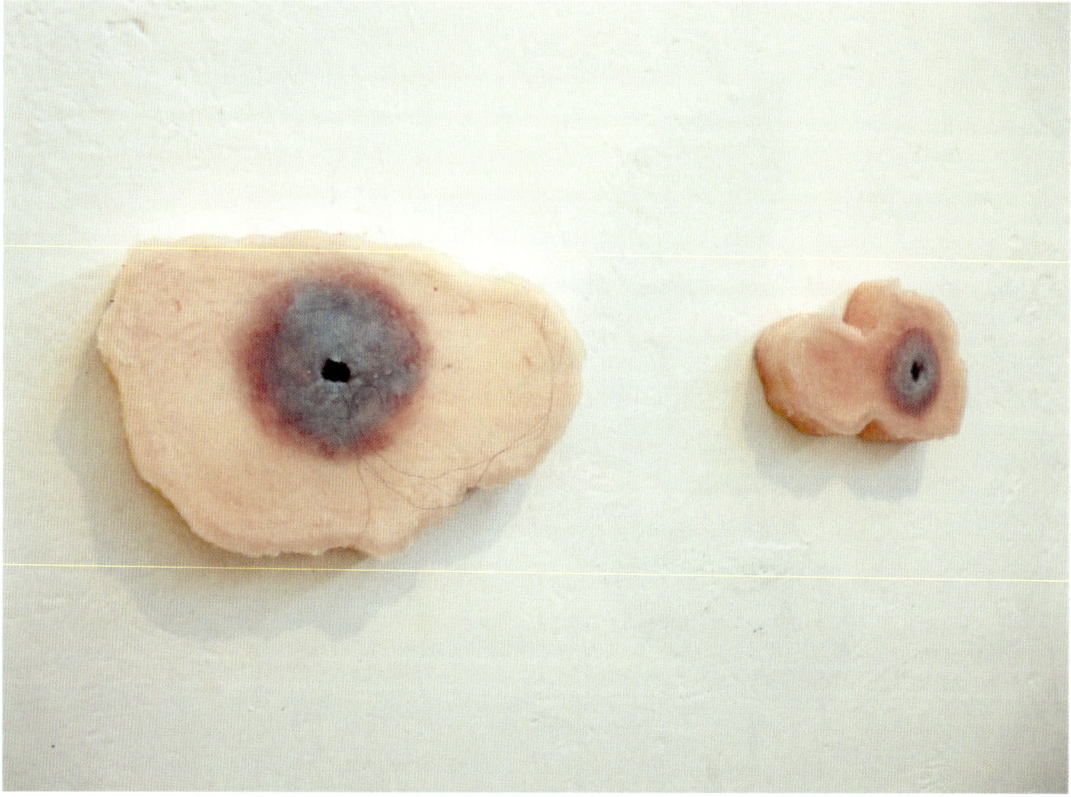

Versi Ragam Hias (Ornament Version)
Glue, Silicone, Hair

装饰物
胶水、硅胶、头发

24×15.5×3cm, 16×11×3cm
2009

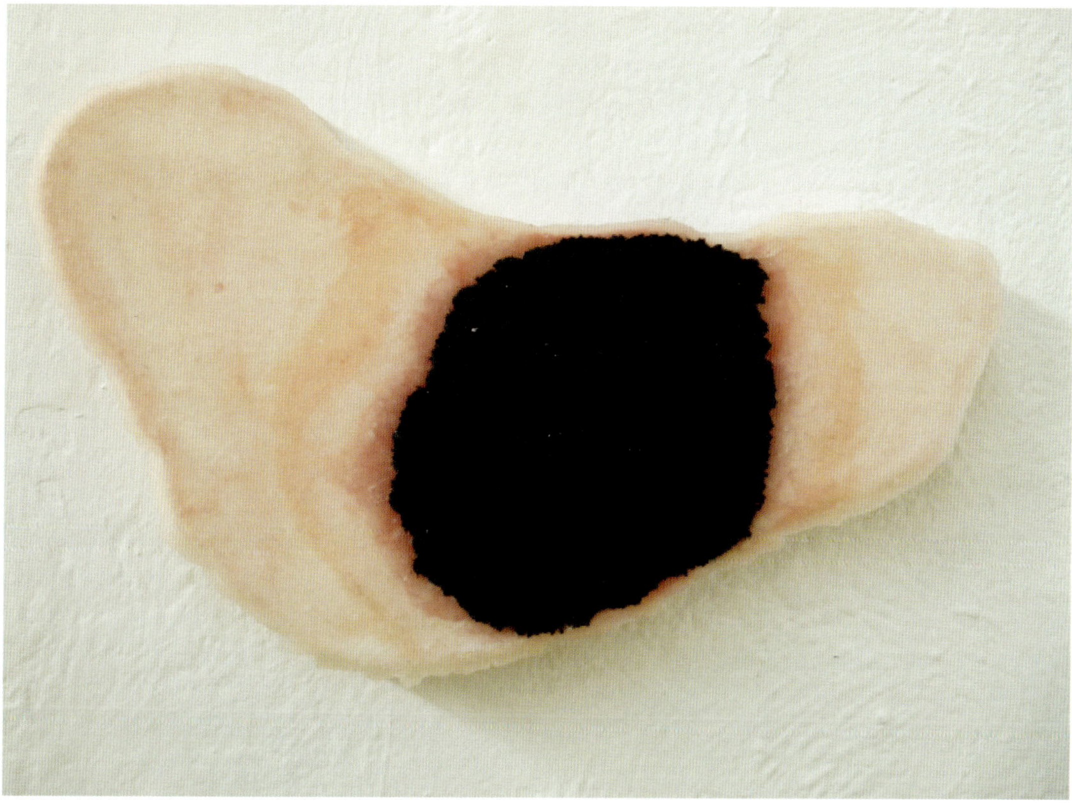

Versi Ragam Hias (Ornament Version)
Glue, Silicone, Wooden Flakes

装饰物
胶水、硅胶、木片

43×28×5cm
2009

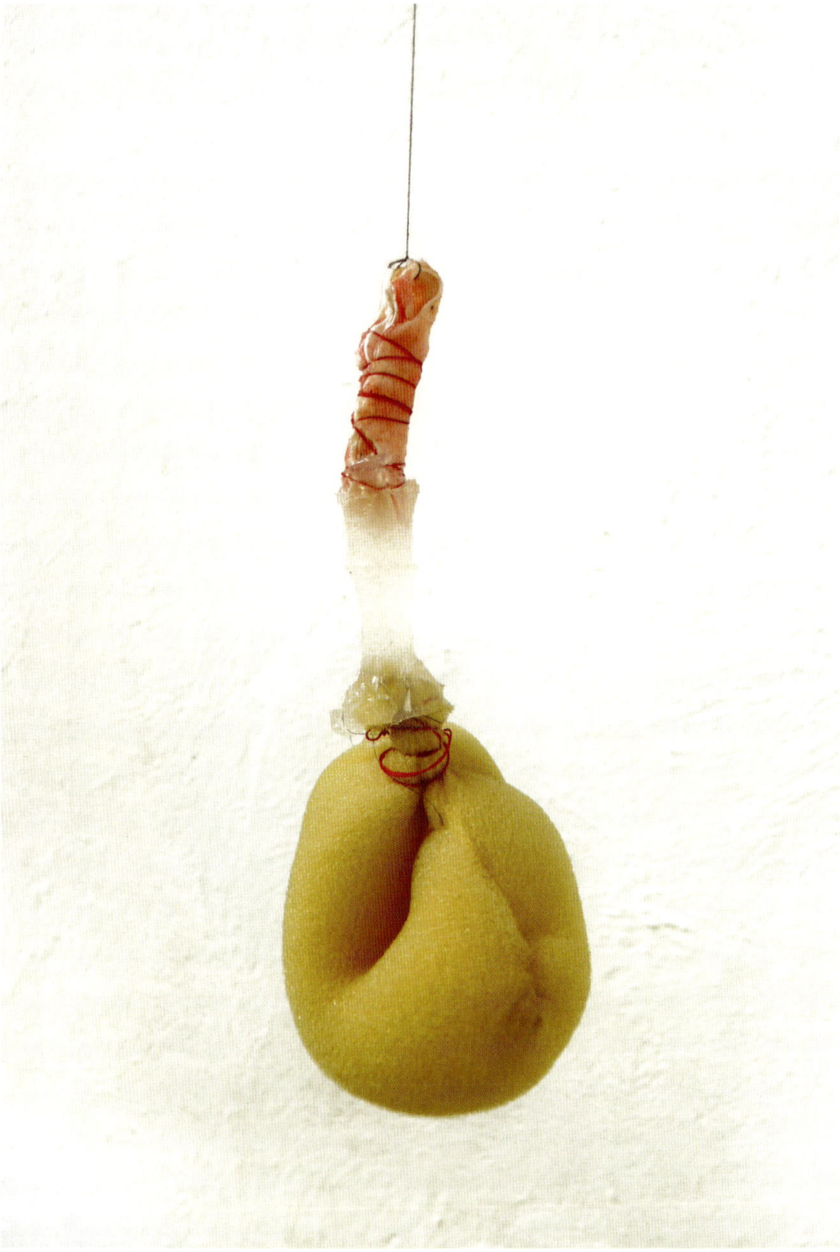

Versi Ragam Hias (Ornament Version)
Glue, Silicone, Sponge

装饰物
胶水、硅胶、海绵

9×5.5×13cm
2009

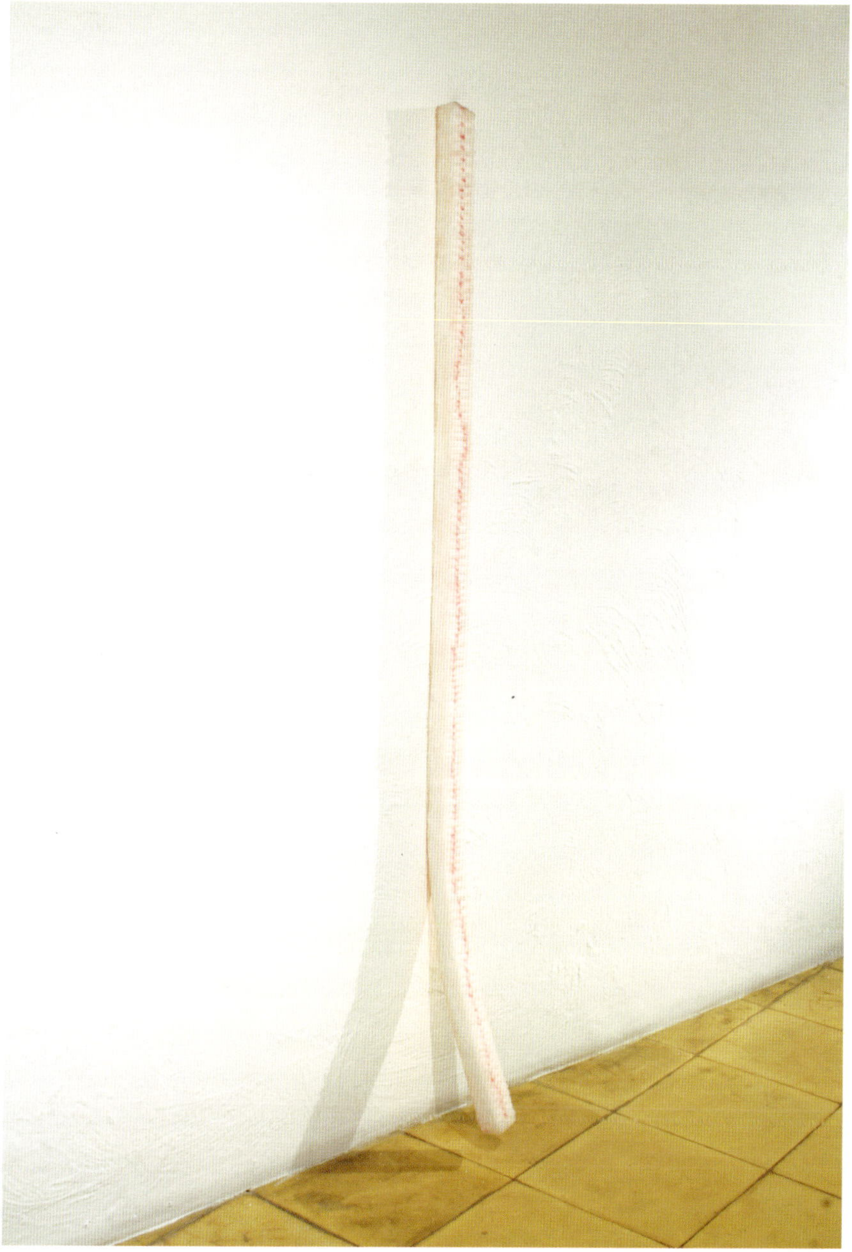

Versi Ragam Hias (Ornament Version)
Glue, Silicone

装饰物
胶水、硅胶

4×5×170cm
2009

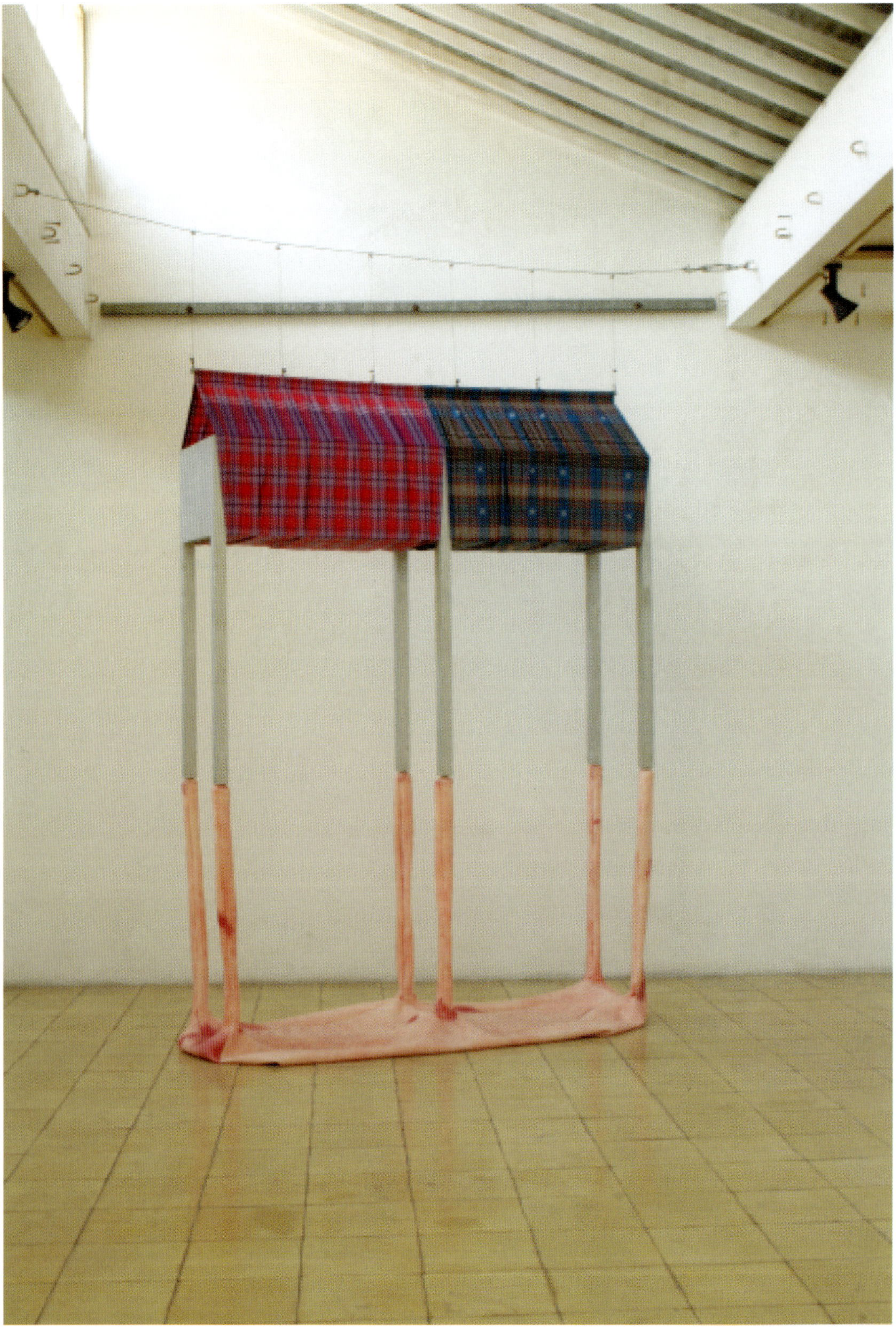

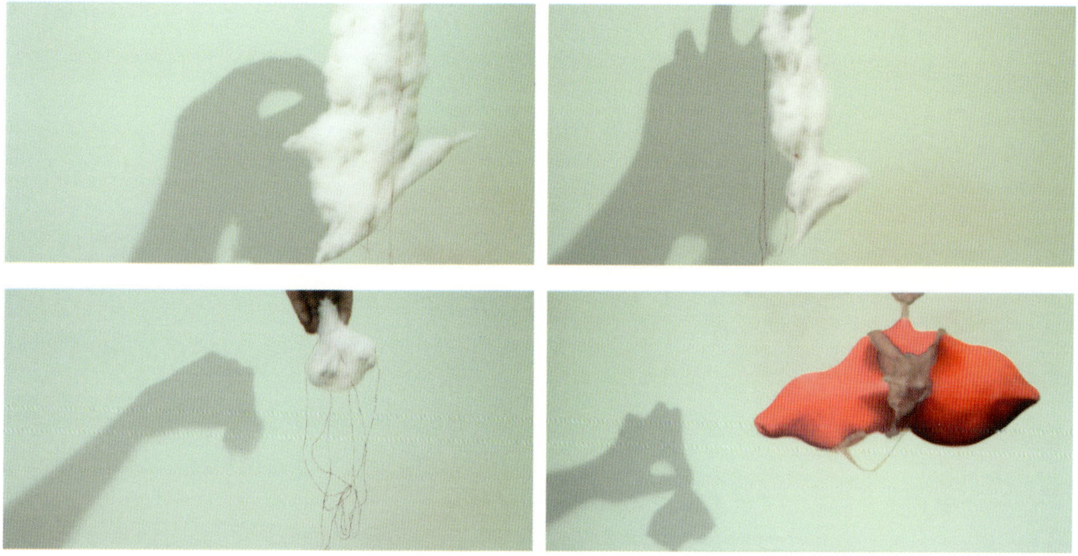

UNTITLED
Sarong, Alumunium Plate, Silicone Glue

无题
纱笼、铝板、硅胶

200×60×300 cm
2009

Seri Benda dan Bayangan (Things and Shadows Series)
Acrylic on Canvas

物体和阴影系列
亚克力布面

100×200 cm (4 panels/版)
2005

Chusin Setiadikara
川森・萨提迪卡亚

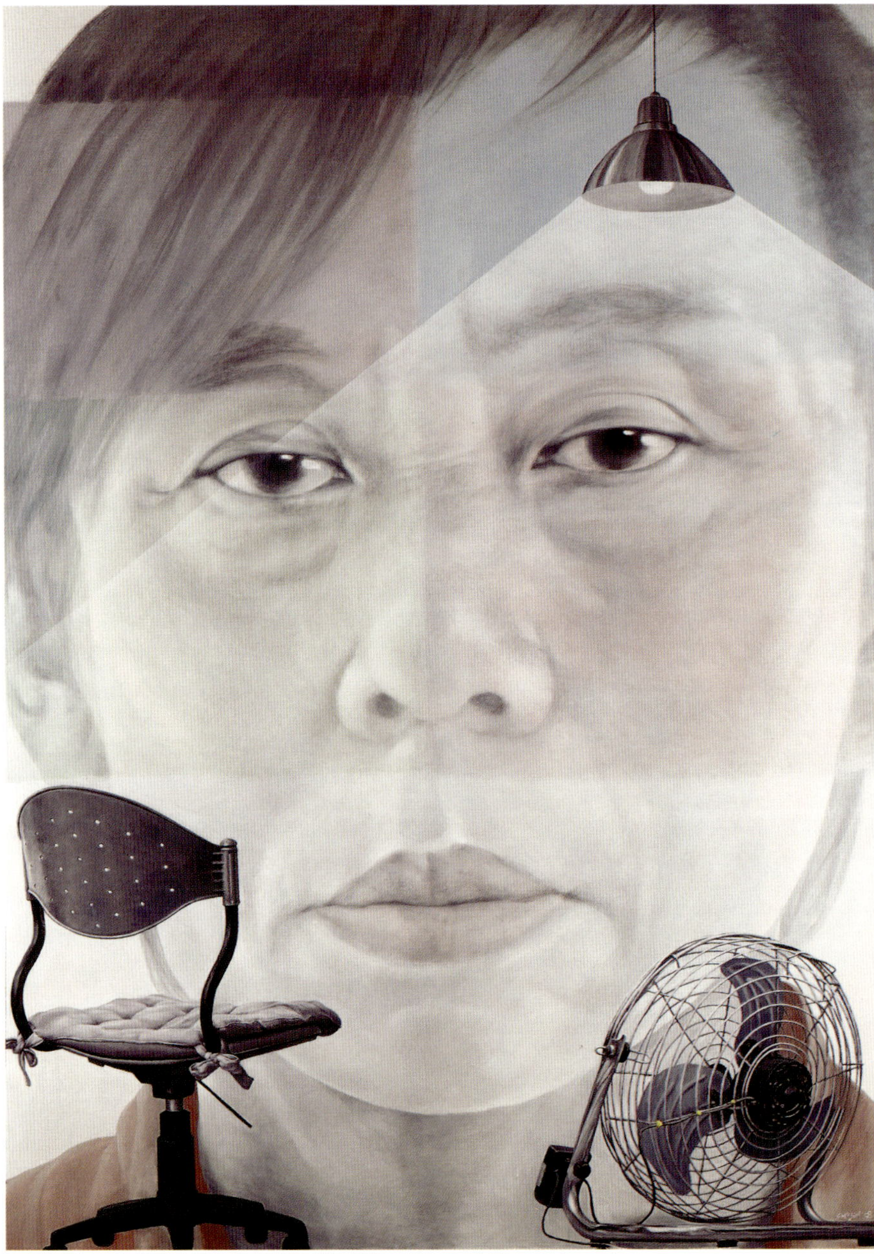

Self
Oil on canvas

自我
布面油画

200×140cm
2008

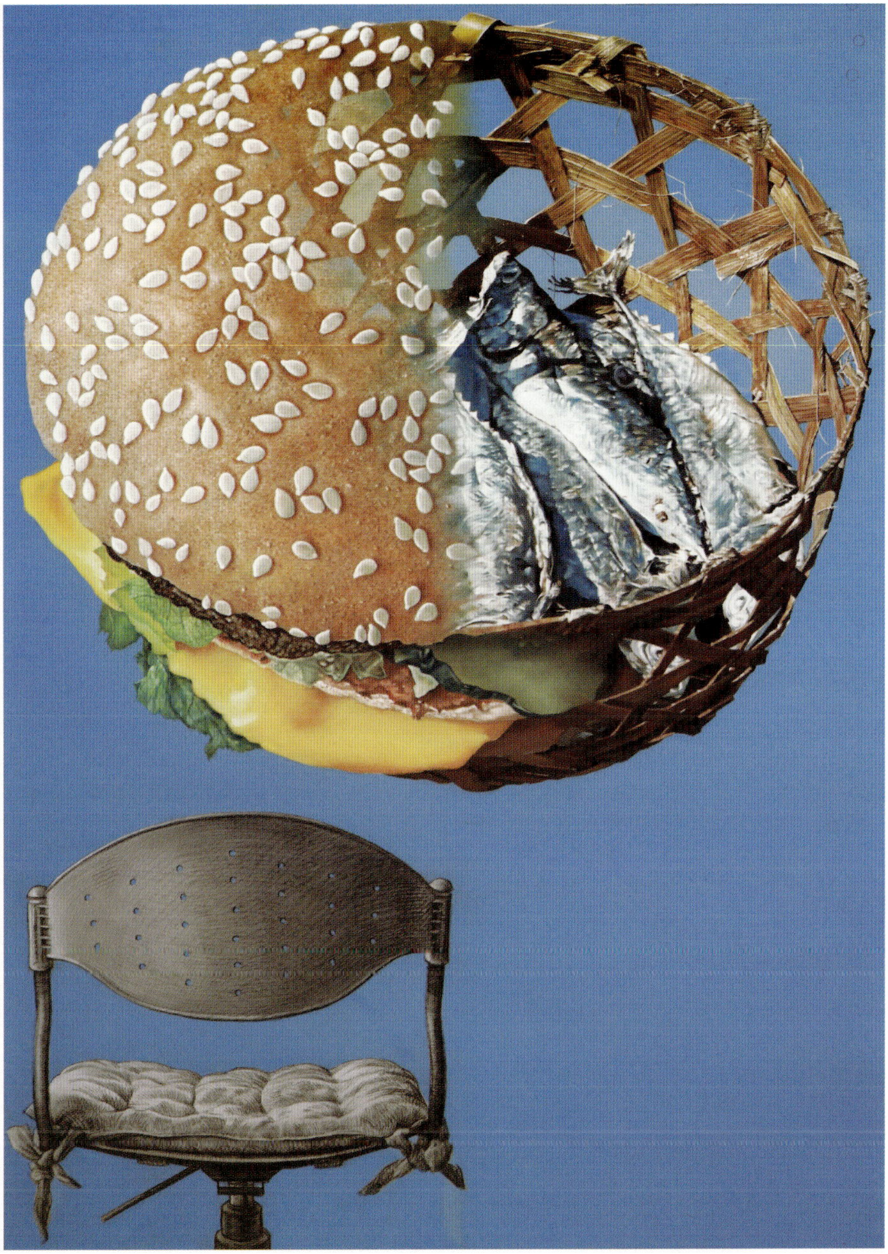

Daily
Oil & charcoal on canvas

每日
布面油画/碳笔画

200×140cm
2010

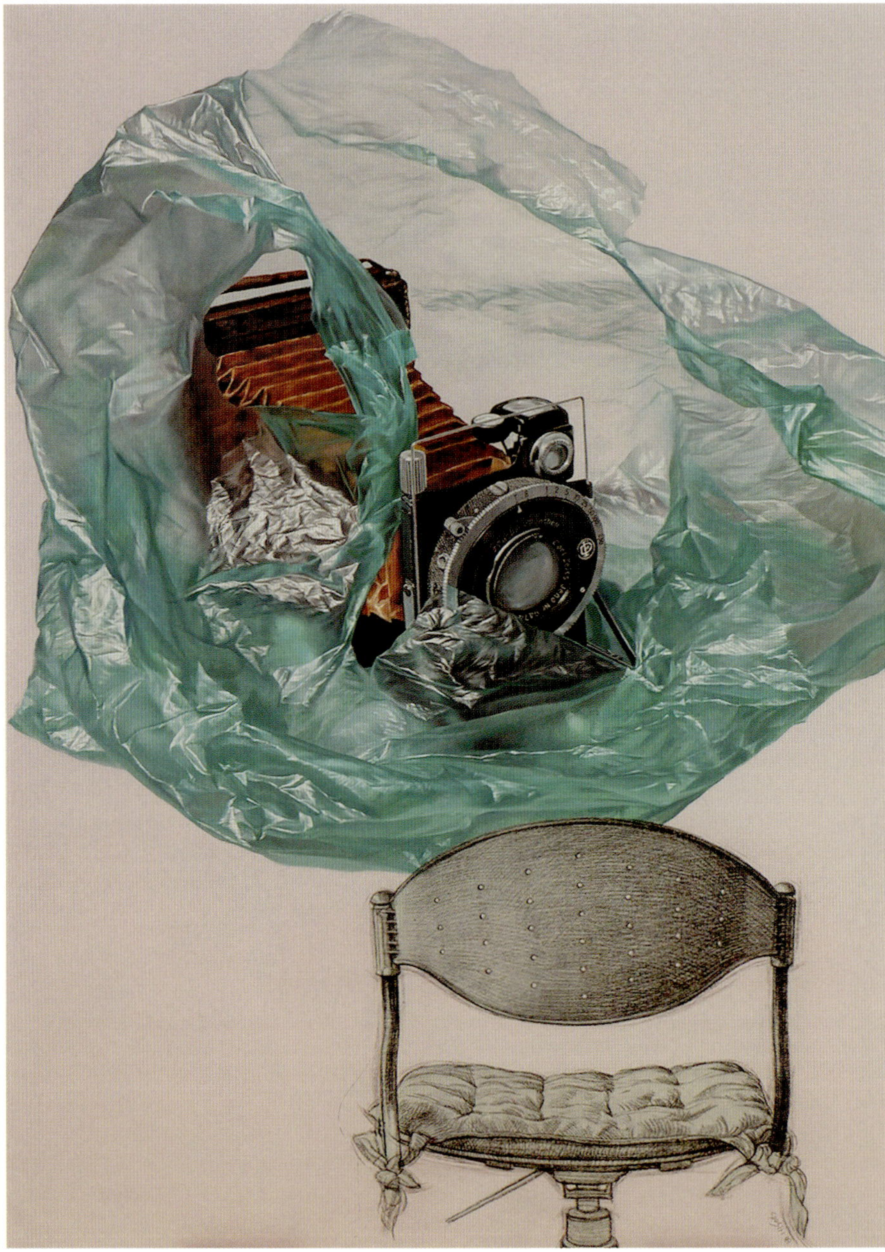

Memory
Oil & charcoal on canvas

记忆
布面油画/碳笔画

200×140cm
2008

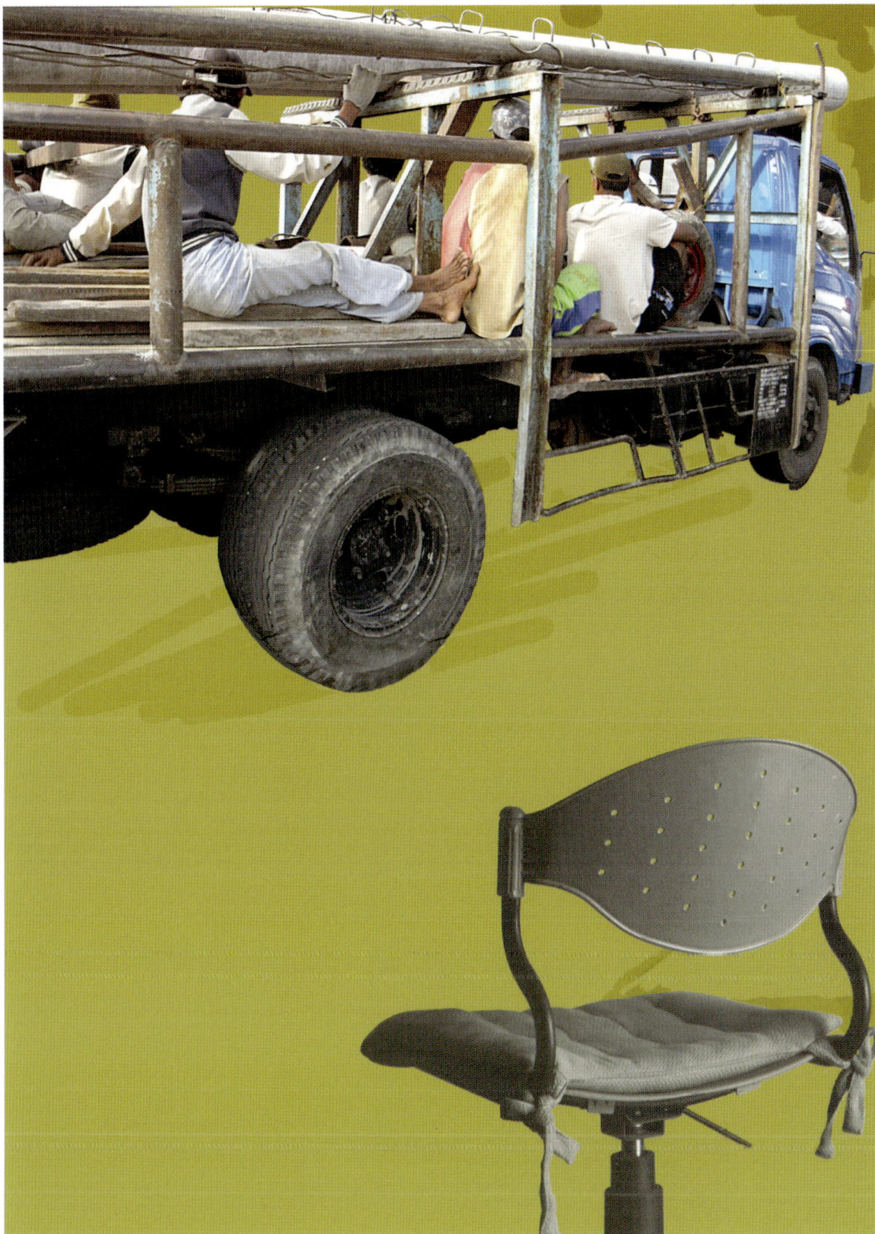

People
Oil & charcoal on canvas

人
布面油画/碳笔画

200×140cm
2010

Pintor Sirait
平托・西瑞特

Victory
Stainless Steel

胜利
不锈钢

318×190×97cm
2008

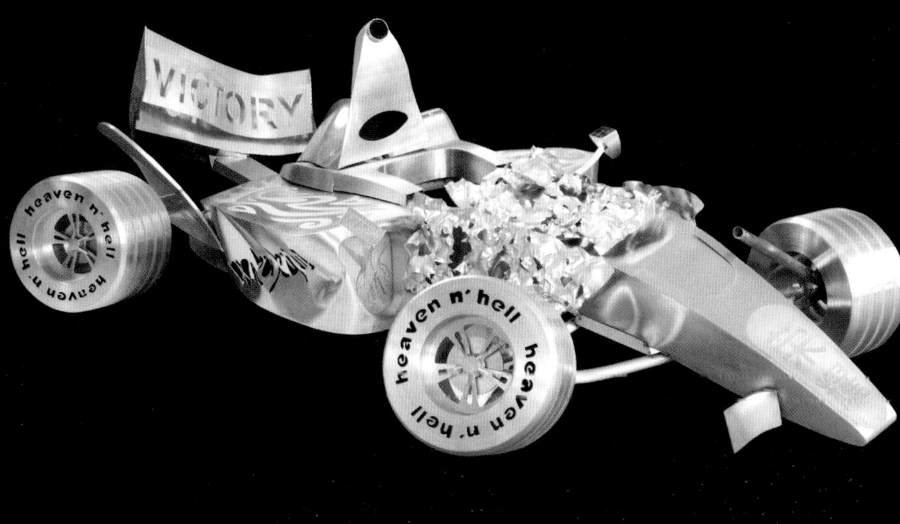
VICTORY
heaven n' hell
heaven n' hell
heaven n' hell
heaven n' hell

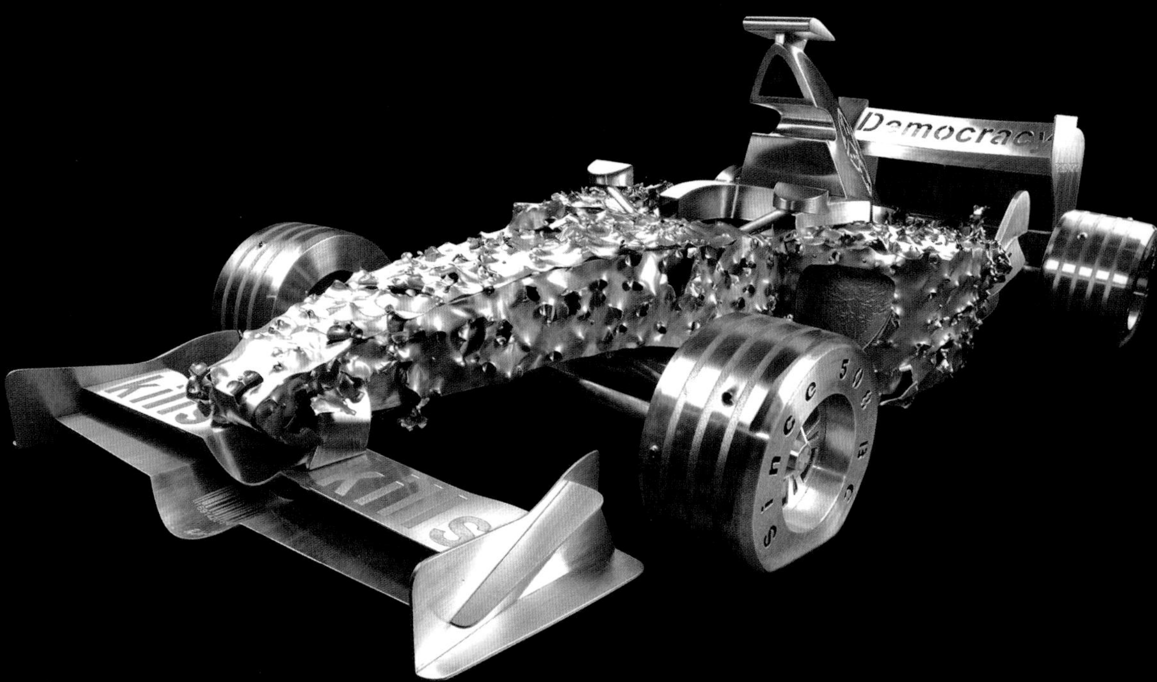
Democracy
Kills

Democracy
Stainless steel, Private collection

民主
不锈钢
私人藏品

100×346×157cm
2009

Putu Sutawijaya
普图·苏塔维嘉亚

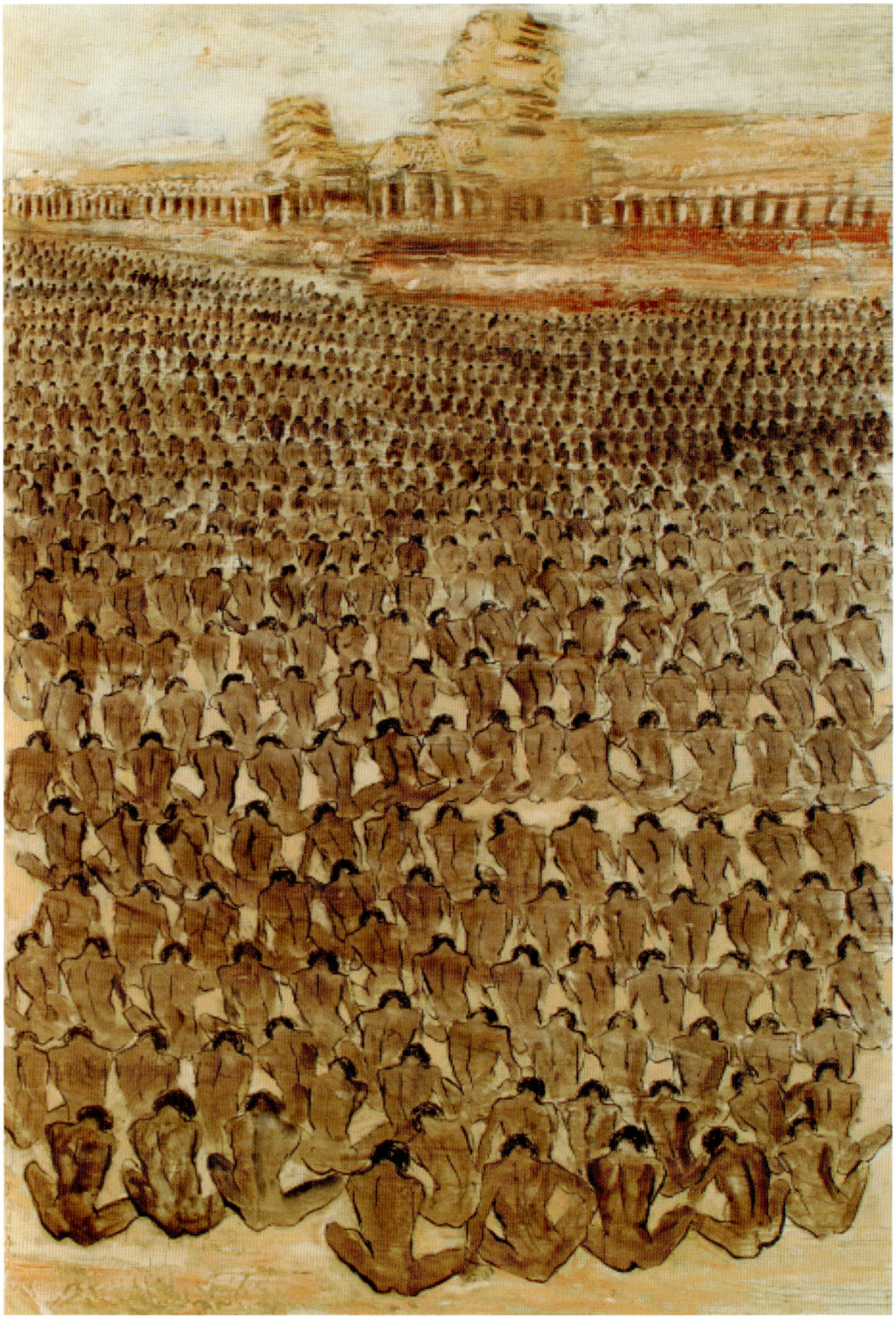

Setelah Sunyi
Mixed Media on Canvas

沉默之后
布面综合材料

300×200cm
2007

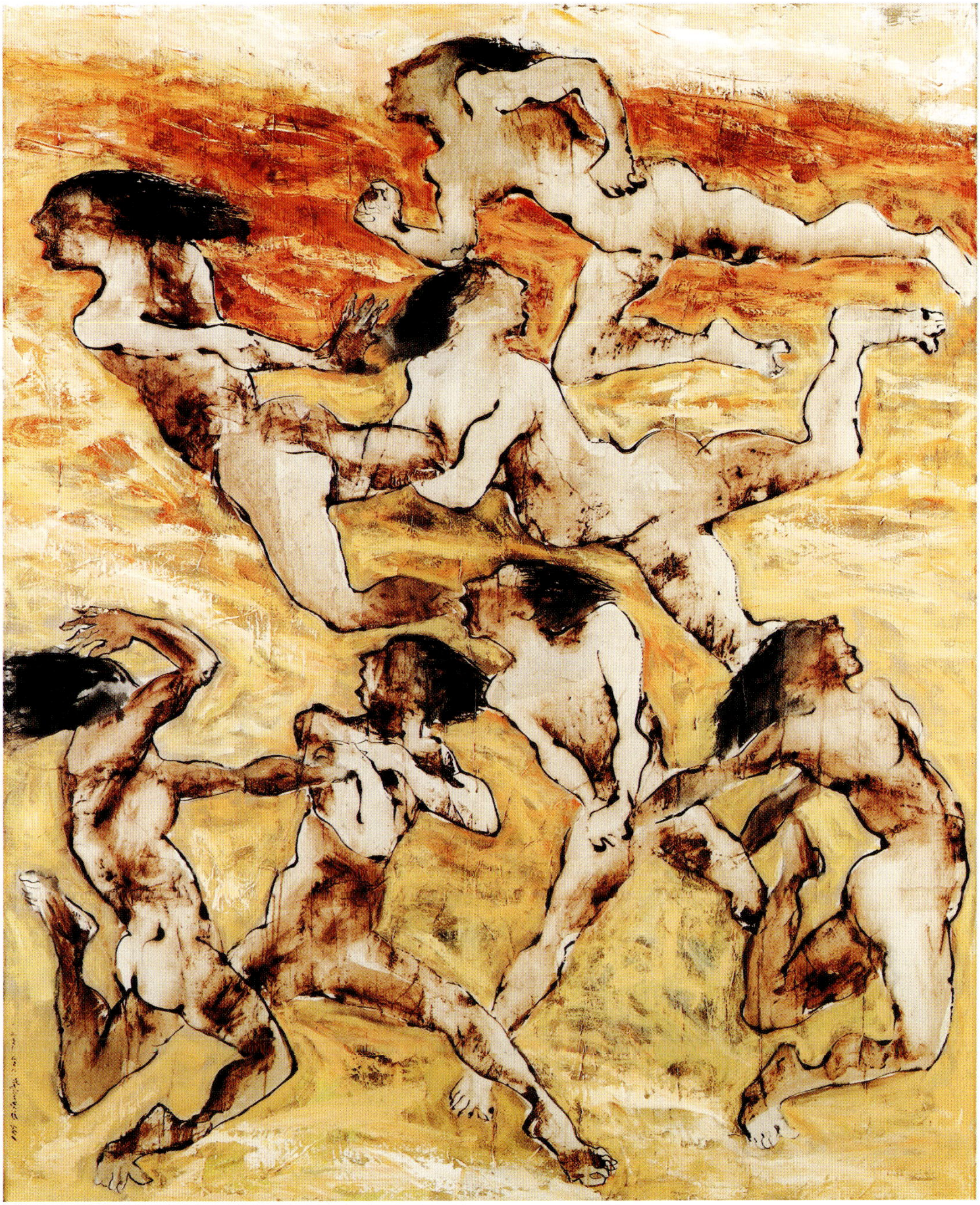

Without Resistance I
Mixed media on canvas
Galeri Canna collection, Jakarta

无阻力I
布面综合材料
雅加达Canna画廊藏品

225×180cm
2003-2007

Agus Suwage
阿顾思・苏瓦吉

Interview with Agus Suwage

Agus Suwage's Studio, Jogjakarta
June 2010

Agus Suwage: **A**
Biljana Ciric: **B**

B: Have you ever considered your work to be of a performative nature? Specifically, the photos you have been taking of yourself and then painting upon?

A: Sometimes what I do is similar to performance. I realized this when my friend pointed it out to me, he said: "Actually, you do performances by yourself," and I realized "Oh, yes." When I was doing the painting performance series, I was continuing in this vein, but using a different approach.

B: Have you ever done actual, live performances?

A: No, I'm too shy.

B: You are too shy?!

A: In my view, it is not pleasing enough to perform. I think if I would try to do a performance I would

阿顾思·苏瓦吉访谈

阿顾思·苏瓦吉工作室，日惹
2010年6月

阿顾思·苏瓦吉：**A**
比利安娜：**B**

B: 你怎么看自己作品中的表演性成份？比如你拍下自己的照片然后再进行绘画创作。

A: 我其实挺喜欢表演的。当我朋友对我说"其实你是自己在进行行为艺术"时，我也意识到"确实如此"。在创作绘画行为系列时，我一直运用不同的方法。

B: 你进行过真正的行为表演吗？

A: 没有，我挺害羞的。

B: 你确实太害羞了！？

A: 我做行为艺术会很难看。我很可能会笑话自己，而且我也不是个好演员。

B: 但是为了绘画，你一直会在镜头前表演。

end up laughing at myself during the performance. And I'm not a good actor.

B: But you always perform in front of the camera for your paintings.

A: Yes, that is something I love to do. And maybe I would love to perform with my music.

B: Have you ever performed publicly?

A: No, not really.

B: So you have been working with music for many years now, but you never actually publicly perform in this way. It seems that you like making self-portraits by taking photos of yourself, but in a way they become like an homage to the performance artist. You practice playing music every single day, and yet you never play this music in front of others…

A: Yes, I think I may be a bit too scared for this, so I perform on my own.

B: You still have the urge to perform though.

A: Not really. Perhaps I do, but mainly I make music for myself. It brings me great satisfaction. Sometimes when I paint I encounter this same feeling. It is like a kind of trance.

B: So you have performed in some way then, right?

A: No.

B: Then why do you practice music?

A: Not really for this reason that you suggest; perhaps I have a little inclination to perform, but mainly just for myself. That's it, this is enough for me. When I play, I forget everything. When I

A: 对，我很喜欢这种形式，还喜欢再配上点音乐。

B: 你有没有在公共场合进行过行为表演?

A: 没有。

B: 多年来，音乐一直是你作品中的重要元素，但你从来没有公开进行过行为表演。从某种意义上讲，照相是你完成自画像的一个手段，同时你也通过这种方式向行为艺术家致敬。你每天都与音乐打交道，但却从未向大家展示过。

A: 没错。或许因为我有一点怯场，所以只表演给自己看。

B: 你有强烈的表演欲望吗?

A: 没有。我只想做自己的音乐而已。这其中的满足感是我所追求的。在进行绘画创作时，我也会有类似的体验。

B: 这一行为系列已经告一段落了吗?

A: 还没有。

B: 你为什么练习音乐演奏呢?

A: 这主要是为了自己，而不全是为了表演。我非常喜欢音乐，仅此而已。当沉浸在音乐的世界中，我似乎可以忘记一切。而在我作画时，我也会忘记一切，仿佛徜徉在艺术的舞池中，我喜欢这种感觉。

B: 你是不是依然相信自己的年龄“玩摇滚太老，而就此辞世又太小”？

A: 我用Jethro Tull的歌来命名我的作品。我的身体可能正在老去，体力确实不如从前。但是，如果可以的话我还是想继续过年少轻狂的日子，我不想

paint, I also forget everything; it becomes something like a dance. That's it, I like that.

B: Tell me about: "you still think you are too old to rock and roll, too young to die."

A: I took the title of this work from a song by Jethro Tull. It is also the title of their song. My body is getting older; my physical strength is not as strong as it used to be. But if I can, I want to continue to live wildly. I don't want to be established and stable. I don't want to be stable at all. I hate being stable, in every sense of the word.

B: When did you start getting involved in music. When did your interest in music spark? Was it very early as well?

A: When I was very young, yes. When I was older I was asked: "What do you want to be when you grow up?" And I would say that I wanted to be a musician. It is my obsession, my obsession since long ago.

B: Really! So you always wanted to be a musician. Who was your idol that you looked to?

A: Led Zeppelin.

B: Did you have a band?

A: Yes, before, while I was in university. In high school I played in different bands, not in a permanent band, and I played with mostly not-yet-established bands, or in some little community groups.

B: If you wanted to be in a band or a musician, why did you start making art? Why did you go to art school?

A: After high school I applied to art school, and if I hadn't been accepted to the official art school,

要安顿下来，我讨厌那种按部就班、波澜不惊的感觉。

B: 你是什么时候开始与音乐结缘的？也是很早以前吗？

A: 小时候当长辈问我长大后想做什么，我会说我要做一个音乐人。那时候我就开始迷恋音乐了。

B: 你一直梦想成为音乐人，对吗？谁是你的偶像？

A: Led Zeppelin。

B: 你有没有组建过乐队？

A: 有，那还是在我上大学以前。我在高中参加过很多乐队，但都是些临时性的。我一般都在玩票性质的乐队或者社团里表演。

B: 既然你想要玩乐队、做音乐人，那又怎么会走上艺术的道路？怎么会想到去艺术学院念书？

A: 高中毕业以后，我申请了艺术学院。如果当时没有被录取，我可能会成为一名音乐人，有自己的乐队，在酒吧或者咖啡馆里演出。直到今天我还是很喜欢音乐，有时自己在工作室里演奏得非常投入，以至于不想再画画、甚至想要放弃艺术了。我在演奏的时候可以忘记一切，这对我的艺术生涯是很危险的。

B: 你会忘记艺术？！

A: 是的，我会变得很懒散，不想再搞艺术了。

B: 那你为什么会从事艺术这一行呢？

A: 这是我的工作、我的职业。

B: 但不是你所迷恋的东西？

I would probably have ended up being a musician and putting together a band, playing in the bars and cafes. I enjoy music very much, and sometimes when I play in my studio I am so concentrated, sometimes I experience the feeling that I don't want to paint or practice art anymore, because I can forget everything while I play music. It's dangerous for my artistic career!

B: You forget about art as well?

A: Yes I become very lazy and do not want to make art.

B: So why make art?

A: It's like my job, my profession.

B: And art is not your obsession?

A: I don't know… my obsession is still music.

B: But what is art in your life then?

A: I don't know. I can't imagine life without art, but I still don't know what is art and what it means in my life. Sometimes art is useless for me, but on the other hand it is also helpful.

B: Do you ever reflect upon yourself as an artist, in the position of an artist, or with regard to the duty or mission of an artist?

A: Yes, I like using the particular benefits of being an artist. As an artist you can do anything. I can wake up late…

B: So you use your position as an artist as an excuse for doing things.

A: I have an advantage as an artist.

B: What's the advantage of being an artist today?

A: 我不知道。不过我迷恋的还是音乐。

B: 艺术在你的生活中扮演着什么角色?

A: 很难说清楚。我无法想象没有艺术的生活，但我又无法对艺术下定义，也说不清它对我的生活究竟意味着什么。艺术对我来说有时候是简直一无是处，有时却又大有裨益。

B: 以艺术家的立场，你有没有想过自己的责任与使命呢?

A: 有啊。我喜欢这个头衔给我带来的许多好处，你可以做任何你想做的事，比如晚起。

B: 你利用艺术家的头衔来为你做的事正名。

A: 我确实可以从中获益很多。

B: 在今天的大环境中，当一名艺术家有哪些好处?

A: 一言难尽啊。比如可以好好打扮一番去见朋友之类的。还可以晚起。

B: 对你来说，作为艺术家可以在行事上获得优势。

A: 也不是。

B: 艺术的哪一点对你来说很重要?

A: 它能激发更多的自由思考，这一点比较重要。

B: 为什么你从来没有组建过真正的乐队?

A: 可能太晚了。

B: 为什么?

A: 坦白说，我在音乐方面缺乏自信，而且组建乐队需要合适的成员。另外，我不喜欢团体的归属

A: I don't know. I have to dress up clean to meet people. I can wake up very late.

B: So for you, the arts are an advantage for doing certain things…

A: No.

B: Is there any other importance for you in art?

A: It allows for more the freedom of thought, and this is very important.

B: Why have you never had a real band?

A: It's too late, maybe.

B: Why?

A: Honestly, I lack the self-confidence to be a musician. And for a band you need to have the right group of people. And also, I don't like the idea of belonging to any single group. I want to remain an individual.

B: So you always act as an individual.

A: Yes, and with one single problem, which is that I am too shy to perform.

感，比较喜欢单打独斗。

B: 所以你一直都是一个人进行行为表演?

A: 是的。而且我还很害羞，不敢表演。

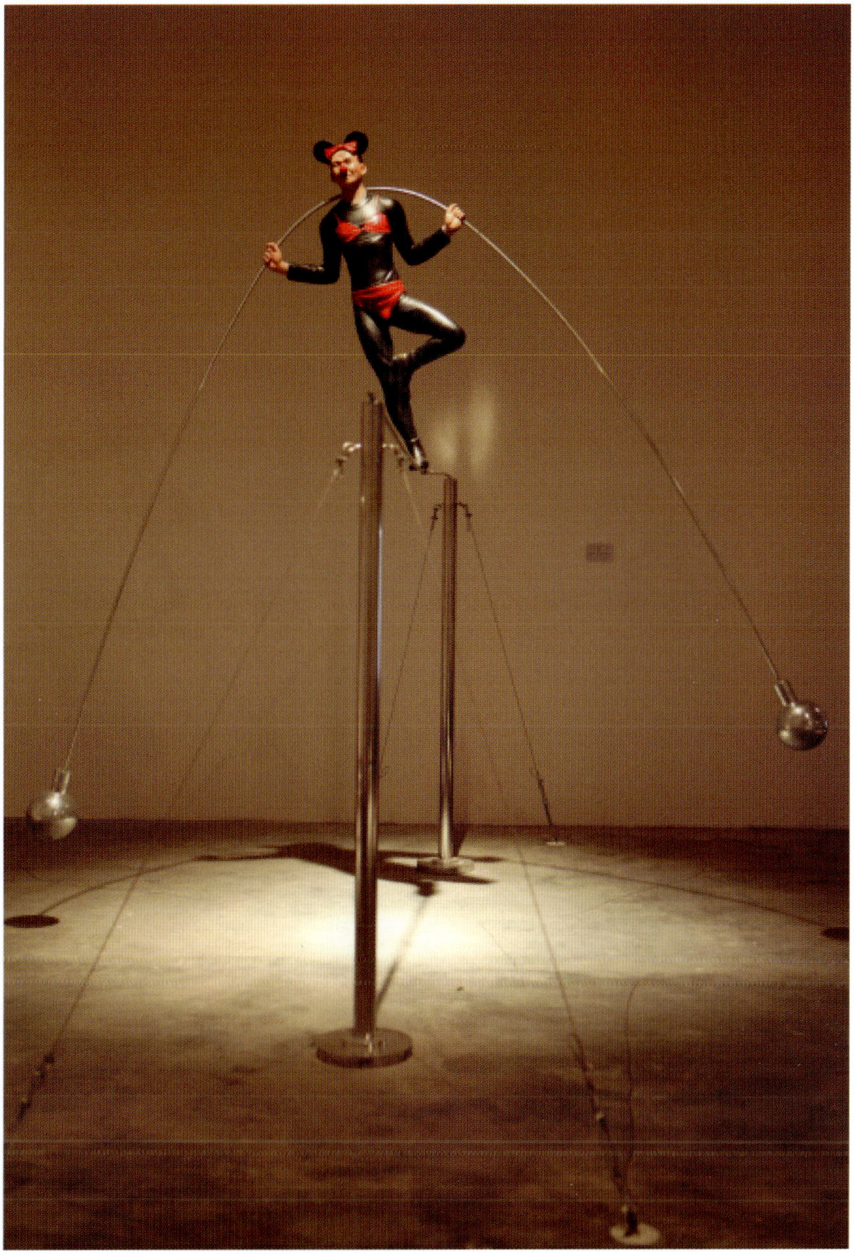

Toys 'S' Us #4
Polyester resin, stainless steel, aluminium and acrylic paint

玩具反斗城 #4
聚酯树脂、不锈钢，铝，丙烯酸颜料

187×120×172cm
2009

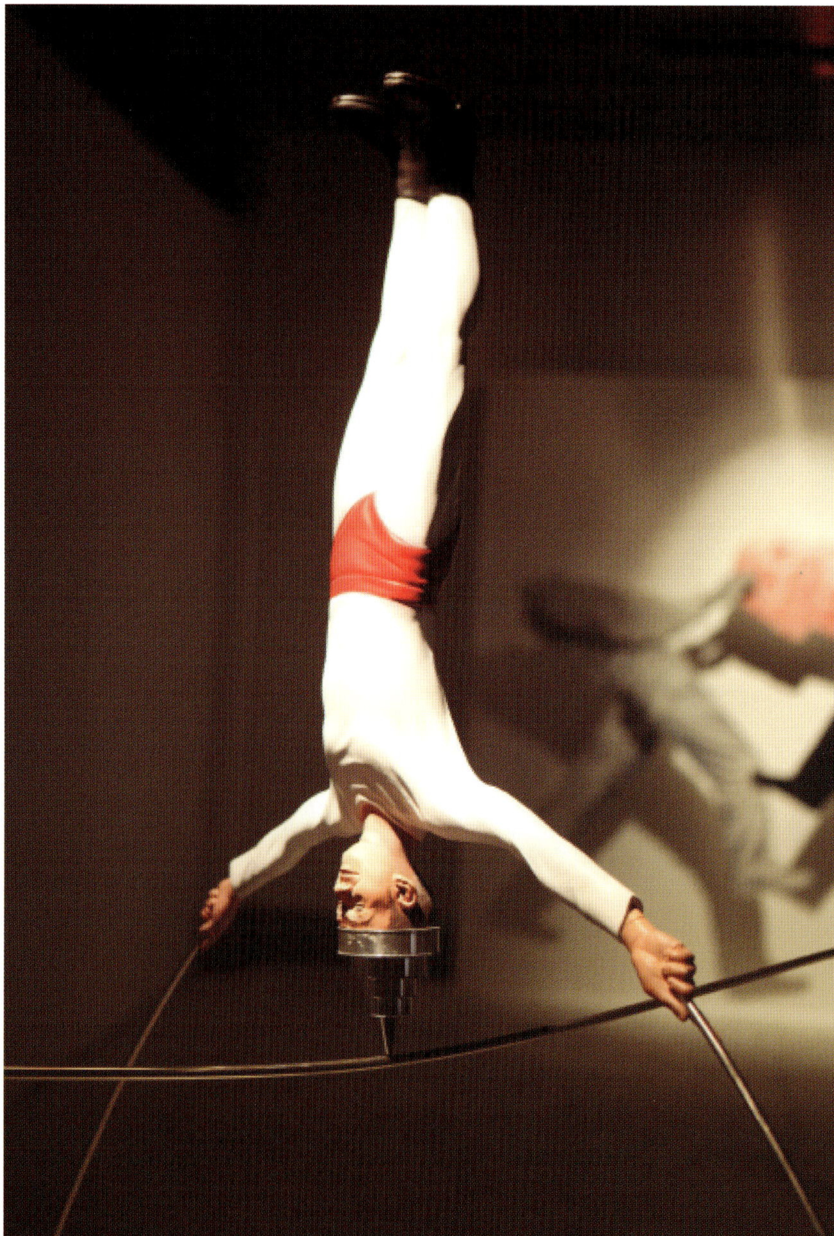

Toys 'S' Us #6
Polyester resin, stainless steel, aluminium and acrylic paint

玩具反斗城 #6
聚酯树脂、不锈钢，铝，丙烯酸颜料

194×130×172cm
2009

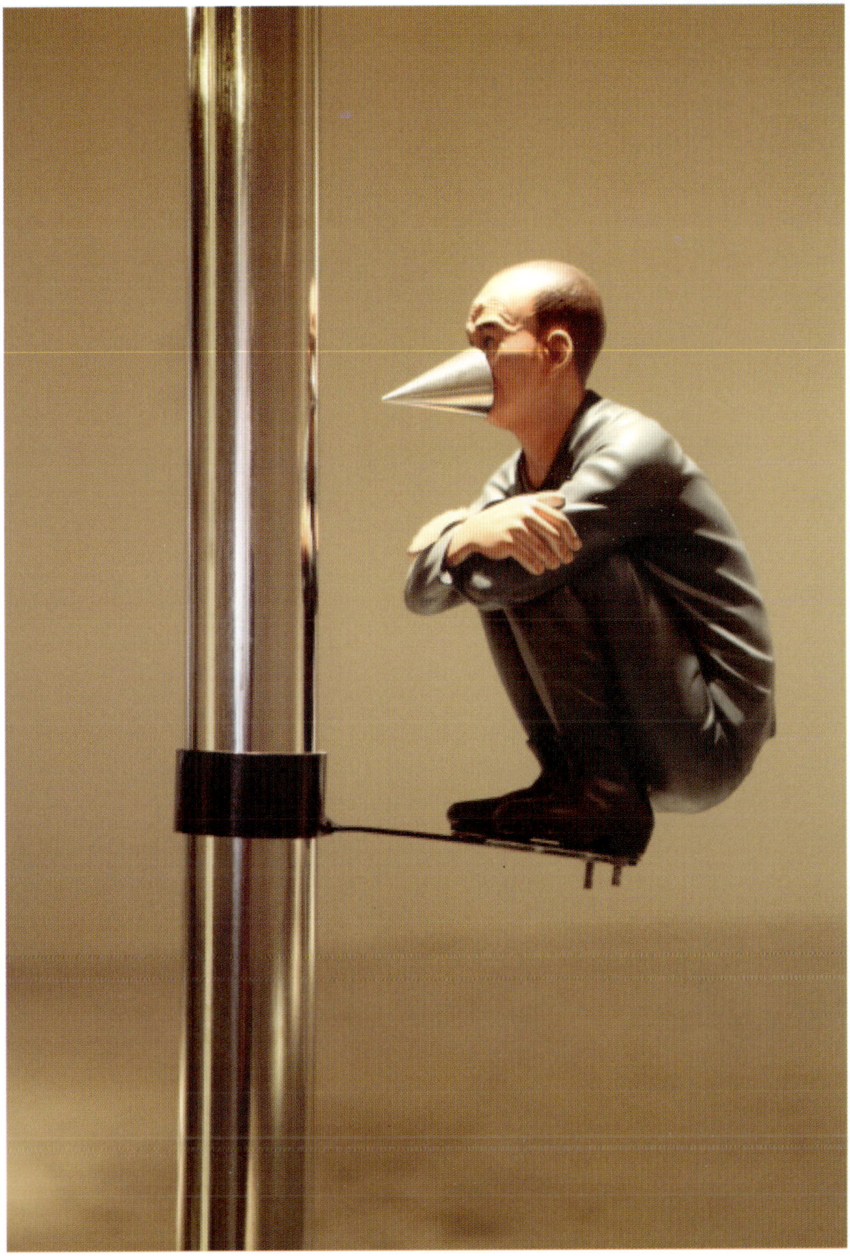

Toys 'S' Us #3
Polyester resin, stainless steel, aluminium and acrylic paint

玩具反斗城 #3
聚酯树脂、不锈钢，铝，丙烯酸颜料

300×13×38 cm
2009

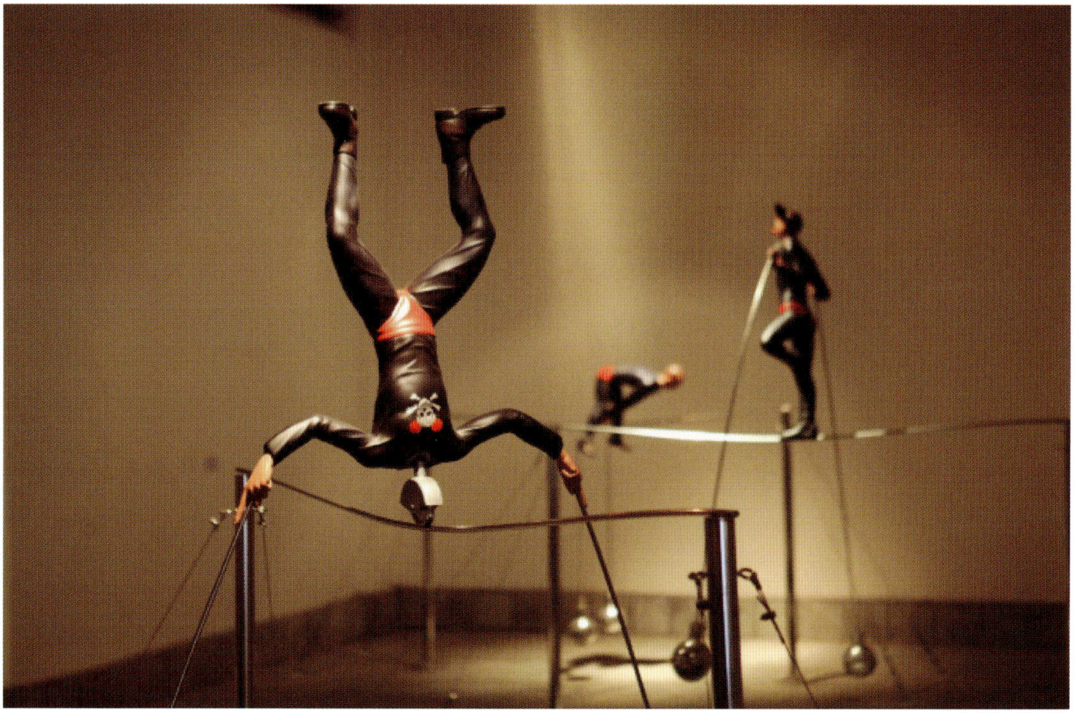

Toys 'S' Us #7
Polyester resin, stainless steel, aluminium, and acrylic paint

玩具反斗城 #7
聚酯树脂、不锈钢，铝，丙烯酸颜料

180×115×172cm
2009

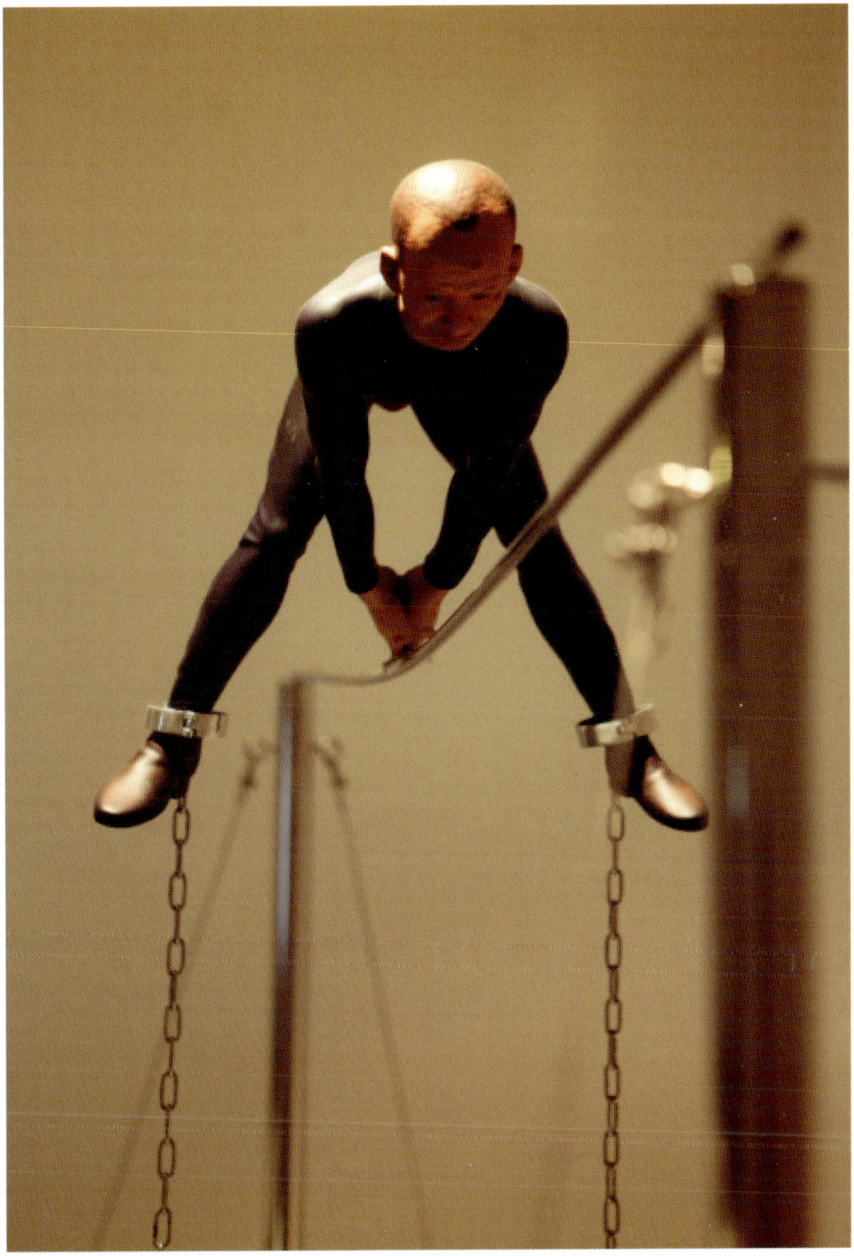

Toys 'S' Us #5
Polyester resin, stainless steel, aluminium and acrylic paint

玩具反斗城 #5
聚酯树脂、不锈钢，铝，丙烯酸颜料

161×49×172cm
2009

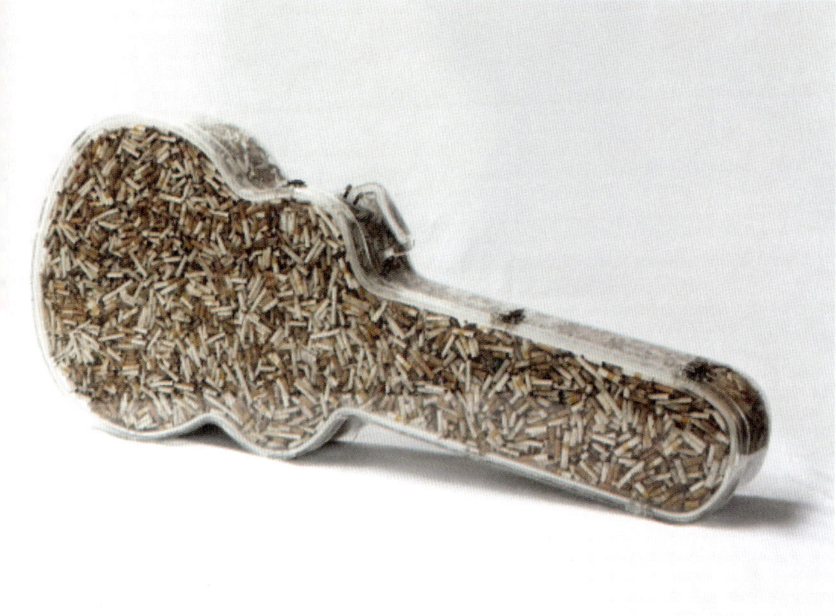

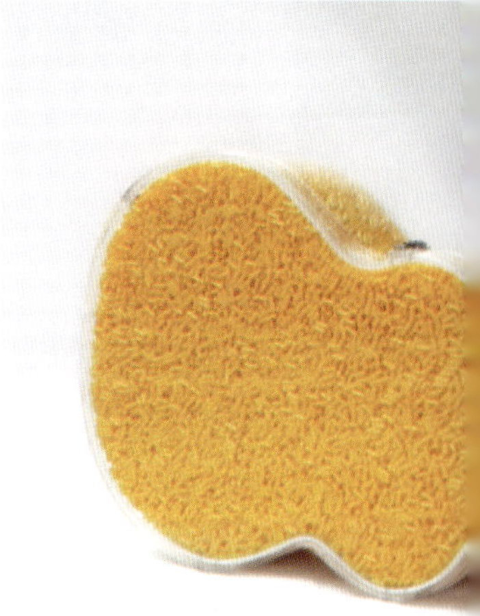

Too Young to Die, Too Old to Rock N' Roll #1 / #2 / #3
Acrylic, cigarette butts, aluminium

生活依旧，年华已逝 #1 / #2 / #3
丙烯、烟蒂、铝

52×119×16cm
2009

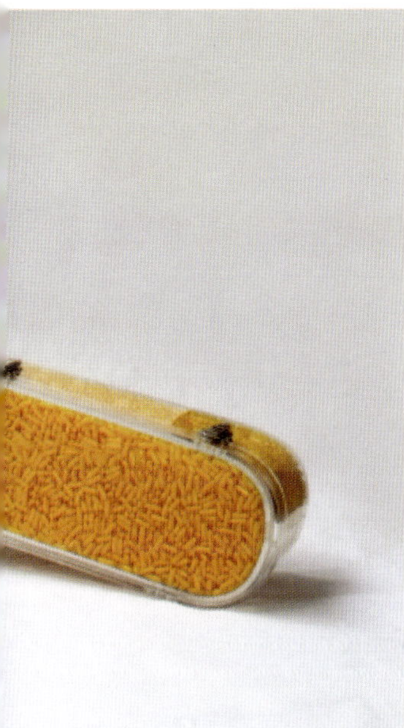

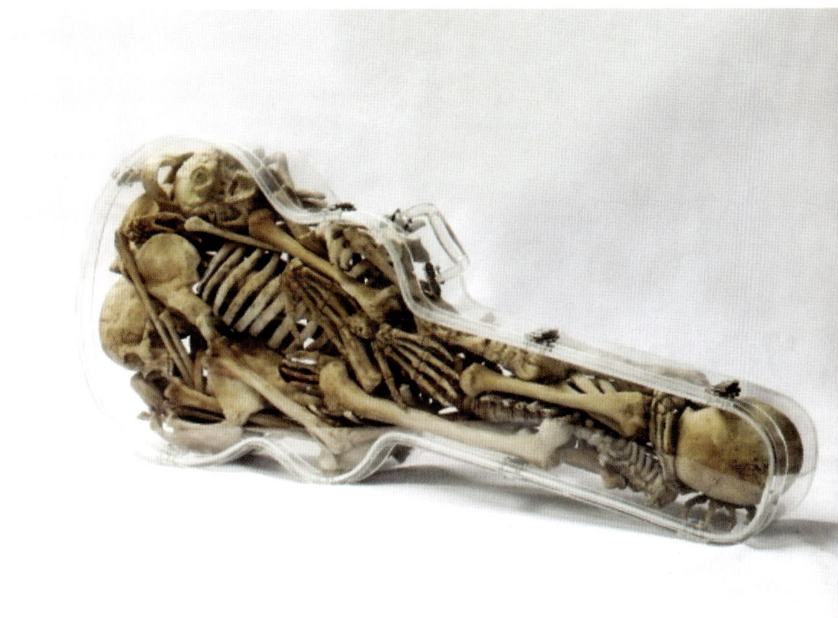

Tromarama
Tromarama艺术小组

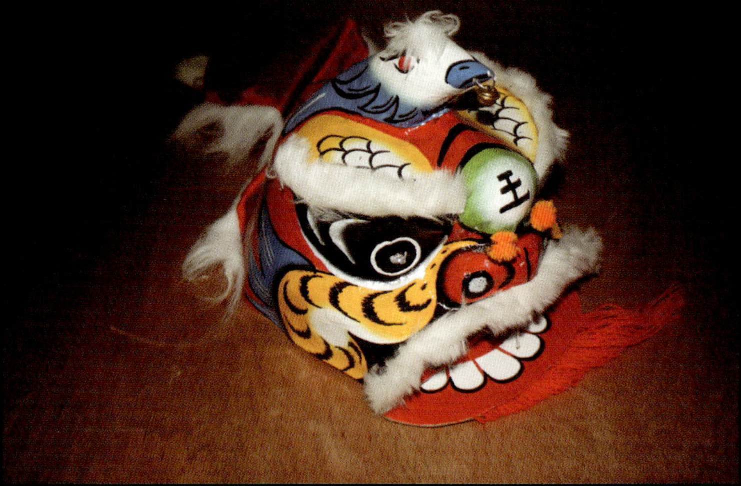

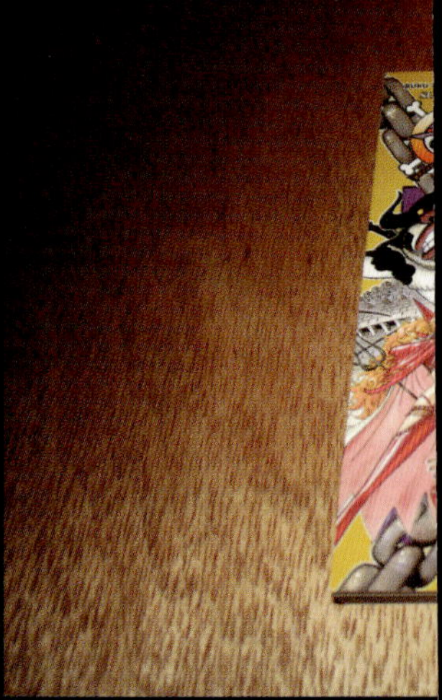

We grew up with television and video entertainment, on VHS, Betamax, Laser Disc and now DVD. Most of the time we watch animated movies. We loved to watch them back then and we still love to watch them today. Studios like Disney, Pixar, and Ghibli produce the majority of them. We also had a love for Sesame Street and The Muppets.
Music videos became our new focus of interest while growing up as teenagers. Back in the mid-90s, when MTV aired in Indonesia, we had the chance to see many music videos from around the world, showcasing many different techniques and approaches. Then we became curious about the "behind the scenes" of each video. So we watched some DVD's on directors and their work, and we learned how they make music videos.
Comics are also among the things that continue to accompany us since childhood. We still love reading comic books, from Japanese anime to graphic novels. We also like to collect toys, such as masks, action figures, animal figures, and so on. These habits do not directly influence our work, but collecting them and having them around keeps us inspired everyday. We also get inspiration from our environment and surrounding things, like our friends, the news on television, gossip, a broken heart, meeting new friends… anything can inspire us.

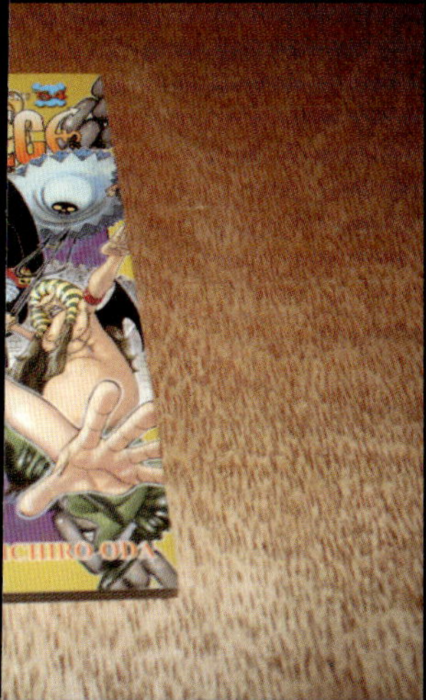

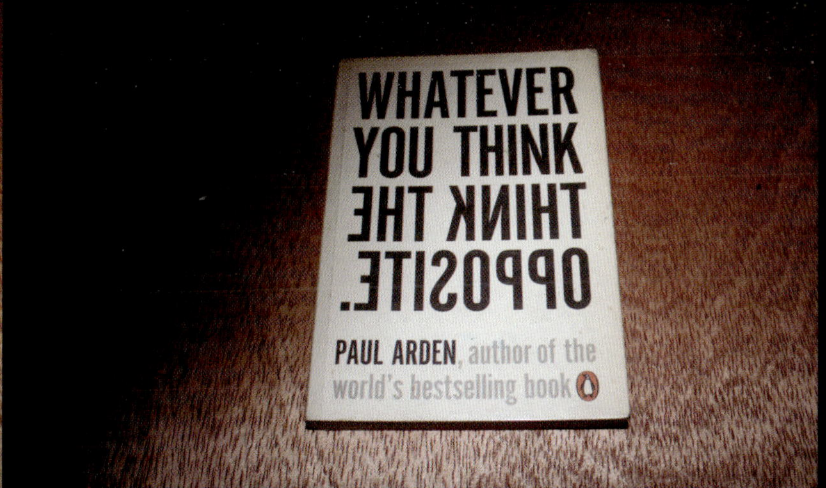
WHATEVER
YOU THINK
THINK THE
OPPOSITE.
PAUL ARDEN, author of the
world's bestselling book

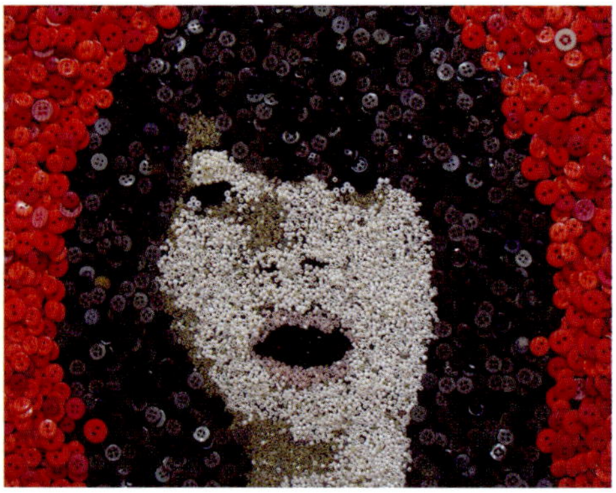

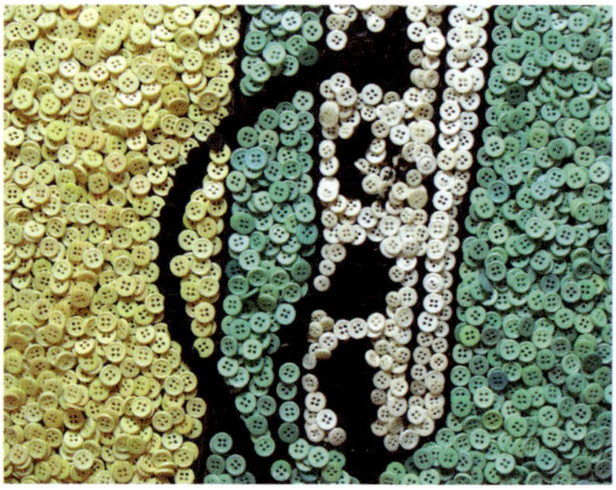

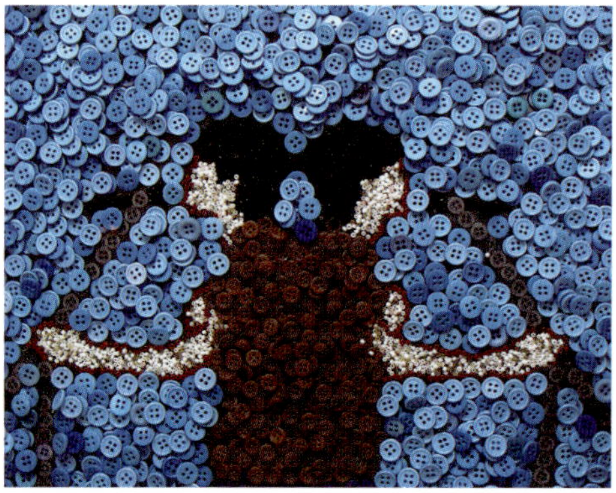

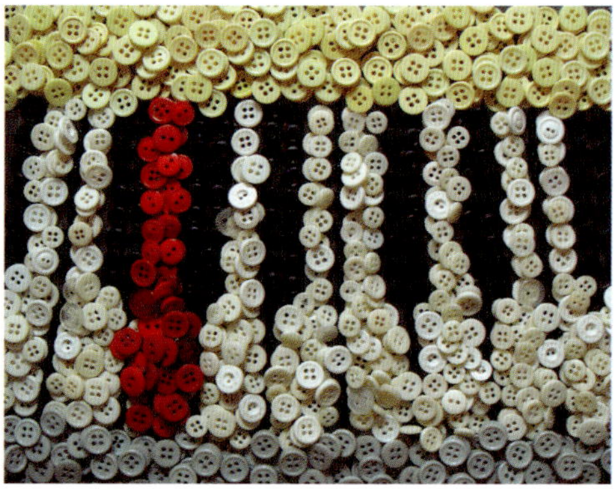

Zsa Zsa Zsu
stop motion animation with buttons and beads
定格动画

4' 54"
2007

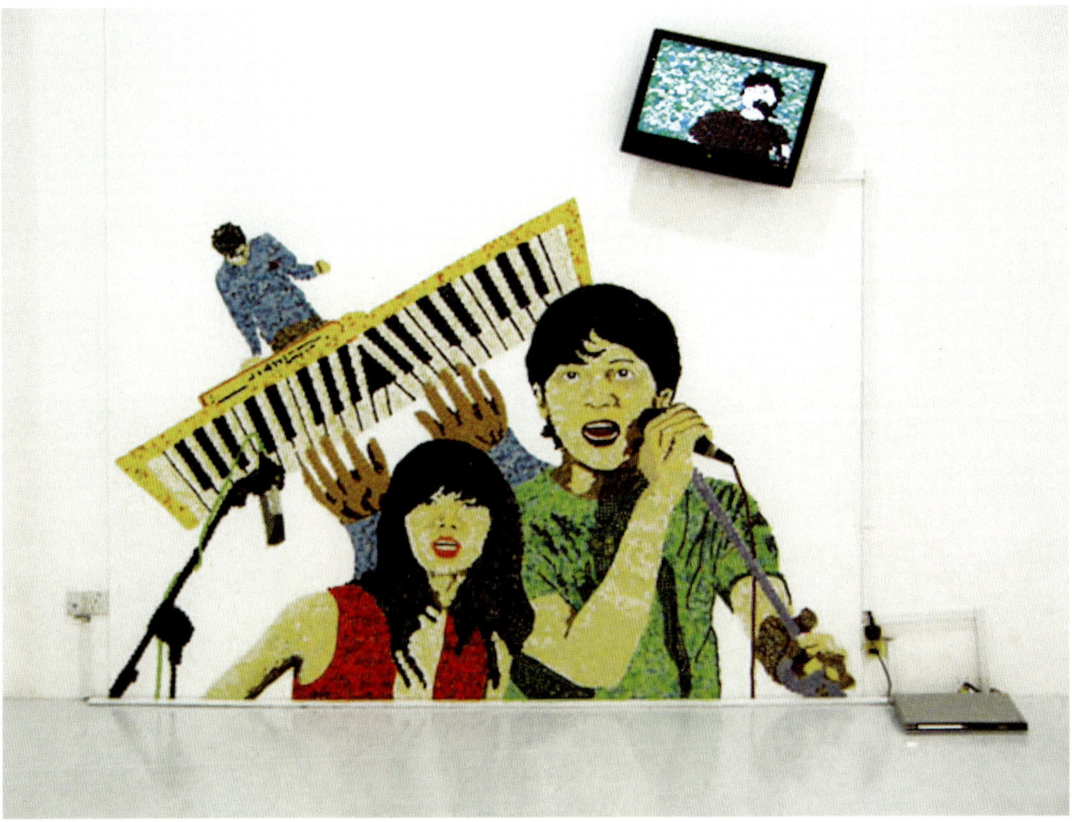

Entang Wiharso
安塔格・维哈梭

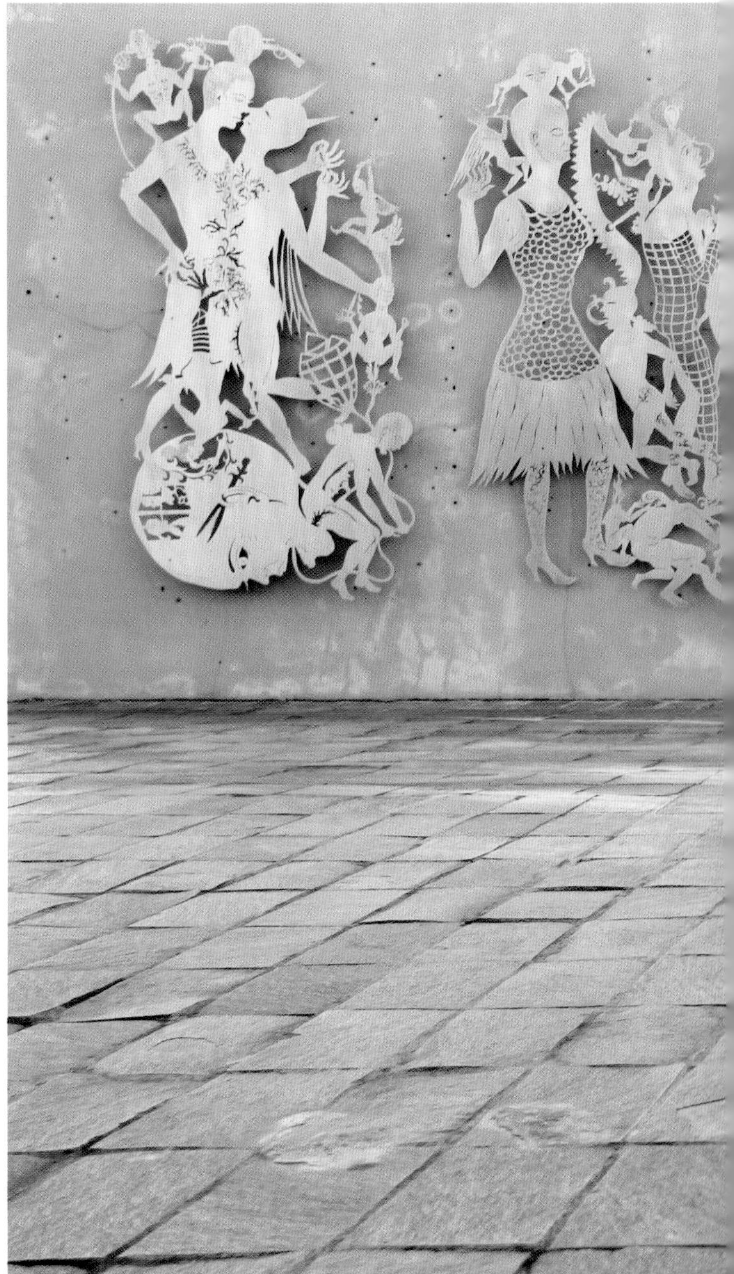

Black Goat VS identity and aesthetic crime (part of)
Alumunium cut out

黑山羊 VS 身份与审美犯罪 (部分)
铝裁剪

200×800cm
2009

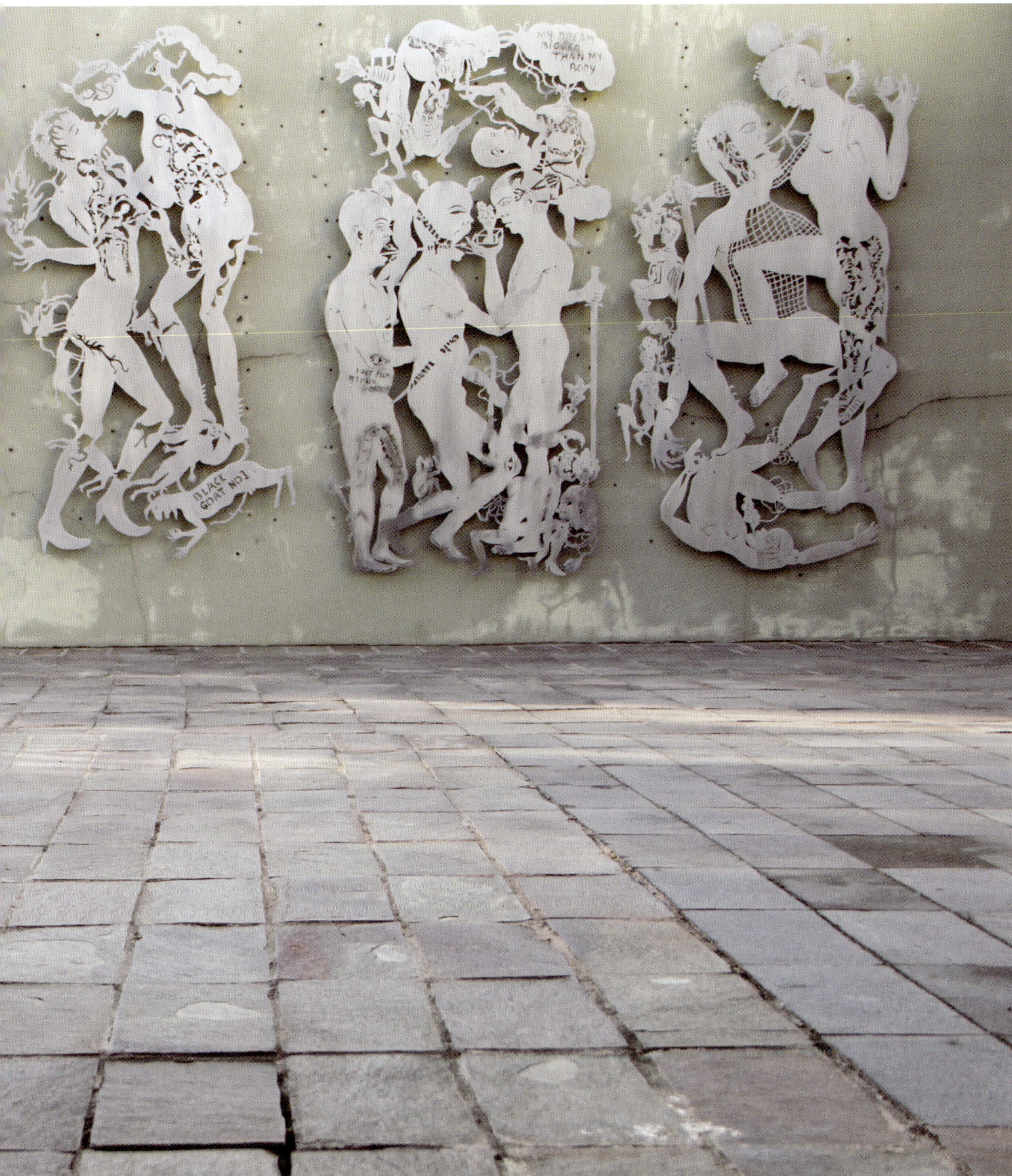
MY DREAM BIGGER THAN MY BODY
BLACK GOAT NO1

Gede Mahendra Yasa
杰德・曼汉德拉・亚萨

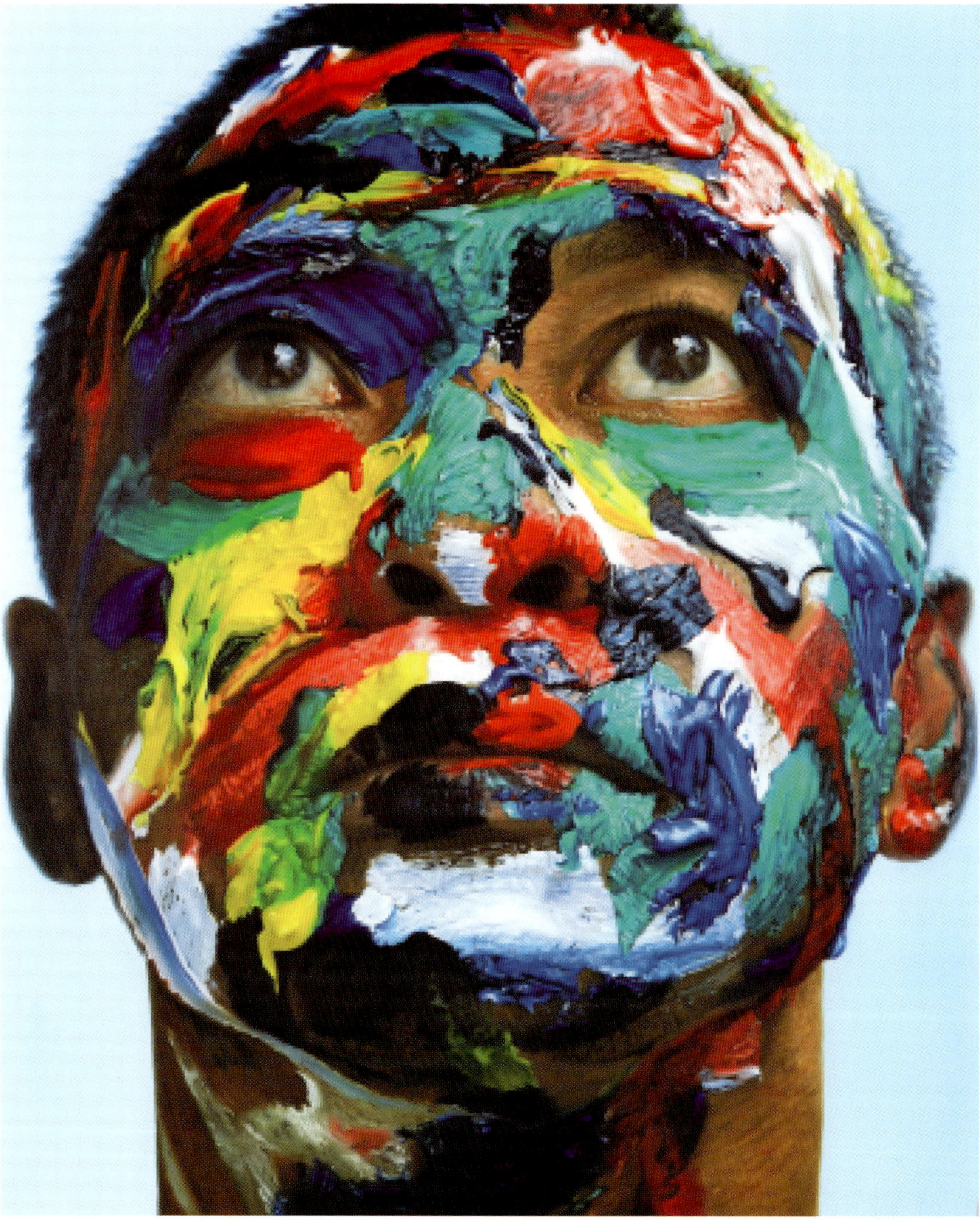

Acrylic Color on Face #3
Oil on canvas

面部彩色丙烯 #3
布面油画

150×120cm
2009

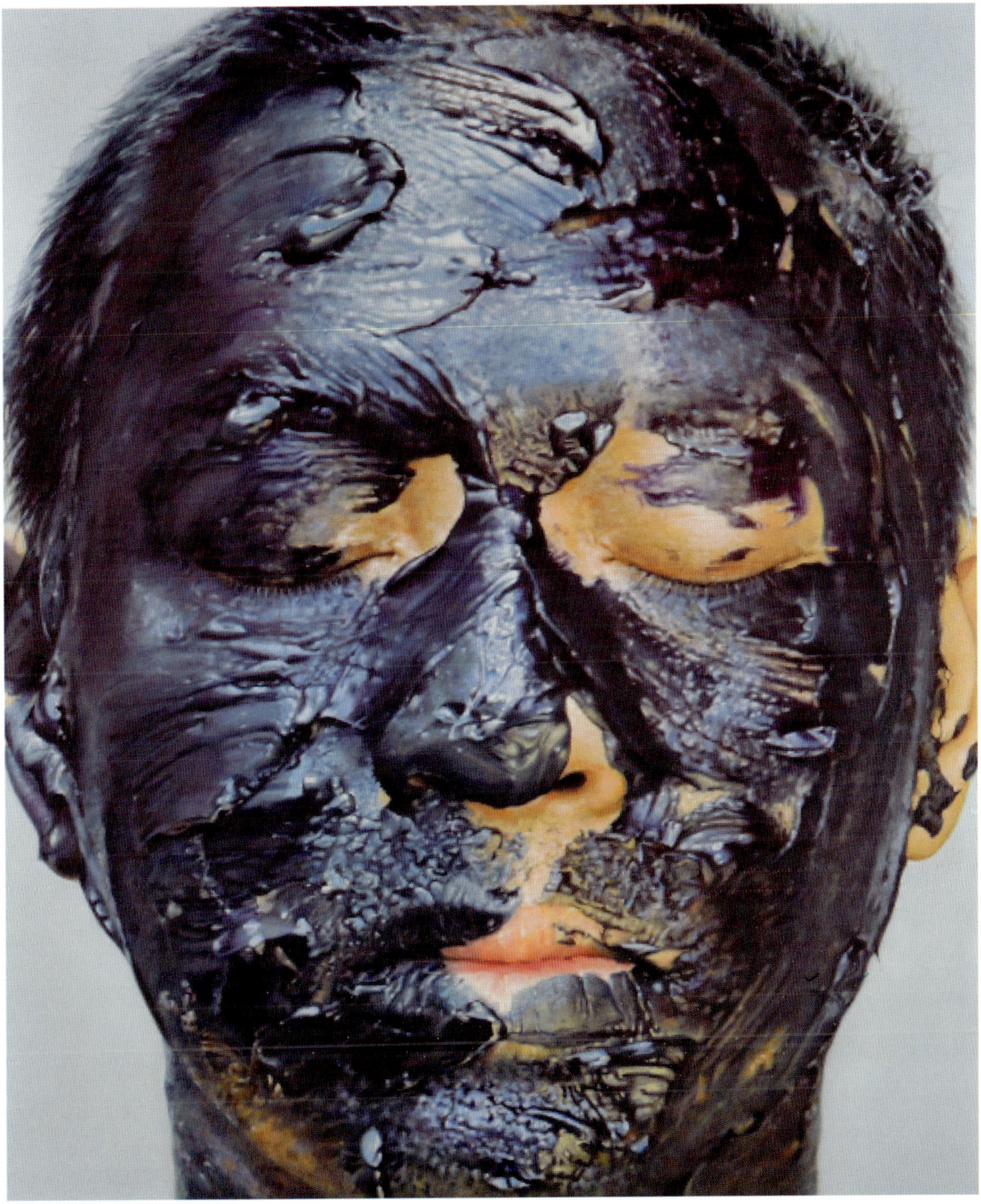

Black Acrylic Paint on Face #1
Oil on canvas

面部黑色丙烯 #1
布面油画

150×120cm
2009

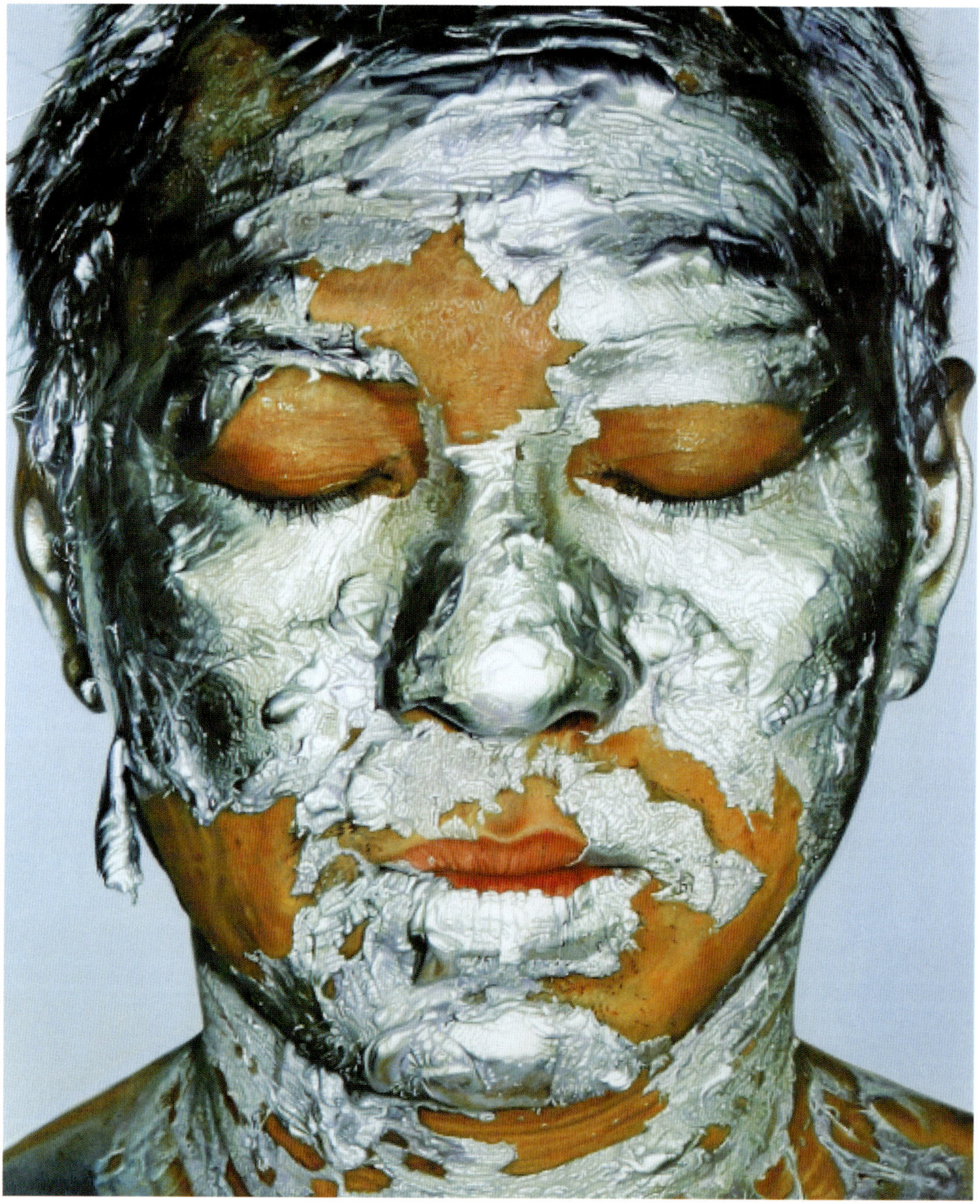

Silver Acrylic Paint on Face #1
Oil on canvas

面部银色丙烯 #1
布面油画

150×120cm
2009

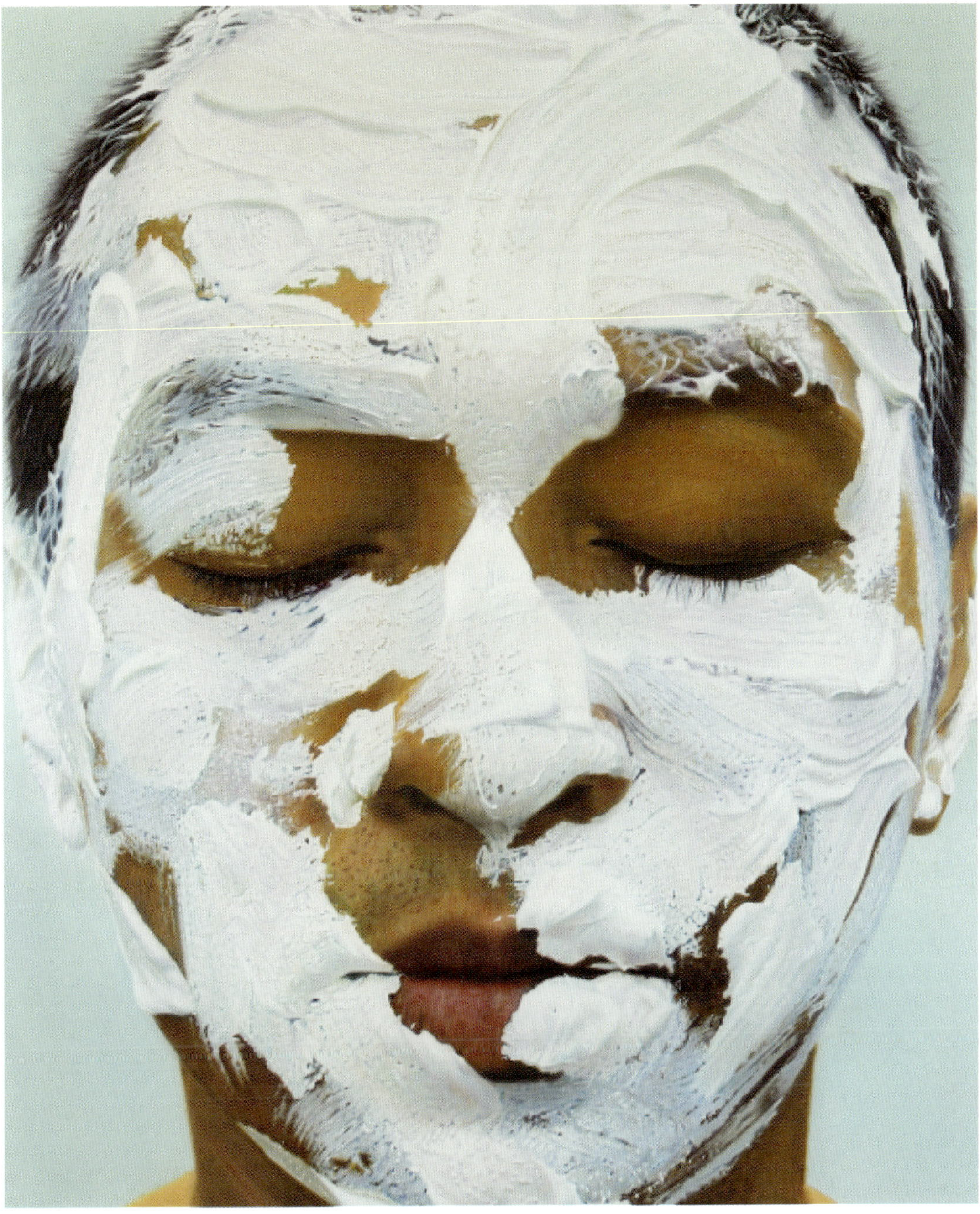

White Acrylic Paint on Face #1
Oil on canvas

面部的白色丙烯 #1
布面油画

150×120cm
2009

Artists' Biographies | 艺术家简历

ARAHMAIANI

Born in Bandung, Indonesia, 1961

Living and working in Yogyakarta, Indonesia

Education

1983

Bachelor of Fine Art in Bandung Institute of Technology, Department of Art, Bandung, Indonesia

1985-1986

Paddington Art School, Sydney, Australia

1991-1992

Academie voor Beeldende Kunst, Enschede, The Netherlands

Selected Group Exhibitions

2010

"Installation I" Campbelltown Art Center, Sydney Festival

I Love You" Ana Tzarev Gallery, NY

2009

"I Don't Want to be a Part of Your Legend" Oberhausen Short Film Festival, Germany

"Produk Gertoli" Charles Darwin University, Australia

Selected Performances

2010

"Make-up or Break-up" Woodford Folk Festival, Brisbane, Australia

2009

"Produk Gertoli" Charles Darwin University, Australia

2008

"Breaking Words" Siliman University, Dumaguette, Phillipines

Selected Bibiliography

2003

Iola Lenzi, "The Pioneering Spirit" Asian Art News Vol 13 No 5 page 51-53, 2003

Iola Lenzi,"Singapore,Thailand & Indonesia at the 50th Venice Biennale" Eyeline no 52, page 40-41, 2003

Edward Lucie-Smith,"Art Tomorrow", 2003

Selected Essays

1999

Whitney Chadwick, "Woman, Art & Society" 3rd Edition,2002, Thames & Hudson

"To The Mother Of The Future Artist" Kompas, 9 May 1999

"The Tabboo Of Naked Body And Orgy Of Violence" Kompas, 8 August 1999

哈拉海麦尼

1961年出生于印尼万隆

现生活工作于印尼日惹

教育背景

1983

万隆科技学院艺术系学士，万隆，印尼

1985-1986

佩丁顿艺术学院，悉尼，澳大利亚

1991-1992

荷兰艺术学院，恩斯赫德，荷兰

部分群展

2010

"装置I"，坎贝尔敦艺术中心，悉尼艺术节

"我爱你"，Ana Tzarey画廊，纽约

2009

"我不想成为你的传奇的一部分"，奥伯豪森短片节，德国

"Produk Gertoli"，查尔斯达尔文大学，澳大利亚

部分演出

2010

"重聚或分手"，伍德福德民间艺术节，布里斯班，澳大利亚

2009

"Produk Gertoli"，查尔斯达尔文大学，澳大利亚

2008

"断裂的语言"，Siliman大学，杜马盖地，菲律宾

文献目录

2003

Iola　Lenzi著《先锋精神》，载于《亚洲艺术新闻》第13卷第5期51-53页，2003

Iola Lenzi著《第50届威尼斯双年展之新加坡、泰国&印尼艺术》，载于《Eyeline》第52期40-41页，2003

Edward Lucie-Smith著《艺术明天》，2003

论文

1999

Whitney Chadwick编著《女性、艺术与社会》(第三版)，Thames & Hudson出版社，2002

《致未来艺术家的母亲》，载于1999年5月9日《罗盘报》

《裸体与暴力狂欢的禁忌》，载于1999年8月8日《罗盘报》

WIMO AMBALA BAYANG

Born 14 October, 1976 in Magelang, Indonesia

Living and working in Yogyakarta, Indonesia

Education

1995-1996

维莫・安巴拉・巴扬

1976年10月14日出生于印尼马格朗

现生活工作于印尼日惹

教育背景

1995-1996

Interior Design, Modern School of Design Yogyakarta, Indonesia.
1996-2006
Photography Department, Indonesian Institute of Art Yogyakarta, Indonesia.

Solo Exhibition
2009
"Wimo Film and Video Festival", Kedai Kebun Forum, Yogyakarta, Indonesia. "CIRCL3" Singapore Tyler Print Institute, Singapore

Selected Group Exhibitions
2009
"Landing Soon #7", Heden, The Hague, The Netherlands.
"South Project", Melbourne Reflection, Melbourne, Australia.
"Landing Soon", Erasmus Huis, Jakarta, Indonesia.
"Look! See?", Nadi Gallery, Jakarta, Indonesia.

Awards
1997
"The Best Black and White Photo Print", Record Media Faculty, Indonesia Institute of Art Yogyakarta
1998
"The Best Art Photography", Indonesia Institute of Arts, Yogyakarta BOOKS

Residencies
2009
"Heden kunst van nu", The Hague, The Netherlands.
"South Project/ Monash", Melbourne, Australia.

EDWIN

Writer/Director's Profile
Edwin, born in Surabaya, 1978
Living and working in Jakarta, Indonesia

In 1999, he decided to move out from Surabaya to study film at The Jakarta Institute of Arts, where he liberated his passion for filmmaking, utilizing 'spontaneous', 'flexible' and 'fun' approaches. In 2005, he left his studies at institute.

In 2005, he wrote and directed, Kara, Anak Sebatang Pohon, which received rave reviews domestically and internationally. The film became the first Indonesian short film screened at the Director's Fortnight, Cannes 2005.

Blind Pig who wants to Fly (2008) is his feature film debut.

Filmography:
Blind Pig Who Wants To Fly had the World Premiere at 13th Pusan IFF, South Korea and had the European premiere at 38th Rotterdam IFF, The Netherlands, which won the FIPRESCI Award. After that, the film has been traveling around the globe to many festivals such as: 11th BAFICI, Buenos Aires, Argentina, 33rd Hongkong, IFF, 35th Seattle IFF, USA, 44th Karlovy Vary IFF, Czech Rep., 58th Melbourne IFF, Australia.

日惹现代设计学院室内设计专业，日惹，印尼
1996-2006
印尼艺术学院摄影系，日惹，印尼

部分个展
2009
"维莫电影与录像节"，Kedai Kebun论坛，日惹，印尼 / "CIRCL3"，新加坡泰勒版画研究院，新加坡

部分群展
2009
"即将登陆#7"，Heden画廊，海牙，荷兰
"南方计划"，墨尔本Reflection画廊，墨尔本，澳大利亚
"即将登陆"，Erasmus Huis画廊，雅加达，印尼
"看！看到了吗？"，Nadi画廊，雅加达，印尼

获奖情况
1997
最佳黑白摄影版画奖，印尼艺术研究院录制媒体系，日惹，印尼
1998
最佳摄影奖，印尼艺术学院，日惹，印尼

驻留项目
2009
"今天的艺术"，海牙，荷兰
"南方计划/莫纳什"，墨尔本，澳大利亚

艾德文

作家/导演
1978年出生于印尼泗水
现工作生活于印尼雅加达

1999年，艾德文离开出生地泗水前往雅加达艺术学院学习电影。在那里，他对于电影制作的热情被点燃，开始实践自己的"自发"、"灵活"而"有趣"的电影手法。2005年，艾德文结束了在雅加达艺术学院的学习，开始了自己的创作道路。

2005年，艾德文创作并导演了《卡拉，树的女儿》，在印尼国际和国际电影界获得了一致的好评。本片于2005年在戛纳国际电影节上展映，成为第一部在"导演双周"展映的印尼短片。

《失明的猪也想飞》(2008)是他的第一部故事片。

影片集锦
《失明的猪也想飞》在第13届釜山国际电影节上举行了全球首映，随后在第38届荷兰鹿特丹国际电影节上举行了欧洲首映，并荣膺费比西影评人奖(FIPRESCI)。

此后，这部影片多次参与全球各大电影节活动，其中包括：第11届BAFICI阿根廷布宜诺斯艾利斯国际独立电影节、第33届香港国际电影节、第35届美国西雅图国际电影节、第44届捷克卡洛维发利国际电影节和第58届墨尔本国际电影节。

The film was screened at MoMa NYC, September 2009. Continue to Viennale, Taipei Golden Horse Intl Film Festival and Thessaloniki Intl Film Festival, and many more…

Selected Awards:

Blind Pig who wants to Fly:

FIPRESCI Prize International, Film Festival Rotterdam. 2009.
NETPAC Award, Taipei Golden Horse Film Festival 2009.
Special Mention, Singapore International Film Festival 2009.
Young Audience Award, Nantes Festival des 3 Continents 2009.
Montgolfière d'argent, Nantes Festival des 3 Continents 2009.
Best New Director, Jakarta International Film Festival 2009.

Hulahoop Soundings:

Second Prize for Best Short Film at Berlin Asian Hot Shot Film Festival.
Nominated as best short film at Berlin Porn Film Festival.

Kara Anak Sebatang Pohon:

Film pendek terbaik, Festival Film Indonesia 2005.
Quinzaine des Realisateur, Cannes International Film Festival, (2005).

Trip to the wound:

Out of competition Short Film, Berlinale International Film Festival (2009)

F.X HARSONO

Born 1949 in Blitar, Indonesia
Living and working in Jakarta, Indonesia

Education

1974
Painting at STSRI 'ASRI', Yogyakarta, Indonesia
1987-1991
Institut Kesenian Jakarta, Indonesia
2005-present
Lecturer, the Faculty of Art and Design, Pelita Harapan University, Tangerang (west Java).

Selected Solo Exhibitions

2010
"FX Harsono: Testimonies", Singapore Art Museum, Singapore
2009
"The Erased Time", National Gallery of Indonesia, Jakarta
"Surviving Memories", Vanessa Art Link, Beijing, China
2008
"Aftertaste", Koong Gallery, Jakarta

Selected Group Exhibitions

2010
"Pleasures of Chaos, Inside New Indonesian Art", Primo Marella Gallery, Milano, Italy
2009
"Beyond The Dutch", Centraal Museum, Utrecht, Netherland

2009年9月，《失明的猪也想飞》在纽约现代艺术馆展映，并于随后相继入围金马奖台北国际电影节和希腊塞萨洛尼基国际电影节等重量级国际电影节。

获奖情况

《失明的猪也想飞》

2009年鹿特丹国际电影节“费比西影评人奖”
2009年金马奖台北国际电影节“亚洲电影促进联盟奖”
2009年新加坡国际电影节“特别提名奖”
2009年法国南特三大洲电影节“青年观众奖”
2009年法国南特三大洲电影节“银气球奖”
2009年雅加达国际电影节“最佳新晋导演奖”

《Hulahoop Soundings》

柏林亚洲热门短片电影节最佳短片二等奖
获柏林电影节最佳短片提名

《卡拉，树的女儿》

2005年印尼电影节最佳短片奖
2005年戛纳国际电影节“导演双周”

《走向创伤之路》

2009年柏林国际电影节非竞赛短片

方济各・沙勿略・哈索诺

1949年出生于印尼布里达
现生活工作于印尼雅加达

教育背景

1974
STSRI 'ASRI绘画专业，日惹，印尼
1987-1991
雅加达艺术学院，印尼
2005-present
希望之光大学艺术设计系讲师，坦格朗(西爪哇省)，印尼

部分个展

2010
“哈索诺个展——证明”，新加坡美术馆，新加坡
2009
“被抹杀的时间”，印尼国家画廊，雅加达，印尼
“幸存的记忆”，华艺莎艺术中心，北京，中国
2008
“余味”，Koong画廊，雅加达，印尼

部分群展

2010
“混沌的欢愉：新印尼艺术”，Primo Marella画廊，米兰，意大利
2009
“荷兰之外”，Centraal博物馆，乌德勒支，荷兰

"Face Value", Exhibition of 4 artists, Agus Suwage, Budi Kustarto, Astari Rasyid and FX Harsono at SIGlarts, Jakarta.
"TechnoSign", Surabaya Art Link, Surabaya
"Milestone", Vanessa Art Link, Jakarta

BUDI KUSTARTO

Born 1972 in Karangbawang, Central Java, Indonesia
Living and working in Yogyakarta, Indonesia

Education

1988-1992
Visual Communication at Sekolah Menengah Senirupa (SMSR/High School of Fine Arts), Yogyakarta, Indonesia.
1993-2003
Sculptural Art at Institut Seni Indonesia (ISI/Indonesian Institute of Fine Arts), Yogyakarta, Indonesia.

Selected Solo Exhibitions

2008
"Among Others" Soka Gallery, Beijing, China
"Ice Creams Series" SOKA Art Centre, Beijing, China
2006
"Hetero; Green" Semarang Gallery, Semarang, Indonesia

Selected Group Exhibitions

2010
"in-difesa" Fondazione 107, Bologna, Italy
"ArtParis 2010", Paris, France
"Art Italy 2010" Bologna
2009
"Next Nature", Vanessa Artlink (Galnas), Jakarta, Indonesia
"Hong Kong Art Fair", Hong Kong

JOMPET KUSWIDANANTO

Born in 16 December 1976, Yogyakarta
Living and working in Yogyakarta, Indonesia

Education

1995-1999
Gadjah Mada University, Faculty of Social and Politics Science, Yogyakarta, Indonesia.

Selected Solo Exhibitions

2009
"Java's Machine: Phantasmagoria", Osage Gallery, Singapore
2008
"Java's Machine: Phantasmagoria", Cemeti Art House, Yogyakarta

Selected Group Exhibitions

2010
"Asia Art Award Exhibition", Seoul Olympic Museum of Art,

"面对价值——四人联展"，SIGlarts画廊，雅加达，印尼
"科技信号"，泗水艺术中心，泗水，印尼
"里程碑"，华艺莎艺术中心，雅加达，印尼

布迪·库斯塔图

1972年出生于印尼中爪哇省卡朗(Karangbawang)
现工作生活于印尼日惹

教育背景

1988-1992
SMSR艺术专科学校视觉传达专业，日惹，印尼
1993-2003
印尼艺术学院雕塑系，日惹，印尼

部分个展

2008
"在陌生人之间"，索卡艺术中心，北京，中国
"冰淇淋系列"，索卡艺术中心，北京，中国
2006
"异·绿"，Semarang画廊，三宝垄，印尼

部分群展

2010
"防"，107基金会，博洛尼亚，意大利
"艺术巴黎2010"，巴黎，法国
"艺术意大利2010"，博洛尼亚，意大利
2009
"下一个自然"，Vanessa Artlink画廊，雅加达，印尼
香港艺术博览会，香港

琼佩特·库斯伟达纳托

1970年12月16日出生于印尼日惹
现生活工作于印尼日惹

教育背景

1995-1999
噶迦玛达大学(Gadjah Mada)社会与政治科学系，日惹，印尼

部分个展

2009
"爪哇机器：千变万化的幻景"，Osage画廊，新加坡
2008
"爪哇机器：千变万化的幻景"，Cemeti艺术之家，日惹，印尼

部分群展

2010
"亚洲艺术奖得奖作品展"，首尔奥林匹克美术馆，首尔，韩国
"即将绿洲"，Maha画廊，巴厘岛，印尼

Seoul, South Korea
"Oasis To Be", Maha Art Gallery, Bali, Indonesia
"The Tradition of The New", Shaksi Gallery, Mumbai
2009
"Jogjakarta Biennale X", Jogja National Museum, Indonesia
"Beyond the Dutch", Centraal Museum Utrecht, The Netherlands

Performances and Visuals On Stage

2009
"Garibaba's Strange World", Dance Theatre with Pappa Tarahumara and Hiroshi Koike
2006
"Mnemosyne", Collaborative work of Kunauka Theatre Company Tokyo and Garasi Theatre Laboratory

Honors and Awards

2010
"Asia Art Award Finalist", Loop Gallery, Seoul, South Korea
2008
"Academic Art Award", Yogyakarta Institute of Art, Yogyakarta

RUDI MANTOFANI

Born in 1973 Padang, West Sumatra
Living and working in Yogyakarta, Indonesia

Education

1996
Indonesian Institute of Art, Yogyakarta, Indonesia

Selected Solo Exhibitions

2006
"The Culture of Things", CP Art Space, Jakarta, Indonesia
2002
"Cakrawala Ganda", Nadi Gallery, Jakarta, Indonesia

Selected Group Exhibitions

2008
"Nostalgia - Indonesia Contemporary Art Exhibition", Michael Ku Gallery, Taipei
I"ndonesian Invasion", Sin Sin Fine Art, Hong Kong, China
2007
"Cilukba: An exhibition by Kelompok Seni Rupa Jendela (Jendela Art Group)", Valentine Willie Fine Art, Kuala Lumpur, Malaysia
2005
"Eksodus Barang", Nadi Gallery, Jakarta, Indonesia
"Jejak-Jejak Drawing", Edwin Gallery, Jakarta, Indonesia
"Pseudo Still Life: Obyek dan Auranya", Semarang Gallery Semarang, Indonesia
"Sculpture Expanded", CP Art Space, Jakarta, Indonesia
"Realis (Me) Banal", Garcia Art Gallery, Surabaya, Indonesia
2004
"Wings of Words, Wings of Color", Langgeng Gallery, Magelang, Indonesia

"新的传统"，Shaksi画廊，孟买，印度
2009
"第十届雅加达双年展"，国家画廊，雅加达，印尼
"荷兰之外"，Centraal博物馆，乌德勒支，荷兰

演出与视觉表演

2009
"加里巴巴的不思议世界"，Pappa Tarahumara/Hiroshi Koike舞蹈戏剧
2006
"记忆女神摩涅莫辛涅"，与Kunauka东京戏剧公司和Garasi戏剧实验室合作

获奖情况

2010
亚洲艺术奖决赛入围者，Loop画廊，首尔，韩国
2008
学术艺术奖，日惹艺术学院，日惹

鲁迪・曼度凡尼

1973年出生于印尼西苏门答腊省巴东
现生活工作于印尼日惹

教育背景

1996年毕业于印尼艺术学院，日惹，印尼

部分个展

2006 "万物的文化"，CP文化空间，雅加达，印尼
2002 "双重水平线"，Nadi画廊，雅加达，印尼

部分群展

2008
"怀旧——印尼当代艺术展"，台北谷公馆，中国台湾
"印尼入侵"，Sin Sin画廊，香港，中国
2007
"Cilukba: Jendela艺术团队展"，Valentine Willie画廊，吉隆坡，马来西亚
2005
"物品外流"，Nadi画廊，雅加达，印尼
"痕迹"，Drawing Edwin画廊，雅加达，印尼
"伪静物：对象和灵气"，三宝垄画廊，三宝垄，印尼
"雕塑扩展"，CP艺术空间，雅加达，印尼
"现实主义与中庸"，Garcia画廊，泗水，印尼
2004
"语言之翼，色彩之翼"，Langgeng画廊，马格朗，印尼
"阅读"，H. Widayat博物馆，马格朗，印尼
"思考・传统"，印尼国家画廊，雅加达，印尼
"客观性"，Nadi画廊，雅加达，印尼

"Membaca Dunia Widayat", H. Widayat Museum, Mungkid Mungkid, Magelang, Indonesia
"Mempertimbangkan Tradisi", The National Gallery of Indonesia
"Object(ify)", Nadi Gallery, Jakarta, Indonesia
"Equatorial Heat", Sichuan Museum, China
"Have We Met?", Foundation Forum, Tokyo, Japan
2003
"30:30", Edwin's Gallery, Jakarta, Indonesia
"Interpellation", CP Open Biennale, The National Gallery of Indonesia, Jakarta, Indonesia
"Kado", Nadi Gallery, Jakarta, Indonesia
"Patung Kecil", Lontar Gallery, Jakarta, Indonesia
"In Search of Peace", Indonesian Contemporary Sculptors, World Trade Center, Jakarta, Indonesia
"Mc (row) Media", Langgeng Gallery, Magelang, Indonesia
"Implotion", Expatri Art Gallery, Jakarta, Indonesia
"Borobudur", H. Widayat Museum Mungkid, Magelang, Java, Indonesia
"Infatuated", Sun Jin Galleries, Singapore
2002
"Ecstaticus Mundi", Chouinard Gallery, Hong Kong, China

I NYOMAN MASRIADI

Born 1973, Gianyar, Bali.
Living and working in Yogyakarta, Indonesia

Education
ISI Yogyakarta, Indonesia
Solo Exhibition
2008
"Masriadi: Black Is My Last Weapon", Singapore Art Museum
Selected Group Exhibitions
2002
"Not Just Political", H. Widayat Museum, Magelang
2000
"Seni Rupa Campur" Exhibition, Beeldende Kunst (DBK), Dordrecth Netherland
1999
"Biennale VI", Purna Budaya, Yogyakarta
"Knalpot" Exhibition, Cemeti Art House, Yogyakarta
Duet Exhibition with I GAK Murniaish, Cement Art House, Yogyakarta
1998
An Exhibition, Museum Rudana, Ubud, Bali
An Exhibition, Imperial Hotel, Kuta, Bali
Sanggar Dewata Indonesia Exhibition, Bentend Vredeburg, Yogyakarta
1997
"Kelompok 7 Exhibition–Sanggar Dewata Indonesian", Bentara

"酷热"，四川博物馆，中国
"我们见过面吗？"，日本基金会论坛，东京，日本
2003
"30：30"，Edwin画廊，雅加达，印尼
"质询——CP露天双年展"，国家画廊，雅加达，印尼
"印尼礼物"，Nadi画廊，雅加达，印尼
"塑像"，Lontar画廊，雅加达，印尼
"寻求和平——印尼当代雕塑展"，世贸中心，雅加达，印尼
"媒介"，Langgeng画廊，马格朗，印尼
"内爆"，Expatri画廊，雅加达，印尼
"Borobudur"，H. Widayat博物馆，马格朗，印尼
"执迷"，Sun Jin画廊，新加坡
2002
"Ecstaticus Mundi"，Chouinard画廊，香港，中国

米斯尼亚迪

1973年出生于印尼巴厘岛
现生活工作于印尼日惹

教育背景
印尼艺术学院，日惹，印尼
部分个展
2008
"米斯尼亚迪：黑色是我最后的武器"，新加坡美术馆，新加坡
部分群展
2002
"不仅是政治"，H. Widayat博物馆，马格朗，印尼
2000
"艺术组合"，DBK画廊，多德雷赫特，荷兰
1999
"第六届日惹双年展"，日惹，印尼
"排气"，Cemeti艺术之家，日惹，印尼
"双人联展"，Cement艺术之家，日惹，印尼
1998
作品展于Rudana博物馆，乌布-巴厘岛，印尼
作品展于帝国酒店，巴厘岛，印尼
作品展于Sanggar Dewata画廊，日惹，印尼
1997
"第七组展览——Sanggar Dewata Indonesian"，Purna Budaya画廊，日惹，印尼
"印尼艺术学院周年展"，日惹，印尼
1996
"双城对话"，Purna Budaya画廊，日惹，印尼
"第七组展览——Sanggar Dewata Indonesian"，Sika画廊，

Budaya, Yogyakarta
"Dies Natalis Indonesian Art Institute Exhibition", Yogyakarta
1996
"Dialog Between Two City" Exhibition, Purna Budaya, Yogyakarta
Kelompok 7 Exhibition–Sanggar Dewata Indonesian, Sika Gallery, Ubud, Bali
"Sanggar Dewata Indonesian Exhibition", Taman Budaya Surakarta, Surakarta
"Young Artist II Exhibition", Bentend Vredebung, Yogyakarta
1995
"Dies Natalis Indonesian Art Institute Exhibition", Yogyakarta
"Collaboration Exhibition with Australian Art Student", Yogyakarta
"Indonesian Art Festival", Bentend Vredebung, Yogyakarta
"Sanggar Dewata Exhibition", Purna Budaya, Yogyakarta
"Sanggar Dewata Indonesian", Sika Gallery, Ubud, Bali
1994
"Hitam Putih + Plus" An Exhibition of Kelompok Prasidha, Indonesian Art Institute, Gampingan Yogyakarta

NASIRUN S.SN

Born in 1965, Cilacap, Indonesia
Living and working in Yogyakarta

Education
1987-1994
Faculty of Art and Design, Indonesian Art Institute (ISI), Yogyakarta, Indonesia
Selected Solo Exhibitions
2002
Nadi Gallery
2000
Galeri Nasional Indonesia
1993
Café Solo Bank Bali, Jl Mangkubumi
Selected Group Exhibitions
2010
"LESBUMI", Pesantren Kali Opak, Jogjakarta, Indonesia
"The Birth of Color", Syang Art Space, Magelang, Indonesia
"Space & Image", Ciputra World, Indonesia
2009
"Vok Populi", BBJ, Indonesia
"Senang-Senang", Tujuh Bintang Art Space, Yogyakarta, Indonesia
Awards
Painting Competition, Dies Sastra UGM, Second Place
The Best Sketch and Art Painting, ISI Jogjakarta, Indonesia
Mc Donald Award on ISI X
Philip Morris Award

乌布–巴厘岛，印尼
"Sanggar Dewata Indonesian展览"，Taman Budaya Surakarta画廊，梭罗，印尼
"年轻艺术家展II"，Bentend Vredebung画廊，日惹，印尼
1995
"印尼艺术学院周年展"，日惹，印尼
"澳大利亚艺术生交流展"，日惹，印尼
"印尼艺术节"，日惹，印尼
"Sanggar Dewata展览"，Purna Budaya画廊，日惹，印尼
"Sanggar Dewata Indonesian展览"，Sika画廊，乌布–巴厘岛，印尼
1994
"白+黑"，印尼艺术学院，日惹，印尼

那室兰 S.Sn

1965年出生于印尼芝拉扎(Cilacap)
现生活工作于雅加达

教育背景
1987-1994
印尼艺术学院(ISI)艺术设计系，雅加达，印尼
部分个展
2002
Nadi画廊
2000
印尼国家画廊
1993
巴厘岛Café河岸画廊
部分群展
2010
"LESBUMI"，Pesantren Kali Opak画廊，雅加达，印尼
"色彩的诞生"，Syang艺术空间，马格朗，印尼
"空间与影像"，Ciputra艺术世界，印尼
2009
"民众的声音"，Tujuh Bintang艺术空间，日惹，印尼
获奖情况
Dies Sastra UGM绘画竞赛二等奖
印尼艺术学院最佳素描与艺术绘画
印尼艺术学院第十届麦当劳艺术奖
菲利普·莫里斯奖

加林·努格罗

1961年出生于印尼日惹
现生活工作于雅加达

教育背景
雅加达艺术学院电影摄制专业，印尼
获奖情况

GARIN NUGROHO

Born 1961, Yogyakarta, Indonesia

Living and working in Jakarta, Indonesia

Education

Filmmaking at Institut Kesenian Jakarta, Indonesia

Awards

Berlin International Film Festival

Puisi Tak Terkuburkan, Singapore International Film Festival

Filmography

2009

Generasi biru (The Blue Generation)

2008

Di Bawah Pohon (Under the Tree)

2006

Serambi

Opera Jawa (Requiem from Java)

2004

Rindu Kami Padamu (Of Love and Eggs)

2002

Rembulan di Ujung Dahan (TV)

Aku Ingin Menciummu Sekali Saja (Bird Man Tale)

2001

Layar hidup: Tanjang priok/Jakarta (Waterfront)

2000

Puisi Tak Terkuburkan (A Poet)

1998

My Family, My Films and My Nation

Daun di Atas Bantal (Leaf on a Pillow)

1995

Dongeng Kancil untuk Kemerdekaan (Kancil's Tale of Freedom)

Bulan Tertusuk Ilalang (...and the Moon Dances)

1994

Surat untuk Bidadari (Letter to an Angel)

1991

Cinta Dalam Sepotong Roti (Love Is a Slice of Bread)

Air dan Romi (Water and Romi)

1989

Tepuk Tangan

1984

Gerbong Satu, Dua (Wagon 1, 2)

EKO NUGROHO

Born in 4 July 1977, Yogyakarta

Living and working in Yogyakarta, Indonesia

Education

1997-2006

Painting Department, Indonesian Art institute, Yogyakarta

柏林国际电影节

《诗人》，新加坡国际电影节

影片目录

2009

《忧郁的一代》

2008

《树下》

2006

《爪哇安魂曲》

《门廊》

2004

《甜心鸡蛋》

2002

《鸟人传说》

2002

《Rembulan di Ujung Dahan》(电视剧)

2001

《海滨》

2000

《诗人》

1998

《枕边叶》

《我的家庭、我的电影和我的国家》

1995

《月之舞》

《坎塞尔的自由故事》

1994

《给天使的信》

1991

《水和罗米》

《爱情是一片面包》

1989

《掌声》

1984

《马车1、2》

艾柯・努格罗荷

1977年7月4日出生于印尼日惹

现生活工作于印尼日惹

教育背景

1997-2006

印尼艺术学院绘画系，日惹

1993-1997

1993-1997

High School for Fine Arts (SMSR), Yogyakarta

Selected Solo Exhibitions

2009

"Solo Exhibition of Eko Nugroho", Galerie Nouvelles Image, Den Haag, Netherlands

"Under The Shadow", Pekin Fine Art, Beijing, China

"In The Name of Pating Tlecek", Nadi Gallery, Jakarta, Indonesia

2008

"It's All About Coalition", National Museum of Singapore

Selected Group Exhibitions

2010

"Lonarte 10 Festival", alongside the beach in Calheta, Madeira Island, Portugal

"The 2010 Next Wave Festival: The Ultimate Time Lapse Megamix", Melbourne, Australia

"The Comical Brothers", National Gallery, Jakarta, Indonesia

"Lihat! Video Art from Indonesia", Galería Jesús Gallardo, Leon Mexico

Selected Performances

2010

"Perseteruan Lendir Bersaudara" at Lembaga Indonesia Perancis, Yogyakarta, Indonesia.

2009

"L'arc En Ciel Sous La Pierre" (Rainbow Beneath A Stone) at the "Open Air Theatre", Vaulx-en-Velin, Lyon, France . Veduta, Lyon "Bienale X", France.

Video Art Works

2009

Dance of The Landlord

2008

Intimacy

ERIK MUHAMMAD

Born 1981 in Bandung, West Java, Indonesia

Education

2009-now

Studiengang Freie Kunst, Hochschule für Bildende Künste Braunschweig, Germany.

2001-2005

Textile Craft and Minor Media Art, Bandung Institute of Technology, Indonesia

Selected Solo Exhibitions

2010

"Indistict Names", Semarang Contemporary Art Gallery, Semarang, Indonesia

2009

"Fictitious Biography", Richard Koh Fine Art, Kuala Lumpur, Ma-

日惹美术专科学校(SMSR)

部分个展

2009

"艾柯·努格罗荷个展"，新镜像画廊，海牙，荷兰

"阴影之下"，北京艺门画廊，北京，中国

"以Pating Tlecek的名义"，Nadi画廊，雅加达，印尼

2008

"都是关于同盟"，新加坡国家博物馆，新加坡

部分群展

2010

"Lonarte 10艺术节"，Calheta海滩，马德拉群岛，葡萄牙

"2010年下一浪艺术节：终极时间流逝"，墨尔本，澳大利亚

"喜剧兄弟"，国家画廊，雅加达，印尼

"Lihat!印尼视频艺术"，Jesús Gallardo画廊，莱昂，墨西哥

部分演出

2010

"兄弟世仇"，印尼法国文化中心，日惹，印尼

2009

"石下的彩虹"，露天剧场，里昂，法国/第十届法国里昂双年展"景观"章节

视频艺术作品

2009

《房东的舞蹈》

2008

《亲密》

埃里克·穆罕穆德

1981年出生于印尼西爪哇省万隆市

教育背景

2009-至今

不伦瑞克造型艺术学院美术系，德国

2001-2005

万隆技术学院纺织工艺与小众媒体艺术系，印尼

部分个展

2010

"模糊的名字"，三宝垄当代艺术画廊，三宝垄，印尼

2009

"虚构的传记"，Richard Koh美术馆，吉隆坡，马来西亚

"面对千变万化的幻景"，Vivi Vip艺术之家，雅加达，印尼

部分群展

2010

"时代对话"，印尼国家画廊，雅加达，印尼

"印尼当代艺术发展的反思"，Lawang Wangi艺术馆，万隆，印尼

laysia
"Face Phantasmagoria", Vivi Yip Art Room, Jakarta, Indonesia

Selected Group Exhibitions

2010
"Percakapan Masa", Galeri Nasional Indonesia
"A reflection upon the development of Indonesian Contemporary Art", Lawang Wangi Art Bandung
2009
"Bandung Expanding", Tony Raka, Bali, Indonesia

Grant, Awards & Scholarships

2010
International Residency, New Museum & Westbeth Artists Housing, New York (Asian Cultural Council)
2007
Goethe-Institut Indonesia (Deutsch Language Scholarship)
2004
Second Winner - Bebegig Installation Art Award, Kota Baru Parahyangan Art Fest

Art Projects, Workshop and Conferences

2010
das zweite AnaDoma-FilmVideoFest, Braunschweig, Germany, ID
2007
The Against The Wall: Grafity Exhibition, FAB vs Ranger Bastard, Buton Kultur 21, Indonesia

GOTOT PRAKOSA

Gotot Prakosa, began making films in 1973 using 8mm, regular-8 and super-8 films.
His first animation film "Sepasang Tanduk" (1975) won an award at the Mini Film Festival, held by the Dewan Kesenian Jakarta (Jakarta Arts Council) in 1976. From that time on, and until 1981, each year consecutively his short films received an award at the Mini Film Festival of the Dewan Kesenian Jakarta.
His first feature-length film, "Tjoet Nja' Dhien," was made for which Eros Djarot was co-director. Gotot Prakosa also co-founded the film company PT. Ekapraya Tata Cipta Film together with Slamet Rahardjo Djarot, Eros Djarot, Christine Hakim and Rahim Latif. The company has to its credit many quality films and has often won national and international awards, including "Langitku Rumahku", "Telegram", "Oh Ibu dan Ayah Selamat Pagi", and "Kantata Takwa", and in all these films Gotot worked as the scriptwriter, producer, cameraman or director. His last feature-length film "Kantata Takwa" (released in 2009) has won 8 international awards and has been shown in over 30 international film festivals around the world.

2009
"万隆扩展"，Tony Raka画廊，巴厘岛，印尼

获奖情况

2010
国际驻留，新博物馆&Westbeth艺术家社区，纽约(亚洲文化委员会)
2007
印尼歌德学院(德语奖学金)
2004
Bebegig装置艺术奖二等奖，巴拉香甘新城艺术节

艺术项目、工作坊活动与会议

2010
AnaDoma电影录像节二等奖，不伦瑞克，德国
2007
靠墙：涂鸦展，Buton Kultur 21画廊，印尼

高托特·普拉考萨

1974年，高托特·普拉考萨完成了高中阶段的学业，并于次年进入雅加达艺术教育学院(LPKI，即现雅加达艺术学院IKJ)，主修导演专业。1978年，普拉考萨完成了三年制文凭课程，并继续进修，分别于1982年个2001年完成了实验动画专业四年制文凭课程和制片专业本科课程。
此后，普拉考萨又于2004年获得印尼日惹市嘎加玛达大学文学院硕士学位。
普拉考萨自1973年开始制作电影，先后采用过8mm、常规8mm和超级8mm胶片。
1976年，他的首部动画电影《一对喇叭》(1975)在雅加达艺术委员会主办的"迷你电影节"中获奖。从1976年至1981年的6年间，普拉考萨的短片每年都在雅加达艺术委员会主办的"迷你电影节"中有所斩获。
《朱月婷》是普拉考萨的第一部剧情长片，拍摄过程中他作为副导演为导演埃罗斯·加罗特(Eros Djarot)提供协助。普拉考萨还与Slamet Rahardjo Djarot、埃罗斯·加罗特、Christine Hakim和Rahim Latif等人一起共同创建了PT. Ekapraya Tata Cipta电影公司。公司出品了一系列经典影片，包括《我的家乡，我的天空》、《电报》、《哦，早安，爸妈！》和《Kantata Takwa》等，多次荣获国内外重量级电影奖项。普拉考萨更是一人身兼编剧、制片人、摄影和导演等多种角色。他的最新剧情长片《Kantata Takwa》(2008)共获得8项国际大奖，并先后在全球30多个国际电影节中进行了展映。

安奇·普班度诺

1971年出生于印尼Cepiring
现生活工作于印尼日惹

教育背景

1994-1999

ANGKI PURBANDONO

Born in 1971 Cepiring, Indonesia

Working and living in Yogyakarta, Indonesia

Education

1994-1999

Indonesia Institute of Art, Yogyakarta, Indonesia

1993-1994

Modern School of Design Yogyakarta, Indonesia

Selected Solo Exhibitions

2010

"2 Folders From Fukuoka", Vivi Yip Art Room 2, Jakarta

2009

"Kissing The Methods", Richard Koh Fine Art, Kuala Lumpur, Malaysia.

2008

"Happy Scan", Biasa Art Space, Seminyak, Bali, Indonesia

2007

"Industrial Fiesta", Cemeti Art House, Yogyakarta, Indonesia

2006

"Industrial Fiesta", Changdong Art Studio, Seoul, South Korea

Selected Group Exhibitions

2010

"Emerging Wave, ASEAN – Korea Contemporary Photo Exhibtion", GoEun Museum of Photography, Busan, South Korea

"Emerging Wave, ASEAN – Korea Contemporary Photo Exhibtion", Hangaram Art Museum, Seoul, South Korea

"Saemangeum Flag Festival 2010, Saemangeum Seawall, Saemangeum, South Korea

2009

"Live and Let Live: Creators of Tomorrow: The 4th Fukuoka Asian Triennal 2009", Fukuoka, Japan

"Kocon 2009 Spring International Digital Design Invitation Exhibition", Silla University in Busan, South Korea

"City Oneminutes Project [Video] Rietveld Arsenale – Venice Biennale", Arsenale Novissimo, Venice

"KOMPILASI : A Survey of Contemporary Indonesia Art [Ruang MES 56]", BUS Gallery Melbourne, Australia

"Jakarta Biennale XIII 2009 ARENA: Zona Pertarungan", Jakarta City, Indonesia

2008

"REFRESH: New Strategies in Indonesian Contemporary Art", Valentine Willie Fine Art Singapore

"Anonymous-Landing Soon Project by Artoteek Den haag and Cemeti Art House", Erasmus Huiz Jakarta, Indonesia

"Manifesto", National Gallery Jakarta, Indonesia

2007

"Kuota: Inbox 2007", National Gallery Jakarta, Indonesia

"Fetish", Biasa Art Space, Denpasar, Indonesia

印尼艺术学院，日惹，印尼

1993-1994

现代设计学院，日惹，印尼

部分个展

2010

“两个来自福冈文件夹”，Vivi Yip艺术空间，雅加达，印尼

2009

“亲吻方法”，Richard Koh画廊，吉隆坡，马来西亚

2008

“快乐扫描”，Biasa艺术空间，巴厘岛，印尼

2007

“工业嘉年华”，Cemeti艺术之家，日惹，印尼

2006

“工业嘉年华”，Changdong国家艺术工作室，首尔，韩国

部分群展

2010

“新浪潮：东盟-韩国当代摄影展”，GoEun摄影博物馆，釜山，韩国

“新浪潮：东盟-韩国当代摄影展”，Hangaram美术馆，首尔，韩国

“2010年新万锦旗节”，新万锦海堤，新万锦，韩国

2009

“自己活也让别人活：明天的缔造者——2009年第4届福冈亚洲三年展”，福冈，日本

“2009年春季国际数字设计邀请展”，新罗大学，釜山，韩国

“城市1分钟项目：里特维尔德军械库——威尼斯双年展”，Arsenale Novissimo，威尼斯

“KOMPILASI：当代印尼艺术调查”，BUS画廊，墨尔本，澳大利亚

“2009年第13届雅加达双年展”，雅加达，印尼

2008

“刷新：印尼等待艺术新策略”，Valentine Willie美术馆，新加坡

“匿名——即将登陆”，Artoteek Den hag/Cemeti艺术之家，雅加达，印尼

“宣言”，国家画廊，雅加达，印尼

2007

“配额：收件箱2007”，国家画廊，雅加达，印尼

“恋物”，Biasa艺术空间，登巴沙，印尼

“三位年轻当代艺术家联展”，Valentine Willie美术馆，吉隆坡，马来西亚

“匿名——即将登陆#1”，Cemeti艺术之家/Cemeti工作室，日惹，印尼

2006

“开放的工作室——Changdong文献展”，Changdong国家艺术工作室，首尔，韩国

"3 Young Contemporary Artists", Valentine Willie Fine Art, Kuala Lumpur, Malaysia
"Anonymous-Landing Soon #1", Cemeti Art House and Cemeti Studio, Yogyakarta, Indonesia
2006
"Open Studio - Document Changdong", Changdong Art Studio, Seoul, South Korea
"Goyang International Art", Goyang, Seoul, South Korea
"Bikini in Winter", LOOP Alternative Space, Seoul, South Korea
"Bitmap International Digital Photo Project", LOOP Alternative Space, Seoul, South Korea
"International Digital Design Invitation Exhibition", Joongbu University, Seoul, South Korea
2005
"Road/Route 1st Pocheon Asian Art Festival", Pocheon City, South Korea
"Space and Shadows - Contemporary Art from Southeast Asia", Haus der Kultur der Welt, Berlin, Germany
"Unfolded City : [Ruang MES 56] Biennale Jogja VIII", Taman Budaya Yogyakarta, Indonesia
"Best Quality : [Ruang MES 56] CP Biennale Indonesia", Bank Museum, Jakarta, Indonesia
"Revolution Ugly-No Beauty", Cemeti Art House, Yogyakarta, Indonesia
"Where troubles melt like lemon drops", Koninklijke Academie voor schone Kunsten Hogeschool Antwerpen, Belgium
"Trans Indonesia", Govett-Browster Art Gallery, New Playmouth, New Zealand
"Top Collection and Beauty Point [Video Art]", Internet Project "Ueber Beauty (http://www.ueber-beauty.com)", Haus der Kulturen der Welt/ House of World Cultures, Berlin, Germany.

MANGU PUTRA

Born 1963, Sangeh, Bali, Indonesia

Education

Graduate from SMSR (Fine Arts High School) Batu Bulan, Bali
Visual Communication Design at Indonesian Art Institute (ISI), Yogyakarta

Selected Solo Exhibitions

2008
"Silent Words", Gajah Gallery, Singapore
2007
"Mandala", Bidadari, Ubud Bali, Indonesia
2006
"Belief", Rupa Gallery, Surabaya
2005
"Spiritual Landscape", Gajah Gallery, Singapore

Selected Group Exhibitions

"高阳国际艺术节"，高阳，首尔，韩国
"冬天的比基尼"，LOOP艺术空间，首尔，韩国
"Bitmap国际数字照片展"，LOOP艺术空间，首尔，韩国
"国际数字设计邀请展"，中部大学，首尔，韩国
2005
"道路/路线——首届抱川亚洲艺术节"，抱川，韩国
"空间与阴影——东南亚当代艺术"，世界文化馆，柏林，德国
"展开的城市——第8届日惹双年展"，Taman Budaya画廊，日惹，印尼
"最佳品质——CP印尼双年展"，河岸博物馆，雅加达，印尼
"革命丑陋——没有美丽"，Cemeti艺术之家，日惹，印尼
"烦恼如柠檬汁般消散"，皇家美术学院，安特卫普，比利时
"跨越印尼"，Govett-Browste画廊，新普利茅斯，新西兰
"顶级收藏与美丽焦点"(http://www.ueber-beauty.com)，世界文化馆，柏林，德国

曼顾・普川

1963年出生于印尼巴厘岛桑给(Sangeh)

教育背景

SMSR美术专科学校，巴土布兰，巴厘岛
印尼艺术学院(ISI)视觉传达系，日惹，印尼

部分个展

2008
"沉默的诂语"，Gajah画廊，新加坡
2007
"曼荼罗"，乌布-巴厘岛，印尼
2006
"信仰"，Rupa画廊，泗水，印尼
2005
"精神景观"，Gajah画廊，新加坡

部分群展

2008
"梅尔蒂地球"，艺术村，三宝垄，印尼
"印尼与主流"，Canna画廊，中艺博国际画廊博览会，北京，中国
2007
"艺术・警戒"，TonyRak画廊，乌布-巴厘岛，印尼
"全球变暖"，TonyRak画廊，乌布-巴厘岛，印尼
2006
"第七届裸体艺术展"，首尔，韩国

获奖情况

2002
2002年Indofood艺术大奖二等奖，雅加达，印尼

2008
"Merti Bumi,Lerep", Art Village, Semarang,Indonesia
"Indonesia and the Mainstream", Canna Gallery at CIGE, Beijing, China
2007
"Ar(t)chepelago Alert", TonyRaka Art Gallery, Ubud-Bali
"Global Warming", TonyRaka Art Gallery, Ubud-Bali, Indonesia
2006
"The 7th Nude", Crouquis Exhibition, Seoul,Korea

Awards

2002
Indofood Art Award 2002, Jakarta
1994
Philip Morris Award for painting titled 'Imagination Under the Sea'
1990
Best of work Visual Coommunication Design,6 th Anniversary of the Indonesian Institute of Art,Yogyakarta

FAOZAN RIZAL

Born in 1973, Tegal, Indonesia
Director of Photography - Cinematographer - Director
Member of Indonesian Society of Cinematographers (INSC)
Lecturer of cinematography and experimental film in the Jakarta Institute of the Arts, Indonesia, since 1999

Education

1998
Master degree graduate from Jakarta Institute of Arts, Indonesia
1998 – 1999
L` Atelier du Cinematographie au Femis, France

As Director

Yasujiro Journey, 48 minutes, Super 16 mm – Paoshas Film Indonesia
Asian Hot Shots Film Festival Berlin 2009
Presented at International Rencontres Paris – Berlin – Madrid 2007
Official selection Jakarta International Film Festival – Indonesia 2005
Official selection Singapore International Film Festival – Singapore 2005 in special program " Faozan Rizal Retrospective"
Official selection PUSAN International Film Festival - Korea 2004
Aries, A Poem For Katia, 80 minute, 35 mm – Kotak Hitam Film Indonesia
Official selection Singapore International Film Festival – Singapore 2005 in special program " Faozan Rizal Retrospective"
Special Screening Bangkok Fringe Festival 2005
Fugu, A sushi tale, 75 minute, DV Cam – Kotak Hitam Film 2006
In Competition Cinema Digital Film Festival – Korea 2009
Official selection Jakarta International Film festival 2009

1994
绘画作品《海洋下的想象》获菲利普·莫里斯大奖
1990
印尼艺术学院第六届视觉传达设计最佳作品奖，日惹，印尼

法赞·利泽尔

1973年出生于印尼直葛(Tegal)
摄影导演/摄影指导/导演
印尼电影摄影师协会(INSC)成员
自1999年起担任印尼雅加达艺术学院摄影与实验电影特约讲师

教育背景

1998年获印尼雅加达艺术学院硕士学位
1998-1999，法国电影摄影工作坊大师班

导演作品

《安二郎之旅》，48分钟，超16mm，印尼PAOSHAS电影公司出品
2009年柏林亚洲热门电影节
2007年国际巴黎–柏林–马德里录像节
2005年印尼雅加达国际电影节
2005年新加坡国际电影节特别单元"法赞·利泽尔回顾展"
2004年韩国釜山国际电影节
《白羊座，一首献给卡蒂娅的诗》，80分钟，35mm，印尼KOTAK HITAM电影公司出品
2005年新加坡国际电影节特别单元"法赞·利泽尔回顾展"
2005年曼谷艺术节
《河豚鱼——寿司的故事》，75分钟，DV拍摄，印尼KOTAK HITAM电影公司出品，2006
2009年韩国数字电影节竞赛单元
2009年雅加达国际电影节

部分纪录片/剧情片

《通往麦加之路》，HD CAM，日本NHK，2008
《亚洲光头》，HD CAM，新加坡，2007
《村庄援助》，HD CAM，新加坡，2007
《每天》，HD CAM，新加坡，2007
《雾都孤儿之亚洲故事》，HDV，新加坡，2007(法德ARTE公共电视网)

获奖情况

1997年雅加达学生电影节最佳摄影
2000年柯达最佳摄影
2000年雅加达短片节最佳影片
2001年雅加达学生电影节最佳影片
2003年捷克布尔诺国际电影节
2005年雅加达舞蹈电影节最佳舞蹈电影

Documentary – Feature(Selection)
Road To Mecca - HD CAM Media Corps-NHK Japan 2008
Skin Heads In Asia – A portrait of an Indonesian leading Skin **Head** - HD CAM - Mediacorps Singapore 2007
Village Help - HD CAM - Mediacorps Singapore 2007
Earth Day - HD CAM - Mediacorps Singapore 2007
Fagin and Oliver The Twist of Asian Story - HDV- Mediacorps Singapore 2007 for Arte - France and Germany.

Awards
Best Cinematography - Jakarta Student Film Fest 1997
Best Cinematography Kodak 2000
Best Short Film Jakarta 2000
Best Student Film Jakarta 2001
Grand Prix Brno Int. Film Festival – Chec 2003
Best Collaboration in Dance Film – Dance Film Festival Jakarta 2005
Golden Panda Shanghai documentary film festival 2007
Best Cinematography FFB (Festival Film Bandung) 2009

S. TEDDY D.
Born in 1970, Padang, Sumatra, Indonesia
Living and working in Yogyakarta, Indonesia

Education
2000
Residency at Ludwig Art Forum, Aachen, Germany
1992-1997
Indonesia Art Institute, Fine Art Department, Yogyakarta, Indonesia
1990-1992
Indonesia Art School, Fine Art Department, Surakarta, Indonesia

Selected Solo Exhibitions
2010
"WAR", Ark Galerie, Jakarta
2009
"Love Tank (The Temple)", National Museum of Singapore
"I Want To Be Your Nest", Emmitan Contemporary Art Gallery, Surabaya, Indonesia
2008
"Meditation of Peanut", CIGE, Organized by Langgeng Gallery, Beijing, China
2007
"Pictura", Nadi Gallery, Jakarta, Indonesia

Selected Group Exhibitions
2010
"Rehorny", Jogja National Museum, Jogjakarta
"Art Amsterdam", RAI Exhibition Centre, Amsterdam, Netherlands
Pameran 102 Kebangkitan Nasional: "PERCAKAPAN MASA",

2007年上海纪录片电影节金熊猫奖
2009年万隆电影节最佳摄影

S. 泰迪·D.
1970年出生于印尼苏门答腊省巴东
现生活工作于印尼日惹

教育背景
2000
路德维格艺术论坛驻留，亚琛，德国
1992-1997
印尼艺术学院美术系，日惹，印尼
1990-1992
印尼艺术专科学校艺术系，梭罗，印尼

部分个展
2010
"战争"，Ark画廊，雅加达，印尼
2009
"爱之神宇"，新加坡国家博物馆，新加坡
"我想成为你的庇护所"，Emmitan 当代艺术画廊，泗水，印尼
2008
"花生的思考"(Langgeng画廊主办)，中艺博国际画廊博览会，北京，中国
2007
"图片"，Nadi画廊，雅加达，印尼

部分群展
2010
"Rehorny"，国家画廊，雅加达，印尼
"艺术阿姆斯特丹"，RAI展览中心，阿姆斯特丹，荷兰
"时代对话"，国家画廊，雅加达，印尼
"后迷幻"，Selasar Sunaryo艺术空间，万隆，印尼
2009
"嗨，六月——两人联展"，Taman Budaya画廊，日惹，印尼
"画"，国家画廊，雅加达，印尼
"多色"，V-Art周年展，BBY画廊，雅加达，印尼
"重新塑型"，国家画廊，雅加达，印尼
"情感绘画"，首尔奥林匹克美术馆绘画中心，首尔，韩国
2008
"走向真实的战略"，S. Sudjojono与印尼当代艺术，NUS博物馆，新加坡
"宣言"，国家画廊，雅加达，印尼
"影像·亚洲：第22届亚洲国际艺术展览会"，Selasar Sunaryo画廊，万隆，印尼
"情感中的绘画"，东京现代艺术馆，东京，日本

Galeri Nasional, Jakarta
"Post Psychedelia", Selasar Sunaryo Art Space, Bandung
2009
"Hi June", with Bob Yudhita, Taman Budaya Yogyakarta
"Drawing", National Gallery of Indonesia, Jakarta
"Polychromatic", V-Art Anniversary, BBY, Yogyakarta
"Re-Form", Jogja National Museum, Yogyakarta
"Emotional Drawing", Drawing Centre, Seoul Olympic Museum of Art, Korea
2008
"Strategies Towards The Real", S. Sudjojono and Contemporary Indonesia Art, NUS Museum, Singapore
"Manifesto", National Gallery, Jakarta, Indonesia
"Imaging Asia : Asian International Art Exhibition 22nd", Selasar Sunaryo, Bandung, West Java, Indonesia
"Drawing in Emotion", Museum of Modern Art Tokyo, Tokyo, Japan
2007
"Book Aid IVAA", Nadi Gallery, Jakarta, Indonesia
"Thermocline of Art : New Asian Waves", ZKM, Karlsruhe, Germany
"100 Tahun Affandi" Taman Budaya Yogyakarta, Yogyakarta, Indonesia
"Artvertising" National Gallery, Jakarta, Indonesia
"Sisa", Technology University of Sydney, Australia
"Neo Nation: Jogja Biennale", Yogyakarta, Indonesia
"Bocor #2", Cemeti Art House, Yogyakarta, Indonesia
"Contemporary Art, Apaan Tuh?", Organized by HeArt Space, Affandi Museum, Yogyakarta, Indonesia
2006
"Draw", Museum dan Tanah Liat, Yogyakarta, Indonesia
"Signed and Dated", 10th Anniversary Valetine Willie Fine Art, Kuala Lumpur, Malaysia
2005
"Culturen in Contact II", Museum Het Oude Raadhuis, Netherland
"Equatorial Heat", Sichuan Museum, China
"Vision and Resonance, Asian Contemporary Inaugural Exhibition, Riverroom Gallery, Asian Civilization Museum, Singapore

HANDIWIRMAN SAPUTRA

Born in January 24, 1975, Bukittinggi, West Sumatra, Indonesia
Living and working in Yogyakarta, Indonesia

Education
1993-1996
Indonesian Institute of Arts (ISI), Yogyakarta
Selected Solo Exhibitions
2009

2007
"IVAA书籍援助"，Nadi画廊，雅加达，印尼
"艺术跃温层——亚洲新潮"，ZMK画廊，卡尔斯鲁厄，德国
"百年Affandi"，Taman Budaya画廊，日惹，印尼
"艺术广告"，国家画廊，雅加达，印尼
"Sisa"，悉尼技术大学，澳大利亚
"新国家：雅加达双年展"，日惹，印尼
"Bocor #2"，Cemeti艺术之家，日惹，印尼
"当代艺术，那是什么？"(HeArt空间主办)，Affandi博物馆，日惹，印尼
2006
"画"，dan Tanah Liat博物馆，日惹，印尼
"签字并注明日期——Valetine Willie画廊十周年特别展"，吉隆坡，马来西亚
2005
"传统文化的联系"，Het Oude Raadhuis博物馆，荷兰
"酷热"，四川博物馆，中国
"视觉与共鸣：亚洲当代艺术揭幕展"，Riverroom画廊/亚洲文明博物馆，新加坡

翰迪怀儿曼・萨普川

1975年1月24日出生于印尼西苏门答腊省布吉丁宜市
现生活工作于印尼日惹

教育背景
1993-1996
印尼艺术学院(ISI)，日惹，印尼
部分个展
2009
"事物——翰迪怀儿曼的秩序"，Cemeti艺术之家，日惹，印尼
2008
"外界，内部观点——内部，外界观点"(Nadi画廊主办)，2008上海当代艺术展，上海
"无一有一无"(Nadi画廊主办)，2008新加坡陈列柜展，新加坡
"语言"(Nadi画廊主办)，中艺博国际画廊博览会，北京，中国
部分群展
2010
"2010艺术香港"，Nadi画廊，香港
"混沌的欢愉：新印尼艺术"，Primo Marella画廊，米兰，意大利
2009
"Kado #2"，Nadi画廊，雅加达，印尼
"2009艺术香港"，Nadi画廊，香港

川森・萨提迪卡亚

1949年出生于印尼万隆
现生活工作于印尼巴厘岛

教育背景

"Things, The Order of Handiwirman", Cemeti Art House, Yogyakarta, Indonesia
2008
"Exterior, Inside View - Interior, Outside View", ShContemporary 08, Shanghai, organized by Nadi Gallery
"Nothing-Something-Nothing", Singapore Show Case 2008, Singapore, organized by Nadi Gallery
"In Lingo", CIGE 2008, Beijing, China, organized by Nadi Gallery
Selected Group Exhibitions
2010
"Art HK 10", Nadi Gallery, Hong Kong
"Pleasures of Chaos – Inside New Indonesian Art", Primo Marella Gallery, Milano, Italy
2009
"Kado #2", Nadi Gallery, Jakarta, Indonesia
"Art HK 09", Nadi Gallery, Hong Kong Performance

CHUSIN SETIADIKARA

Born in 1949, Bandung
Living and working in Bali, Indonesia

Education
1976-1980
Study drawing and painting from Barli Sasmitawinata
Selected Solo Exhibitions
2004
"Massa Kintamani", CP Art Space, Jakarta, Indonesia
2002
"Post Photo Realistic Portrayal", National Gallery, Jakarta, Indonesia
"Solo Exhibition", CP Art Space, Washington DC, USA
Selected Group Exhibitions
2009
"Indonesia Contemporary Drawing", National Gallery, Jakarta, Indonesia
2008
"A New Force In Southeast Asia", Asia Art Center, Beijing, China
2007
"BALANCE Art", Helligendamm, Germany
Selected Honors And Awards
2005
"Float and the Might 1" received the "excellent work Award
1996
Winner of 5 best Philip Morris Asian Art Awards

PINTOR SIRAIT

Born in 1962, Braunschweig, Germany
Living and working in Bali, Indonesia

Education
1985-1988
Bachelors degree, Liberal Arts, University of Nevada-Reno

1976-1980
师从巴里・沙斯密塔威纳塔(Barli Sasmitawinata)学习绘画
部分个展
2004
"玛莎・金塔玛尼"，CP艺术空间，雅加达，印尼
2002
"后相片现实写照"，国家画廊，雅加达，印尼
"川森・萨提迪卡亚个展"，CP艺术空间，华盛顿特区，美国
部分群展
2009
"印尼当代绘画"，国家画廊，雅加达，印尼
2008
"东南亚新势力——印尼当代艺术大展"，亚洲艺术中心，北京，中国
2007
"平衡艺术"，海利根旦姆，德国
获奖情况
2005
作品"漂浮与力量1"获最佳作品奖
1996
菲利普・莫里斯亚洲艺术大奖

平托・西瑞特

1962年出生于不伦瑞克，德国
现生活工作于印尼巴厘岛

教育背景
1985-1988
内华达大学里诺校区艺术学士，内华达州，美国
1989-1990
万隆技术学院石雕工作室，印尼
1990-1992
内华达大学里诺校区雕塑专业特等生
部分个展
2009
"平托・西瑞特的赛车"，ION Orchard，新加坡
2008
"他的和她的"，华艺莎艺术空间，北京，中国
部分群展
2009
"Darga画廊展"，Darga画廊，巴厘岛，印尼
"进行中的传说"，国家画廊，雅加达，印尼
2008
"维特根斯坦的浴缸"，Sierra艺术画廊，里诺，内华达州，美国

(UNR), Nevada, USA.
1989-1990
Stone Carving work-shop, Institute of Technology, Bandung, Indonesia
1990-1992
Graduate Special Sculpture Student, UNR.
Selected Solo Exhibitions
2009
"Pintor Sirait's Race Cars", ION Orchard, Singapore
2008
"His and Hers", Vannessa Art Space, Beijing, China.
Selected Group Exhibitions
2009
"Darga Gallery Exhibition", Darga Gallery, Bali, Indonesia.
"The Living Legends", Galeri Nasional, Jakarta, Indonesia.
2008
"Wittgenstein's Bath", Sierra Arts Gallery, Reno, NV, USA.
"Indonesian Contemporary Art", Glerum, Amsterdam Netherlands.
Award
1994
Public Award from the French Government at the 6th Symposium d'Arts Plastiques, De La Ville De Perigueux, France.

PUTU SUTAWIJAYA

Born in 27 November 1971, Angseri,Tabanan,Bali.
Living and working in Yogyakarta, Indonesia

Education
1991-1998
Indonesia Institute of Fine Art(ISI) Yogyakarta
Selected Solo Exhibitions
2008
"Man, Mountain", CIGE, Beijing, China
"Legacy of Sagacity", Nasional Gallery, Jakarta, Indonesia
2007
"Fullmoon", Sin Sin Art Gallery,Hong Kong
"Poem of Nature", Valentine Willes Fine Art, Kuala Lumpur, Malaysia
Selected Group Exhibitions
2010
"Romansa 91", Sangkring Art Space, Yogyakarta, Indonesia
"The Grass Is Greener Where You Water It", Grand Palais Art Paris, Paris, France
"The Birth of Colours", Syang Art, Magelang, Indonesia
2009
" Humanities" Ben Cabrera, Ahmad Zakii Anwar, Putu Sutawijaya, Andrer Shire Gallery, Los Angeles, Cal, USA
"2D 3D", Sin Sin Fine Art ,Hong Kong

"印尼当代艺术"，Glerum画廊，阿姆斯特丹，荷兰
获奖情况
1994
第六届视觉艺术研讨会获得法国政府颁发的公共艺术奖

普图·苏塔维嘉亚

1971年11月27日出生于印尼巴厘岛
现生活工作于印尼日惹

教育背景
1991-1998
印尼艺术学院(ISI)，日惹，印尼
部分个展
2008
"人，山"，中艺博国际画廊博览会，北京，中国
"睿智的遗产"，国家画廊，雅加达，印尼
2007
"满月"，Sin Sin画廊，香港
"自然之诗"，Valentine Willes画廊，吉隆坡，马来西亚
部分群展
2010
"浪漫91"，Sangkring艺术空间，日惹，印尼
"有水滋养的草地格外鲜绿"，巴黎大皇宫，巴黎，法国
"色彩的诞生"，Syang艺术空间，马格朗，印尼
2009
"人性——四人联展"，Andrer Shire画廊，洛杉矶，加州，美国
"2D 3D"，Sin Sin画廊，香港
获奖情况
2000
印尼Sanggar Dewata LEMPAD艺术奖
1999
菲利斯·莫里斯国际艺术奖十佳作品

阿顾思·苏瓦吉

1959年出生于印尼中爪哇省普沃勒佐市
现生活工作于印尼日惹

教育背景
1979-1986
万隆科技学院美术与设计系平面设计专业，万隆，印尼
部分个展
2009
"多年之后，疯狂依然"，日惹国家博物馆，日惹/Selasar Sunaryo艺术空间，万隆，印尼

Awards

2000

Lempad Prize from Sanggar Dewata Indonesia

1999

Best 10 Phillip Morris – International Art Award

AGUS SUWAGE

Born in 1959, Purworejo, Central Java, Indonesia

Living and Working in Yogyakarta, Indonesia

Education

1979 – 1986

Graphic Design at Bandung Institute of Technology, Faculty of Fine Art and Design, Bandung, Indonesia

Selected Solo Exhibitions

2009

"Still Crazy After All These Years", Jogja National Museum, Yogyakarta & Selasar Sunaryo Art Space, Bandung, Indonesia

"CIRCL3", Singapore Tyler Print Institute, Singapore

2008

Beauty in the Dark", Avanthay Contemporary Gallery, Zurich, Switzerland

Selected Group Exhibitions

2010

"Almost White Cube", the 12th Anniversary of CGartspace, Jakarta, Indonesia

"Pleasures of Chaos", Primo Marella gallery, Milan, Italy

2009

"Group", Galerie Christian Hosp, Berlin

"Post-Tsunami Art", Primo Marella, Gallery Milano, Italia

"Simple Art of Parody", Museum of Contemporary Art, Taipei, Taiwan

Selected Catalogues

2008

"Inanimate Performance" published by Soka Art Center, Taipei, Taiwan

Selected Books

2010

"Still Crazy After All These Years" published by Studio Biru

2009

"Pause/Replay" Agus Suwage, published by Studio Biru

2007

"Thermocline of Art" New Asian Waves, published by Hatje Cantz Verlag

"Indonesian Contemporary ArtNow", published by SNP International Publishing

"CIRCL3"，新加坡泰勒版画研究院，新加坡

2008

"黑暗中的美丽"，Avanthay当代画廊，苏黎世，瑞士

部分群展

2010

"几乎白盒子——CGartspace画廊12周年纪念展"，CGartspace画廊，雅加达，印尼

"混沌的愉悦"，Primo Marella画廊，米兰，意大利

2009

"团体"，Christian Hosp画廊，柏林，德国

"后海啸艺术"，Primo Marella画廊，米兰，意大利

"派乐地"，台北当代艺术馆，中国台湾

画册

2008

《无生命演出》，索卡艺术中心，台北，中国台湾

专著

2010

《多年之后，疯狂依然》，Biru工作室出版

2009

《暂停/重放》，Biru工作室出版

2007

《艺术跃温层——亚洲新潮》，Hatje Cantz Verlag出版社

《印尼当代艺术的现在》，SNP国际出版社

TROMARAMA艺术小组

费比・贝比罗斯

1985年出生于印尼雅加达

2008年获万隆技术学院艺术与设计系版画工作室学士学位

赫伯特・汉斯・马鲁利

1984年出生于印尼雅加达

2008年获万隆技术学院艺术与设计系视觉传达设计专业学士学位

鲁迪・亚历山大・哈图曼那

1984年出生于巴林

2007年获万隆技术学院艺术与设计系视觉传达设计专业学士学位

部分群展

2010

"我会穿越你：版画、雕刻与其他雕刻艺术"，书籍艺术中心，纽约，美国

"变化中的表面：数字媒体时代中的版画"，当代艺术中心，萨克拉曼多，美国

"Lihat! ——来自印尼的视频艺术"，Jesus Gallardo画廊，莱昂，墨西哥

"Philagrafika 2010：无意识图形"，费城，美国

TROMARAMA

Febie Babyrose

Born in Jakarta 1985

2008 BFA, Printmaking Studio, Faculty of Art and Design, Bandung Institute of Technology

Herbert Hans Maruli

Born in Jakarta 1984

2008 BA, Visual Communication Design, Faculty of Art and Design, Bandung Institute of Technology

Ruddy Alexander Hatumena

Born in Bahrain 1984

2007 BA, Visual Communication Design, Faculty of Art and Design, Bandung Institute of Technology

Selected Group Exhibitions

2010

"I will cut thrU: Pochoirs", Carvings, and Other Cuttings, The Center for Book Arts, New York City, USA

"A Changing Surface: Prints in the Age of Digital Media", Center for Contemporary Art, Sacramento, USA

"Lihat! Video Art from Indonesia", Gallery Jesus Gallardo, Leon, Mexico

"Philagrafika 2010: The Graphic Unconscious", Philadelphia, USA

2009

"Jakarta Contemporary Ceramics Biennale #1", North Art Space, Jakarta

"Tropical Lab", Praxis Space, Lasalle College of Arts, Singapore

"OK. VIDEO COMEDY, 4TH Jakarta International Video Festival", National Gallery, Jakarta

"Cross Animate", space*c Coreana art & culture complex , Seoul, South Korea

2008

"Wonder", Singapore Biennale 2008, Singapore

2006

"Chapter One: Der Ach , Paper Model and Custom Sneakers Exhibition", Bandung

"Bandung New Emergence", Selasar Sunaryo Art Space, Bandung

Screenings

2010

Children's Season, Moving Image Gallery, SAM 8Q, Singapore

Arts for Health, Singapore National Eye Centre

2009

A Window to the World, Hiroshima City Museum of Contemporary Art, Japan

Workshop

2009 Tropical Lab, Presented by Lasalle College of Arts, Singapore

2009

第一届雅加达当代陶艺双年展，北方艺术空间，雅加达，印尼

"热带实验室"，实践空间，新加坡Lasalle艺术学院，新加坡

"OK，录像喜剧——第四届雅加达国际录像节"，国家画廊，雅加达，印尼

"十字动画"，韩国艺术与文化空间，首尔，韩国

2008

"奇迹——2008年新加坡双年展"，新加坡

2006

"第一章：纸模与特制运动鞋展"，万隆，印尼

"万隆新势力"，Selasar Sunaryo艺术空间，万隆，印尼

放映

2010

"儿童季"，Moving Image画廊(SAM 8Q)，新加坡

"健康艺术"，新加坡国家眼中心

2009

"世界之窗"，广岛当代艺术城市博物馆，日本

工作室

2009

"热带实验室"，新加坡Lasalle艺术学院

安塔格·维哈梭

1967年出生于印尼中爪哇省直葛市

现生活工作于印尼日惹

教育背景

1987-1994

印尼艺术学院绘画系学士，日惹，印尼

部分个展

2008

"黑山羊作为我最后的防御"，5 Traverse画廊，普罗维登斯，RI，美国(出版画册)

"黑山羊空间"，Ark画廊，雅加达，印尼(出版画册)

2007

"无毒"，艺术之家，三宝垄，印尼(出版画册)

部分群展

2010

"混沌的欢愉：新印尼艺术"，Primo Marella画廊，米兰，意大利(出版画册)

"跳马系列"，新贝德福德艺术馆，马萨诸塞，美国

2009

"拓展绘画3——第四届布拉格双年展"，捷克(出版画册)

"常识"，印尼国家画廊，雅加达，印尼(出版画册)

部分演出

ENTANG WIHARSO

Born in 1967, Tegal, Central Java, Indonesia

Living and working in Yogyakarta

Education

1987-1994

Bachelors of Fine Art in Painting, Indonesian Art Institute, Yogyakarta, Indonesia

Selected Solo Exhibitions

2008

"Black Goat as My Last Defense", 5 Traverse Gallery, Providence, RI, USA (catalogue)

"Black Goat Space", Ark Gallery, Jakarta Indonesia, Indonesia (catalogue)

2007

"InToxic", Rumah Seni Yaitu, Semarang, Central Java, Indonesia (catalogue)

Selected Group Exhibitions

2010

"PLEASURES OF CHAOS: Inside New Indonesian Art", Primo Marella Gallery, Milan, Italy (catalogue)

"Vault Series", New Bedford Art Museum, MA, USA

2009

" Expanded Painting 3", Prague Biennale 4, Czech Republic (catalogue)

"Common Sense", Indonesia National Gallery, Jakarta, Indonesia (catalogue)

Selected Performances

2009

"Desire : Eating Identity", Primo Marella Gallery, Milan, USA

2007

"Eating Identity", Mead Art Museum, Amherst, MA, USA

Awards, Residencies & Grants

2007

Copeland Fellowship, Amherst College, Amherst, MA, USA

Pollock – Krasner Foundation Grant

2006

Vasl International Artists' Workshop, Karachi, Pakistan

Speaking Engagements

2008

"Menjadi Sang Liyan (Becoming the Other)" NeoNation, Jogja Biennale, Yogyakarta, Indonesia

2007

"Cultural Identity Today", Amherst Collage, Amherst, MA, USA

GEDE MAHENDRA YASA

Education

1998 – 2002

2009

"欲望：吃掉身份"，Primo Marella画廊，米兰，意大利

2007

"吃掉身份"，Mead美术馆，安姆斯特，马萨诸塞州，美国

获奖情况

2007

Copeland学术奖金，安姆斯特学院，安姆斯特，马萨诸塞州，美国

Pollock – Krasner基金会奖金

2006

Vasl国际艺术节工作坊，卡拉奇，巴基斯坦

演讲活动

2008

"成为其他"，日惹双年展《NeoNation》，日惹，印尼

2007

"文化身份・今天"，安姆斯特学院，安姆斯特，马萨诸塞州，美国

杰德・曼汉德拉・亚萨

教育背景

1998-2002

印尼艺术学院，登巴沙，巴厘岛

部分个展

2010

"当脸庞不再透露灵魂"，SIGIarts画廊，雅加达，印尼

2009

"亨德拉的女人：重新构造德库宁"，SIGIarts画廊，雅加达，印尼

2008

"画家的调色板"，Aryaseni艺术画廊，新加坡

"白色系列：绘画的寓言"，Richard Koh美术馆，吉隆坡，马来西亚

部分群展

2010

"混沌的欢愉：新印尼艺术"，Primo Marella画廊，米兰，意大利

2009

"后海啸艺术：东南亚崛起"，Primo Marella画廊，米兰，意大利

"杂交"，北方艺术空间，雅加达，印尼

"第四届布拉格双年展"，布拉格，捷克

Indonesian Art Institute, Denpasar, Bali

Selected Solo Exhibitions

2010

"As the Face No Longer Bespeaks the Soul", SIGIarts, Jakarta

2009

"Hendra's Woman: Reframing De Kooning", SIGIarts, Jakarta

2008

"The Painter's Palette", The Aryaseni Art Gallery, Singapore

"White Series: Allegory of Painting", Richard Koh Fine Art, Kuala Lumpur, Malaysia

Selected Group Exhibitions

2010

"Pleasure of Chaos, Inside New Indonesian Art", Primo Marella Gallery Milan, Italy

2009

"Post-Tsunami Art, South East B(l)ooming", Primo Marella Gallery Milan, Italy

"Hybridization", North Art Space, Jakarta

"Prague Biennale 4", Prague, Czech Republic

Contributors' Biographies | 作者简历

JIM SUPANGKAT

Jim Supangkat was born in Makassar, Indonesia in 1948. He entered the Faculty of Fine Art and Design, Bandung Institute of Technology, in 1970. Before graduating in 1975, he studied esthetics under noted philosopher, Dick Hartoko in the city of Yogyakarta, between 1974-1975.

In 1975, Supangkat founded 'Indonesia New Art Movement', which proclaimed the re-definition of art and the search of Indonesian subversive perception on art. Debate on the movement's principles persisted for ten years and is now regarded as the beginning of contemporary art discourse in Indonesia.

In 1992, Supangkat decided to change course. Aware of the need of professional curators in Indonesia, he left his work as a lecturer and even as an artist. He has initiated several international contemporary art exhibitions in Indonesia—Contemporary Art of the Non-Aligned Countries (1995), CP Biennale I (2003) and CP Biennale II (2005). As an independent curator, he was involved in many Asian contemporary art exhibits between 1992 - 2000. He has written several books and a number of essays introducing contemporary art in Asia and Indonesia to the international art world. In 1997, he received the Prince Claus Award for this attempt.

BILJANA CIRIC

Biljana Ciric received her M.A in Art history from East China Normal University in Shanghai. She was the director of the Curatorial Department at the Shanghai Duolun Museum of Modern Art and the China networking curator for the 2006 Singapore Biennale. Her ambitious ongoing project "Migration Addicts" was presented at the 52nd Venice Biennale in the 2007 Collateral Events and in the Shenzhen/Hong Kong Bi-city Biennale of Urbanism and Architecture. Her exhibition projects include 'Strategies from Within - Contemporary Art Practices in Vietnam and Cambodia" (Ke Center of Contemporary Arts), major retrospective of Yoko Ono (Ke Center for Contemporary Art, Guangdong Museum of Art). Biljana Ciric was curator of public art project "Intrude: Art & Life 366" in 2008 and curated "History in Making: Shanghai 1979-2009, 30 Years Retrospective of Shanghai Contemporary Culture" in 2009. Currently she is working as an independent curator based in Shanghai.

ANTARIKSA

Antariksa (b. 1975) is a writer with focus of interest on Indonesian art and culture. He studied philosophy (at Gadjah Mada University, Yogyakarta) and history (at Lembaga Studi Realino, Yogyakarta). He is a co-director of Indonesia Contemporary Art Network (iCAN, http://canmanage.net) dan a founding member of KUNCI Cultural Studies Center (http://kunci.or.id). His publications including Tuan Tanah Kawin Muda: Hubungan LEKRA-Seni Rupa 1950-1965 [The Connection Between LEKRA and the Arts

杰姆·苏潘凯特

杰姆·苏潘凯特于1948年生于印尼的Makassar。1970年，他进入万隆科技学院的现代艺术与设计系。在1975年毕业之前，他于1974-1975年在Yogyakarta跟随著名哲学家Dick Hartoko学习美学。

1975年，Supangkat发起“印尼新艺术运动”，提倡重新定义艺术，并提出寻找印尼文化的颠覆性感知。关于该运动的辩论持续了十年，现在这项运动被誉为印尼当代艺术对话的起源。

1992年，Supangkat决定改变人生轨迹。当他发现印尼缺乏专业策展人时，便毅然放弃讲师甚至艺术家的工作。他在印尼举行了数次国际当代艺术展——Contemporary Art of the Non-Aligned Countries (1995)、CP Biennale I (2003) 和CP Biennale II (2005)。他也撰写了几本书和一系列文章，向国际艺术界介绍亚洲及印尼的当代艺术。1997年，他因对艺术领域的卓越贡献而荣获克劳斯亲王奖(Prince Claus Award)。

比利安娜·思瑞克

比利安娜·思瑞克荣获上海的华东师范大学艺术历史系文学硕士学位。她曾担任上海多伦现代美术馆策展部主任，并且担任2006年新加坡双年展的中国网络策展人。她倾注心血的力作“迁移嗜好者”受邀参加2007年第52届威尼斯双年展的特别机构邀请展以及深圳及香港的都市及建筑双城双年展。她策划的展览包括“在野策略——柬埔寨越南当代艺术展”(可当代艺术中心)，艺术家小野洋子的首次中国个展(可当代艺术中心，广东美术馆)。比利安娜·思瑞是2008年公共艺术项目“介入：艺术生活366天”的策展人，并在2009年策划了“上海滩1979—2009”上海当代艺术30年的大型回顾展。目前，她是常住上海的独立策展人。

安塔瑞克沙

安塔瑞克沙(1975-)，作家，主要以印尼艺术与文化为关注点。他先后在印尼日惹的噶迦玛达大学和Realino研究所学习哲学和历史。安塔瑞克沙现为印尼当代艺术网络(iCAN, http://canmanage.net)负责人，同时，也是KUNCI文化研究中心(http://kunci.or.id)创始人之一。出版的著作包括《LEKRA与艺术之间的联系1950-1965》(2005)、《荷印20世纪初期电影与现代性》(2006)等。

印尼当代艺术网络(iCAN)致力于对话网络的构建，推动印尼当代视觉艺术界中的对话与协作，组织各种艺术项目与论坛，并为各项研究和艺术批评活动提供支持。

托尼·高夫雷

托尼·高夫雷，新加坡苏富比艺术学院当代艺术系主任。最新著作

1950-1965] (2005) and Bioskop dan Modernitas di Hindia Belanda Awal Abad ke-20 [Cinema and Modernity in the Early 20th Century Netherland Indies] (2006).

TONY GODFREY

Tony Godfrey is Head of Contemporary Art at Sotheby's Institute Singapore. His most recent book [Painting Today] was published by Phaidon press in 2009. He writes regularly inter alia for [LEAP] and [C Arts Magazine]. He is currently working on a book on painting throughout East Asia.

SIMON GUAN

Simon Guan, Freelance Art Critic; a lecturer of English language and literature in the early years; now working as Creative Center Director for a multinational company; author and translater of several books and essays on psychology, literature, art and music.

NURAINI JULIASTUTI

Nuraini Juliastuti (b. 1975) is a co-founder of KUNCI Cultural Studies Center. She gained her Bachelor's degree in Communication Studies at the Gadjah Mada University, and Master's degree in Contemporary Asian Studies from University of Amsterdam. She lives and works in Yogyakarta.

DR. SANENTO YULIMAN

Sanento Yuliman (1941-1992) was an art historian who defended his doctoral thesis on Indonesian modern art at University of Paris VII, Paris, France, in 1980. This lecturer of art history and art criticism at the Faculty of Art and Design, Bandung Institute of Technology, was a socialist who was close with Indonesian artists. Since 1970, he had maintained a shrewd outlook toward history, the concept of fine art, and modernism. He played a role in the establishment of the New Art Movement (Gerakan Seni Rupa Baru) in Indonesia in 1975, an early sign of the Indonesian contemporary art emergence. Sanento Yuliman was renowned as an eminent art critic who also wrote literary and theater criticism. His articles were mostly published in the national news weekly, Tempo. The following essay was published in three consecutive pieces in the newspaper Pikiran Rakyat, November 1983. (introduction text written by Jim Supangkat)

《当代绘画》(Painting Today)于2009年由Phaidon出版社发行。此外，托尼・高夫雷也是《LEAP艺术界》和印尼当代艺术双语杂志《C Arts》等刊物的特约撰稿人。目前，高夫雷正在撰写一本关于东亚绘画的新作。

肖蒙

肖蒙(本名：关颖)，自由艺评人。早年从事大学英语教学。现供职于某跨过公司任创意中心总监。发表过心理学，文学艺术音乐等方面专著译著数百万字。

努拉伊妮・朱丽阿斯图缇

努拉伊妮・朱丽阿斯图缇(1975-)， KUNCI文化研究中心创始人之一。朱丽阿斯图缇先后获得噶迦玛达大学传播研究学士学位和阿姆斯特丹大学当代亚洲研究硕士学位，现在印尼日惹生活、工作。

KUNCI文化研究中心是一个非盈利性的独立机构，旨在通过普及教育推动当代文化对话和批判性思维。KUNCI于1999年9月在印尼日惹成立，一直积极组织并参与跨学科学者、独立研究人员/观察员、学生、评论家和其他相关从业人员之间的合作与讨论，致力于推动理念交流和批判性思维，并努力构建跨越国界的对话网络，就各大关键性文化事项展开探讨。

未来两年中，KUNCI的活动将主要围绕印尼的媒体和技术结合项目，旨在探索本土文化如何在日常生活中推动媒体和技术的发展，以及日常的技术实践如何为印尼的社会文化转型提供新的机遇与挑战。

萨能托・于利曼 博士

萨能托・于利曼(1941-1992)，艺术史学家，1980年获巴黎第七大学博士学位，专攻印尼现代艺术研究。于利曼博士为万隆技术学院艺术与设计系艺术史与艺术评论专题讲师，是一名与印尼艺术家关系密切的社会主义者。自1970年起，于利曼始终对历史、艺术和现代主义保持着密切的关注与敏锐的观察。他曾参与了1975年发生的标志印尼当代艺术兴起的“新艺术运动”。此外，他不仅是一名著名的艺术评论家，同时也从事文学和戏剧批评研究。他的文章经常在印尼全国性新闻周刊《Tempo》上发表。本文于1983年11月在《人民思想报》(Pikiran Rakyat)上分三期连载。(文字介绍由杰姆・苏潘凯特撰写)

“当代性：印度尼西亚的当代艺术”展览
“CONTEMPORANEITY: CONTEMPORARY ART OF INDONESIA” EXHIBITION

展览主办 / Organized by

上海当代艺术馆
Museum of Contemporary Art, Shanghai

印尼AKR集团
AKR Group

中国金慈善基金会
China Gold Charity Foundation

浩然艺术与教育基金会
H2 Foundation for Arts and Education

赞助商 / Sponsored by

Mandiri银行 / Bank Mandiri

印度尼西亚航空公司 / Garuda Indonesia

特别鸣谢 / Special Thanks

H. E. Mrs. Mari Pangestu
印度尼西亚共和国贸易部部长 / Minister of Trade of the Republic of Indonesia
H. E. Mr. Fauzi Bowo
印度尼西亚共和国雅加达市市长 / The Governor of Jakarta
Mr. Adi Harsono
印度尼西亚共和国驻上海商会主席 / Chairman of Indonesian Business Association Shanghai

Mrs. Deborah Iskandar
Mrs. Katerina Valdivia Bruch
Mr. F.X Harsono
Mr. Roslisham Ismail aka Ise
Mr. Russel Storer

支持机构 / Supporting Institutions

雅加达歌德学院 / Goethe Institute Jakarta
Cemeti Art House
MES 56
KUNCI文化研究中心 / KUNCI Cultural Studies Center
上海宝铭文化传播 / Shanghai Powerful Means Advertising Company
Set Film

媒体合作伙伴 / Media Partners

上海当代艺术馆
MUSEUM OF CONTEMPORARY ART, SHANGHAI

馆长 / Director
龚明光 / Samuel Kung

副馆长 / Deputy Director
周志聪 / Joe Zhou

创意总监 / Creative Director
陆蓉之 / Victoria Lu

主席办公室展览项目顾问 / Exhibition & Project Advisor, Chairman's Office
马迪 / Mati Cuenca

策展部 / Exhibition Department
王慰慰 / Weiwei Wang, 董文晶 / Jenny Dong, 徐婧 / Jane Xu

教育部 / Education Department
丁秋怡 / Emily Ding, 房洁 / J Fang, 戴敏豪 / David Demres

市场媒体部 / Marketing & Media Department
王颖 / Ying Wang

行政部 / Administration Department
李玲 / Lillian Li, 马洁 / Maggie Ma, 王宇澄 / Nelson Wang, 孔婷婷 / Elva Kong, 王慧 / Katt Wang, 龚富强 / Fred Gong

设计部 / Design Department
陈聪 / Sansan Chen
朱盈易 / Yiyi Zhu

财务部 / Accounting Department
郭素珍 / Susan Guo, 夏冰 / Ben Xia, 龚爱伦 / Allen Gong

技术部 / Technician
黄建兴 / Jianxing Huang, 顾强生 / Qiangsheng Gu, 刘学冰 / Xuebing Liu
叶国芳 / Guofang, Ye 曹国明 / Guoming Cao, 朱春跃 / Chunyue Zhu

上海当代艺术馆
Museum of Contemporary Art, Shanghai
www.mocashanghai.org

上海南京西路231号人民公园 200003
People's Park, 231 Nan Jing West Road, Shanghai, 20002, China
Tel: +86 21 63279900
Fax: +86 21 63271257
Email: info@mocashanghai.org

本画册作为“当代性：印度尼西亚的当代艺术”展览出版物

上海当代艺术馆
2010年7月23日至2010年8月19日
展览策展人：Jim Supangkat, 比利安娜·思瑞克
展览主办方：上海当代艺术馆, 印尼AKR集团, 中国金慈善基金会, 浩然艺术与教育基金会
展览支持：Mandiri银行, 印度尼西亚航空公司

THE CATALOGUE WAS PUBLISHED IN CONJUNCTION WITH THE EXHIBITION CONTEMPORANEITY: CONTEMPORARY ART OF INDONESIA

Museum of Contemporary Art, Shanghai
23 July 2010- 19 August 2010
Curators: Jim Supangkat and Biljana Ciric
The exhibition is organized by Museum of Contemporary Art, Shanghai, AKR Group, China Gold Charity Foundation, H2 Foundation for Arts and Education with support from Bank Mandiri and Garuda Indonesia

编辑 / Editor
比利安娜·思瑞克 / Biljana Ciric

翻译 / Translation
邬晨云 / Wu Chenyun, 周辰 / Zhou Chen, Rani Elsanti, Myrna Lim, Henny Rolan

校对 / Proofreading
Steven L. Bridges, 廖文峰 / Liao Wenfeng

设计 / Designer
曹巍 / Cao Wei

项目协调 / Project Coordinators
Martha Soemantri, 廖文峰 / Liao Wenfeng

艺术家访谈主编 / Artists Interviews
比利安娜·思瑞克 / Biljana Ciric

艺术家访谈视频编辑 / Artists Interviews Video Editing
廖文峰 / Liao Wenfeng

timezone 8

Published by Timezone 8 Limited
19A Entertainment Building
30 Queen's Road Central
Hong Kong
e-mail: info@timezone8.com
www.timezone8.com

ISBN 13: 978-988-18907-7-1

Editor/Author: Biljana Ciric

Cover Credits: Cao Wei

Printed in China.

Price / 定价: 200 RMB